Ten Suttas from Dīgha Nikāya

Collection of Long Discourses of the Buddha

SĪLAKKHANDHA VAGGA

MAHĀ VAGGA

PĀTHIKA VAGGA

TRANSLATED BY BURMA PIṬAKA ASSOCIATION

MPE

MPA Pariyatti Editions
an imprint of
Pariyatti Publishing
www.pariyatti.org

First published in 1984 by the Burma Pitaka Association.
First Pariyatti Edition, 2025

ISBN: 978-1-68172-808-7 (hardback)
ISBN: 978-1-68172-811-7 (paperback)
ISBN: 978-1-68172-264-1 (PDF)
ISBN: 978-1-68172-262-7 (ePub)
ISBN: 978-1-68172-263-4 (Mobi)
Library of Congress Control Number: 2019943800

Namo tassa bhagavato arahato sammāsambuddhassa

Veneration to the Exalted One
the Homage-Worthy
the Perfectly Self-Enlightened

The Buddha is an Arahat and he is worthy of the highest veneration. All beings including devas and Brahmās venerate the Buddha because the Buddha is the Supreme One, who has extinguished all defilements, who has become perfectly self-enlightened through realization of the Four Noble Truths, and who is endowed with the six great qualities of glory, namely, *Issariya* (supremacy), *Dhamma* (knowledge of the Path to Nibbāna), *Yasa* (fame and following), *Sirī* (noble splendour of appearance), *Kāma* (power of accomplishment) and *Payatta* (diligent mindfulness).

CONTENTS

Introduction

The Burma Piṭaka Association was founded on 20th August, 1980, by U Nu, former Prime Minister of Burma, with the concurrence of the Government of the Socialist Republic of the Union of Burma headed by the then President, U Ne Win. The primary aim of the Association is to promote through translations in English an understanding of the Piṭaka texts as interpreted and accepted in Theravāda Buddhism. After this translation of the original sources is completed, it is intended further to translate the Commentaries and the Sub-Commentaries of the Theravāda school of Buddhism, as well as explications and expositions by eminent scholar-monks of Burma.

The Burma Piṭaka Association now has twenty-nine members, thirteen from Rangoon and sixteen from the districts. To supervise the work being done under its sponsorship, the Association holds two (sometimes three) meetings a month, but members from the districts attend only quarterly meetings to hear reports and to decide on policy matters. They may also attend other meetings of the Association if they happen to be in Rangoon.

As is generally known, the Piṭaka texts are in the Pāḷi language. These texts are divided into three Divisions which are known as the Three Piṭakas. (*Piṭaka* literally means 'basket'.) Thus they are called Tipiṭaka in Pāḷi, (*ti* meaning 'three'). The three Piṭakas are the Vinaya (containing the Rules of Discipline for the Order of monks), the Suttanta (consisting of Suttas or Discourses), and the Abhidhamma (which deals with more profound philosophical and psychological aspects of Buddhism). The overall term for all the texts in these three Piṭakas is just Piṭaka.

According to this Piṭaka classification the Suttanta Piṭaka consists of five Nikāyas or Collections. These five Nikāyas are: Dīgha Nikāya or Collection of long discourses of the Buddha; Majjhima Nikāya or Collection of middle-length discourses; Saṃyutta Nikāya or Collection of groups of connected discourses; Aṅguttara Nikāya or Collection of numerically graduated discourses; and lastly, Khuddaka Nikāya or Collection of miscellaneous works or books, an omnibus Collection which contains compilations of Suttas (i.e., Discourses and Narrative Accounts).

The Dīgha Nikāya or Collection of the long discourses of the Buddha has three compilations, which we can call books, known as the Sīlakkhandha Vagga or Division of discourses on morality (containing thirteen suttas or discourses), the Mahā Vagga or Large Division (containing ten suttas) and the Pāthika Vagga or the Pāthika Division (containing eleven suttas). This last Division takes its name from the first sutta in this Division.

The Majjhima Nikāya also has three compilations, each containing a fair number of suttas. The Saṃyutta Nikāya is divided into five compilations, each called a Division (Vagga), and each has a large number of short suttas. The Aṅguttara Nikāya, Collection of numerically graduated discourses, has eleven parts or books, ranging from the first part consisting of discourses dealing with just one point or subject-matter, to the eleventh containing discourses each enumerating eleven things or points The Khuddaka Nikāya contains eighteen books of miscellaneous suttas, as accepted by the Sixth International Buddhist Synod of 1954–56.

When the Pāḷi Texts as a whole are divided into Nikāyas, the five books of Vinaya and the seven books of Abhidhamma are included in the Khuddaka Nikāya.

Thus there are fifty-two Pāḷi works or books which are collectively termed the Piṭaka. Of these, all but seven have been officially translated into Burmese.

After the Burma Piṭaka Association was founded, there was an intensive search in Burma for qualified English-speaking translators. The whole of the year 1981 was taken up with this task and with the assigning of particular books to these translators who were accepted after some testing. Translation manuscripts started coming in towards the end of 1981, and continued coming in through the year 1982. Not all translators completed their assignments, and a fair number of the completed assignments were found to be unsatisfactory on subsequent examination. However, twenty translators completed the translation of thirty-two books. Eleven more books are works-in-progress. The remaining nine books have not yet been assigned for translation.

From the beginning the translations were regarded as raw material which would need to be processed considerably. An editorial board was formed early on. One method after another of editing the translation manuscripts was tried. Towards the end of 1982, a new editorial committee was formed with U Shwe Mra as Chairman.

Three staff-members were assigned to the editorial committee to assist in the work of editing, and another staff-member was assigned the task of card-indexing translated terms.

Sayadaw U Kumāra of Bhamo Monastery, Mandalay, a member of the Saṅgha Advisory Board of the Association, acted as Adviser throughout the editing period of these ten suttas, and the final drafts were submitted to this learned Sayadaw for scrutiny.

A very important member of the editorial committee was the Consultant on doctrinal points of the Dhamma, Sayagyi U Kyaw Htut, a very learned scholar who early in life passed the highest examinations in the Dhamma and had earned the title Dhammācariya (Teacher of Dhamma). In editing a translation manuscript, it was collated with the Pāḷi text officially approved by the Sixth International Buddhist Synod held in Rangoon (1954–56). The Burmese Version of the text was also used as an aid. When difficult points on the Dhamma arose in the course of editing, or when doubtful renderings of a word, or a sentence, or a passage were in question, the relevant Aṭṭhakathā (the Commentary) and the Ṭīkā (the Sub-Commentary) were constantly referred to, and the Dhamma Consultant had a busy time explaining points of significance to the other members of the editorial committee. Sometimes when such difficult points could not be resolved by the committee, or when there was disagreement amongst the members on a particular point, the matter was put up for decision to one of the eminently learned chief monks on the Saṅgha Advisory Board of the Association.

From the time the translation work started, early in 1981, four learned Dhamma Consultants were always on hand at the headquarters of the Association, and were available for consultation by the translators who were strongly exhorted to seek their guidance on doctrinal matters, to ask them for elucidation of perplexing words, phrases or passages, to obtain from them explanation of difficult Dhamma concepts, and to approach them for amplification upon points which needed to be explicated according to the Commentaries. Nevertheless, much editing work remained to be done on the translation manuscripts.

When the editorial committee was formed towards the end of 1982, it was decided to take ten suttas from the three books of the Dīgha Nikāya, (comprising three from the first book, three from the second book and four from the third book), and to edit their translations first so as to be able to publish these ten sutta-translations in collected form by the middle of 1983. Although the first editing process was finished by the middle of 1983, it was felt necessary to revise and review those edited versions again and again. Even after that, it was found that many of the sentences and passages in the translation text needed to be expanded and elucidated according to the Commentary, if they were to be understood fully. Therefore, it is only now (November, 1983) that we have completed the work of editing the ten sutta-translations to be published in this collection.

The above editorial procedure has been described rather fully, because a new editorial and translation scheme is to be introduced in order to speed up the editing process and publication.

We should now like to describe our approach to the editing process. Our aim generally has been to produce a translation which is not too literal but which is as close as possible to the original Pāḷi text. We have done our best to realize this aim.

Since, however, we are fully conscious of the fact that the reader we have in mind is a person who knows English fairly well, and who is interested in finding out from the primary sources what Buddhism says, but who is not familiar with Buddhist concepts or with the way these concepts are expressed, we have endeavoured to help him. This means that sometimes an approximation in English to the Pāḷi expression, amounting to a paraphrase, has had to be preferred to a strictly exact rendering. It also means that sometimes explicatory material from the Commentary has to be incorporated in the translation text itself, since if that is not done what is read by the kind of reader we have in mind would be mere words, without conveying the sense intended. This will be seen especially in the translation of the Mahāsatipaṭṭhāna Sutta.

We find that in several places of the translations the reader we have in mind will be unable to understand correctly and completely what is intended to be conveyed, unless he is helped. Footnotes and appendices do not seem to be sufficient to meet the case. He will have no one to turn to for explanation, no readable annotations explaining the very points that puzzle him in the phraseology or the subject-matter of the passage before him.

The need is immediate for our reader who has a particular translation before him and who wants to understand what a certain phrase or a certain passage signifies. Therefore we have tried to help him in several places in the translations. In our anxiety to help such a reader, we have inserted in the body of the translation, either in a paragraph or between paragraphs, explanatory or amplificatory material or synopses, in brackets.

We wish to assure the readers that in the coming publications, we will do our very best to give them better help, so that they will be in a good position to understand what they read.

As in the case of some people engaged in a similar task, but for a different religion, we have not felt obliged to make an effort to render the same Pāḷi word everywhere by the same English word. By exploiting a wide range of English words covering a similar area of meaning and association, we feel that the meaning of the sentence as a whole is conveyed more effectively. This sort of approach applies also to structure. For instance, we have felt free to use the Active Voice where the Pāḷi text uses the Passive Voice, and vice versa. To try to follow closely the idiom of Pāḷi in an English rendering is to make it, at the least, awkward reading. But we have tried to keep a little of the flavor of Pāḷi, if not the flavor of words or tone, at least the flavor of modes of thought or modes of exposition, the latter being due to the early tradition of oral transmission. Thus, the reader will find many repetitious phrases, paragraphs and passages. But where the Pāḷi text has a letter-symbol indicating the omission of a repeated passage, we have used either the symbol (p), standing for the Pāḷi word *peyyāla*, or dots (e.g., ... (p) ...).

The reader may be puzzled by the numbering sequence of the paragraphs in some places. The actual numbering follows that of the Pāḷi text as approved by the Sixth International Buddhist Synod held at Rangoon. This numbering is consecutive for all the suttas in a particular book. But for this first publication of translations by the Association, we have taken the first, the second and the ninth suttas from Book One of the Dīgha Nikāya. Thus there is a gap in paragraph numbers between the second and the following sutta. The first sutta from Mahāvagga in this publication, the fourth one here, starts with paragraph No.95, because this actually is the second sutta in Book Two. When the three books of the Dīgha Nikāya are published in their entirety, the suttas in the present publication will come in their proper place and the numbering of the paragraphs will be consecutive in each book.

Wherever we have used Pāḷi words, and this we have done fairly liberally, English renderings of these Pāḷi words are provided the first few times. The use of Pāḷi words, we hope, will help to obviate ambiguity for those who have some knowledge of Pāḷi, and secondly, we again hope, will help the reader who is keenly interested in Buddhism to familiarize himself with significant terms, each of which carries a whole bundle of meaning in Buddhism.

We are glad to acknowledge our debt to both western and oriental writers on Buddhism from the Theravāda point of view, and to previous translators of Pāḷi texts, especially those from Sri Lanka, even though in many places we have diverged. Also, Pāḷi-English dictionaries compiled by both western and oriental scholars have been of great help in our task.

We have tried to avoid using English words or terms which carry connotations or associations closely connected, especially in the mind of a western reader, with fundamental ideas or practices in another religion. Thus, we have avoided words such as 'sin', 'salvation', 'deliverance' and 'Heaven'. In the Mahānidāna Sutta, the sutta which sets forth the Doctrine of Dependent Origination, *Paṭiccasamuppāda*, we have deliberately avoided the term 'becoming' or 'the process of becoming' for *bhava*, in spite of a whole book justifying the term, which was published by an eminent western scholar in 1937, but which, in our opinion, is not in conformity with the Theravāda view. This term has been accepted and used even by later Theravāda scholars and translators who have overlooked the implications of the term, and we can only think that this is due to etymological considerations which, we venture to say, are sometimes misleading.

We have had to weigh carefully the choice of English equivalents for certain Pāḷi words. To give only one or two instances, the Pāḷi word *nibbidā*, which is on the surface very simple and is usually translated as 'disgust' or 'weariness', cannot be translated adequately by a single word; a phrase should really be used, but that is awkward sometimes since the smooth flow of the text is disturbed. Another word that has often been superficially translated because of etymological considerations is *abhiññā*. Since it has more than one meaning, we have rendered it 'Magga Insight', following the Commentary, where the context calls for such a rendering.

We say in all humility and without false modesty that the translations as edited by us must necessarily be inadequate. Burma is a land of many eminent scholars of Buddhism, ranging from the very learned and revered Sayadaws (chief monks) to the Dhammācariyas (i.e., those who have been awarded the title of Teacher of the Dhamma, both monks and laymen), and these eminent scholars have a profound understanding of the Dhamma and can interpret it effectively in Burmese. But with a very few exceptions, they are not able to translate the Pāḷi texts into English as they do not have an adequate command of English for this task. Because of this situation, the members of this editorial committee have had to attempt an uphill task. We are conscious of our short-comings and our limitations. Our task has been made possible only because of the guidance we have had from our Dhamma Consultants and because of the support we have had from members of our Advisory Body of Revered Saṅghas.

We do not regard the translations we have edited and produced as the final word on the subject. We therefore sincerely invite scholars of the Dhamma from all over the world to assist us by sending in criticisms, comments and suggestions, so that later editions of these translations issued by us may be better and more correct.

May the Buddha's Teaching Shine
Forth Like the Radiant Sun.

The Editorial Committee
Burma Piṭaka Association
Visākhā Hall,
Kabā-Aye Pagoda Estate,
Rangoon.

Full Moon Day of Tazaungmon, 1345 BE.
The Nineteenth Day of November, 1983.

BURMA PIṬAKA ASSOCIATION

List of Members (Rangoon)

U Nu	President
Thado Maha Thray Sithu	
U Chan Htoon	General Secretary
Mahā Thray Sithu	
U San Maung	Auditor
Sithu	
U Nyun	Treasurer
U Doe	Joint Treasurer
Thray Sithu	
U Kyaw Khine	Chairman (Editorial Board)
Thray Sithu	
U Shwe Mra	Joint Chairman (Editorial Board)
Thiripyanchi	
U Soe Ya	Joint Chairman (Editorial Board)
U Myint Too	Librarian
U Kyaw	
Daw Mya Tin	
Dr. Maung Maung Kha	
U Aye Maung	

List of Members (Regional)

U Sao Tha Tint	(Shan State)
U Ba Aye	(Rakhine State)
U San Tun Aung	(Rakhine State)
U San Ohn	(Mon State)
Mahn Tun Yone	(Irrawaddy Division)
U Sein Maung	(Irrawaddy Division)
U Pu	(Tenasserim Division)
U Myint Oo	(Pegu Division)
U Kyan	(Pegu Division)
Dr. Tha Dun	(Sagaing Division)
U Kyaw	(Mandalay Division)
Saya Hti	(Mandalay Division)
U Pu	(Mandalay Division)
U Bo Bo	(Mandalay Division)
U Tauk Htein	(Mandalay Division)
U Kyan Tin	(Magwe Division)

Burma Piṭaka Association Editorial Committee

Doctrinal Adviser	Sayadaw U Kumāra, B.A., Dhammacariya (Siromani, Vajamsaka).
Chairman	U Shwe Mra, B.A., I.C.S. Retd., Former Special Adviser, Public Administration Division, E.S.A., United Nations Secretariat.
Members	U Chan Htoon, L.L.B., Barrister-At-Law; Former President, World Fellowship of Buddhists.
	U Nyun, B.A., I.C.S. Retd., Former Executive Secretary, United Nations Economic Commission for Asia and the Far East; Vice-President, World Fellowship of Buddhists.
	U Myint Too, B.Sc., B.L., Barrister-At-Law, Vice-President, All Burma Buddhist Association.
	Daw Mya Tin, M.A., Former Head of Geography Department, Institute of Education, Rangoon.
Doctrinal Consultant	U Kyaw Htut, Dhammācariya; Former Editor-In-Chief of the Board for Burmese Translation of the Sixth Synod Pāḷi Texts.
Editors	U Myo Min, M.A., B.L., Former Professor of English, Rangoon University.
	U Ko Lay, M. Sc., Former Vice-Chancellor, Mandalay University.
	U Thein Maung, B.A., B.L.
	U Hla Maung, B.A., B.L.
Secretary	U Tin Nwe, B.Sc.

Contents of Each Sutta

Ten Suttas from
Dīgha Nikāya

Collection of Long Discourses of the Buddha

THREE SUTTAS

FROM

SĪLAKKHANDHA VAGGA

Division Concerning Morality

Brahmajāla Sutta
Sāmaññaphala Sutta
Poṭṭhapāda Sutta

Namo tassa bhagavato arahato sammāsambuddhassa

BRAHMAJĀLA SUTTA

I. BRAHMAJĀLA SUTTA

(Discourse on the Net of Perfect Wisdom)

PARIBBĀJAKA KATHĀ
About the (two) Wandering Ascetics

1. Thus have I heard:

Once the Bhagavā[1] (the Exalted One) made a long journey from Rājagaha to Nāḷandā with a large company of bhikkhus[2] numbering five hundred. Suppiya, a wandering ascetic, was also making a long journey from Rājagaha to Nāḷandā together with his pupil, the youth Brahmadatta.

In the course of the journey Suppiya, the wandering ascetic, maligned the Buddha, the Dhamma and the Saṅgha in many ways. The youth Brahmadatta, the pupil of Suppiya, however, praised the Buddha, the Dhamma and the Saṅgha in many ways. Thus the teacher and the pupil, each saying things directly contradictory to the other, followed behind the Bhagavā and the company of bhikkhus.

2. Then the Bhagavā went up to the King's Rest House at the Ambalaṭṭhikā garden to put up there with his company of bhikkhus for one night. The wandering ascetic, Suppiya, approached the same Rest House with his pupil, the youth Brahmadatta, to put up there for one night. At the garden also, the wandering ascetic, Suppiya, maligned the Buddha, the Dhamma and the Saṅgha in many ways, whereas his pupil, the youth Brahmadatta, praised the Buddha, the Dhamma and the Saṅgha in many ways. And in this manner the teacher and the pupil were each saying things directly contradictory to the other.

3. Then, as the night ended and the day dawned, the bhikkhus congregated in the pavilion when the following conversation arose: "Friends! How wonderful! And, indeed, how marvelous, friends, that what has never happened before has now happened! The Exalted One, the All-knowing, the All-seeing, the Homage-worthy, the Perfectly Self-Enlightened, understands with clear penetration the varied dispositions of sentient beings. (As an example of how there are varied dispositions of sentient beings, the bhikkhus continued to say:)[3] This wandering ascetic,

---

1. *Bhagavā*: This is the most frequently used appellation of the Buddha in the Suttanta Piṭaka.
2. *Bhikkhus*: a bhikkhu is a member of the Buddhist Order (the Saṅgha).
3. As explained in the Commentary.

Suppiya, maligned the Buddha, the Dhamma and the Saṅgha in many ways, whereas his pupil, the youth Brahmadatta, praised the Buddha, the Dhamma and the Saṅgha in many ways. The teacher and the pupil, each saying things directly contradictory to the other, followed behind the Bhagavā and the company of bhikkhus."

4. The Bhagavā, knowing the subject of their talk,[4] came to the pavilion, took the seat prepared for him and asked: "Bhikkhus! What were you talking about as you are assembled here? What was the subject of your unfinished conversation before I came?" On thus being questioned, the bhikkhus told the Bhagavā thus:

"Venerable Sir! As the night ended and the day dawned, we congregated in this pavilion and the following conversation arose:

'Friends! How wonderful! And, indeed, how marvellous, friends, that what has never happened before has now happened! The Exalted One, the All-knowing, the All-seeing, the Homage-Worthy, the Perfectly Self-Enlightened, understands with clear penetration the varied dispositions of sentient beings. This wandering ascetic, Suppiya, maligned the Buddha, the Dhamma and the Saṅgha in many ways, whereas his pupil, the youth Brahmadatta, praised the Buddha, the Dhamma and the Saṅgha in many ways. The teacher and the pupil, each saying things directly contradictory to the other, followed behind the Bhagavā and the company of bhikkhus.'

"This, Venerable Sir, was the unfinished conversation before the Bhagavā came in."

5. Bhikkhus! If others should malign the Buddha, the Dhamma and the Saṅgha, you must not feel resentment, nor displeasure, nor anger on that account.

Bhikkhus! If you feel angry or displeased when others malign the Buddha, the Dhamma and the Saṅgha, it will only be harmful to you (because then you will not be able to practice the dhamma).

Bhikkhus! If you feel angry or displeased when others malign the Buddha, the Dhamma and the Saṅgha, will you be able to discriminate their good speech from bad?

"No, indeed, Venerable Sir!" said the bhikkhus.

---

4. The Buddha, through his faculty of knowing other people's minds and through his omniscience, already knew all that had happened and all that had been discussed in his absence. But it was customary for him to ask the bhikkhus or lay disciples what they had been discussing, as an introduction to a discourse he would give on the subject.

If others malign me, or the Dhamma, or the Saṅgha, you should explain (to them) what is false as false, saying 'It is not so. It is not true. It is, indeed, not thus with us. Such fault is not to be found among us.'

6. Bhikkhus! If others should praise the Buddha, the Dhamma and the Saṅgha, you should not feel pleased, or delighted, or elated on that account.

Bhikkhus! If you feel pleased, or delighted, or elated, when others praise me, or the Dhamma, or the Saṅgha, it will only be harmful to you.[5]

Bhikkhus! If others praise me, or the Dhamma, or the Saṅgha, you should admit what is true as true, saying 'It is so. It is true. It is, indeed, thus with us. In fact, it is to be found among us.'

CŪḶA SĪLA
(Short Section on Morality)[6]

7. Bhikkhus! When a worldling[7] praises the Tathāgata[8] he might do so only in respect of matters of a trifling and inferior nature, of mere morality.[9] And what are those matters of a trifling and inferior nature, of mere morality, by which a worldling might praise the Tathāgata?

8. Bhikkhus! In his praise of the Tathāgata, a worldling might say thus: 'Samaṇa Gotama abandons all thoughts of taking life and abstains

---

5. Feeling of pleasure or delight due to faith in and devotion to the Buddha is meritorious (*kusala dhamma*). But when the feeling of pleasure or delight is tainted with personal attachment to the Buddha, it becomes demeritorious (*akusala dhamma*). Thus it will be an obstacle in practising the dhamma, and will be harmful to the striving for *Jhāna, magga, phala*.

6. **Morality**: The titles Cūḷa Sīla, Majjhima Sīla and Mahā Sīla are descriptive of the lengths of the text in each section. These should not be taken as indicating that the latter two are higher than the first. In fact the most serious sīlas, including the five precepts and the Path factors of Right Action and Right Speech, are mentioned in the first section, Cūḷa Sīla. See note 4 below, as well.

7. **Worldling**: Puthujjana, one who has not attained any *magga*.

8. *Tathāgata*: lit., "Thus come or Thus gone" (following the course and the practice of the former Buddhas). This appellation, meaning he who has won the Four Noble Truths, is used frequently by the Buddha in referring to himself or to former Buddhas. The Commentary gives eight interpretations of this term.

9. **Mere Morality**: This is not to say that Morality is unimportant. It is the foundation of the practice. Morality (*sīla*) is only considered trifling and inferior when compared with concentration (*samādhi*) and wisdom (*paññā*). In other words, mere Morality by itself is not sufficient to gain liberation.

from destruction of life, setting aside the stick and sword, ashamed to do evil, and he is compassionate and dwells with solicitude for the welfare of all living beings.'

Bhikkhus! In his praise of the Tathāgata, a worldling might say thus: 'Samaṇa Gotama abandons all thoughts of taking what is not given and abstains from taking what is not given. He accepts only what is given, wishing to receive only what is given. He establishes himself in purity by abstaining from committing theft.'

Bhikkhus! In his praise of the Tathāgata, a worldling might say thus: 'Samaṇa Gotama abandons all thoughts of leading a life of unchastity and practices chastity, remaining virtuous and abstinent from sexual intercourse, the practice of lay people.'

9. Bhikkhus! In his praise of the Tathāgata, a worldling might say thus: 'Samaṇa Gotama abandons all thoughts of telling lies and abstains from telling lies, speaking only the truth, combining truth with truth, remaining steadfast (in truth), trustworthy and not deceiving.'

Bhikkhus! In his praise of the Tathāgata, a worldling might say thus: 'Samaṇa Gotama abandons all thoughts of slandering and abstains from slander. Hearing things from these people he does not relate them to those people to sow the seed of discord among them. Hearing things from those people he does not relate them to these people to sow the seed of discord among them. He reconciles those who are at variance. He encourages those who are in accord. He delights in unity, loves it and rejoices in it. He speaks to create harmony.'

Bhikkhus! In his praise of the Tathāgata, a worldling might say thus: 'Samaṇa Gotama abandons all thoughts of speaking harshly and abstains from harsh speech. He speaks only blameless words, pleasing to the ear, affectionate, going to the heart, courteous, pleasing to many and heartening to many.'

Bhikkhus! In his praise of the Tathāgata, a worldling might say thus: 'Samaṇa Gotama abandons all thoughts of talking frivolously and abstains from frivolous talk. His speech is appropriate to the occasion, being truthful, beneficial, consistent with the Doctrine and the Discipline, memorable, timely and opportune, with reasons, confined within limits and conducive to welfare.'

10. In his praise of the Tathāgata, a worldling might say thus: 'Samaṇa Gotama abstains from destroying all seeds and vegetation.

'Samaṇa Gotama takes only one meal a day, not taking food at night and fasting after mid-day.

Samaṇa Gotama abstains from dancing, singing, music and watching (entertainments) that is a stumbling block to the attainment of morality.

Samaṇa Gotama abstains from wearing flowers, using perfumes and anointing with unguents.

'Samaṇa Gotama abstains from the use of high and luxurious beds and seats.

'Samaṇa Gotama abstains from the acceptance of gold and silver.

'Samaṇa Gotama abstains from the acceptance of uncooked cereals.

'Samaṇa Gotama abstains from the acceptance of uncooked meat.

'Samaṇa Gotama abstains from the acceptance of women and maidens.

'Samaṇa Gotama abstains from the acceptance of male and female slaves.

'Samaṇa Gotama abstains from the acceptance of goats and sheep.

'Samaṇa Gotama abstains from the acceptance of chickens and pigs.

'Samaṇa Gotama abstains from the acceptance of elephants, cattle, horses and mares.

'Samaṇa Gotama abstains from the acceptance of cultivated or uncultivated land.

'Samaṇa Gotama abstains from acting as messenger or courier.

'Samaṇa Gotama abstains from buying and selling.

'Samaṇa Gotama abstains from using false weights and measures and counterfeits.

'Samaṇa Gotama abstains from such dishonest practices as bribery, cheating and fraud.

'Samaṇa Gotama abstains from maiming, murdering, holding persons in captivity, committing highway robbery, plundering villages and engaging in dacoity.'

O Bhikkhus! Such are things that might be said should a worldling praise the Tathāgata.

End of the Short Section on Morality

Majjhima Sīla
(Middle-length Section Morality)

11. And then there are certain respected samaṇas and brāhmaṇas (recluses in general) who, living on the food offered out of faith (in *kamma* and its results), are given to destroying such things as seeds and vegetation. And what are such things? They are of five kinds, namely, root-germs, stem-germs, node-germs, plumule-germs and seed-germs. Samaṇa Gotama abstains from destroying such seeds and vegetation. Bhikkhus! A Worldling might praise the Tathāgata in this manner.

12. And then there are certain respected samaṇas and brāhmaṇas who, living on the food offered out of faith (in *kamma* and its results), are given to storing up and using things offered, such as cooked rice, beverages, clothing, sandals, beds, unguents and eatables. Samaṇa Gotama abstains from storing up and using such things. Bhikkhus! A worldling might praise the Tathāgata in this manner.

13. And then there are certain respected samaṇas and brāhmaṇas who, living on the food offered out of faith (in *kamma* and its results), are given to watching (entertainments) that is a stumbling block to the attainment of morality. And what are such entertainments? They are: dancing, singing, music, shows, recitations, hand-clapping, brass-instrument-playing, drum-playing, art exhibitions, playing with an iron ball, bamboo raising games, rituals of washing the bones of the dead, elephant-fights, horse-fights, buffalo-fights, bull-fights, goat-fights, sheep-fights, cockfights, quail-fights, fighting with quarter-staffs, boxing, wrestling, military tattoos, military reviews, route marches and troop-movements. Samaṇa Gotama abstains from watching (entertainments) which is a stumbling block to the attainment of morality. Bhikkhus! A worldling might praise the Tathāgata in this manner.

14. And then there are certain respected samaṇas and brāhmaṇas who, living on the food offered out of faith (in *kamma* and its results), are given to gambling (and taking part in sports and games) that weakens one's vigilance (in the practice of morality). And what are such sports and games? They are: playing chess on eight-squared or ten-squared boards; playing imaginary chess using the sky as a chess-board; playing chess on moon-shaped chessboards; flipping cowries with thumb and finger; throwing dice; playing tipcat; playing with brush and paints; playing marbles; playing at whistling with folded leaves; playing with miniature ploughs; acrobatics; turning palm-leaf wheels; measuring

with toy-baskets made of leaves; playing with miniature chariots; playing with small bows and arrows; alphabetical riddles; mind-reading and simulating physical defects. Samaṇa Gotama abstains from gambling (and taking part in such sports and games) that weakens one's vigilance (in the practice of morality). A worldling, bhikkhus, might praise the Tathāgata in this manner.

15. And then there are certain respected samaṇas and brāhmaṇas who, living on the food offered out of faith (in *kamma* and its results), are given to using high and luxurious beds and their furnishings. And what are they? They are: high couches; divans raised on sculptured legs; long-fleeced carpets; woollen coverlets with quaint (geometrical) designs; white woollen coverlets; woollen coverlets with floral designs; mattresses stuffed with cotton; woollen coverlets with pictorial designs; woollen coverlets with fringes on one or both sides; gold-brocaded coverlets; silk coverlets; large carpets (wide enough for sixteen dancing girls to dance on); saddle cloth and trappings for elephants and horses; upholstery for carriages, rugs made of black panther's hide, rugs made of antelope's hide, red canopies and couches with red bolsters at each end. Samaṇa Gotama abstains from using such high and luxurious beds and their furnishings. A worldling, bhikkhus, might praise the Tathāgata in this manner.

16. And then there are certain respected samaṇas and brāhmaṇas who, living on the food offered out of faith (in *kamma* and its results), are given to beautifying or adorning themselves. And what are such embellishments and adornments? They are: using perfumed cosmetics, getting massaged, taking perfumed baths, developing one's physique, using mirrors, painting eye-lashes dark, decorating (oneself) with flowers, applying powder and lotion to the body, beautifying the face with powder and lotion, wearing bangles, tying the hair into a top-knot, carrying walking sticks or ornamented hollow cylinders (containing medicinal herbs) or swords, using multi-coloured umbrellas or footwear (with gorgeous designs), wearing a turban or hair-pin set with rubies, carrying a Yak-tail fan and wearing long white robes with fringes. Samaṇa Gotama abstains from such embellishment and adornment. A worldling, bhikkhus, might praise the Tathāgata in this manner.

17. And then there are certain respected samaṇas and brāhmaṇas who, living on the food offered out of faith (in *kamma* and its results), are given to engaging themselves in unprofitable talk (that is contrary to correct practice conducive to the attainment of deva realms and

Nibbāna), such as talk about kings, thieves, ministers, armed forces, calamities, battles, food, drinks, clothing, beds, flowers, unguents, relatives, vehicles, villages, market-towns, cities, provinces, womenfolk, heroes, streets, waterfronts, the dead and the departed, trivialities, the universe, the oceans, prosperity, adversity, and so on.[10] Samaṇa Gotama abstains from engaging himself in such unprofitable talk. A worldling, bhikkhus, might praise the Tathāgata in this manner.

18. And then there are certain respected samaṇas and brāhmaṇas who, living on the food offered out of faith (in *kamma* and its results), are given to mutually disparaging disputes. And what are they? (They are as follows:) "You do not know this Doctrine and Discipline. I know this Doctrine and Discipline. How can you ever know this Doctrine and Discipline? Your practice is wrong. My practice is right. My speech is coherent and sensible. Your speech is not coherent and sensible. What you should say first, you say last; and what you should say last, you say first. What you have long practiced to say has been upset now. I have exposed the faults in your doctrine. You stand rebuked. Try to escape from this censure or explain it if you can." Samaṇa Gotama abstains from such mutually disparaging disputes. A worldling, bhikkhus, might praise the Tathāgata in this manner.

19. And then there are certain respected samaṇas and brāhmaṇas who, living on the food offered out of faith (in *kamma* and its results), are given to serving as messengers or couriers. And what are such services? They are: going from this place to that place, or coming from that place to this place and taking things from this place to that place, or bringing things from that place to this place, on behalf of kings, ministers, brahmins, householders and youths. Samaṇa Gotama abstains from serving as messenger or courier. A worldling, bhikkhus, might praise the Tathāgata in this manner.

20. And then there are certain respected samaṇas and brāhmaṇas who, living on the food offered out of faith (in *kamma* and its results), practice deceitful pretensions (to attainments), flattery (for gain), subtle insinuation by signs and indications (for gain), using pressure (to get offerings) and the seeking of more gain by cunning offer of gifts. Samaṇa Gotama abstains from such pretension and flattery. A worldling, bhikkhus, might praise the Tathāgata in this manner.

End of the Middle-length Section on Morality

---

10. **And so on**: by this is meant 'forests, mountains, rivers and islands.'

Mahā Sīla
(Long Section on Morality)

21. And then there are certain respected samaṇas and brāhmaṇas who, living on the food offered out of faith (in *kamma* and its results), make a wrongful living by means of low arts contrary to correct practice conducive to the attainment of deva realms and Nibbāna. And what are such low arts? They are: fortune telling from a study of physical characteristics, or of signs and omens, or of lightning; interpreting dreams; reading physiognomy; prognosticating from a study of rat-bites; indicating benefits from fire-oblation with different kinds of firewood, or with different kinds of ladles, with husks, broken rice, whole rice, clarified butter, oil, oral spells, or with blood; reading physiognomy while chanting spells; forecasting good or bad fortune from the signs and marks of a piece of land; being versed in state affairs; reciting spells in the graveyard to eliminate danger; reciting spells to overcome evil spirits; using magical formulae learnt in a mud-house; charming snakes and curing snake-bites; treating poisoning: curing scorpion-stings or rat-bites; interpreting animal and bird sounds and the cawing of crows; foretelling the remaining length of life; diverting the flight of arrows; and identifying the cries of animals. Samaṇa Gotama abstains from making a wrongful living by such means. A worldling, bhikkhus, might praise the Tathāgata in this manner.

22. And then there are certain respected samaṇas and brāhmaṇas who, living on the food offered out of faith (in *kamma* and its results), make a wrongful living by means of low arts contrary to correct practice conducive to the attainment of deva realms and Nibbāna. And what are they? They are: reading the portents of gems, dresses, sticks, daggers, swords, arrows, bows and other weapons; reading the characteristics of women, men, young men, young women, male slaves, female slaves, elephants, horses, buffaloes, bulls and other cattle, goats, sheep, chickens, quails, iguanas, pointed-eared animals,[11] tortoises and game-beasts. Samaṇa Gotama abstains from making a wrongful living by such means. A worldling, bhikkhus, might praise the Tathāgata in this manner.

23. And then there are certain respected samaṇas and brāhmaṇas who, living on the food offered out of faith (in *kamma* and its results), make a wrongful living by means of low arts contrary to correct practice

11. **Pointed-eared animals**: Kaṇṇikā: The Commentary here says this term means pinnacles of houses or points of ear-ornaments.

conducive to the attainment of deva realms and Nibbāna. And what are they? They are: making predictions about kings going to war; about kings coming back from war; about kings advancing in battle from their home country; about kings from foreign countries retreating; about kings from foreign countries advancing in battle; about kings retreating to their home country; about kings from their home country proving victorious; about kings from foreign countries losing battles; about kings from foreign countries winning battles; about kings in their home country losing battles; and about probabilities of victories and losses of warring kings. Samaṇa Gotama abstains from making a wrongful living by such means. A worldling, bhikkhus, might praise the Tathāgata in this manner.

24. And then there are certain respected samaṇas and brāhmaṇas who, living on the food offered out of faith (in *kamma* and its results), make a wrongful living by means of low arts contrary to correct practice conducive to the attainment of deva realms and Nibbāna. And what are they? They are: making predictions about the eclipse of the moon, or of the sun; about the conjunction of a group of stars with a planet; about the correct or incorrect course of the moon, the sun and the planets; about meteors, comets, earthquakes and thunder; about the rising and setting of the moon, the sun and the planets; about the phenomena of darkness and brightness following such rising and setting; about the effects of the eclipse of the moon, or of the sun, or of the planets; about the effects of the moon or the sun taking the right course; about the effects of the moon or the sun taking the wrong course; about the effects of the planets taking the right course; about the effects of the planets taking the wrong course; about the effects of meteors, comets, and thunder; about the effects of the rising and setting of the moon, or of the sun, or of the planets; and about the effects of the phenomena of darkness or brightness following such rising and setting. Samaṇa Gotama abstains from making a wrongful living by such means. A worldling, bhikkhus, might praise the Tathāgata in this manner.

25. And then there are certain respected samaṇas and brāhmaṇas who, living on the food offered out of faith (in *kamma* and its results), make a wrongful living by means of low arts contrary to correct practice conducive to the attainment of deva realms and Nibbāna. And what are they? They are: predicting rainfall or drought, abundance or famine, peace or calamity, disease or health; and knowledge of counting on the fingers or of arithmetical or mathematical calculations, of versification, and of treatises of controversial matters (such as the origin of the universe etc.).

Samaṇa Gotama abstains from making a wrongful living by such means. A worldling, bhikkhus, might praise the Tathāgata in this manner.

26. And then there are certain respected samaṇas and brāhmaṇas who, living on the food offered out of faith (in *kamma* and its results), make a wrongful living by means of low arts contrary to correct practice conducive to the attainment of deva realms and Nibbāna. And what are they? They are: bringing the bride to the bridegroom; leading away the bride from her father's home; arranging betrothal, or divorce; making predictions relating to acquisition or distribution of property; causing gain or loss of fame and prosperity; curing the tendency to abort or miscarry; casting spells to cause immobility of the tongue or the jaws; reciting a spell to stop an attacking hand or to cause inability to speak or to hear; conducting seances with the aid of mirrors, or employing young women or female slaves as mediums; propitiating the sun or the Brahmā; making fire issue from the mouth by means of a spell; and making invocations to the goddess of glory. Samaṇa Gotama abstains from making a wrongful living by such means. A worldling, bhikkhus, might praise the Tathāgata in this manner.

27. And then there are certain respected samaṇas and brāhmaṇas who, living on the food offered out of faith (in *kamma* and its results), make a wrongful living by means of low arts contrary to correct practice conducive to the attainment of deva realms and Nibbāna. And what are they? They are: propitiating the devas by promises of offerings; making offerings to devas for favours granted; causing possession by spirits or exorcising them; casting spells with magical formulae learnt in a mud-house; turning a eunuch into a man; turning a man into a eunuch; practising the art of choosing building-sites; propitiating the devas while choosing building-sites; practising the profession of mouth-washing or bathing; fire-worshipping; causing vomiting; giving purgatives; using emetics, or catharses; letting out phlegm etc. from the head; preparing ear-drops or eye drops; preparing medicinal snuff, or eye ointment to remove cataracts; preparing eye-lotions; curing cataracts; doing surgery; practising paediatrics; preparing basic drugs and dressing sores and removing the dressing. Samaṇa Gotama abstains from making a wrongful living by such means. A worldling, bhikkhus, might praise the Tathāgata in this manner.

Bhikkhus! These are the matters of a trifling and inferior nature, of mere morality, in respect of which a worldling might speak when praising the Tathāgata.

End of the Long Section on Morality

Exposition on Wrong Views

28. Bhikkhus! Besides morality there are other dhammas[12] which are profound, hard to see, hard to comprehend, tranquil, noble, surpassing logic, subtle and intelligible only to the *paṇḍita, ariyas* who have attained one of the four maggas. The Tathāgata has set them forth after realization of these dhammas by himself through *sabbaññuta ñāṇa* (Perfect Wisdom).[13] Anyone wishing to praise correctly the true virtues of the Tathāgata should do so in terms of these dhammas. And what are the dhammas which are profound, hard to see, hard to comprehend, tranquil, noble, surpassing logic, subtle and intelligible only to the *ariyas*?

(The Buddha answered this question by means of a graduated discourse, beginning with eighteen wrong views relating to the past as follows.)

Eighteen Wrong Views Relating to the Past (Pubbantānudiṭṭhi)

Note: [A Synopsis is inserted here to facilitate understanding of the eighteen wrong views relating to the past.]

Synopsis of Wrong Views

The Brahmajāla Sutta sets forth sixty-two kinds of wrong views which are held by samaṇas and brāhmaṇas. These sixty-two kinds of wrong views are classified into two categories, namely, Pubbantānudiṭṭhi and Aparantanudiṭṭhi.

Pubbantānudiṭṭhi means the group of wrong views which are based on the past existences. Aparantānudiṭṭhi means the group of wrong views which are thoughts or speculations on the future.

Pubbantānudiṭṭhi is further classified into five sub-categories. They are as follows:

(1) Sassata diṭṭhi
(2) Ekacca sassata diṭṭhi
(3) Antānanta diṭṭhi
(4) Amarāvikkhepa diṭṭhi
(5) Adhiccasamuppanna diṭṭhi

The following are brief explanations on the above-mentioned five subcategories.

12. *Dhammas*: The Commentary says that here the dhammas referred to are sabbaññuta ñāṇa.

13. The Buddha's *sabbaññuta ñāṇa* encompasses Magga Insight.

(1) *Sassata diṭṭhi* is a group of false views of eternity, which says that *atta* as well as *loka* is eternal. There are four different views in this group, namely, the first eternity view, the second eternity view, the third eternity view, and the fourth eternity view.

(2) *Ekacca Sassata diṭṭhi* is a group of false views of eternity, which says that *atta* and *loka* are in some cases eternal and in other cases not eternal. There are four different dualistic views in this group, namely, the first dualistic view of eternity, the second dualistic view of eternity, the third dualistic view of eternity, and the fourth dualistic view of eternity.

(3) *Antānanta diṭṭhi* is a group of false views on the finiteness or otherwise of the world system (as represented by the mental image of the earth-device used in meditation). There are four different views in this group, namely, the first view which says the world system is finite, the second view which says it is infinite, the third view which says it is finite vertically and infinite horizontally, and the fourth view which says it is neither finite nor infinite.

(4) *Amarāvikkhepa diṭṭhi* (false views that make one sit on the fence, to be on the safe side). For example, a question is put to a person who does not know the answer. He does not want to admit that he does not know. At the same time, he fears that the wrong answer would cause him distress, which might be harmful to him. Therefore, he answers the question thus: "I don't take it this way; neither do I take it that way; and I don't take it the other way; neither do I take it not this way, nor that way, nor the other way, and also I don't take it that it is otherwise."

There are four causes that make the samaṇas and brāhmaṇas in this group sit on the fence. The first sits on the fence because of the fear that the wrong answer would cause him distress, which might be harmful to him. The second sits on the fence because of the fear that the wrong answer might cause the arising in him of mental defilements, which would in turn cause distress that might be harmful to him. The third sits on the fence because of the fear of his being taken to task for the wrong answer. The fourth sits on the fence because of lack of wisdom.

(5) *Adhiccasamuppanna diṭṭhi* (false views that *atta* as well as *loka* arises without a cause).

There are two groups of persons who hold this view.

(a) The persons belonging to the first group were asaññasatta brahmās in their previous existence. These brahmās are so called because they are the brahmās who have only body and no mind. In order to achieve this kind of rebirth, those who are desirous of having it have to practice the Saññā virāga bhāvanā. In simple terms, it means bhāvanā for the extermination of mind. Even though it is so called, it does not exterminate mind. It only suspends the arising of mind. When the effects of Saññā virāga bhāvanā come to an end, the mental process that has been suspended arises generally as the paṭisandhi citta (the first citta) of a human being. In simple terms, it can be said thus: When an asaññasatta brahmā dies, he is generally reborn as a human being. When he comes of age he may acquire through the practice of meditation a psychic power which would enable one to recall the past. Since, however, he was an asaññasatta brahmā in his previous existence, his psychic power cannot take him beyond his paṭisandhi citta. Therefore he says that *atta* and *loka* arise by themselves, without anything to cause their appearance.

(b) The persons belonging to the second group base on speculation their view that *atta* and loka arise without a cause.

This is the end of the synopsis on Pubbantānu diṭṭhi, which consists of eighteen false views.

29. There are, bhikkhus, certain samaṇas and brāhmaṇas who speculate on the past and who adhere to views relating to it. They assert on eighteen different grounds their various wrong views based on the past. On what authority and on what basis do these respected samaṇas and brāhmaṇas speculate on the past, adhere to views relating to it, and assert on eighteen different grounds their various wrong views based on the past?

Four Kinds of Eternity View (Sassata Diṭṭhi)

30. There are, bhikkhus, certain samaṇas and brāhmaṇas who hold the view of eternity. They give four reasons to demonstrate the eternal existence of *atta* as well as *loka.*[14] On what authority and on what basis do these respected samaṇas and brāhmaṇas demonstrate on four grounds[15] that *atta* as well as *loka* is eternal?

---

14. The Commentary explains *atta* as well as *loka* as one of the five khandhas. The Sub-Commentary expands this by saying that (i) when the four mental khandhas are taken as *atta* by those who believe in *atta* (soul), the remaining khandha is taken as *loka*; or (ii) when one of the five khandhas is taken as *atta*, the rest of the khandhas are taken as *loka*; or (iii) when all the five khandhas of oneself are taken as *atta*, the khandhas outside oneself are taken as *loka* by those who believe in *atta.*

15. See Appendix A 1.

The First Category of Eternity View

31. In this world, bhikkhus, a certain samaṇa or brāhmaṇa achieves utmost mental concentration by dint of ardent, steadfast, persevering exertion, mindfulness and right attentiveness. When his mind has thus gained the highest concentration, he recollects many past existences.[16] And what does he recollect?

He recollects one past existence, or two, or three, or four, or five, or ten, or twenty, or thirty, or forty, or fifty, or a hundred, a thousand, a hundred thousand existences, or many hundred, many thousand, many hundred thousand existences in this way: "In that past existence I was known by such a name. I was born into such a family. I was of such an appearance. I was thus nourished. I enjoyed pleasure thus. I suffered pain thus. My life-span was such. I died in that existence. I was born in another existence. In that (new) existence I was known by such a name. I was born into such a family. I was of such an appearance. I was thus nourished. I enjoyed pleasure thus. I suffered pain thus. My life-span was such. I died in that existence. Then I was born in this existence." In this way he recollects many past existences together with their characteristics and related facts (such as names and clans).

He says thus:

"*Atta* as well as *loka* is eternal, barren,[17] standing like a mountain peak and firm like a gate post.

Beings transmigrate, go the round of rebirths, die and are born again. *Atta* or *loka*, however, is permanent like all things of an unchanging and enduring nature. It must be so because I have achieved utmost mental concentration by dint of ardent, steadfast, persevering exertion, mindfulness and right attentiveness. When my mind has thus gained the highest concentration, I can recollect many past existences. And what do I recollect?

I recollect one past existence, or two, or three, or four, or five, or ten, or twenty, or thirty, or forty, or fifty, or a hundred, a thousand, a hundred thousand existences, or many hundred, many thousand, many hundred thousand existences in this way: 'In that past existence I was known by such a name. I was born into such a family. I was of such an appearance. I was thus nourished. I enjoyed pleasure thus. I suffered

---

16. **Recollects many past existences:** See Appendix A 2.

17. **Barren:** just as a barren woman cannot bear any children, *atta* as well as *loka* cannot produce another *atta* or *loka*.

pain thus. My life-span was such. I died in that existence. I was born in another existence. In that (new) existence I was known by such a name. I was born into such a family. I was of such an appearance. I was thus nourished. I enjoyed pleasure thus. I suffered pain thus. My life-span was such. I died in that existence. Then I was born in this existence.' In this way I recollect many past existences together with their characteristics and related facts (such as names and clans). And so I say that I know this:

Atta as well as *loka* is eternal, barren, standing like a mountain peak and firm like a gate post. Beings transmigrate, go the round of rebirths, die and are born again. *Atta* or *loka*, however, is permanent like all things of an unchanging and enduring nature."

Bhikkhus! This is the first line of reasoning and it is based on this, holding on to this, that certain samaṇas and brāhmaṇas demonstrate that *atta* as well as *loka* is eternal. (1)

The Second Category of Eternity View

32. And secondly, on what authority and on what basis do the respected samaṇas and brāhmaṇas who hold the eternity view demonstrate that *atta* as well as *loka* is eternal?

In this world, bhikkhus, a certain Samaṇa or brāhmaṇa achieves utmost mental concentration by dint of ardent, steadfast, persevering exertion, mindfulness and right attentiveness. When his mind has thus gained the highest concentration, he recollects many past existences. And what does he recollect?

He recollects one cycle of dissolution and development, or two, or three, or four, or five, or ten cycles in this way: "In that past existence I was known by such a name. I was born into such a family. I was of such an appearance. I was thus nourished. I enjoyed pleasure thus. I suffered pain thus. My life-span was such. I died in that existence. I was born in another existence. In that (new) existence I was known by such a name. I was born into such a family. I was of such an appearance. I was thus nourished. I enjoyed pleasure thus. I suffered pain thus. My life-span was such. I died in that existence. Then I was born in this existence." In this way he recollects many past existences together with their characteristics and related facts (such as names and clans).

He says thus:

"*Atta* as well as *loka* is eternal, barren, standing like a mountain peak and firm like a gate post. Beings transmigrate, go the round of rebirths, die and are born again. *Atta* or *loka*, however, is permanent like all things of an unchanging and enduring nature. It must be so because I have achieved utmost mental concentration by dint of ardent, steadfast, persevering exertion, mindfulness and right attentiveness. When my mind has thus gained the highest concentration, I can recollect many past existences. And what do I recollect?

I recollect one cycle of dissolution and development, or two, or three, or four, or five, or ten cycles in this way: 'In that past existence I was known by such a name. I was born into such a family. I was of such an appearance. I was thus nourished. I enjoyed pleasure thus. I suffered pain thus. My life-span was such. I died in that existence. I was born in another existence. In that (new) existence I was known by such a name. I was born into such a family. I was of such an appearance. I was thus nourished. I enjoyed pleasure thus. I suffered pain thus. My life-span was such. I died in that existence. Then I was born in this existence.' In this way I recollect many past existences together with their characteristics and related facts (such as names and clans). And so I say that I know this:

Atta as well as *loka* is eternal, barren, standing like a mountain peak and firm like a gate post. Beings transmigrate, go the round of rebirths, die and are born again. *Atta* or *loka*, however, is permanent like all things of an unchanging and enduring nature."

Bhikkhus! This is the second line of reasoning and it is based on this, holding on to this, that certain samaṇas and brāhmaṇas demonstrate that *atta* as well as *loka* is eternal. (2)

The Third Category of Eternity View

33. And thirdly, on what authority and on what basis do the respected samaṇas and brāhmaṇas who hold the eternity view demonstrate that *atta* as well as *loka* is eternal?

In this world, bhikkhus, a certain samaṇa or brāhmaṇa achieves utmost mental concentration by dint of ardent, steadfast, persevering exertion, mindfulness and right attentiveness. When his mind has thus gained the highest mental concentration, he recollects many past existences. And what does he recollect?

He recollects ten cycles of dissolution and development, or twenty, or thirty, or forty cycles in this way: "In that past existence I was known by such a name. I was born into such a family. I was of such an appearance. I was thus nourished. I enjoyed pleasure thus. I suffered pain thus. My life-span was such. I died in that existence. I was born in another existence. In that (new) existence I was known by such a name.

I was born into such a family. I was of such an appearance. I was thus nourished. I enjoyed pleasure thus. I suffered pain thus. My life-span was such. I died in that existence. Then I was born in this existence." In this way he recollects many past existences together with their characteristics and related facts (such as names and clans).

He says thus:

"*Atta* as well as *loka* is eternal, barren, standing like a mountain peak and firm like a gate post. Beings transmigrate, go the round of rebirths, die and are born again. *Atta* or *loka*, however, is permanent like all things of an unchanging and enduring nature. It must be so because I have achieved utmost mental concentration by dint of Ardent, steadfast, persevering exertion mindfulness and right attentiveness. When my mind has thus gained the highest concentration, I can recollect many past existences. And what do I recollect?

I recollect ten, or twenty, or thirty or forty, cycles of dissolution and development in this way: 'In that past existence I was known by such a name. I was born into such a family. I was of such an appearance. I was thus nourished. I enjoyed pleasure thus. I suffered pain thus. My life-span was such. I died in that existence. I was born in another existence. In that (new) existence I was known by such a name. I was born into such a family. I was of such an appearance. I was thus nourished. I enjoyed pleasure thus. I suffered pain thus. My life-span was such. I died in that existence. Then I was born in this existence.' In this way I recollect many past existences together with their characteristics and related facts (such as names and clans). And so I say that I know this:

Atta as well as *loka* is eternal, barren, standing like a mountain peak and firm like a gate post. Beings transmigrate, go the round of rebirths, die and are born again. *Atta* or *loka*, however, is permanent like all things of an unchanging and enduring nature."

Bhikkhus! This is the third line of reasoning, and it is based on this, holding on to this, that certain samaṇas and brāhmaṇas demonstrate that *atta* as well as *loka* is eternal. (3)

The Fourth Category of Eternity View

34. And fourthly, on what authority and on what basis do the respected samaṇas and brāhmaṇas demonstrate that *atta* as well as *loka* is eternal?

In this world, bhikkhus, a certain Samaṇa or brāhmaṇa is given to logic and investigation. He uses various methods of reasoning, conducts investigations and gives his views, saying:

'*Atta* as well as *loka* is eternal, barren, standing like a mountain peak and firm like a gate post. Beings transmigrate, *go* the round of rebirths, die and are born again. *Atta* or *loka*, however, is permanent like all things of an unchanging and enduring nature.'

Bhikkhus! This is the fourth line of reasoning, and it is based on this, holding on to this, that certain samaṇas and brāhmaṇas demonstrate that *atta* as well as *loka* is eternal. (4)

35. Bhikkhus! The samaṇas and brāhmaṇas who hold the eternity view demonstrate that *atta* as well as *loka* is eternal in the four ways thus cited above.

Bhikkhus! When any samaṇas and brāhmaṇas who hold the eternity view demonstrate that *atta* as well as *loka* is eternal, all of them proffer these four, or one of these four, lines of reasoning and no other besides them.

36. Bhikkhus! The Tathāgata knows the destination, the next existence in which one holding these four views would be reborn, if these views are thus held on to, if these views are thus grasped.

The Tathāgata knows these four views. He also knows the dhamma which surpasses them. Knowing that dhamma, he does not view it in the wrong way.[18] Since he does not view it in the wrong way, he realizes by himself the extinction of defilements (i.e., greed, anger, and ignorance of the Four Ariya Truths.)

Bhikkhus! Since the Tathāgata rightly knows the arising of feeling[19] (*vedanā*) and its cause, the cessation of feeling and its cause, its pleasantness, its faults, and freedom from attachment to it, he becomes liberated without any clinging, (i.e., he realizes Nibbāna).

37. Thus, bhikkhus, these are the dhammas[20] which are profound, hard to see, hard to comprehend, tranquil, noble, surpassing logic, subtle and intelligible only to the *ariyas*. The Tathāgata has set them forth after realization of these dhammas by himself through *Sabbaññuta ñāṇa* (Perfect Wisdom). Anyone wishing to praise correctly the true virtues of the Tathāgata should do so in terms of these dhammas.

End of the first portion for recitation (bhāṇa vāra)[21]

---

18. **In the wrong way**: See Appendix A 3.
19. **Feeling**: see Appendix A 4.
20. *Dhammas:* see footnote 1 of para 28.
21. *Bhāṇa vāra* means the portion of the text which can be recited at a stretch by an average bhikkhu. If the text is in the *gāthā* form, one *bhāṇa vāra* may roughly have two hundred and fifty stanzas. If it is in the prose form, it may roughly have eight thousand words.

FOUR VIEWS OF ETERNITY AND NON-ETERNITY (Ekacca Sassata Diṭṭhi)

38. There are, bhikkhus, some samaṇas and brāhmaṇas who, holding the dualistic view of eternity and non-eternity, put forward four reasons to show that *atta* as well as *loka* is in some cases eternal and in others not eternal. On what authority and on what basis do these respected samaṇas and brāhmaṇas, holding the dualistic view of eternity and non-eternity, put forward four reasons to show that *atta* as well as *loka* is in some cases eternal and in others not eternal?

THE FIRST CATEGORY OF EKACCA SASSATA DIṬṬHI

39. There, indeed, is such a time, bhikkhus, as when this world system gets dissolved, as it does at times, after a lapse of many aeons. When the world system becomes thus dissolved, beings are reborn mostly in the Abhassara[22] plane of existence (of radiant Brahmās). When they are born there because of *Jhāna* mind, they are nurtured by rapture, resplendent with light from their own bodies, sojourning in the heavens and living in splendour. And they remain there for aeons.

40. There, indeed, is such a time, bhikkhus, as when this world system rises again, as it does at times, after a lapse of many aeons. When the world system thus rises again, there appears a palatial Brahmā-abode (brahmā-vimāna, one or all three of Brahmā realms of first *Jhāna*), void of all life. At that time, a certain being from the Ābhassara plane of existence dies, either at the end of his span of life, or on the exhaustion of the stock of his meritorious deeds, and is reborn in that empty palatial Brahmā realm. When he is born there because of *Jhāna* mind, he is nurtured by rapture, resplendent with light from his own body, sojourning in the heavens and living in splendour. Thus he remains there for aeons.

41. Living there alone for aeons, there arises in him mental weariness and a longing for company thus: "Would that some other beings come to this place!" And then other beings from the Ābhassara plane of existence die either at the end of their span of life, or on the exhaustion of the stock of their meritorious deeds, and are reborn in

---

22. The Ābhassara plane of existence, to which Brahmās of flashing radiance belong, is the third of the three Second Jhāna Brahmā realms in the thirty-one planes of existence. See Appendix A5 for the thirty-one planes of existence.

that palatial Brahmā realm. When they are born there because of *Jhāna* mind, they are nurtured by rapture, resplendent with light from their own bodies, sojourning in the heavens and living in splendour. Thus they remain there for aeons.

42. Then, bhikkhus, the being who was the first to be reborn there thinks to himself thus:

> "I am the Brahmā, the great Brahmā, the conqueror, the unconquered, the all-seeing, the subjector of all to his wishes, the omnipotent, the maker, the creator, the supreme, the controller, the one confirmed in the practice of Jhāna, and father to all that have been and shall be. I have created these other beings. Why can I say so? I can say so because awhile ago I thought to myself: 'Would that some other beings come to this place!' As I wished so, other beings have appeared in this place."

And then other beings who appeared later think to themselves:

> "This honourable personage is the Brahmā, the great Brahmā, the conqueror, the unconquered, the all-seeing, the subjector of all to his wishes, the omnipotent, the maker, the creator, the supreme, the controller, the one confirmed in the practice of Jhāna, and father to all that have been and shall be. This honourable Brahmā has created us. Why can we say so? We can say so because, as we see, he appeared in this place first, whereas we appeared only after him."

43. Among them, bhikkhus, the one who appeared first lives longer, and is more beautiful and more powerful (than the others). Those beings who appeared later have a shorter life, and are less beautiful and less powerful (than the one who first appeared).

44. Then, bhikkhus, there arises this possibility. A being dies in the Brahmā plane of existence and is reborn in this human world; and there he renounces the worldly life for the homeless life of a recluse. And having thus renounced the worldly life and become a homeless recluse, he achieves utmost mental concentration by dint of ardent, steadfast, persevering exertion, mindfulness and right attentiveness. Having established his mind in highest concentration, he can recollect that former existence (of a Brahmā); but he cannot recollect beyond that.

He says thus:

> "That honourable personage is the Brahmā, the great Brahmā, the conqueror, the unconquered, the all-seeing, the subjector of all to his wishes, the omnipotent, the maker, the creator, the supreme, the

controller, the one confirmed in the practice of Jhāna, and father to all that have been and shall be. That honourable Brahmā has created us. He is permanent, stable, eternal, immutable and as everlasting as all things eternal. We, who were created by the honourable Brahmā, are impermanent, changeable, short-lived and mortal. Thus have we come into this human world."

This, bhikkhus, is the first possibility. It is based on this, holding on to this, that some samaṇas and brāhmaṇas, holding the dualistic view of eternity and non eternity, propound that *atta* as well as *loka* is in some cases eternal and in others not eternal. (4+1=5)

The Second Category of Ekacca Sassata Diṭṭhi

45. In the second category (of *ekacca sassata diṭṭhi*) on what authority and on what basis do the respected samaṇas and brāhmaṇas, holding the dualistic view of eternity and non-eternity, propound that *atta* as well as *loka* is in some cases eternal and in others not eternal?

Bhikkhus! There are devas known as Khiḍḍāpadosikas who, absorbed in merry-making and pleasure-seeking for a long time, forget to take nutriment and through such forgetfulness die in that abode of the devas.

46. Then, bhikkhus, there arises this possibility. A certain being dies in that world of devas and is reborn in this human world; and there he renounces the worldly life for, the homeless life of a recluse. And having thus renounced the worldly life and become a homeless recluse, he achieves utmost mental concentration by dint of ardent, steadfast, persevering exertion, mindfulness and right attentiveness. Having established his mind in highest concentration, he can recollect that former existence (of a deva); but he cannot recollect beyond that.

He says thus:

"Those honourable devas, who are not Khiḍḍāpadosikas, are not absorbed in merrymaking and pleasure-seeking for a long time. And as they are not absorbed in merry-making and pleasure-seeking for a long time, they do not forget to take nutriment. And since they are not forgetful they do not die in that abode of the devas. They remain permanent, stable, eternal, immutable and as everlasting as all things eternal. But we Khiḍḍāpadosikas were absorbed in merry-making and pleasure-seeking for a long time; and because we were absorbed in merry-making and pleasure-seeking for a long time, we forgot to take nutriment. Through such forgetfulness we died in that world of the devas. We are impermanent, changeable, short lived and mortal. Thus have we come into this human world."

This, bhikkhus, is the second possibility. It is based on this that some samaṇas and brāhmaṇas, holding the dualistic view of eternity and non-eternity, propound that *atta* as well as *loka* is in some cases eternal and in others not eternal. (4+2=6)

The Third Category of Ekacca Sassata Diṭṭhi

47. In the third category (of *ekacca sassata diṭṭhi*) on what authority and on what basis do the respected samaṇas and brāhmaṇas, holding the dualistic view of eternity and non-eternity, propound that *atta* as well as *loka* is in some cases eternal and in others not eternal?

Bhikkhus! There are devas known as Manopadosikas who stare hard and long at one another (with jealousy). Staring hard and long thus at one another, they develop mutual hatred; becoming exhausted both physically and mentally, they die in that world of devas.

48. Then, bhikkhus, there arises this possibility. A certain being dies in that world of devas and is reborn in this human world; and there he renounces the worldly life for the homeless life of a recluse. And having thus renounced the worldly life and become a homeless recluse, he achieves utmost mental concentration by dint of ardent, steadfast, persevering exertion, mindfulness and right attentiveness. Having established his mind in highest concentration, he can recollect that former existence (of a deva); but he cannot recollect beyond that.

He says thus:

"Those honourable devas who are not Manopadosikas do not stare hard and long at one another (with jealousy). They do not, therefore, develop mutual hatred. Not becoming exhausted both physically and mentally they do not die in that world of devas. They remain permanent, stable, eternal, immutable and as everlasting as all things eternal. But we Manopadosikas, who stared hard and long at one another (with jealousy), developed mutual hatred and became exhausted both physically and mentally. And we died in that world of devas. We are impermanent, changeable, short-lived and mortal. Thus have we come into this human world."

This, bhikkhus, is the third possibility. It is based on this that some samaṇas and brāhmaṇas, holding the dualistic view of eternity and non-eternity, propound that *atta* as well as *loka* is in some cases eternal and in others not eternal. (4+3=7)

The Fourth Category of Ekacca Sassata Diṭṭhi

49. In the fourth category (of *ekacca sassata diṭṭhi*) on what authority and on what basis do the respected samaṇas and brāhmaṇas, holding the dualistic view of eternity and non-eternity, propound that *atta* as well as *loka* is in some cases eternal and in others not eternal?

Bhikkhus! In this world a certain Samaṇa or brāhmaṇa is given to logic and investigation. He uses various methods of reasoning, conducts investigations and gives his views, saying:

> "This which is called eye, ear, nose, tongue and the physical body is the *atta* which is impermanent, unstable, not eternal and mutable. But this which is called mind, thought or consciousness, is the *atta* which is permanent, stable, eternal, immutable and as everlasting as things eternal."

Bhikkhus! This is the fourth possibility. It is based on this that some samaṇas and brāhmaṇas, holding the dualistic view of eternity and non-eternity, propound that *atta* as well as *loka* is in some cases eternal and in others not eternal. (4+4=8)

50. Bhikkhus! These samaṇas and brāhmaṇas, holding the dualistic view of eternity and non-eternity, demonstrate on these four grounds that *atta* as well as *loka* is in some cases eternal and in others not eternal.

Bhikkhus! When any samaṇas and brāhmaṇas, holding the dualistic view of eternity and non-eternity, demonstrate that *atta* as well as *loka* is in some cases eternal and in others not eternal, all of them proffer these four, or one of these four, lines of reasoning and not any other line of reasoning.

51. Bhikkhus! The Tathāgata knows the destination, the next existence in which one holding these four views would be reborn, if these views are thus held on to, if these views are thus grasped.

The Tathāgata knows these four views. He also knows the dhamma which surpasses them. Knowing that dhamma, he does not view it in the wrong way. Since he does not view it in the wrong way, he realizes by himself the extinction of defilements (i.e., greed, anger, and ignorance of the Four Ariya Truths).

Bhikkhus! Since the Tathāgata rightly knows the arising of feeling (*vedanā*) and its cause, the cessation of feeling and its cause, its pleasantness, its faults, and freedom from attachment to it, he becomes liberated without any clinging, (i.e., he realizes Nibbana).[23]

52. Thus, bhikkhus, these are the dhammas which are profound, hard to see, hard to comprehend, tranquil, noble, surpassing logic, subtle and intelligible only to the *ariyas*. The Tathāgata has set them forth after realization of these dhammas by himself through *Sabbaññuta ñāṇa* (Perfect Wisdom). Anyone wishing to praise correctly the true virtues of the Tathāgata should do so in terms of these dhammas.

FOUR VIEWS OF THE WORLD BEING FINITE OR INFINITE (Antānanta Diṭṭhi)

53. There are, bhikkhus, some samaṇas and brāhmaṇas, who hold that the world is finite. There are also samaṇas and brāhmaṇas, who hold that the world is infinite. They put forward four grounds to support their respective views. On what authority and on what basis do these respected samaṇas and brāhmaṇas put forward four grounds to support their respective views?

THE FIRST ANTĀNANTA DIṬṬHI

54. In this world, bhikkhus, a certain Samaṇa or brāhmaṇa achieves utmost mental concentration by dint of ardent, steadfast, persevering exertion, mindfulness and right attentiveness. Having thus established his mind in highest concentration, he abides in the view that the world (as represented by the purified mental image, paṭibhāga nimitta,[24] of the earth-device used in meditation) is finite.

---

23. The Buddha achieved four maggas, by means of four Satipaṭṭhānas. In this paragraph, the Buddha was referring to Vedanānupassanā Satipaṭṭhāna, which is one of the four.

Vedanānupassanā Satipaṭṭhāna requires one to be mindful of feeling, whenever it appears, before any train of thought takes place. If he can do so steadfastly, he will perceive the *anicca, dukkha, anattā* nature of the five khandhas. This perception is conducive to the achievement of maggas.

By means of Vedanānupassanā Satipaṭṭhāna, the Bodhisatta perceived the impermanent, oppressive, soulless nature of *vedanā*. This perception was conducive, to his achievement of freedom from *dukkha*, where there was absolute extinction of *kilesas* (defilements).

This paragraph is meant to disillusion those who believe "*vedanā* (feeling)" to be *atta*.

24. See Appendix A6 on Paṭibhāga Nimitta.

He says thus:

"This world is finite. It is circumscribed. Why can it be said so? It can be said so because having achieved utmost mental concentration by dint of ardent, steadfast, persevering exertion, mindfulness and right attentiveness, and having established my mind in highest concentration, I abide in the view that the world is finite. Based on this I know that the world is finite and that it is circumscribed."

This, bhikkhus, is the first possibility. Basing themselves on this authority and on this ground, some samaṇas and brāhmaṇas holding the view that the world is finite, and some samaṇas and brāhmaṇas holding the view that the world is infinite, demonstrate their respective points of view — the finiteness or the infiniteness of the world. (8+1=9)

The Second Antānanta Diṭṭhi

55. In the second category of *antānanta diṭṭhi*, on what authority and on what basis do the respected samaṇas and brāhmaṇas propound either that the world is finite or that the world is infinite?

In this world, bhikkhus, a certain samaṇa or brāhmaṇa achieves utmost mental concentration by dint of ardent, steadfast, persevering exertion, mindfulness and right attentiveness. Having thus established his mind in highest concentration, he abides in the view that the world (as represented by the purified mental image of the earth-device used in meditation) is infinite.

He says thus:

"This world is infinite, with no limit. Those samaṇas and brāhmaṇas who assert that the world is finite and that it is circumscribed are wrong. In fact, this world is infinite, with no limit. Why can it be said so? It can be said so because having achieved utmost mental concentration by dint of ardent, steadfast, persevering exertion, mindfulness and right attentiveness, and having established my mind in highest concentration, I abide in the view that the world is infinite. Based on this I know that the world is infinite, with no limit."

This, bhikkhus, is the second possibility. Basing themselves on this authority and on this ground, some samaṇas and brāhmaṇas holding the view that the world is finite, and some samaṇas and brāhmaṇas holding the view that the world is infinite, demonstrate their respective points of view — the finiteness or the infiniteness of the world. (8+2=10)

The Third Antānanta Diṭṭhi

56. In the third category of *antānanta diṭṭhi*, on what authority and on what basis do the respected samaṇas and brāhmaṇas propound either that the world is finite or that the world is infinite?

In this world, bhikkhus, a certain samaṇa or brāhmaṇa achieves utmost mental concentration by dint of ardent, steadfast, persevering exertion, mindfulness and right attentiveness. Having thus established his mind in highest concentration, he abides in the view that the world (as represented by the purified mental image of the earth-device used in meditation) is finite vertically, but infinite horizontally.

He says thus:

"This world is finite, and, at the same time, infinite. Those samaṇas and brāhmaṇas who assert that the world is finite and is circumscribed are wrong. And so are the samaṇas and brāhmaṇas who assert that the world is infinite, with no limit. Why can it be said so? It can be said so because having achieved utmost mental concentration by dint of ardent, steadfast, persevering exertion, mindfulness and right attentiveness, and having established my mind in highest concentration, I abide in the view that the world is finite vertically, and is infinite horizontally. Based on this I know that the world is finite, and, at the same time, infinite."

This, bhikkhus, is the third possibility. Basing themselves on this authority and on this ground, some samaṇas and brāhmaṇas holding the view that the world is finite, and some samaṇas and brāhmaṇas holding the view that the world is infinite, demonstrate their respective points of view — the finiteness or the infiniteness of the world. (8+3=11)

The Fourth Antānanta Diṭṭhi

57. In the fourth category of *antānanta diṭṭhi*, on what authority and on what basis do the respected samaṇas and brāhmaṇas propound either that the world is finite or that the world is infinite?

In this world, bhikkhus, a certain samara or brāhmaṇa is given to logic and investigation. He uses various methods of reasoning, conducts investigations and gives his views, saying:

"This World is neither finite nor infinite. Those samaṇas and brāhmaṇas who assert that the world is finite and that it is circumscribed are wrong. And so are those samaṇas and brāhmaṇas who assert that the world is infinite, with no limit. And so also are those samaṇas and brāhmaṇas who assert that the world is finite as well as infinite. This world is neither finite nor infinite."

This, bhikkhus, is the fourth possibility. Basing themselves on this authority and on this ground, some samaṇas and brāhmaṇas holding the view that the world is finite, and some samaṇas and brāhmaṇas holding the view that the world is infinite, demonstrate their respective points of view — the finiteness or the infiniteness of the world. (8+4=12)

58. Bhikkhus! Those samaṇas and brāhmaṇas who hold that the world is finite and those samaṇas and brāhmaṇas who hold that the world is infinite support their respective views on these four grounds.

Bhikkhus! When any samaṇas and brāhmaṇas who hold that the world is finite or when any samaṇas and brāhmaṇas who hold that it is infinite support their respective views, all of them proffer these four, or any one of the four, lines of reasoning and not any other line of reasoning.

59. Bhikkhus! The Tathāgata knows the destination, the next existence in which one holding these four views would be reborn, if these views are thus held on to, if these views are thus grasped.

The Tathāgata knows these four views. He also knows the dhamma which surpasses them. Knowing that dhamma, he does not view it in the wrong way. Since he does not view it in the wrong way, he realizes by himself the extinction of defilements (i.e., greed, anger, and ignorance of the Four Ariya Truths).

Bhikkhus! Since the Tathāgata rightly knows the arising of feeling (*vedanā*) and its cause, the cessation of feeling and its cause, its pleasantness, its faults, and freedom from attachment to it, he becomes liberated without any clinging, (i.e., he realizes Nibbāna).

60. Thus, bhikkhus, these are the dhammas which are profound, hard to see, hard to comprehend, tranquil, noble, surpassing logic, subtle and intelligible only to the *ariyas*. The Tathāgata has set them forth after realization of these dhammas by himself through *Sabbaññuta ñāṇa* (Perfect Wisdom). Anyone wishing to praise correctly the true virtues of the Tathāgata should do so in terms of these dhammas.

Four Kinds of Indecisive Evasion
(Amarāvikkhepa Diṭṭhi)

61. Bhikkhus, there are certain samaṇas and brāhmaṇas who by means of indecisive speech evade questions put to them on any matter;

they evade answering them, (behaving elusively like amarā fish)[25] and speak in ambiguous terms, because of four reasons.

What are the four reasons that cause those respected samaṇas and brāhmaṇas to be elusive, to evade questions put to them on any matter and to speak in ambiguous terms?

The First Amarāvikkhepa Diṭṭhi

62. In this world, bhikkhus, a certain samaṇa or brāhmaṇa does not understand correctly what is merit[26] or what is demerit.[27]

He thinks thus:

"I do not understand correctly what is merit or what is demerit. If I were to say what is merit, without really understanding it as

---

25. **amarā fish**: a kind of slippery fish which cannot be caught because of its skill in diving into and jumping out of water.

26. Merit means *dāna* (charity), *sīla* (self-control to refrain from doing and speaking what is evil), *bhāvanā* (*samatha* and *vipassanā*). *Samatha* is the means for attaining *rūpa jhānas* and *arūpa jhānas*; *rūpa jhānas* can cause those who have them to be reborn as corporeal brahmās; *arūpa jhānas* can cause those who have them to be reborn as incorporeal brahmās. *Vipassanā* is the means for attaining *maggas* and *phalas* that will give one who has them freedom from *dukkha*.

27. Demerit is a synonym for *akusala kammapatha*.

Ten Akusala Kamamapathas

Akusala Kammapatha means the path to evil or demerit. There are ten such paths:

(a) killing,
(b) stealing,
(c) using improper means to satisfy one's sensual desires, e.g., committing adultery, taking intoxicants,
(d) telling lies,
(e) setting one against another,
(f) using rough and abusive words,
(g) indulging in unbeneficial speech,
(h) belief in false theories,
(i) ill will,
(j) covetousness.

Causes of Akusala Kammapathas

There are three causes. They are *lobha, dosa, moha* (greed, anger, ignorance).

Causes of Kusala Kammapathas

There arc three causes. They are *alobha, adosa, amoha* (absence of greed, anger and ignorance).

being merit, or what is demerit, without really understanding it as being demerit, I may be stating a falsehood. This false statement of mine would cause me distress. Such distress might be harmful to me." (The thought that I have told a lie will cause me distress. Such distress will be a very serious obstacle in my path to higher rebirths and achievement of maggas and phalas.)

He who thus fears and detests making a false statement declines to say what is merit or what is demerit. If he were asked to answer the question (as to what is merit or what is demerit), he would reply: 'I don't take it this way; neither do I take it that way; and I don't take it the other way; neither do I take it not this way, not that way, not the other way; and, also, I don't take it that it is otherwise."

Bhikkhus! This is the first possibility. It is based on this reason that some samaṇas and brāhmaṇas who are elusive evade questions put to them on any matter and speak in ambiguous terms. (12+1=13)

The Second Amarāvikkhepa Diṭṭhi

63. What is the second reason that causes respected samaṇas and brāhmaṇas to be elusive, to evade questions put to them on any matter and to speak in ambiguous terms?

In this world, bhikkhus, a certain samaṇa or brāhmaṇa does not understand correctly what is merit or what is demerit.

He thinks thus:

"I do not understand correctly what is merit or what is demerit. If I were to say what is merit, without really understanding it as being merit, or what is demerit, without really understanding it as being demerit, my answer might cause satisfaction and pleasure, or dissatisfaction and displeasure, to arise in me. These feelings of satisfaction, pleasure, dissatisfaction or displeasure would cling to me. This clinging would cause me distress. Such distress might be harmful to me." (If some learned persons approve of my answer, I shall think highly of myself. This thought will arouse in me either satisfaction or pleasure. If some learned persons disapprove of my answer, I shall think poorly of myself. This thought will arouse in me either dissatisfaction or displeasure with myself. These feelings of satisfaction and pleasure or dissatisfaction and displeasure will cling to me. This clinging will cause me distress. Such distress will be a very serious obstacle in my path to higher rebirths and achievement of maggas and phalas.)

He who thus fears and detests making a wrong statement declines to say what is merit or what is demerit. If he were asked to answer the question (as to what is merit or what is demerit), he would reply: "I don't take it this way; neither do I take it that way; and I don't take it the other way; neither do I take it not this way, not that way, not the other way; and, also, I don't take it that it is otherwise."

Bhikkhus! This is the second possibility. It is based on this reason that some samaṇas and brahmanas who are elusive evade questions put to them on any matter and speak in ambiguous terms. (12+2=14)

The Third Amarāvikkhepa Diṭṭhi

64. What is the third reason that causes respected samaṇas and brahmanas to be elusive, to evade questions put to them on any matter and to speak in ambiguous terms?

In this world, bhikkhus, a certain samaṇa or brāhmaṇa does not understand correctly what is merit or what is demerit.

He thinks thus:

> "I do not understand correctly what is merit or what is demerit. If I were to say what is merit, without really understanding it as being merit, or what is demerit, without really understanding it as being demerit, those samaṇas and brahmanas who are learned, subtle, well-versed in other creeds, skilled in saying things straight to the point (like a skilful archer able to split the tail hair of an animal) and who are given to smashing all other views by their knowledge, might question (my views), ask reasons for them, and pass strictures on them. If they should thus question me, ask for reasons and pass strictures on my views, 1 might not be able to give them an adequate reply. In that case it would cause me distress. Such distress might be harmful to me." (Such distress would be a very serious obstacle in my path to higher rebirths and achievement of maggas and phalas.)

He who thus fears and detests such questioning declines to say what is merit or what is demerit. If he were asked to answer the question (as to what is merit, or what is demerit), he would reply: "I don't take it this way; neither do I take it that way; and 1 don't take it the other way; neither do 1 take it not this way, not that way, not the other way; and, also, I don't take it that it is otherwise."

Bhikkhus! This is the third possibility. It is based on this reason that some samaṇas and brāhmaṇas who are elusive evade questions put to them on any matter and speak in ambiguous terms. (12+3=15)

The Fourth Amarāvikkhepa Diṭṭhi

Note:

(i) Thirty-One Bhūmis

According to Buddhism, there are thirty-one bhūmis. A bhūmi means an abode, where beings live. Bhūmi is sometimes translated as "plane of existence", or "realm".

(a) Twenty brahmā (Higher Celestial) bhūmis:

Arūpa brahmās (brahmās with mind and no body) live in four arūpa brahmā bhūmis. Rūpa brahmās (with mind and body) live in fifteen rūpa brahmā bhūmis. Asaññasatta brahmās (rūpa brahmās with body and no mind) live in the asaññasatta brahmā bhūmi. Brahmās are superior to devas.

(b) Six deva (Celestial) bhūmis:
Devas live in the six deva bhūmis.

(c) One manussa (human) bhūmi:
Human beings live in this manussa bhūmi.

(d) Four apāya (nether) bhūmis:

Niraya (beings in realms of continuous suffering), tiracchāna (animals), peta (miserable and ever hungry beings), asurakāyas (miserable and frightened beings) live in these four bhūmis.

(ii) Four types of Birth

According to Buddhism, there are four types of birth. They are (a) aṇḍaja (oviparous), (b) jalābuja (viviparous), (c) saṃsedaja (moisture-sprung), (d) opapātika (fully-fledged birth).

(iii) Opapātika

In the case of brahmās, devas, asurakāyas, petas and nirayas, as soon as paṭisandhi mind (first mind of the new life) takes place, they — unlike humans and animals, — attain full maturity. They appear as fully-fledged beings. This kind of birth is called opapātika birth. Unlike jalābujas, opapātikas do not leave behind dead bodies when they die. Simultaneously with their death, their bodies disappear.

The birth of beings in these thirty-one bhūmis takes place in accordance with their kammas. Kamma is the abbreviated term for deeds, words and thoughts, which one has done, spoken and conceived.

(iv) Bad Kammas

Killing, stealing, satisfying one's sensual desire by improper means — committing adultery and taking intoxicants are improper means, — telling lies, setting one against another, using rough and abusive words indulging in unbeneficial talk, covetousness, anger, having faith in wrong beliefs — these are bad kammas. They can cause one to have rebirths in the four apāya bhūmis.

(v) Good Kammas

Charity and self-control to refrain from doing and saying what is evil. These are good kammas. They can cause one to have rebirths in deva bhūmis.

(vi) Better Kammas

Four rūpa jhānas (refined mental states of concentration) which one will gain as a result of practising samatha bhāvanā. They are better kammas. They can cause rebirths in rūpa Brahmā bhūmis.

(vii) Best Kammas

Four maggas and phalas which one will gain as a result of practising *vipassanā* bhāvanā. They will enable one to perceive Nibbāna. These four maggas will uproot seven anusayas, which are the causes of endless rebirths. Extinction of rebirths will cause one to gain freedom from *dukkha.*

65. "What is the fourth reason that causes respected samaṇas and brāhmaṇas to be elusive, to evade questions put to them on any matter and to speak in ambiguous terms?

In this world, bhikkhus, a certain samaṇa or brāhmaṇa is lacking in wisdom and is very bewildered. He evades questions put to him on any matter and speaks in ambiguous terms (in the following manner) as he is lacking in wisdom and is very bewildered.

"If I were asked, 'Is there another world?' and if I took it that there is, I should answer, 'There is another world'. But I would not say this way, nor that way, nor the other way; neither would I say not this way, not that way, not, the other way; nor would I say otherwise.

If I were asked:

whether there is not another world ...

whether there is, and also is not, another world ...

whether there neither is, nor is not, another world ...

whether there is opapātika birth of beings ...

whether there is no opapātika birth of beings ...

whether there is, and also there is not, opapātika birth of beings ...

whether it is not that there is, and also there is not, opapātika birth of beings ...

whether a good or a bad kamma produces results ...

whether a good or a bad kamma produces no results

whether it is that a good or a bad kamma produces results, and also does not produce results ...

whether it is not that a good or a bad kamma produces results, and also does not produce results ...

whether there is life after death[28] ...

28. Lit., whether a sentient being exists after death.

whether there is no life after death ...

whether there is life as well as no life after death ...

whether it is not that there is life as well as no life after death, and if I took it that it is not that there is life as well as no life after death, I should answer: 'It is not that there is life as well as no life after death.' But I would not say this way, nor that way, nor the other way; neither would I say not this way, not that way, not the other way; nor would I say otherwise."

Bhikkhus! This is the fourth possibility. It is based on this reason that some samaṇas and brāhmaṇas who are elusive evade questions put to them on any matter and speak in ambiguous terms. (12+4=16)

66. Bhikkhus! These are the four reasons that cause those samaṇas and brāhmaṇas to be elusive, to evade questions put to them on any matter and to speak ambiguously.

Bhikkhus! When any of the samaṇas and brāhmaṇas who are elusive, evade questions put to them on any matter, all of them do so either for these four, or any one of the four, reasons and not for any other reason. The Tathāgata knows ... (as in paras 59 and 60) ... Anyone wishing to praise correctly the true virtues of the Tathāgata should do so in terms of these dhammas.

Two Doctrines of Non-causality
(Adhiccasamuppanna Vāda)

67. There are, bhikkhus, some samaṇas and brāhmaṇas who, holding the doctrine of non-causality, propound in two ways that *atta* as well as *loka* arises without a cause.

On what authority and on what basis do those respected samaṇas and brāhmaṇas propound in two ways that *atta* as well as *loka* arises without a cause?

The First Adhiccasamuppanna Vāda

68. There are, bhikkhus, Brahmās who are known as *asaññasatta*, beings devoid of *saññā*, (lit., perception; here, the Commentary says, mind and mental concomitants are meant). When these Brahmās pass away from that realm, they are reborn in a sensual existence with *saññā*. There is a possibility that when a being thus passes away from that realm, he is reborn in this human world. Having been thus reborn, he renounces the worldly life for the homeless life of a recluse. He then

achieves utmost mental concentration by dint of ardent, steadfast, persevering exertion, mindfulness and right attentiveness. When he has thus established his mind in highest concentration, he can recollect the arising of *saññā* (birth-linking consciousness) in the present existence, but cannot recollect beyond that.

He says thus:

> "*Atta* as well as *loka* arises without a cause. Why can I say so? I can say so because formerly I was not in existence, but now I actually exist although I had not existed before."

Bhikkhus! This is the first possibility. It is based on this that some samaṇas and brāhmaṇas, holding the doctrine of non-causality, propound that *atta* as well as *loka* arises without a cause. (16+1=17)

The Second Adhiccasamuppanna Vāda

69. Secondly, bhikkhus, on what authority and on what basis do the respected samaṇas and brāhmaṇas, holding the doctrine of non-causality, propound that *atta* as well as *loka* arises without a cause?

In this world, bhikkhus, a certain Samaṇa or brāhmaṇa is given to logic and investigation. He uses various methods of reasoning, conducts investigations and gives his views thus:

"*Atta* as well as *loka* arises without a cause."

This, bhikkhus, is the second possibility. It is based on this that some samaṇas and brāhmaṇas, holding the doctrine of non-causality, declare that *atta* as well as *loka* arises without a cause. (16+2=18)

70. Bhikkhus! Those samaṇas and brāhmaṇas who hold the doctrine of non-causality demonstrate on these two grounds that *atta* as well as *loka* arises without a cause. When any of the samaṇas and brāhmaṇas who hold the doctrine of non-causality demonstrate that *atta* as well as *loka* arises without a cause, all of them do so on these two, or one of the two, grounds and on no other ground. The Tathāgata knows ... (as in paras 59 & 60) ... Anyone wishing to praise correctly the true virtues of the Tathāgata should do so in terms of these dhammas.

71. Bhikkhus! Those samaṇas and brāhmaṇas who speculate on the past and who adhere to views relating to it assert in these eighteen ways their many and varied wrong views about the past.

Bhikkhus! When any of those samaṇas and brāhmaṇas who speculate on the past and adhere to views relating to it declare their many and varied wrong views about the past, all of them do so in these eighteen, or one of the eighteen, different ways and in no other way.

72. Bhikkhus! The Tathāgata knows the destination, the next existence in which one holding these eighteen views would be reborn, if these views are thus held on to, if these views are thus grasped.

The Tathāgata knows these eighteen views. He also knows the dhamma which surpasses them. Knowing that dhamma, he does not view it in the wrong way. Since he does not view it in the wrong way, he realizes by himself the extinction of defilements (i.e., greed, anger, and ignorance of the Four Ariya Truths).

Bhikkhus! Since the Tathāgata rightly knows the arising of feeling (*vedanā*) and its cause, the cessation of feeling and its cause, its pleasantness, its faults, and freedom from attachment to it, he becomes liberated without any clinging, (i.e., he realizes Nibbāna).

73. Thus, bhikkhus, these are the dhammas which are profound, hard to see, hard to comprehend, tranquil, noble, surpassing logic, subtle and intelligible only to the *ariyas*. The Tathāgata has set them forth after realization of these dhammas by himself through *Sabbaññuta Ñāṇa* (Perfect Wisdom). Anyone wishing to praise correctly the true virtues of the Tathāgata should do so in terms of these dhammas.

End of the second portion for recitation

Forty-four Views Relating to the Future (Aparantānudiṭṭhi)

74. There are, bhikkhus, certain samaṇas and brāhmaṇas who speculate on the future and adhere to beliefs relating to it. They assert in forty-four ways their many and varied wrong views relating to the future. On what authority and on what basis do these respected samaṇas and brāhmaṇas speculate on the future, adhere to beliefs relating to it, and declare them in forty-four ways?

Sixteen Kinds of Belief in the Existence of Saññā after Death (Uddhamāghātanika Saññī Vāda)

75. There are, bhikkhus, certain samaṇas and brāhmaṇas who believe in the existence of *saññā*[29] after death. They declare in sixteen ways their belief in the existence of *atta* with *saññā* after death. On what

29. *Saññā*: lit., perception; in most cases it stands for mind and mental concomitants.

authority and on what basis do these respected samaṇas and brāhmaṇas, believing in the existence of *atta* with *saññā* after death, demonstrate in sixteen ways the existence of *atta* with *saññā* after death?

76. They declare that: (1) *atta* is corporeal; it does not decay after death; and it has *saññā; ...*

(This view is held by a person who has attained a *rūpa Jhāna* and who takes as *atta* the purified mental image, *paṭibhāga nimitta*, which is the object of his Jhāna concentration. This purified mental image is taken by him as having the nature of corporeality because of its similarity to the original *kasiṇa* object of meditation, or because it has the nature of changeability, as it is small before being enlarged mentally and as it becomes large when expanded mentally. The Jhāna mind which is concentrated on this purified mental image is taken by this person to be *saññā*, and thus he believes that the *atta* identified with the purified mental image has *saññā*. However, a person who believes in *atta* and who has not attained any Jhāna just takes it through some sort of reasoning that *atta* is corporeal and has *saññā*. Both these two kinds of persons firmly believe that after death in the present existence *atta* is not subject to decay or disintegration, and therefore is eternal.)

or that: (2) *atta* is incorporeal; it does not decay after death; and it has *saññā; ...*

(This view is held by one who has attained an *arūpa Jhāna* and whose object of Jhāna concentration is some abstract thing such as *ākāsa* or space; this abstract object of concentration is taken by him as *atta*. Such objects of Jhāna concentration, being abstract, do not have the nature of corporeality. The *arūpa Jhāna* mind concentrating on such an object is taken as *saññā*. Thus, this *atta* has *saññā* and is eternal.)

or that: (3) *atta* is both corporeal and incorporeal; ...

(This view is held by a person who first attains an *arūpa Jhāna* and believes in the corporeality of *atta*, through concentrating on the purified mental image of a kasiṇa object; then, after progressing further in concentration, when he attains an *arūpa Jhāna*, he comes to believe also that the *atta* identified with the abstract object of *arūpa Jhāna* concentration is incorporeal.)

or that: (4) *atta* is neither corporeal nor incorporeal; ...

(This view is held by a person who has not attained any *Jhāna*, and who has heard such a statement from others or who has thought it out on his own.)

or that: (5) *atta* is finite; ...

(This view is held by a person who believes in the finiteness of the world, *loka*, as represented by the purified mental image, *paṭibhāga nimitta*, of the kasiṇa object of meditation, as in Para 54. This purified mental image is at first of the same size as the original kasiṇa object. When much stronger concentration is gained, the purified mental image can be mentally enlarged and expanded, either before or after *Jhāna*, in one of three ways: with finite limits; or endlessly, that is, without finite limits; or with finite limits vertically, and endlessly without finite limits horizontally. Here the person concerned has mentally enlarged the purified mental image, *paṭibhāga nimitta*, within finite limits, and he takes this enlarged and defined image itself as *atta.* Thus he says '*atta* is finite; it does not decay after death; and it has *saññā.*' In Para 54, the person concerned was speculating about the past; here the person concerned is speculating about the future. The same applies to the next three persons.)

or that: (6) *atta* is infinite; ...

(This view is held by a person who has mentally expanded the purified mental image endlessly.)

or that: (7) *atta* is both finite and infinite; ...

(This view is held by a person who has mentally expanded the purified mental image with definite limits vertically and endlessly without definite limits horizontally.)

or that: (8) *atta is* neither finite nor infinite; ...

(This view is held by a person who has not attained any *Jhāna*, but who may have come to this conclusion either through his own reasoning or because he has heard the contradictory views above.)

or that: (9) *atta* has only one kind of *saññā; ...*

(This view is held by a person who is immersed in *Jhāna;* while immersed in *Jhāna*, he takes the mind as *atta*, and that *atta* being concentrated on only one object of *Jhāna* concentration, he believes that *atta* has only one kind of *saññā.*)

or that: (10) *atta* has various kinds of *saññā; ...*

(This view is held by a person who, not being immersed in any *Jhāna*, is conscious of several kinds of objects of the senses; thus he believes *atta* has various kinds of *saññā.*)

or that: (11) *atta* has limited *saññā*; ...

(This view is held by a person who has attained *Jhāna*, but who has not mentally enlarged the purified mental image of the kasiṇa object, which therefore appears to him to be small or limited. His *Jhāna saññā* concentrates on this small or limited mental image as its object, and he takes the *Jhāna* mind or *saññā* as *atta*, and he concludes that *atta* has a small or limited *suññā*. Other persons believe that *atta* itself is as small as a thumb, or a paddy seed, or an atom, and therefore *atta* has a small or limited *saññā*.)

or that: (12) *atta* has unlimited *saññā*; ...

(This view is held by a person whose *Jhāna* concentration has as its object the purified mental image which has been mentally enlarged or expanded by him, and who therefore concludes that *atta* has a very large or unlimited *saññā*. Other persons believe that *atta* exists in every animate or inanimate thing and thus it has immeasurably numerous *saññā*.)

or that: (13) *atta* indeed has bliss; ...

(This view is held by a person who has attained the divine power of sight, *dibba-cakkhu abhiññā*, and who by this power sees those in the three lowest rūpa bhūmis abiding in *Jhāna* and experiencing blissful sensation. He therefore concludes that *atta* indeed has and will have bliss.)

or that: (14) *atta* indeed has suffering; ...

(This view is held by a person who through divine power of sight sees those in the abodes of intense continuous suffering. He therefore concludes that *atta* indeed has and will have suffering.)

or that: (15) *atta* has both happiness and suffering; ...

(This view is held by a person who sees beings in the human world experiencing both happiness and suffering.)

or that: (16) *atta* has neither happiness nor suffering; it does not decay after death; and it has *saññā*.

(Here, neither happiness nor suffering means equanimity. This view is held by a person who through the divine power of sight sees the Vehapphala Brahmās who are given to abiding in the *Jhāna* of equanimity.) (18+16=34)

77. Bhikkhus, these are the sixteen ways in which those samaṇas and brāhmaṇas who believe in the existence of *saññā* after death declare their belief in the existence of *atta* with *saññā* after death. When any of those samaṇas and brāhmaṇas who believe in the existence of *saññā* after death demonstrate the existence of *atta* with *saññā* after death, all of them do so in these sixteen, or in one or other of these sixteen ways

and in no other way. The Tathāgata knows ... (as in Paras 72, 73) ... Anyone wishing to praise correctly the true virtues of the Tathāgata, should do so in terms of these dhammas.

Eight Kinds of Belief in the Non-existence of Saññā after Death (Uddhamāghātanika Asaññī Vāda)

78. There are, bhikkhus, some samaṇas and brāhmaṇas who believe in the non-existence of *saññā* after death. They declare in eight ways their belief in the existence of *atta* devoid of *saññā* after death.

On what authority and on what basis do those respected samaṇas and brāhmaṇas, believing in the existence of *atta* devoid of *saññā* after death, demonstrate in eight ways their belief in the "existence of *atta* devoid of *saññā* after death?

79. They declare that: (1) *atta* is corporeal; it does not decay after death; and it has no *saññā; ...*

(This view is held by a person who, like the person in item (1) of Para 76, takes the *paṭibhāga nimitta* as *atta*, and believes that *atta* is corporeal and eternal. But this person sees those who have reached after death the *asaññasatta* Brahmā realm, with only body and no mind, and thus he believes that *atta* has no *saññā* after death.)

or that: (2) *atta* is incorporeal; it does not decay after death; and it has no *saññā; ...*

(This view is held by a person who takes as *atta* the *saññākkhandha*, the aggregate of Perception, from amongst the five Aggregates or Khandhas. As there is no other kind of *saññā* apart from this *saññākkhandha*, this person takes it that there is no *saññā* after death.)

or that: (3) *atta* is both corporeal and incorporeal; ...

(This view is held by a person who takes as *atta* all the aggregates of physical and mental phenomena, including *saññā*, and as this *atta* has no additional *saññā* apart from *saññākkhandha*, either before or after death, he takes it that there is no *saññā* after death, since he is speculating about future existence.)

or that: (4) *atta* is neither corporeal nor incorporeal; ...

(This view is held by a person who has either heard it from other persons, or thought it out on his own.)

or that: (5) *atta* is finite; ...

(This view is held by a person who takes as *atta* the purified mental image of which he has not mentally enlarged or expanded. As this purified mental image of the kasiṇa object does not have *saññā*, the person takes it that there is no *saññā* after death.)

or that: (6) *atta* is infinite; ...

or that: (7) *atta* is both finite and infinite; ...

or that: (8) *atta* is neither finite nor infinite; it does not decay after death; and it has no *saññā.*

(These three views, (6), (7), (8) may be interpreted on the lines of views, (6), (7), (8), of Para 76, except that here *atta* is taken as having no *saññā.*) (3 4 +8=42)

80. Bhikkhus! Those samaṇas and brāhmaṇas who believe in the existence of *atta* devoid of *saññā* after death demonstrate in these eight ways their belief in the existence of *atta* devoid of *saññā* after death.

Bhikkhus! When any of the samaṇas and brāhmaṇas propound their belief in the existence of *atta* devoid of *saññā* after death, all of them do so in these eight, or one of the eight, ways and in no other way. The Tathāgata knows ... (as in Paras 72, 73) ... Anyone wishing to praise correctly the true virtues of the Tathāgata should do so in terms of these dhammas.

Eight Kinds of Belief in the Existence of neither Saññā nor Non-Saññā After Death (Uddhamāghātanika Nevasaññī Nāsaññī Vāda)

81. There are, bhikkhus, some samaṇas and brāhmaṇas who believe in the existence of neither *saññā* nor non-*saññā*[30] after death. They declare in eight ways their belief in the existence of *atta* in a state of neither *saññā* nor non-*saññā* after death.

On what authority and on what basis do those respected samaṇas and brāhmaṇas, believing in the existence of neither *saññā* nor *non-saññā* after death, demonstrate in eight ways their belief in the existence of *atta* in a state of neither *saññā* nor non-*saññā* after death?

82. They declare that: (1) *atta* is corporeal; it does not decay after death; and it has neither *saññā* nor non-*saññā*; ...

(This view is held by a person who maintains that as *saññā* is extremely weak at the moment of death and at the moment of conception

---

30. *Saññā*: lit., perception. Here it stands for mind and mental concomitants. (See Para 68.) Thus *saññā* may be rendered 'consciousness'.

in the next existence, *saññā* cannot be said to exist definitely, nor can it be said to not exist since it still exists in a very delicate and refined form. Thus *atta* has neither *saññā* nor *asaññā*, i.e., non-*saññā*.)

or that: (2) *atta* is incorporeal; ...

or that: (3) *atta* is both corporeal and incorporeal; ...

or that: (4) *atta* is neither corporeal nor incorporeal; ...

or that: (5) *atta* is finite; ...

or that: (6) *atta* is infinite; ...

or that: (7) *atta* is both finite and infinite; ...

or that: (8) *atta* is neither finite nor infinite; it does not decay after death; it has neither *saññā* nor non-*saññā*. (42+8=50)

83. Bhikkhus! Those samaṇas and brāhmaṇas who believe in the existence of neither *saññā* nor *non-saññā* after death demonstrate in these eight ways their belief in the existence of *atta* in a state of neither *saññā* nor non-*saññā* after death.

Bhikkhus! When any of the samaṇas and brāhmaṇas who believe in the existence of neither *saññā* nor non-*saññā* after death propound their belief in the existence of *atta* in a state of neither *saññā* nor non-*saññā* after death, all of them do so in these eight, or one of the eight, ways and in no other way. The Tathāgata knows ... (as in Paras 72, 73) ... Anyone wishing to praise correctly the true virtues of the Tathāgata should do so in terms of these dhammas.

Seven Kinds of Belief in Annihilation (Uccheda Vāda)

84. There are, bhikkhus, some samaṇas and brāhmaṇas who believe in annihilation. They declare in seven ways their belief in the annihilation, destruction and (future) non-existence of beings presently living.[31]

On what authority and on what basis do those respected samaṇas and brāhmaṇas declare in seven ways their belief in the annihilation, destruction and (future) non-existence of beings presently living?

85. In this world, bhikkhus, a certain Samaṇa or brāhmaṇa asserts and holds the (following) view:

"Friend! This *atta* is corporeal; made up of four great primary elements; born of the union of father and mother; annihilated and

---

31. *Satosattassa*: the Commentary qualifies *sato* with *vijjamanassa*, meaning "visibly or apparently existing".

destroyed on the dissolution of the physical body and it does not exist after death. In this manner, this *atta* becomes entirely extirpated."

Thus do some declare the belief in the annihilation, destruction and (future) non-existence of beings presently living. (1) (50+1=51)

86. To him someone else says:

"Friend! The *atta* that you speak of does exist. I do not say it does not exist. But *atta* is not by this much entirely annihilated. There is another *atta* of the sensuous world (kāmāvacara) of the devas, having corporeality, nourished by solid nutriments. You do not know that *atta*; neither can you see it. But I know it; and I see it. Friend, with the dissolution of the physical body, that *atta* becomes annihilated and destroyed. It does not exist after death. In this manner, this *atta* becomes entirely extirpated."

Thus do some declare their belief in the annihilation, destruction and (future) non-existence of beings presently living. (2) (50+2=52)

87. To him, again, someone else says:

"Friend! The *atta* that you speak of does exist. I do not say it does not exist. But *atta* is not by this much entirely annihilated. There is another *atta* of the world of Brahmās, having corporeality, caused by the *Jhāna* mind and endowed completely with (all the minor and major) physical organs, and not deficient in any of the faculties of the senses. You do not know that *atta;* neither can you see it. But I know it; and I see it. Friend, with the dissolution of the physical body, that *atta* becomes annihilated and destroyed. It does not exist after death, in this manner, this *atta* becomes entirely extirpated."

Thus do some declare their belief in the annihilation, destruction and (future) non-existence of beings presently living. (3) (50+3=53)

88. To him, again, someone else says:

"Friend! The *atta* that you speak of does exist. I do not say it does not exist. But *atta* is not by this much entirely annihilated. There is another *atta* of one who, by concentrating (through *kasiṇa* meditation) on the concept "Space is Infinite", has reached the (non-corporeal) Realm of Infinity of Space (*ākāsānañcāyatana* plane of the Brāhmās) where all forms of *saññā* that turn on corporeality (*rūpa saññā*) have been completely transcended, all forms of *saññā* arising out of contact between the senses and their objects (*paṭigha saññā*) have vanished, and other forms of *saññā*, many and varied, (*nānatta saññā*) are not paid attention to. You do not know that *atta*; neither can you see it. But I know it; and I see it. Friend, with the dissolution of that one's mental aggregates, that *atta* becomes annihilated and destroyed. It does not exist after death. In this manner, this *atta* becomes entirely extirpated."

Thus do some declare their belief in the annihilation, destruction and (future) non-existence of beings presently living. (4) (50+4=54)

89. To him, again, someone else says:

"Friend! The *atta* that you speak of does exist. I do not say it does not exist. But *atta* is not by this much entirely annihilated. There is another *atta* of one who has reached the (non-corporeal) Realm of Infinity of Consciousness (*viññāṇañcāyatana* plane of the Brahmās), by concentrating on the concept "Consciousness is Infinite", having totally gone beyond the *Jhāna* of Infinity of Space. You do not know that *atta;* neither can you see it. But I know it; and I see it. Friend, with the dissolution of that one's mental aggregates, that *atta* becomes annihilated and destroyed. It does not exist after death. In this manner this *atta* becomes entirely extirpated."

Thus do some declare their belief in the annihilation, destruction and (future) non-existence of beings presently living. (5) (50+5=55)

90. To him, again, someone else says:

"Friend! The *atta* that you speak of does exist. I do not say it does not exist. But *atta* is not by this much entirely annihilated. There is another *atta* of one who has reached the (non-corporeal) Realm of Nothingness (*ākiñcaññāyatana* plane of the Brahmās), by concentrating on the concept "Nothing is there", having totally gone beyond the *Jhāna* of Infinity of Consciousness. You do not know that *atta*; neither can you see it. But I know it; and I see it. Friend, with the dissolution of that one's mental aggregates, that *atta* becomes annihilated and destroyed. It does not exist after death. In this manner, this *atta* becomes entirely extirpated."

Thus do some declare their belief in the annihilation, destruction and (future) non-existence of beings presently living. (6) (50+6=56)

91. To him, again, someone else says:

"Friend! The *atta* that you speak of does exist. I do not say it does not exist. (But) *atta* is not by this much entirely annihilated. There is another *atta* of one who has reached the (non-corporeal) Realm of neither *saññā* nor non-*saññā* (*Nevasaññānāsaññāyatana* plane of the Brahmās), by concentrating on the mental object "This (Third Arūpa *Jhāna* Consciousness) is tranquil; this is sublime", having totally gone beyond the *Jhāna* of Nothingness. You do not know that *atta;* neither can you see it. But I know it; and I see it. Friend, with the dissolution of that one's mental aggregates, that *atta* becomes annihilated and destroyed. It does not exist after death. In this manner, this *atta* becomes entirely extirpated."

Thus do some declare their belief in the annihilation, destruction and (future) non-existence of beings presently living. (7) (50+7=57)

92. Bhikkhus! Those samaṇas and brāhmaṇas declare in these seven ways their belief in the annihilation, destruction and (future) non-existence of beings presently living.

Bhikkhus! When any of the samaṇas and brāhmaṇas who believe in annihilation, propound their belief in the annihilation, destruction and (future) non-existence of beings presently living, all of them do so in these seven, or one of the seven, ways and in no other way. The Tathāgata knows ... (as in Paras 72, 73) ... Anyone wishing to praise correctly the true virtues of the Tathāgata should do so in terms of these dhammas.

Five Kinds of Belief in (Mundane) Nibbāna as Realizable in this Very Life (Diṭṭhadhamma Nibbāna Vāda)

93. There are, bhikkhus, some samaṇas and brāhmaṇas who hold the view that (mundane) Nibbana[32] is realizable in this very life by beings presently living. They declare in five ways the nature of the supreme (mundane) immediate Nibbāna of beings presently living.

On what authority and on what basis do those respected samaṇas and brāhmaṇas, holding the view that (mundane) Nibbāna is realizable in this very life by beings presently living, declare in five ways the nature of the supreme (mundane) immediate Nibbāna of beings presently, living?

94. In this world, bhikkhus, a certain Samaṇa or brāhmaṇa puts forward this view and adheres to it, saying:

"Friend! This *atta* fully and thoroughly enjoys the five kinds of sensual pleasures. Thus, friend, this *atta* has reached the supreme (mundane) immediate Nibbāna."

In this way some declare the nature of the supreme (mundane) immediate Nibbāna of beings presently living. (1) (57+1=58)

95. To him someone else says:

"Friend! The *atta* that you speak of does exist. I do not say it does not exist. (But) *atta* by this means has not yet reached the supreme (mundane) immediate Nibbāna. Why? It is because sensual pleasures

---

32. The Nibbāna of the holders of these views is entirely different from the Nibbāna of the Buddha's Teaching.

are impermanent, painful and subject to change. Out of the nature of their changeableness and instability arise grief, lamentation, pain, distress and despair. Friend! Being detached from sensual pleasures and demeritorious factors, this *atta* achieves and remains in the first *Jhāna* which is accompanied by *vitakka* (initial application of the mind), *vicāra* (sustained application of the mind), *pīti* (delightful satisfaction) and *sukha* (bliss) born of detachment from hindrances (*nīvaraṇa*). It is only in this manner, friend, that this *atta* reaches the supreme (mundane) immediate Nibbāna."

Thus do some declare the nature of the supreme (mundane) immediate Nibbāna of beings presently living. (2) (57+2=59)

96. To him someone else says:

"Friend! The *atta* that you speak of does exist. I do not say it does not exist. (But) *atta* by this means has not yet reached the supreme (mundane) immediate Nibbāna. Why? It is because the first *Jhāna* is considered coarse since *vitakka* and *vicāra* are still extant. Indeed, friend, this *atta*, having calmed *vitakka* and *vicāra*, achieves and remains in the second *Jhāna*, with internal tranquillity, with enhancement of one-pointedness of Concentration, devoid of *vitakka* and *vicāra*, with *pīti* and *sukha* born of (first *Jhāna*) concentration. It is only in this manner, friend, that this *atta* reaches the supreme (mundane) immediate Nibbāna."

Thus do some declare the nature of the supreme (mundane) immediate Nibbāna of beings presently living. (3) (57+3=60)

97. To him someone else says:

"Friend! The *atta* that you speak of does exist. I do not say it does not exist. (But) *atta* by this means has not yet reached the supreme (mundane) immediate Nibbāna. Why? It is because the second *Jhāna* is considered coarse since there still is elation of mind which is *pīti.* Indeed, friend, this *atta*, having been detached from *pīti*, dwells with mindfulness and clear comprehension in equanimity, and experiences mental and physical well-being. It achieves and remains in the third *Jhāna*, that which causes a person who attains it to be praised by the Ariyas as one who has equanimity and mindfulness, one who abides in *sukha.* It is only in this manner, that this *atta* reaches the supreme (mundane) immediate Nibbāna."

Thus do some declare the nature of the supreme (mundane) immediate Nibbāna of beings presently living. (4) (57+4=61)

98. To him someone else says:

"Friend! The *atta* that you speak of does exist. I do not say it does not exist. (But) *atta* by this means has not yet reached the supreme (mundane) immediate Nibbāna. Why? It is because the third *Jhāna* is considered coarse since in that *Jhāna* there still is *sukha* constantly in mind. Indeed, friend, this *atta*, by dispelling both pain and pleasure, and by the previous disappearance of sadness and gladness, achieves and remains in the fourth *Jhāna*, without pain and pleasure, a state of equanimity and absolute purity of mindfulness. It is only in this manner, friend, that it reaches the supreme (mundane) immediate Nibbāna."

Thus do some declare the nature of the supreme (mundane) immediate Nibbāna of beings presently living. (5) (57+5=62)

99. Bhikkhus! Those samaṇas and brāhmaṇas declare in these five ways their belief in the supreme (mundane) immediate Nibbāna of beings presently living. Bhikkhus! When any of the samaṇas and brāhmaṇas declare the supreme (mundane) immediate Nibbāna of beings presently living, all of them do so in these five, or one of five, ways and in no other way. The Tathāgata knows ... (as in Paras 72, 73) ... Anyone wishing to praise correctly the true virtues of the Tathāgata should do so in terms of these dhammas.

100. Bhikkhus! Those samaṇas and brāhmaṇas who speculate on the future and adhere to beliefs relating to it, assert their many and varied wrong views about the future in these forty-four different ways.

Bhikkhus! When any of the samaṇas and brāhmaṇas propound the many and varied wrong views about the future, all of them do so in these forty-four, or one of the forty-four, different ways and in no other way. The Tathāgata knows ... (as in Paras 72, 73) ... Anyone wishing to praise correctly the true virtues of the Tathāgata should do so in terms of these dhammas.

101. Bhikkhus! Those samaṇas and brāhmaṇas who speculate on the past, or the future, or both the past and the future and adhere to beliefs relating to them assert their many and varied wrong views in these sixty-two different ways.

102. Bhikkhus! When any of the samaṇas and brāhmaṇas who speculate on the past, or the future, or both the past and the future propound their many and varied wrong views, all of them do so in these sixty-two, or one of the sixty-two, ways and in no other way.

103. Bhikkhus! The Tathāgata knows the destination, the next existence in which one holding these sixty-two views would be reborn, if these views are thus held on to, if these views are thus grasped.

The Tathāgata knows these sixty-two views. He also knows the dhamma which surpasses them. Knowing that dhamma, he does not view it in the wrong way. Since he does not view it in the wrong way, he realizes by himself the extinction of defilements (i.e., greed, anger, and ignorance of the Four Ariya Truths).

Bhikkhus! Since the Tathāgata rightly knows the arising of feeling (*vedanā*) and its cause, the cessation of feeling and its cause, its pleasantness, its faults, and freedom from attachment to it, he becomes liberated without any clinging, (i.e., he realizes Nibbāna).

104. Thus, bhikkhus, these are the dhammas which are profound, hard to see, hard to comprehend, tranquil, noble, surpassing logic, subtle and intelligible only to the *ariyas*. The Tathāgata has set them forth after realization of these dhammas by himself through Sabbaññuta Ñāṇa (Perfect Wisdom). Anyone wishing to praise correctly the true virtues of the Tathāgata should do so in terms of these dhammas.

Agitation Conditioned by Wrong Views and Craving (Paritassita Vipphandita Vāra)

105. Bhikkhus, of those (holding the wrong views), those samaṇas and brāhmaṇas who hold the view of eternity declare on four grounds that *atta* as well as *loka* is eternal, (based on their own personal feeling of satisfaction in their view). That (feeling) being felt by those respected samaṇas and brāhmaṇas who do not know and who do not see (the truth) and who are seized by craving, is agitated through longing.[33]

106. Bhikkhus, of those (holding the wrong views), those samaṇas and brāhmaṇas who hold the view that there is eternity as well as non-eternity declare on four grounds that *atta* as well as *loka* is in some cases eternal and in others not eternal, (based on their own personal feeling of satisfaction in their view). That (feeling), too, being felt by those respected samaṇas and brāhmaṇas who do not know and who do not see (the truth) and who are seized by craving, is agitated through longing.

107. Bhikkhus, of those (holding the wrong views), those samaṇas and brāhmaṇas who view the world as finite and those who view the world as infinite declare on four grounds that the world is finite or that it is infinite, (based on their own personal feeling of satisfaction in their view). That (feeling), too, being felt by those respected samaṇas and brāhmaṇas who do not know and who do not see (the truth) and who are seized by craving, is agitated through longing.

---

33. **Longing**: *Paritassita*: by this is meant 'wrong view' and 'craving'.

108. Bhikkhus, of those (holding the wrong views), those samaṇas and brāhmaṇas who are elusive evade questions put to them and remain ambiguous in four ways, (based on their own personal feeling of satisfaction, in their view). That (feeling), too, being felt by those respected samaṇas and brāhmaṇas who do not know and who do not see (the truth) and who are seized by craving, is agitated through longing.

109. Bhikkhus, of those (holding the wrong views), those samaṇas and brāhmaṇas who hold the view of non-causality declare on two grounds that *atta* as well as *loka* arises without a cause, (based on their own personal feeling of satisfaction in their view). That (feeling), too, being felt by those respected samaṇas and brāhmaṇas who do not know and who do not see (the truth) and who are seized by craving, is agitated through longing.

110. Bhikkhus, of those (holding the wrong views), those samaṇas and brāhmaṇas who speculate on the past and adhere to beliefs relating to it declare in eighteen ways their many and varied wrong views relating to the past, (based on their own personal feeling of satisfaction in their view). That (feeling), too, being felt by those respected samaṇas and brāhmaṇas who do not know and who do not see (the truth) and who are seized by craving, is agitated through longing.

111. Bhikkhus, of those (holding the wrong views), those samaṇas and brāhmaṇas who believe in the existence of *saññā* after death declare in sixteen ways that *atta* exists with *saññā* after death, (based on their own personal feeling of satisfaction in their view), That (feeling), too, being felt by those respected samaṇas and brāhmaṇas who do not know and who do not see (the truth) and who are seized by craving, is agitated through longing.

112. Bhikkhus, of those (holding the wrong views), those samaṇas and brāhmaṇas who believe in the nonexistence of *saññā* after death declare in eight ways that *atta* exists devoid of *saññā* after death, (based on their personal feeling of satisfaction in their view). That (feeling), too, being felt by those respected samaṇas and brāhmaṇas who do not know and who do not see (the truths and who are seized by craving, is agitated through longing.

113. Bhikkhus, of those (holding the wrong views), those samaṇas and brāhmaṇas who hold the view that there is neither *saññā* nor non-*saññā* (*asaññā*) after death declare in eight ways that *atta* exists in a state of neither *saññā* nor *non-saññā* after death, (based on their own personal feeling of satisfaction in their view). That (feeling), too, being felt by those

respected samaṇas and brāhmaṇas who do not know and who do not see (the truth) and who are seized by craving, is agitated through longing.

114. Bhikkhus, of those (holding the wrong views), those samaṇas and brāhmaṇas who hold the belief in annihilation declare in seven ways their belief in the annihilation, destruction and (future) non-existence of beings presently living, (based on their own personal feeling of satisfaction in their view). That (feeling), too, being felt by those respected samaṇas and brāhmaṇas who do not know and who do not see (the truth) and who are seized by craving, is agitated through longing.

115. Bhikkhus, of those (holding the wrong views), those samaṇas and brāhmaṇas who believe in (mundane) immediate Nibbāna declare in five ways their view of the supreme (mundane) immediate Nibbāna of beings presently living, (based on their own personal feeling of satisfaction in their view). That (feeling), too, being felt by those respected samaṇas and brāhmaṇas who do not know and who do not see (the truth) and who are seized by craving, is agitated through longing.

116. Bhikkhus, of those (holding the wrong views), those samaṇas and brāhmaṇas who speculate on the future and adhere to beliefs relating to it assert in forty-four ways their many and varied wrong views about the future, (based on their own personal feeling of satisfaction in their view). That (feeling), too, being felt by those respected samaṇas and brāhmaṇas who do not know and who do not see (the truth) and who are seized by craving, is agitated through longing.

117. Bhikkhus, of those (holding the wrong views), those samaras and brāhmaṇas who speculate on the past, or the future, or both the past and the future and adhere to beliefs relating to them assert in sixty-two ways their many and varied wrong views relating to the past and the future, (based on their own personal feeling of satisfaction in their view). That (feeling), too, being felt by those respected samaṇas and brāhmaṇas who do not know and who do not see (the truth) and who are seized by craving, is agitated through longing.

Contact as Cause
(Phassa Paccaya)

118. Bhikkhus, of those (holding the wrong views), those samaṇas and brāhmaṇas who hold the eternity view declare on four grounds that *atta* as well as *loka* is eternal, (based on their own personal feeling of satisfaction in their view). That (feeling) arises because of contact.

119. Bhikkhus, of those (holding the wrong views), those samaṇas and brāhmaṇas who hold the view that there is eternity as well as non-eternity declare on four grounds that *atta* as well as *loka* is in some cases eternal and in others not eternal, (based on their own personal feeling of satisfaction in their view). That (feeling), too, arises because of contact.

120. Bhikkhus, of those (holding the wrong views), those samaṇas and brāhmaṇas who view the world as finite and those who view the world as infinite declare on four grounds that the world is finite or that it is infinite, (based on their own personal feeling of satisfaction in their view). That (feeling), too arises because of contact.

121. Bhikkhus, of those (holding the wrong views), those samaṇas and brāhmaṇas who are elusive evade questions put to them and remain ambiguous in four ways, (based on their own personal feeling of satisfaction in their view). That (feeling), too, arises because of contact.

122. Bhikkhus, of those (holding the wrong views), those samaṇas and brāhmaṇas who hold the view of non-causality declare on two grounds that *atta* as well as *loka* arises without a cause, (based on their own personal feeling of satisfaction in their view). That (feeling), too, arises because of contact.

123. Bhikkhus, of those (holding the wrong views), those samaṇas and brāhmaṇas who speculate on the past and adhere to beliefs relating to it declare in eighteen ways their many and varied wrong views relating to the past, (based on their own personal feeling of satisfaction in their view). That (feeling), too, arises because of contact.

124. Bhikkhus, of those (holding the wrong views), those samaṇas and brāhmaṇas who believe in the existence of *saññā* after death declare in sixteen ways that *atta* exists with *saññā* after death, (based on their own personal feeling of satisfaction in their view). That (feeling), too, arises because of contact.

125. Bhikkhus, of those (holding the wrong views), those samaṇas and brāhmaṇas who believe in the non- existence of *saññā* after death declare in eight ways that *atta* exists devoid of *saññā* after death, (based on their own personal feeling of satisfaction in their view) That (feeling), too, arises because of contact.

126. Bhikkhus, of those (holding the wrong views), those samaṇas and brāhmaṇas who hold the view that there is neither *saññā* nor *non-saññā* after death declare in ēight ways that *atta* exists in a state of neither *saññā* nor non-*saññā* after death, (based on their own personal feeling of satisfaction in their view). That (feeling), too, arises because of contact.

127. Bhikkhus, of those (holding the wrong views), those samaṇas and brāhmaṇas who hold the belief in annihilation declare in seven ways their belief in the annihilation, destruction and (future) non-existence of beings presently living, (based on their own personal feeling of satisfaction in their view). That (feeling), too, arises because of contact.

128. Bhikkhus, of those (holding the wrong views), those samaṇas and brāhmaṇas who believe in (mundane) immediate Nibbāna declare in five ways their view of the supreme (mundane) immediate Nibbāna of beings presently living, (based on their own personal feeling of satisfaction in their view). That (feeling), too, arises because of contact.

129. Bhikkhus. of those (holding the wrong views), those samaṇas and brāhmaṇas who speculate on the future and adhere to beliefs relating to it assert in forty-four ways their many and varied wrong views about the future, (based on their own personal feeling of satisfaction in their view). That (feeling), too, arises because of contact.

130. Bhikkhus, of those (holding the wrong views), those samaṇas and brāhmaṇas who speculate on the past, or the future, or both the past and the future and adhere to beliefs relating to them assert in sixty-two ways their many and varied wrong views relating to the past and the future, (based on their own personal feeling of satisfaction in their view). That (feeling), too, arises because of contact.

No Possibility of Feeling without Contact (Netaṃ Ṭhānaṃ Vijjati Vāra)

131. Bhikkhus, of those (holding the wrong views), those samaṇas and brāhmaṇas who hold the view of eternity declare on four grounds that *atta* as well as *loka* is eternal, (based on their own personal feeling of satisfaction in their view). Indeed, they can in no way experience that (feeling) without contact.

132. Bhikkhus, of those (holding the wrong views), those samaṇas and brāhmaṇas who hold the view that there is eternity as well as non-eternity declare on four grounds that *atta* as well as *loka* is in some cases eternal and in others not eternal, (based on their own personal feeling of satisfaction in their view). Indeed, they can in no way experience that (feeling) without contact.

133. Bhikkhus, of those (holding the wrong views), those samaṇas and brāhmaṇas who view the world as finite and those who view the world as infinite declare on four grounds that the world is finite or

that it is infinite, (based on their own personal feeling of satisfaction in their view). Indeed, they can in no way experience that (feeling) without contact.

134. Bhikkhus, of those (holding the wrong views), those samaṇas and brāhmaṇas who are elusive evade questions put to them and remain ambiguous in four ways, (based on their own personal feeling of satisfaction in their view). Indeed, they can in no way experience that (feeling) without contact.

135. Bhikkhus, of those (holding the wrong views), those samaṇas and brāhmaṇas who hold the view of non-causality declare on two grounds that *atta* as well as *loka* arises without a cause, (based on their own personal feeling of satisfaction in their view). Indeed, they can in no way experience that (feeling) without contact.

136. Bhikkhus, of those (holding the wrong views), those samaṇas and brāhmaṇas who speculate on the past and adhere to beliefs relating to it declare in eighteen ways their many and varied wrong views relating to the past, (based on their own personal feeling of satisfaction in their view). Indeed, they can in no way experience that (feeling) without contact.

137. Bhikkhus, of those (holding the wrong views), those samaṇas and brāhmaṇas who believe in the existence of *saññā* after death declare in sixteen ways that *atta* exists with *saññā* after death, (based on their own personal feeling of satisfaction in their view). Indeed, they can in no way experience that (feeling) without contact.

138. Bhikkhus, of those (holding the wrong views), those samaṇas and brāhmaṇas who believe in the non-existence of *saññā* after death declare in eight ways that *atta* exists devoid of *saññā* after death, (based on their own personal feeling of satisfaction in their view). Indeed, they can in no way experience that (feeling) without contact.

139. Bhikkhus, of those (holding the wrong views), those samaṇas and brāhmaṇas who hold the view that there is neither *saññā* nor non-*saññā* after death declare in eight ways that *atta* exists in a state of neither *saññā* nor non-*saññā* after death, (based on their own personal feeling of satisfaction in their view). Indeed, they can in no way experience that (feeling) without contact.

140. Bhikkhus, of those (holding the wrong views), those samaṇas and brāhmaṇas who hold the belief in annihilation declare in seven ways their belief in the annihilation, destruction and (future) non-existence of beings presently living, (based on their own personal feeling of

satisfaction in their view). Indeed, they can in no way experience that (feeling) without contact.

141. Bhikkhus, of those (holding the wrong views), those samaṇas and brāhmaṇas who believe in (mundane) immediate Nibbāna declare in five ways their view of the supreme (mundane) immediate Nibbāna of beings presently living, (based on their own personal feeling of satisfaction in their view). Indeed, they can in no way experience that (feeling) without contact.

142. Bhikkhus, of those (holding the wrong views), those samaṇas and brāhmaṇas who speculate on the future and adhere to beliefs relating to it assert in forty-four ways their many and varied wrong views about the future, (based on their own personal feeling of satisfaction in their view). Indeed, they can in no way experience that (feeling) without contact.

143. Bhikkhus, of those (holding the wrong views), those samaṇas and brāhmaṇas who speculate on the past, or the future, or both the past and the future assert in sixty-two ways their many and varied wrong views about the past and the future, (based on their own personal feeling of satisfaction in their view). Indeed, they can in no way experience that (feeling) without contact.

Of the Round of Suffering Caused by Wrong Views (Diṭṭhigatikadhiṭṭhāna Vaṭṭa Kathā)

144. Bhikkhus, of those (holding the wrong views), those samaṇas and brāhmaṇas who hold the view of eternity declare on four grounds that *atta* as well as *loka* is eternal. Also those samaṇas and brāhmaṇas who hold the view that *atta* as well as *loka* is in some cases eternal and in others not eternal ... (p) ... Also those samaṇas and brāhmaṇas who hold the view of the world as finite or those who hold it as infinite ... (p) ... Also those samaras and brāhmaṇas who elusively evade questions ... (p) ... Also those samaṇas and brāhmaṇas who hold the view of non-causality ... (p) ... Also those samaṇas and brāhmaṇas who speculate on the past, and adhere to beliefs relating to it ... (p) ... Also those samaṇas and brāhmaṇas who believe in the existence of *saññā* after death ... (p) ... Also those samaṇas and brāhmaṇas who believe in the non-existence of *saññā* after death ... (p) ... Also those samaṇas and brāhmaṇas who believe that there is neither *saññā* nor *non-saññā* after death ... (p) ... Also those samaṇas and brāhmaṇas who believe in annihilation ... (p) ... Also those samaṇas and brāhmaṇas who believe in (mundane) immediate Nibbāna ... (p) ... Also those samaṇas and brāhmaṇas who speculate on the future

... (p) ... Also those samaṇas and brāhmaṇas who speculate on the past, or the future, or both, and adhere to beliefs relating to them, assert in sixty-two ways their many and varied wrong views relating to the past and the future. They experience feeling as a result of repeated contact through the six sense bases. In them feeling gives rise to craving; craving gives rise to clinging; clinging gives rise to current existence (*upapatti bhava*) and the kammic causal process (*kamma bhava*); the kammic causal process gives rise to rebirth; and rebirth gives rise to ageing, death, grief, lamentation, pain, distress and despair.

Discourse on the Cessation of the Round of Rebirths (Vivaṭṭa Kathādi)

145. Bhikkhus! When a bhikkhu knows correctly the origin of the six sense bases of contact, their cessation, their pleasantness, their danger and the way of escape from them, he realizes the dhammas (Morality, *sīla;* Concentration, *samādhi;* Wisdom, *paññā;* Liberation, *vimutti*) that surpass all these (wrong) views.

146. Bhikkhus! When any of the samaṇas and brāhmaṇas who speculate on the past, or the future, or both the past and the future, and adhere to beliefs relating to them, assert the many and varied (wrong) views about the past, or the future, or both, all of them are caught in the net of this discourse with all their sixty-two categories of wrong views, and if they try to rise (or sink), they rise (or sink) within the net, for all their views fall within the net of this discourse.

Take this simile, bhikkhus! When a skilful fisherman or his apprentice spreads out a finely meshed net on the waters of a small lake, it may occur to him thus:

'As all big creatures in the lake have been caught in the finely meshed net, if they rise to the surface (or sink), they do so within the net. As they are all contained in the net, if they rise (or sink), they do so all within the finely meshed net.'

In the same manner, bhikkhus, when all samaṇas and brāhmaṇas, speculating on the past, or the future, or both, and adhering to beliefs relating to them, assert their many and varied (wrong) views they do so in sixty-two ways, which all fall within the net of this discourse. And as this discourse encompasses all those (wrong) views, if any one of the views comes up, it does so within the compass of this discourse.

147. The Tathāgata's physical body stands cut off from the bonds of craving for existence. Men and devas will behold him for so long as

his physical body remains. They will not behold him when his physical body dissolves at the end of his life.

Just as, bhikkhus, when the stalk is cut off, all mangoes hanging on it go with it; so, bhikkhus, the physical body of the Tathāgata stands cut off from craving for existence.

Men and devas will behold him for so long as his physical body remains. They will not behold him when his physical body dissolves at the end of his life.

Conclusion

148. When the Bhagavā had delivered this discourse, the Venerable Ānanda addressed him thus: "Marvellous indeed, Venerable Sir! Extraordinary indeed, Venerable Sir! What is the name of this exposition of the dhamma?"

"Ānanda!" said the Bhagavā, "Bear in mind that this exposition of the dhamma is called Atthajāla, the Net of Essence, as well as Dhammajāla, the Net of the Dhamma, as well as Brahmajāla, the Net of Perfect Wisdom, as well as Diṭṭhijāla, the Net of Views, as well as Anuttarasaṅgāma Vijaya, the Incomparable Victory in Battle." Thus said the Bhagavā.

149. Delighted, the bhikkhus rejoiced at the words of the Bhagavā. On the delivery of this discourse ten thousand world systems quaked.

End of the Brahmajāla Sutta, the first sutta from division one (*Sīlakkhandha Vagga*)

Namo tassa bhagavato arahato sammāsambuddhassa

SĀMAÑÑAPHALA SUTTA

II. SĀMAÑÑAPHALA SUTTA

(The Fruits of the Life of a Samaṇa)

Of the King and His Ministers

150. Thus have I heard:

At one time, the Bhagavā was residing in Rājagaha at the mango grove of Jīvaka, the adopted son of the Prince (Abhaya), together with a large company of bhikkhus, numbering twelve hundred and fifty.

At that time King Ajātasattu of Magadha, the son of Queen Vedehī, was resting on the upper terrace of his palace with a retinue of ministers, on the night of the fasting day, the fullmoon day of the month at the end of the four-month rainy season when the white lotus bloomed.

On that day of fasting, King Ajātasattu of Magadha, the son of Queen Vedehī, made a solemn utterance thus:

> "Pleasant, indeed, is the moonlit night, friends! Beautiful, indeed, is the moonlit night, friends! Fair to behold, indeed, is the moonlit night, friends! Lovely, indeed, is the moonlit night, friends! Remarkable, indeed, is the moonlit night,[34] friends! Which Samaṇa or brāhmaṇa shall I attend on today? Which Samaṇa or brāhmaṇa can make my (troubled) mind clear and calm when I attend on him?"

151. When King Ajātasattu of Magadha, the son of Queen Vedehī, had made this utterance, a certain minister addressed him thus:

> "Your Majesty! There is this Pūraṇa Kassapa, who has a group of disciples, with his own sect, being the teacher of his sect, reputed and well-known, the founder of a school of thought, acclaimed by many as virtuous, ripe with experience, having spent long years as an ascetic, with knowledge of the olden days, and far advanced in age. Let Your Majesty attend on that Pūraṇa Kassapa. If Your Majesty should attend on him, your mind might become clear and calm."

King Ajatāsattu of Magadha, the son of Queen Vedehī, remained silent.

152. Another of the ministers addressed King Ajātasattu of Magadha, the son of Queen Vedehī, thus:

> "Your Majesty! There is this Makkhali Gosāla, who has a group of disciples, with his own sect, being the teacher of his sect, reputed and well-known, the founder of a school of thought, acclaimed by

---

34. Remarkable, by illumining the paths of the heavenly bodies, according to the Commentary.

many as virtuous, ripe with experience, having spent long years as an ascetic, with knowledge of the olden days, and far advanced in age. Let Your Majesty attend on that Makkhali Gosāla. If Your Majesty should attend on him, your mind might become clear and calm."

King Ajātasattu of Magadha, the son of Queen Vedehī, remained silent.

153. Another of the ministers addressed King Ajātasattu of Magadha, the son of Queen Vedehī, thus:

"Your Majesty! There is this Ajita Kesakambala, who has a group of disciples, with his own sect, being the teacher of his sect, reputed and well-known, the founder of a school of thought, acclaimed by many as virtuous, ripe with experience, having spent many years as an ascetic, with knowledge of the olden days, and far advanced in age. Let Your Majesty attend on that Ajita Kesakambala. If Your Majesty should attend on him, your mind might become clear and calm."

King-Ajātasattu of Magadha, the son of Queen Vedehī, remained silent.

154. Another of the ministers addressed King Ajātasattu of Magadha, the son of Queen Vedehī, thus:

"Your Majesty! There is this Pakudha Kaccāyana, who has a group of disciples, with his own sect, being the teacher of his sect, reputed and well-known, the founder of a school of thought, acclaimed by many as virtuous, ripe with experience, having spent long years as an ascetic, with knowledge of the olden days, and far advanced in age. Let Your Majesty attend on that Pakudha Kaccāyana. If Your Majesty should attend on him, your mind might become clear and calm."

King Ajātasattu of Magadha, the son of Queen Vedehī, remained silent.

155. Another of the ministers addressed King Ajātasattu of Magadha, the son of Queen Vedehī, thus:

"Your Majesty! There is this Sañcaya Belaṭṭhaputta, who has a group of disciples, with his own sect, being the teacher of his sect, reputed and well-known, the founder of a school of thought, acclaimed by many as virtuous, ripe with experience, having spent long years as an ascetic, with knowledge of the olden days, and far advanced in age. Let Your Majesty attend on that Sañcaya Belaṭṭhaputta. If Your Majesty should attend on him, your mind might become clear and calm."

King Ajātasattu of Magadha, the son of Queen Vedehī, remained silent.

156. Another of the ministers addressed King Ajātasattu of Magadha, the son of Queen Vedehī, thus:

"Your Majesty! There is this Nigaṇṭha Nāṭaputta, who has a group of disciples, with his own sect, being the teacher of his sect, reputed and well-known, the founder of a school of thought, acclaimed by many as virtuous, ripe with experience, having spent long years as an ascetic, with knowledge of the olden days, and far advanced in age. Let Your Majesty attend on that Nigaṇṭha Nātaputta. If Your Majesty should attend on him, your mind might become clear and calm."

King Ajātasattu of Magadha, the son of Queen Vedehī, remained, silent.

Concerning Jīvaka, Adopted Son of a Prince

157. At that time, Jīvaka, the adopted son of the Prince (Abhaya), was seated in silence, not far from King Ajātasattu of Magadha, the son of Queen Vedehī, who then asked: "Friend Jīvaka! "Why do you remain silent?"

"Your Majesty! (said Jīvaka) "The Exalted One, the Homage-Worthy, the Perfectly Self-Enlightened, is now dwelling in our mango grove with a large company of bhikkhus, numbering twelve hundred and fifty. His fame has spread far and wide in this way:

'It has been said of the Bhagavā that he is worthy of special veneration (Arahaṃ); that he truly comprehends the dhammas by his own intellect and insight (Sammā-sambuddha); that he possesses supreme knowledge and the perfect practice of morality (Vijjācaraṇa-sampanna); that he speaks only what is beneficial and true (Sugata); that he knows all the three *lokas*[35] (Lokavidū); that he is incomparable in taming those who deserve to be tamed (Anuttaropurisadammasārathi); that he is the Teacher of devas and men (Satthā-devamanussānaṃ); that he is the Enlightened One, knowing and teaching the Four Noble Truths (Buddha); that he is the Most Exalted (Bhagavā).'

"Let Your Majesty attend on the Bhagavā, and if you should attend on him, your mind might become clear and calm."

158. "If that be so, Friend Jīvaka, make the riding elephants ready."

Saying "Very well, Your Majesty!" to King Ajātasattu of Magadha, the son of Queen Vedehī, Jīvaka, the adopted son of the Prince (Abhaya), had five hundred cow-elephants together with the King's elephant made

35. The three *lokas* are: the animate world (Sattaloka), the inanimate world (Okāsaloka) and the world of the conditioned (Sankhāraloka).

ready, and informed him, "Your Majesty! The riding elephants are ready. Your Majesty can proceed at will."[36]

159. Then King Ajātasattu of Magadha, the son of Queen Vedehī, had the female attendants mounted on the five hundred cow-elephants, one on each, and himself riding on his state elephant, with dignity befitting royalty, attended by torch-bearers, set forth from Rājagaha to the mango grove of Jīvaka, the adopted son of the Prince (Abhaya).

On getting near the mango grove, King Ajātasattu of Magadha, the son of Queen Vedehī, was seized with fear and alarm which caused the hairs on his body to stand erect. Frightened and agitated, with hairs standing on end, King Ajātasattu of Magadha, the son of Queen Vedehī, said to Jīvaka, the adopted son of the Prince (Abhaya):

> "Friend Jīvaka! Are you sure that you are not deceiving me? Friend Jīvaka! Are you sure that you are not playing me tricks? Friend Jīvaka! Are you sure you are not giving me into the hands of enemies? How is it that there is no sound, not even a sneeze nor a cough nor a spoken word among so large an assemblage of bhikkhus numbering twelve hundred and fifty?"

"Great King," (said Jīvaka,) "Be not afraid! Great King! Be not afraid! Noble King, I am not deceiving you; Noble King, I am not playing you tricks; Noble King, I am not giving you into the hands of enemies. Proceed, Great King, proceed! The lamps are burning bright in the pavilion."

Questions on the Fruits of the Life of a Samaṇa

160. Then King Ajātasattu of Magadha, the son of Queen Vedehī, having gone on the elephant as far as it should go, dismounted and approached on foot the door of the pavilion and said to Jīvaka, the adopted son of the Prince (Abhaya), "But, Friend Jīvaka, where is the Bhagavā?"

Jīvaka said, "Great King, this is the Bhagavā. The One sitting against the middle pillar and facing east, in front of the bhikkhus, is the Bhagavā."

161. Then King Ajātasattu of Magadha, the son of Queen Vedehī, approached the Bhagavā, paid him homage and standing in a suitable place, looked again and again at the bhikkhus of the assemblage who were seated in perfect silence and calm as the waters of a clear lake. Then he made this solemn utterance:

36. A literal translation would read: "Now you know the time."

"Would that my son, Prince Udayabhadda, be as peaceful as this assembly of the bhikkhus!"

"Indeed, Great King," said the Bhagavā, "your thoughts have gone where affection leads."

"Venerable Sir," said the King, "I love Udayabhadda, the young Prince. Now this assembly of bhikkhus is very peaceful. May the young Prince, Udayabhadda, have the peace that this assembly possesses."

162. Then King Ajātasattu of Magadha, the son of Queen Vedehī, made obeisance to the Bhagavā, paid respect to the assembly of bhikkhus with joined palms raised (to the forehead) and took a suitable seat. And he addressed the Bhagavā thus:

"Venerable Sir! If the Bhagavā would permit me to put a question, I would like to ask something on a certain subject."

"You may ask, Great King," said the Bhagavā, "whatever you wish to ask."

163. "Venerable Sir! There are (men of) various callings. And what are they? They are:

Elephant riders; horse riders; charioteers; archers; standard-bearers; military strategists; commandos; men of royal birth prominent as warriors; members of striking forces; men brave as elephants; men of valour; mail-clad warriors; trusted servants; confectioners; barbers; bath attendants; cooks; garland-makers; washermen; weavers; reed-mat makers; potters; arithmeticians; and accountants. Besides them, there are men of many other callings. All those skilled in them enjoy the fruits of their proficiency in this very life. They make themselves well-fed and happy. And so do they make their mothers and fathers well-fed and happy, their wives and children well-fed and happy, and their friends well-fed and happy. They engage themselves in the practice of making gifts to samaṇas and brāhmaṇas with a view to attaining the higher realms, the abodes of devas, and obtaining happy and beneficial results. Can you, Venerable Sir, reveal to me the advantages to be gained in this very life from being a samaṇa, similar to the advantages accruing from these callings?"

164. "Do you remember, Great King, ever putting the same question to other samaṇas and brāhmaṇas?"

"I do remember, Venerable Sir, putting the same question to other samaṇas and brāhmaṇas."

"Great King, if it is not burdensome for you to tell me how other samaṇas and brāhmaṇas answered your questions, tell me."

"In the presence of the Bhagavā, or a personage like him, it will not be burdensome for me."

"If that be so, speak. Great King!"

The Creed of Pūraṇa Kassapa

165. Once, Venerable Sir, I went to Pūraṇa Kassapa and exchanged glad greetings with him. Having exchanged courteous and memorable greetings, I sat in a suitable place and put to him this question:

"O Kassapa! There are (men of) various callings. And what are they? They are:

Elephant riders; horse riders; charioteers; archers; standard-bearers; military strategists; commandos; men of royal birth prominent as warriors; members of striking forces; men brave as elephants; men of valour; mail-clad warriors; trusted servants; confectioners; barbers; bath attendants; cooks; garland-makers; washermen; weavers; reed-mat makers; potters; arithmeticians; and accountants. Besides them, there are men of many other callings. All those skilled in them enjoy the fruits of their proficiency in this very life. They make themselves well-fed and happy. And so do they make their mothers and fathers well-fed and happy, their wives and children well-fed and happy, and their friends well-fed and happy. They engage themselves in the practice of making gifts to samaṇas and brāhmaṇas with a view to attaining the higher realms, the abodes of devas, and obtaining happy and beneficial results. Can you, O Kassapa, reveal to me the advantages to be gained in this very life from being a Samaṇa, similar of the advantages accruing from these callings?"

166. At this, Venerable Sir, Pūraṇa Kassapa made this reply:

"Great King! One who acts or causes others to act, one who mutilates or causes others to mutilate, one who torments or causes others to torment, one who inflicts sorrow or causes others to inflict sorrow, one who oppresses and causes others to oppress, one who threatens or causes others to threaten, one who kills or causes others to kill, one who steals or causes others to steal, one who breaks into houses or causes others to break into houses, one who raids or causes others to raid villages, one who robs or causes others to rob, one who commits or causes others to commit highway robbery, one who commits or causes others to commit adultery or one who tells lies or causes others to tell lies is not deemed to have done evil even though he has done (these things). Even if one cuts up all beings on this earth into a pile or a heap of flesh with a grinding wheel fitted with razors, evil will not be caused. No evil ensues therefrom. Even if anyone living on the south bank of the Ganges should kill or cause others to kill, mutilate or cause others to mutilate, or torment or cause others to torment, no evil is done. No evil ensues therefrom. Even if anyone living on the north bank of the Ganges should give alms or cause others to give alms, or make offerings or cause others to make offerings, no meritorious action is done. No merit ensues therefrom. Such actions as giving in charity, controlling the senses, observing morality and speaking the truth will not bring about meritoriousness. No merit ensues therefrom."

Venerable Sir! I asked Pūraṇa Kassapa about the advantages in this very life of being a samaṇa, and he replied by expounding the doctrine of *Akiriya*, non-causative action or non-kamma. It is as if, when asked about a mango tree, he explains what a mountain-jack[37] is and when asked about a mountain-jack he explains what a mango tree is. Similarly, Pūraṇa Kassapa, when asked about the advantages in this very life of being a samaṇa, explained to me the doctrine of *Akiriya*, non-kamma. At that, it occurred to me thus, Venerable Sir!

"Why should a king like me think of blaming the samaṇas and brāhmaṇas living in my realm?"

Venerable Sir! I was not pleased with what Pūraṇa Kassapa told me. But I did not say that I rejected what he said. Although I neither liked it nor rejected it and said nothing about my displeasure, I arose and departed from his presence without accepting what he said or paying any heed to it.

The Creed of Makkhali Gosāla

167. Once, Venerable Sir, I went to Makkhali Gosāla and exchanged glad greetings with him. Having exchanged courteous and memorable greetings, I sat in a suitable place and put to him this question.

"O Gosāla! There are (men of) various callings ... (p) ... Can you, O Gosāla, reveal to me the advantages in this very life to be gained from being a samaṇa similar to advantages accruing from these callings?"

168. At this, Venerable Sir, Makkhali Gosāla made this reply:

"Great King! There exists no cause or condition for beings to become defiled; they are defiled without cause or condition. There exists no

37. **Mountain-jack**: labuja; some translate this term as breadfruit tree.

cause or condition for beings to become absolutely pure; they are absolutely pure without cause or condition. There is no such thing as action done by oneself, nor action done by another for the sake of oneself, nor action done by men. There is no power, no energy, no human strength and no human endeavour. All sentient beings, all those that breathe, all those that exist, all those that possess the principle of life are devoid of power, energy, strength and endeavour. They just happen naturally, by chance and according to their own individual character. They experience pleasure and pain in accordance with the various positions they occupy in their hierarchy of six kinds of births. There are one million four hundred and six thousand six hundred main types of beings. There are five hundred kinds of actions (*kamma*), or else five, or else three; and there are complete actions as well as half actions. There are sixty-two methods of religious practices, sixty-two world cycles, six categories of special castes, eight stages of man, four thousand and nine hundred modes of living, four thousand and nine hundred kinds of wandering ascetics, four thousand and nine hundred abodes of nāga serpents, two thousand faculties of the senses, three thousand abodes of suffering (*niraya*), thirty-six repositories of atoms of dust, seven kinds of rebirth with consciousness (*saññā*), seven kinds of rebirth without consciousness, seven kinds of reproduction by budding and grafting, seven kinds of devas, seven kinds of human beings, seven kinds of sprites, seven kinds of lakes, seven kinds of great prominences, seven hundred small prominences, seven great chasms, seven hundred small chasms, seven major dreams and seven hundred minor dreams. And then there are eighty-four hundred thousand great cycles of time during which the fool and the wise alike, wandering from one existence to another, will at last put an end to the round of suffering. In the meanwhile there will be no end (of it). No one can say: 'By the practice of this morality and conduct, of this austerity, of this chastity, I shall make my immature actions grow into maturity, at the same time destroying mature actions by repeated encounters.' All happiness and misery have been measured in the measuring basket; and the round of rebirths is in this way delimited, with no extension or reduction. When a ball of string is thrown forward, it will go as far as the length of the string allows. In like manner both the fool and the wise would wander from one existence to another as far as they can go, and ultimately make an end of the round of suffering."

169. Venerable Sir! I asked Makkhali Gosāla about the advantages in this very life of being a samaṇa and he replied by expounding the doctrine of *saṃsāra suddhi*, purification by means of the round of suffering. It is as if, when asked about a mango tree, he explains what a mountain-jack is and when asked about a mountain-jack, he explains what a mango tree is. Similarly, Makkhali Gosāla, when asked about the advantages in this very life of being a Samaṇa, explained to me the doctrine of purification by means of the round of suffering. At that, it occurred to me thus, Venerable Sir!

"Why should a king like me think of blaming the samaṇas and brāhmaṇas living in my realm?"

Venerable Sir! I was not pleased with what Makkhali Gosāla told me. But I did not say that I rejected what he said. Although I neither liked it nor rejected it and said nothing about my displeasure, I arose and departed from his presence without accepting what he said or paying any heed to it.

The Creed of Ajita Kesakambala

170. Once, Venerable Sir, I went to Ajita Kesakambala and exchanged glad greetings with him. Having exchanged courteous and memorable greetings, I sat in a suitable place and put to him this question.

"O Ajita! There are (men of) various callings ... (p) ... Can you, O Ajita, reveal to me the advantages to be gained in this very life from being a samaṇa, similar to the advantages accruing from these callings?"

171. At this, Venerable Sir. Ajita Kesakambala made this reply:

"Great King! There is no (consequence to) almsgiving, sacrifice or oblation. A good or bad action produces no result. This world does not exist, nor do other worlds. There is no mother, no father, (all good or evil done to them producing no result). There is no rebirth of beings after death. In this world, there are no samaṇas or brāhmaṇas, established in the Noble Path and accomplished in good practice, who through direct knowledge (i.e., *magga* insight) acquired by their own efforts, can expound on this world and other worlds. This being is but a compound of the four great primary elements; after death, the earth-element (or element of extension) returns and goes back to the body of the earth, the water-element (or element of cohesion) returns and goes back to the body of water, the fire-element (or element of thermal energy) returns and goes back to the body of fire, and the air-element (or element of motion) returns and goes back to the body of air, while the mental faculties pass on into space. The four pall-bearers and the bier (constituting the fifth) carry the corpse. The remains of the dead can be seen up to the cemetery where bare bones lie greying like the colour of the pigeons. All almsgiving ends in ashes. Fools prescribe alms-giving; and some assert that there is such a thing as merit in alms-giving; but their words are empty, false and nonsensical. Both the fool and the wise are annihilated and destroyed after death and dissolution of their bodies. Nothing exists after death."

172. Venerable Sir! I asked Ajita Kesakambala about the advantages in this very life of being a Samaṇa, and he replied by expounding the doctrine of annihilation. It is as if, when asked, about a mango tree, he explains what a mountain-jack is and when asked about a mountain-jack, he explains what a mango tree is. Similarly, Ajita Kesakambala, when asked about the advantages in this very life of being a samaṇa, explained to me the doctrine of annihilation. At that, it occurred to me thus, Venerable Sir!

"Why should a king like me think of blaming the samaṇas and brāhmaṇas living in my realm?"

Venerable Sir! I was not pleased with what Ajita Kesakambala told me. But I did not say that I rejected what he said. Although I neither liked it nor rejected it and said nothing about my displeasure, I arose and departed from his presence without accepting what he said or paying any heed to it.

The Creed of Pakudha Kaccāyana

173. Once, Venerable Sir, I went to Pakudha Kaccāyana and exchanged glad greetings with him. Having exchanged courteous and memorable greetings, I sat in a suitable place and put to him this question.

"O Kaccayāna! There are (men of) various callings ... (p) ... Can you, O Kaccāyana, reveal to me the advantages to be gained in this very life from being a samaṇa, similar to the advantages accruing from these callings?"

174. At this, Venerable Sir, Pakudha Kaccāyana made this reply:

"Great King! There is this group of seven which is neither made nor caused to be made, and neither created nor caused to be created. These seven are sterile, permanent as a mountain peak and firm as a gate post. They are unshakable, immutable, unable to harm one another and incapable of causing pleasure or pain or both pleasure and pain to one another. And what are those seven? They are: the body of earth, of water, of fire, of air; pleasure, pain and the soul.[38]

"These seven are neither made nor caused to be made, and neither created nor caused to be created. They are sterile, permanent as a mountain peak and firm as a gate post. They are unshakable, immutable, unable to harm one another and incapable of causing pleasure or pain or both pleasure and pain to one another. Among the seven there is neither killer nor one who causes killing, neither hearer nor one who causes hearing, neither knower nor one who causes knowing. When one cuts off another's head with a sharp weapon, it does not mean that one has killed the other, for the weapon only falls through the space in between the seven."

175. Venerable Sir! I asked Pakudha Kaccāyana about the advantages in this very life of being a samaṇa and he replied by substituting another subject. It is as if, when asked about a mango tree, he explains what a mountain-jack is and when asked about a mountain-jack, he explains what a mango tree is. Similarly, Pakudha Kaccāyana, when asked about the advantages in this very life of being a samaṇa, substituted another subject. At that, it occurred to me thus, Venerable Sir!

"Why should a king like me think of blaming the samaṇas and brāhmaṇas living in my realm?"

Venerable Sir! I was not pleased with what Pakudha Kaccāyana told me. But I did not say that I rejected what he said. Although I neither liked it nor rejected it and said nothing about my displeasure, I arose and departed from his presence without accepting what he said or paying any heed to it.

The Creed of Nigaṇṭha Nātaputta

176. Once, Venerable Sir, I went to Nigaṇṭha Nātaputta and exchanged glad greetings with him. Having exchanged courteous and memorable greetings, I sat in a suitable place and put to him this question.

"O Aggivessana![39] There are (men of) various callings ... (p) ... Can you, O Aggivessana, reveal to me the advantages to be gained in this very life from being a samaṇa, similar to the advantages accruing from these callings?"

38. **The soul:** *jiva*; another meaning of *jiva* is "life" or "life-principle".
39. Aggivessana is the family name of Nigaṇṭha Nātaputta.

177. At this, Venerable Sir, Nigaṇṭha Nātaputta made this reply:

"Great King! In this world a Nigaṇṭha is disciplined in four kinds of self-restraint. And what are they? They are as follows. A Nigaṇṭha abstains from taking cold water from all sources. He abstains from all (evil), and by such complete abstinence, throws off all (evil), and achieves[40] perfect restraint. O King! A Nigaṇṭha who is disciplined in these four kinds of self-restraint is deemed to have become perfected in self-discipline, self-restraint and steadfastness."

178. Venerable Sir! I asked Nigaṇṭha Nātaputta about the advantages in this very life of being a samaṇa, and he replied by expounding the fourfold self-discipline. It is as if, when asked about a mango tree, he explains what a mountain-jack is and when asked about a mountain-jack, he explains what a mango tree is. Nigaṇṭha Nātaputta, when asked about the advantages in this very life of being a samaṇa, expounded the fourfold self-discipline. At that, it occurred to me thus, Venerable Sir!

"Why should a king like me think of blaming the samaṇas and brāhmaṇas living in my realm?"

Venerable Sir! I was not pleased with what Nigaṇṭha Nātaputta told me. But I did not say that I rejected what he said. Although I neither liked it nor rejected it and said nothing about my displeasure, I arose and departed from his presence without accepting what he said or paying any heed to it.

The Creed of Sañcaya Belaṭṭhaputta

179. Once, Venerable Sir, I went to Sañcaya Belaṭṭhaputta and exchanged glad greetings with him. Having exchanged courteous and memorable greetings, I sat in a suitable place and put to him this question.

"O Sañcaya! There are (men of) various callings ... (p) ... Can you, O Sañcaya, reveal to me the advantages to be gained in this very life from being a samaṇa, similar to the advantages accruing from these callings?"

180. At this, Venerable Sir, Sañcaya Belaṭṭhaputta made this reply:

"If I were asked, 'Is there another world?'and if I took it that there is, I should answer 'There is another world.' But I would not say this

40. **Achieves**: lit., comes into contact with.

way, nor that way, nor the other way; neither would I say not this way, not that way, not the other way; nor would I say otherwise.

If I were asked:

whether there is not another world ...

whether there is, and also is not, another world ...

whether there neither is, nor is not, another world ...

whether there is opapātika birth[41] of beings ...

whether there is no opapātika birth of beings ...

whether there is, and also there is not, opapātika birth of beings ...

whether it is not that there is, and also there is not, opapātika birth of beings ...

whether a good or a bad kamma produces results ...

whether a good or a bad kamma produces no results ...

whether it is that a good or a bad kamma produces results and also does not produce results ...

whether it is not that a good or a bad kamma produces results and also does not produce results ...

whether there is life after death[42] ...

whether there is no life after death ... whether there is life as well as no life after death...

whether it is not that there is life as well as no life after death, and if I took it that it is not that there is life as well as no life after death, I should answer 'It is not that there is life as well as no life after death.' But I would not say this way, nor that way, not the other way; neither would I say not this way, not that way, not the other way; nor would I say otherwise."

181. Venerable Sir! I asked Sañcaya Belaṭṭhaputta about the advantages in this very life of being a samaṇa, and he replied by expounding the creed of evasion. It is as if, when asked about a mango tree, he explains what a mountain-jack is, and when asked about a mountain-jack, he explains what a mango tree is. Similarly, Sañcaya Belaṭṭhaputta, when asked about the advantages in this very life of being a samaṇa, expounded the creed of evasion. At that, it occurred to me thus. Venerable Sir!

"Of all samaṇas and brāhmaṇas, this man is the most foolish and bewildered. Why did he tell me the creed of evasion when I asked

---

41. See para 65, Brahmajāla Sutta.
42. Literally: whether a sentient being exists after death.

him about the advantages in this very life of being a samaṇa? Why should a king like me think of blaming the samaṇas and brāhmaṇas living in my realm?"

Venerable Sir! I was not pleased with what Sañcaya Belaṭṭhaputta told me. But I did not say that I rejected what he said. Although I neither liked it nor rejected it and said nothing about my displeasure, I arose and departed from his presence without accepting what he said or paying any heed to it.

First Advantage of a Samaṇa's Life Experienced Here and Now

182. Venerable Sir! Let me ask of you also. There are (men of) various callings. And what are they? They are: "Elephant riders; horse riders; charioteers; archers; standard-bearers; military strategists; commandos; men of royal birth prominent as warriors; members of striking forces; men brave as elephants; men of valour; mail-clad warriors; trusted servants; confectioners; barbers; bath attendants; cooks; garland-makers; washermen; weavers; reed-mat makers; potters; arithmeticians; and accountants. Besides them, there are men of many other callings. All those skilled in them enjoy the fruits of their proficiency in this very life. They make themselves well-fed and happy. And so do they make their mothers and fathers well-fed and happy, their wives and children well-fed and happy, and their friends well-fed and happy. They engage themselves in the practice of making gifts to samaṇas and brāhmaṇas with a view to attaining the higher realms, the abodes of devas, and obtaining happy and beneficial results. Can you, Venerable Sir, reveal to me the advantages to be gained in this very life from being a samaṇa, similar to the advantages accruing from these callings?"

183. I can, Great King! But in order to tell you about this, let me put a counter-question to you. Answer it as you like. Now what do you think of this?

Suppose you had a household servant, whose habit was to get up from bed earlier and retire later than his master, and who was ready to act at his master's bidding, performing duties to give pleasure to his master, affable in speech, and observant of his master's demeanour to know what he wanted. Suppose it occurred to him thus:

'Friends! How wonderful and extraordinary is the state of existence conditioned by meritorious deeds and the resultant effect of such deeds! Here is King Ajātasattu of Magadha, the son of Queen Vedehī, who is a man; and I also am a man. But King Ajātasattu of Magadha, the son of Queen Vedehī, enjoys to the full the five pleasures of the senses as if he were a deva. I am but a servant, getting up from bed earlier and retiring later than my master, ready to act at his bidding, performing duties to give pleasure to him, affable in speech and observant of his demeanour to know what he wants. Had I done meritorious deeds I could have been a king like him. Now it were better for me to shave off my hair and beard, don the bark-dyed robe, renounce hearth and home, and become a recluse leading the homeless life.'

Suppose that afterwards that man shaved off his hair and beard, donned the bark-dyed robe, renounced hearth and home, and became a recluse leading the homeless life. Having become a recluse he exercised self-control in bodily, verbal and mental actions, content with what he could get for food and clothing and delighting in solitude. Then suppose your attendants, reported to you thus:

'Your Majesty! Please know this. Your Majesty's servant, who used to get up from bed earlier and retire later than you, ready to act at your bidding, performing his duties to give pleasure to you, affable in speech and observant of your demeanour to know what you wanted, has shaved off his hair and beard, donned the bark-dyed robe, renounced hearth and home, and has become a recluse leading the homeless life. Having thus become a recluse he exercised self-control in bodily, verbal and mental actions, content with what he could get for food and clothing, and delighting in solitude.'

If he were thus reported, would it be appropriate for you to say:

'Men! Let that man come back to me! Let him be a servant again, rising up from bed earlier and retiring later than I, ready to act at my bidding, performing duties to give pleasure to me, affable in speech and observant of my demeanour to know what I want.'?

184. "No, Venerable Sir! Indeed we should pay respect to him, welcome him and beg him to be seated. We should even invite him to accept our offerings of such requisites as robe, food, shelter, and medicine for use in illness. And we should also provide protection and security for him according to law."

185. If that be so, Great King, what do you think of this? Is there or is there not any personally experienced advantage in being a Samaṇa?

"Venerable Sir, there is certainly a personally experienced advantage in being a Samaṇa."

Great King! This, I say to you, is the first advantage of being a Samaṇa, personally experienced in this very life.

Second Advantage of a Samaṇa's Life Experienced Here and Now

186. "Can you, Venerable Sir, reveal to me any other similar advantage of being a samaṇa personally experienced in this very life?"

I can, Great King. But in order to tell you about this, let me put a counter-question to you. Answer it as you like. Now what do you think of this? Suppose you had in your kingdom a landholder cultivating his own land and paying taxes to increase (the country's) wealth. Suppose it occurred to him thus:

> 'Friends! How wonderful and extraordinary is the state of existence conditioned by meritorious deeds and the resultant effect of such deeds! Here is King Ajātasattu of Magadha, the son of Queen Vedehī, who is a man; and I also am a man. But King Ajātasattu of Magadha, the son of Queen Vedehī, enjoys to the full the five pleasures of the senses as if he were a deva. I am but a landholder cultivating my own land and paying taxes to increase (the country's) wealth. Had I done meritorious deeds I could have been a king like him. Now it were better for me to shave off my hair and beard, don the bark-dyed robe, renounce hearth and home, and become a recluse leading the homeless life.'

Suppose that afterwards that man gave up his wealth, great or small, leaving his relatives, be they few or be they many, shaved off his hair and beard, donned the bark-dyed robe, renounced hearth and home and became a recluse leading the homeless life. Having thus become a recluse, he exercised self-control in bodily, verbal and mental actions, content with what he could get for food and clothing, delighting in solitude. Suppose, then, your attendants reported to you thus:

> 'Your Majesty! Please know this. Your Majesty's landholder who used to cultivate his own land and pay taxes to increase (the country's) wealth has shaved off his hair and beard, donned the bark-dyed robe, renounced hearth and home, and has become a recluse leading the homeless life. Having thus become a recluse, he exercised self-control in bodily, verbal and mental actions, content with what he could get for food and clothing, delighting in solitude.'

If he were thus reported, would it be appropriate for you to say:

'Men! Let that man come back to me! Let him be a landholder again, cultivating his own land and paying taxes to increase (the country's) wealth.'?

187. "No, Venerable Sir! Indeed we should pay respect to him, welcome him and beg him to be seated. We should even invite him to accept our offerings of such requisites as robe, food, shelter, and medicine for use in illness. And we should also provide protection and security for him according to law."

188. If that be so, Great King, what do you think of this? Is there or is there not any personally experienced advantage in being a samaṇa?

"Venerable Sir! There is certainly a personally experienced advantage in being a Samaṇa."

Great King! This, I say to you, is the second advantage of being a samaṇa, personally experienced in this very life.

Higher and Better Advantage of a Samaṇa's Life

189. "Can you, Venerable Sir, reveal to me any other advantage, higher and better, of being a Samaṇa, personally experienced in this very life?"

I can, Great King! Listen and pay good attention. I shall speak.

"Very well, Venerable Sir!" said King Ajātasattu of Magadha, the son of Queen Vedehī.

190. Then the Bhagavā spoke thus:

Great King! There arises in this world the Tathāgata who is worthy of special veneration, who truly comprehends all Dhammas by his own intellect and insight, who possesses supreme knowledge and perfect practice of morality, who speaks only what is beneficial and true, who knows all the three *lokas*, who is incomparable in taming those who deserve to be tamed, who is the Teacher of devas and men, who is the Enlightened One, knowing and teaching the Four Noble Truths, and who is the Most Exalted. Through Perfect Wisdom, he personally realizes the nature of the universe with its devas, māras and Brahmās, and also the world of human beings with its samaṇas and brāhmaṇas, kings and men, and knowing it, he expounds on it. He proclaims the dhamma which is excellent at the beginning, excellent at the middle, and excellent at the end, with richness in meaning and words. He makes clear the completeness and purity of the Noble Practice.[43]

191. A householder, or his son, or anyone belonging to any caste, listens to that dhamma. On hearing the dhamma he develops faith in the Tathāgata. When faith is thus developed, he considers thus:

> 'Confined is the life of a householder; it is a path laden with dust (of defilement). A samaṇa's life is like an open plain. Difficult it is for a layman to pursue the Noble Practice in all its fullness, in all its purity, like a polished conch. Now, it were better for me to shave off my hair and beard, don the bark-dyed robe, renounce hearth and home, and become a recluse leading the homeless life.'

192. Afterwards, he gives up his wealth, great or small, leaving his relatives, be they few or be they many, shaves off his hair and beard, dons the bark-dyed robe, renounces hearth and home, and becomes a recluse leading the homeless life.

193. When he has thus become a samaṇa, he practices self-restraint in accordance with the fundamental precepts (*pātimokkhasaṃvara Sīla*). He is endowed with good practice and resorts only to suitable places.[44] He now sees danger even in the least offences. He observes the precepts well. Being possessed of good deeds and good words, he pursues a pure livelihood. He is endowed with morality. He has his sense-doors guarded. He attains mindfulness and clearness of comprehension. He is contented.

CŪḶA SĪLA
(Short Section on Morality)

194. Great King! How is a bhikkhu endowed with morality? In this matter, Great King, a bhikkhu abandons all thoughts of taking life and abstains from destruction of life, setting aside the stick and the sword, ashamed to do evil, and he is compassionate and dwells with solicitude for the welfare of all living beings. This is one of the precepts of his morality.

He abandons all thoughts of taking what is not given and abstains from taking what is not given. He accepts only what is given, wishing to

---

43. **Noble Practice**: Brahmacariya: The Noble Practice of morality (*sīla*), concentration (*samādhi*) and wisdom (*paññā*) as practised by the Buddha and the Ariyas.

44. "**Resorts ... places**": *Gocara*; another interpretation of this term is "a suitable subject for constant meditation."

receive only what is given. He establishes himself in purity by abstaining from committing theft. This also is one of the precepts of his morality.

He abandons all thoughts of leading a life of un-chastity and practices chastity, remaining virtuous and abstinent from sexual intercourse, the practice of lay people. This also is one of the precepts of his morality.

He abandons all thoughts of telling lies and abstains from telling lies, speaking only the truth, combining truth with truth, and remaining steadfast (in truth), trustworthy and not deceiving. This also is one of the precepts of his morality.

He abandons all thoughts of slandering and abstains from slander. Hearing things from these people he does not relate them to those people to sow the seed of discord among them. Hearing things from those people he does not relate them to these people to sow the seed of discord among them. He reconciles those who are at variance. He encourages those who are in accord. He delights in unity, loves it and rejoices in it. He speaks to create harmony. This also is one of the precepts of his morality.

He abandons all thoughts of speaking harshly and abstains from harsh speech. He speaks only blameless words, pleasing to the ear, affectionate, going to the heart, courteous, pleasing to many and heartening to many. This also is one of the precepts of his morality.

He abandons all thoughts of talking frivolously and abstains from frivolous talk. His speech is appropriate to the occasion, being truthful, beneficial, consistent with the Doctrine and the Discipline, memorable, timely and opportune, with reasons, confined within limits and conducive to welfare. This also is one of the precepts of his morality.

He abstains from destroying all seeds and vegetation ... (p) ...

He takes only one meal a day, not taking food at night and fasting after mid-day.

He abstains from dancing, singing, music and watching (entertainments) that is a stumbling block to the attainment of morality.

He abstains from wearing flowers, using perfumes and anointing with unguents.

He abstains from the use of high and luxurious beds and seats.

He abstains from the acceptance of gold and silver.

He abstains from the acceptance of uncooked cereals.

He abstains from the acceptance of uncooked meat.

He abstains from the acceptance of women and maidens.

He abstains from the acceptance of male and female slaves.

He abstains from the acceptance of goats and sheep.

He abstains from the acceptance of chickens and pigs.

He abstains from the acceptance of elephants, cattle, horses and mares.

He abstains from the acceptance of cultivated or uncultivated land.

He abstains from acting as messenger or courier.

He abstains from buying and selling.

He abstains from using false weights and measures and counterfeits.

He abstains from such dishonest practices as bribery, cheating and fraud.

He abstains from maiming, murdering, holding persons in captivity, committing highway robbery, plundering villages and committing dacoity.

This also is one of the precepts of his morality.

End of the Short Section on Morality

Majjhima Sīla
(Middle-length Section on Morality)

195. There are certain respected samaṇas and brāhmaṇas who, living on the food offered out of faith (in *kamma* and its results), are given to destroying such things as seeds and vegetation. And what are such things? They are of five kinds, namely, root-germs, stem-germs, node-germs, plumule-germs and seed-germs. A bhikkhu abstains from destroying such seeds and vegetation. This is one of the precepts of his morality.

196. And then there are certain respected samaṇas and brāhmaṇas who, living on the food offered out of faith (in *kamma* and its results), are given to storing up and using things offered, such as cooked rice, beverages, clothing, sandals, beds, unguents and eatables. A bhikkhu abstains from storing up and using such things. This also is one of the precepts of his morality.

197. And then there are certain respected samaṇas and brāhmaṇas who, living on the food offered out of faith (in *kamma* and its results), are given to watching (entertainments) that is a stumbling block to the attainment of morality. And what are such entertainments? They are: dancing, singing, music, shows, recitations, hand-clapping, brass-instrument-playing, drum-playing, art exhibitions, playing with an iron ball, bamboo raising games, rituals of washing the bones of the dead, elephant-fights, horse-fights, buffalo-fights, bull-fights, goat-fights, sheep-fights, cock-fights, quail-fights, fighting with quarter-staffs, boxing, wrestling, military tattoos, military reviews, route-marches and troop-movements. A bhikkhu abstains from watching (entertainments)

that is a stumbling block to the attainment of morality. This also is one of the precepts of his morality.

198. And then there are certain respected samaṇas and brāhmaṇas who, living on the food offered out of faith (in *kamma* and its results), are given to betting (and taking part in sports and games) that weakens one's vigilance (in the practice of morality). And what are such sports and games? They are: playing chess on eight-squared or ten-squared boards; playing imaginary chess using the sky as a chess-board; playing chess on a moon-shaped chess-board; flipping cowries with thumb and finger; throwing dice; playing tipcat; playing with brush and paints; playing marbles; playing whistling games with folded leaves; playing with miniature ploughs; acrobatics; turning palm-leaf wheels; measuring with toy-baskets made of leaves; playing with miniature chariots; playing with small bows and arrows; alphabetical riddles; mind-reading and simulating physical defects. A bhikkhu abstains from betting (and taking part in such sports and games) that weakens one's vigilance (in the practice of morality). This also is one of the precepts of his morality.

199. And then there are certain respected samaṇas and brāhmaṇas who, living on the food offered out of faith (in *kamma* and its results), are given to using high and luxurious beds and their furnishings. And what are they? They are: high couches; divans raised on sculptured legs; long-fleeced carpets; woollen carpets with quaint (geometrical) designs; white woollen coverlets; woollen coverlets with floral designs; mattresses stuffed with cotton; woollen coverlets with pictorial designs; woollen coverlets with fringes on one or both sides; gold-brocaded coverlets; silk coverlets; large carpets (wide enough for sixteen dancing girls to dance on); saddle cloth and trappings for elephants and horses; upholstery for carriages; rugs made of black panther's hide; rugs made of antelope's hide; red canopies and couches with red bolsters at each end. A bhikkhu abstains from using such high and luxurious beds and their furnishings. This also is one of the precepts of his morality.

200. And then there are certain respected samaṇas and brāhmaṇas, who, living on the food offered out of faith (in *kamma* and its results), are given to beautifying or adorning themselves. And what are such embellishments and adornments? They are: using perfumed cosmetics; getting massaged; taking perfumed baths; developing one's physique; using mirrors; painting eyelashes dark; decorating (oneself) with flowers; applying powder and lotion to the body; beautifying the face with

powder and lotion; wearing bangles; tying the hair into a top-knot; carrying walking sticks or ornamented hollow cylinders (containing medicinal herbs) or swords; using multi-coloured umbrellas or footwear (with gorgeous designs); wearing a turban, or a hair-pin set with rubies; carrying a yak-tail fan; and wearing long white robes with fringes. A bhikkhu abstains from such embellishments and adornments. This also is one of the precepts of his morality.

201. And then there are certain respected samaṇas and brāhmaṇas who, living on the food offered out of faith (in *kamma* and its results), are given to engaging themselves in unprofitable talk (that is contrary to correct practice conducive to the attainment of deva realms and Nibbāna), such as talk about kings, thieves, ministers, armed forces, calamities, battles, food, drinks, clothing, beds, flowers, unguents, relatives, vehicles, villages, market-towns, cities, provinces, womenfolk, heroes, streets, water-fronts, the dead and the departed, trivialities, the universe, the oceans, prosperity, adversity, and so on. A bhikkhu abstains from engaging himself in such unprofitable talk. This also is one of the precepts of his morality.

202. And then there are certain respected samaṇas and brāhmaṇas who, living on the food offered out of faith (in *kamma* and its results), are given to mutually disparaging disputes. And what are they? (They are as follows:) "You do not know this Doctrine and Discipline. I know this Doctrine and Discipline. How can you ever know this Doctrine and Discipline? Your practice is wrong. My practice is right. What I say is coherent and sensible. What you say is not coherent and sensible. What you should say first, you say last; and what you should say last, you say first. What you have long practiced to say has been upset now. I have exposed the faults in your doctrine. You stand rebuked. Try to escape from this censure, or explain it if you can." A bhikkhu abstains from such mutually disparaging disputes. This also is one of the precepts of his morality.

203. And then there are certain respected samaṇas and brāhmaṇas who, living on the food offered out of faith (in *kamma* and its results), are given to serving as messengers or couriers. And what are such services? They are: going from this place to that place, or coming from that place to this place and taking things from this place to that place, or bringing things from that place to this place, on behalf of kings, ministers, brahmins, house-holders and youths. A bhikkhu abstains from serving as messenger or courier. This also is one of the precepts of his morality.

204. And then there are certain respected samaṇas and brāhmaṇas who, living on the food offered out of faith (in *kamma* and its results), practice deceitful pretension (to attainments), flattery (for gain), subtle insinuation by signs or indications (for gain), using pressure (to get offerings) and the seeking of more gain by cunning offer of gifts. A bhikkhu abstains from such pretension and flattery. This also is one of the precepts of his morality.

End of the Middle-length Section on Morality

Mahā Sīla
(Long Section on Morality)

205. And then there are certain respected samaṇas and brāhmaṇas who, living on the food offered out of faith (in *kamma* and its results), make a wrongful living by means of low arts contrary to correct practice conducive to the attainment of deva realms and Nibbāna. And what are such low arts? They are: fortune telling from a study of physical characteristics, or of signs and omens, or of lightning; interpreting dreams; reading physiognomy; prognosticating from a study of rat-bites; indicating benefits from fire-oblation with different kinds of firewood, or with different kinds of ladles, or with husks, broken rice, whole rice, clarified butter, oil, oral spells, or with blood; reading physiognomy while chanting spells; forecasting good or bad fortune from the signs and marks of a piece of land; being versed in state affairs; reciting spells in the graveyard to eliminate dangers; reciting spells to overcome evil spirits; using magical formulae learnt in a mud-house; charming snakes and curing snake-bites; treating poisoning; curing scorpion-stings or rat-bites; interpreting animal and bird sounds and the cawing of crows; foretelling the remaining length of life; diverting the flight of arrows; and identifying the cries of animals. A bhikkhu abstains from making a wrongful living by such means. This also is one of the precepts of his morality.

206. And then there are certain respected samaṇas and brāhmaṇas who, living on the food offered out of faith (in *kamma* and its results), make a wrongful living by means of low arts contrary to correct practice conducive to the attainment of deva realms and Nibbāna. And what are they? They are: reading the portents of gems, dresses, sticks, daggers, swords, arrows, bows and other weapons; reading the characteristics of women, men, young men, young women, male slaves, female slaves, elephants, horses, buffaloes, bulls and other cattle, goats, sheep, chickens,

quails, iguanas, pointed-eared animals,[45] tortoises and game-beasts. A bhikkhu abstains from making a wrongful living by such means. This also is one of the precepts of his morality.

207. And then there are certain respected samaṇas and brāhmaṇas who, living on the food offered out of faith (in *kamma* and its results), make a wrongful living by means of low arts contrary to correct practice conducive to the attainment of deva realms and Nibbāna. And what are they? They are: making predictions about kings going to war; about kings coming back from war; about kings advancing in battle from their home country; about kings from foreign countries retreating; about kings from foreign countries advancing in battle; about kings retreating to their home country; about kings from their home country winning battles; about kings from foreign countries losing battles; about kings from foreign countries winning battles; about kings in their home country losing battles; and about probabilities of victories and losses of warring kings. A bhikkhu abstains from making a wrongful living by such means. This also is one of the precepts of his morality.

208. And then there are certain respected samaṇas and brāhmaṇas who, living on the food offered out of faith (in *kamma* and its results), make a wrongful living by means of low arts contrary to correct practice conducive to the attainment of deva realms and Nibbāna. And what are they? They are: making predictions about the eclipse of the moon, or of the sun; about the conjunction of a group of stars with a planet; about the correct or incorrect course of the moon, the sun and the planets; about meteors, comets, earthquakes and thunder; about the rising and setting of the moon, the sun and the planets; about the phenomena of darkness and brightness following such rising and setting; about the effects of the eclipse of the moon, or of the sun, or of the planets; about the effects of the moon or the sun taking the right course; about the effects of the moon or the sun taking the wrong course; about the effects of the planets taking the right course; about the effects of the planets taking the wrong course; about the effects of meteors, comets, earthquakes and thunder; about the effects of the rising and setting of the moon, or of the sun, or of the planets; and about the effects of the phenomena of darkness or brightness following such rising and setting. A bhikkhu abstains from making a wrongful living by such means. This also is one of the precepts of his morality.

---

45. See footnote to Para 22, Brahmajāla Sutta.

209. And then there are certain respected samaṇas and brāhmaṇas who, living on the food offered out of faith (in *kamma* and its results), make a wrongful living by means of low arts contrary to correct practice conducive to the attainment of deva realms and Nibbāna. And what are they? They are: predicting rainfall or drought, abundance or famine, peace or calamity, disease or health; and knowledge of counting on the fingers or of arithmetical or mathematical calculations, of versification, and of treatises on controversial matters (such as the origin of the universe etc.). A bhikkhu abstains from making a wrongful living by such means. This also is one of the precepts of his morality.

210. And then there are certain respected samaṇas and brāhmaṇas who, living on the food offered out of faith (in *kamma* and its results), make a wrongful living by means of low arts contrary to correct practice conducive to the attainment of deva realms and Nibbāna. And what are they? They are: bringing the bride to the bridegroom, leading away the bride from her father's home; arranging betrothal, or divorce; making predictions relating to acquisition or distribution of property; causing gain or loss of fame and prosperity; curing the tendency to abort or miscarry; casting spells to cause immobility of the tongue or the jaws; reciting a spell to stop an attacking hand; or to cause inability to speak or to hear; conducting seances with the aid of mirrors, or employing young women or female slaves as mediums; propitiating the sun or the Brahmā; making fire issue from the mouth by means of a spell; and making invocations to the goddess of glory. A bhikkhu abstains from making a wrongful living by such means. This also is one of the precepts of his morality.

211. And then there are certain respected samaṇas and brāhmaṇas who, living on the food offered out of faith (in *kamma* and its results), make a wrongful living by means of low arts contrary to correct practice conducive to the attainment of deva realms ana Nibbāna. And what are they? They are: propitiating the devas by promises of offerings; making offerings to the devas for favours granted; causing possession by spirits or exorcising them; casting spells with magical formulae learnt in a mud-house; turning a eunuch into a man; turning a man into a eunuch; practising the art of choosing building-sites; propitiating the devas while choosing building-sites; practising the profession of mouth-washing or bathing; fire-worshipping; causing vomiting; giving purgatives; using emetics, or catharses; letting out phlegm etc. from the head; preparing ear-drops or eye-drops; preparing medicinal snuff, or eye ointment to

remove cataracts; preparing eye-lotions; curing cataracts; doing surgery; practising paediatrics; preparing basic drugs; and dressing sores and removing the dressing. A bhikkhu abstains from making a wrongful living by such means. This also is one of the precepts of his morality.

212. Great King! A bhikkhu thus endowed with morality encounters no danger in any way arising out of his practice of morality. A sovereign, duly anointed and installed as king after having defeated his enemies, can encounter no danger whatsoever from his enemies. In the same way, a bhikkhu thus endowed with morality encounters no danger in any way arising out of his practice of morality. That bhikkhu, possessing this noble group of moral precepts, enjoys within himself happiness that is free from blame. Thus is a bhikkhu endowed with morality.

End of the Long Section on Morality

Guarding the Sense Faculties
(Indriya Saṃvara)

213. How, Great King, does a bhikkhu keep the doors closed at the faculties of the senses? (i.e., How does he guard the sense faculties?) In this matter whenever a bhikkhu sees a visible object with the eye, he does not take in its appearance (such as male or female), nor its characteristics (such as movement or behaviour). If the faculty of sight is left unguarded, such depraved states of mind as covetousness and dissatisfaction stemming from that would overpower him as he fails to control his senses. So he sets himself to the task of guarding his faculty of sight, keeps watch on it, and gains control over it.

Whenever he hears a sound with the ear ... (p) ...

Whenever he smells an odour with the nose ... (p) ...

Whenever he tastes a flavor with the tongue ... (p) ...

Whenever he makes contact with the body ... (p) ...

Whenever he cognizes a mind-object with the mind, he does not take in its appearance (such as male or female), nor its characteristics (such as movement or behaviour). If the faculty of mind is left unguarded, such depraved states of mind as covetousness and dissatisfaction stemming from that would overpower him as he fails to control his senses. So he sets himself to the task of guarding his faculty of mind, keeps watch on it, and gains control over it.

And the bhikkhu, endowed with this noble control of the sense faculties, enjoys within himself happiness unalloyed (with defilements of the mind). In this way, Great King, a bhikkhu keeps the doors closed at the faculties of the senses.

MINDFULNESS AND AWARENESS
(Sati-sampajañña)

214. Great King! How is a bhikkhu endowed with mindfulness and clear comprehension (of what he does)? In this matter, a bhikkhus keeps himself completely aware, in moving forward or back; keeps himself completely aware, in looking forward or sideways; keeps himself completely aware, in bending or stretching his limbs; keeps himself completely aware, in carrying or wearing the great robe (i.e., double-layered robe), alms-bowl and the other two robes; keeps himself completely aware, in eating, drinking, chewing and savouring (food and beverages); keeps himself completely aware, in urinating and defecating; keeps himself completely aware, in walking, standing, sitting, falling asleep, waking, speaking and observing silence. Thus, Great King, is a bhikkhu endowed with mindfulness and clear comprehension (of what he does).

CONTENTMENT
(Santosa)

215. Great King! How does a bhikkhu become contented? In this matter, Great King, a bhikkhu remains contented with robes just sufficient to protect his body and with food just sufficient to sustain him. Wherever he goes, that bhikkhu carries with him all his requisites. Wherever a winged bird flies, it flies only with its burden of wings. In the same way, Great King, a bhikkhu is content with his robes that protect his body, and his food that sustains him. Wherever he goes, he carries with him all his requisites. Thus, Great King, does a bhikkhu remain contented.

DISSOCIATION FROM THE FIVE HINDRANCES
(Nīvaraṇappahāna)

216. Then that bhikkhu, endowed with this noble group of moral precepts, this noble self-control, this noble mindfulness and clear comprehension, and this noble contentedness, chooses for habitation a lonely spot in the woods or at the foot of a tree or on a hillside, or in a gully, or in a mountain cave, or in a cemetery, or in a thicket, or on an open plain, or on a heap of straw.

Returning from the round of alms and having had his meal, he sits down cross-legged and upright and establishes mindfulness in meditation.

217. Then that bhikkhu dissociates himself from coveting the world (of the five aggregates of clinging) and abides with his mind free from covetousness, thereby cleansing himself of covetousness altogether. He dissociates himself from ill will, abides with his mind free from ill will and develops goodwill towards all living beings, thereby cleansing himself of ill will altogether. He dissociates himself from sloth and torpor, abides with his mind free from sloth and torpor, with clear perception, mindfulness and comprehension, thereby cleansing himself of sloth and torpor altogether. He dissociates himself from restlessness and worry and abides with his mind in calmness and develops inner peace, thereby cleansing himself of restlessness and worry altogether. He dissociates himself from doubt, abides with his mind free from doubt, and does not waver (in his faith) in meritorious dhammas, thereby cleansing himself of doubt altogether.

218. Great King! Take the example of a man who did business with borrowed money. As his business prospered, he paid up his old debts. He also acquired profit with which he could maintain his family. Then it occurred to him thus:

> 'Formerly I worked on borrowed money. Now my business has prospered. I have paid up my old debts and acquired profit with which I have been able to maintain my family.'

Thereby that man became pleased and delighted.

219. Great King! Take another example, that of a man afflicted with disease, suffering pain, extremely ill, having no appetite and losing physical strength. Afterwards he recovered from that disease. His appetite returned and he gained physical strength. Then it occurred to him thus:

> 'Formerly I was afflicted with disease, suffering pain, extremely ill, losing appetite and physical strength. Now I have recovered from that disease. My appetite has returned and I have regained physical strength.'

Thereby that man became pleased and delighted.

220. Great King! Take another example, that of a man confined in a prison. Later he was released from prison, safe and sound and without losing any property. Then it occurred to him thus:

> 'Formerly I was confined in a prison. Now I have been released from prison, safe and sound and without losing any property.'

Thereby that man became pleased and delighted.

221. Great King! Take another example, that of a slave who was not his own master but subject to another, unable to go about as he pleased. Later he was freed from slavery, becoming once again his own master, not subject to another and able to go about as he pleased. Then it occurred to him thus:

> 'Formerly I was a slave, not my own master but subject to another, unable to go about as I pleased. Now I have been freed from slavery, becoming once again my own master, not subject to another and able to go about as I please.'

Thereby that man was pleased and delighted.

222. Great King! Take another example, that of a man who, carrying all his treasures and wealth, travelled on a long, difficult and dangerous journey where the threat of famine was present. Later he completed that difficult journey and arrived at a village where there was peace and security. Then it occurred to him thus:

> 'Formerly I travelled on a long, difficult and dangerous journey where the threat of famine was present. Now I have completed the difficult journey and arrived at the village where there is peace and security.'

Thereby that man was pleased and delighted.

223. Great King! A bhikkhu clearly sees the five hindrances which have not been got rid of from within himself as indebtedness, disease, imprisonment, enslavement, and a difficult and dangerous journey.

224. Great King! A bhikkhu clearly sees the discarding of the five hindrances from within himself as gaining freedom from indebtedness, disease, imprisonment, enslavement and as reaching a place of safety.

225. That bhikkhu who clearly sees that the five hindrances have been got rid of becomes gladdened. This gladness gives rise to *pīti* (delightful satisfaction) and the delighted mind of the bhikkhu generates calm. The bhikkhu who enjoys calmness experiences *sukha* (bliss). Being blissful, his mind gains concentration.

The First Jhāna as an Advantage for a Samaṇa

226. Being detached from sensual pleasures and demeritorious factors, that bhikkhu achieves and remains in the first *jhāna* which is accompanied by *vitakka* (initial application of the mind), *vicāra* (sustained application of the mind), and which has *pīti* (delightful satisfaction) and *sukha* (bliss), born of detachment from the hindrances (*nīvaraṇā*). He soaks, drenches, permeates and suffuses his body with *pīti* and *sukha*, born of detachment from the hindrances. There is no place in his body not suffused with *pīti* and *sukha*, born of detachment from the hindrances.

227. Great King! Take the example of a skilful bath attendant or his assistant, who strews bath powder into a brass dish and sprinkles water on it and makes it into a mass. Water, permeating through that mass to form a cake soaked with unguents inside and out, is unable to seep out.

Great King! In the same way, that bhikkhu soaks, drenches, permeates and suffuses his body with *pīti* and *sukha*, born of detachment from the hindrances. There is no place in his body not suffused with *pīti* and *sukha*, born of detachment from the hindrances.

Great King! This is an advantage of being a Samaṇa, personally experienced, which is more pleasing and higher than the advantages previously mentioned.

The Second Jhāna as an Advantage for a Samaṇa

228. And again, Great King, having got rid of *vitakka* and *vicāra*, the bhikkhu achieves and remains in the second *jhāna*, with internal tranquillity, with enhancement of one-pointedness of Concentration, devoid of *vitakka* and *vicāra*, but with *pīti* and *sukha* born of Concentration. He soaks, drenches, permeates and suffuses his body with *pīti* and *sukha* born of Concentration. There is no place in his body not suffused with *pīti* and *sukha* born of Concentration.

229. Great King! Take the example of a deep lake with water welling up from a spring below. There is no inlet from either east or south or west or north. It does not rain heavily or regularly there. And yet cool water which wells up from that spring soaks, drenches, permeates and suffuses the lake and there is no place in that lake not suffused with it.

Great King! In the same way, that bhikkhu soaks, drenches, permeates and suffuses his body with *pīti* and *sukha* born of Concentration. There is no place in his body not suffused with them.

Great King! This also is an advantage of being a samaṇa, personally experienced, which is more pleasing and higher than the advantages previously mentioned.

The Third Jhāna as an Advantage for a Samaṇa

230. And again, Great King, having been detached from *pīti*, that bhikkhu dwells in equanimity with mindfulness and clear comprehension and experiences *sukha* in mind and body. He achieves and remains in the third *jhāna*, that which causes a person who attains it to be praised by the Ariyas as one who has equanimity and mindfulness, one who abides in *sukha*. He soaks, drenches, permeates and suffuses his body with *sukha* detached from *pīti*. There is no place in his body not suffused with *sukha* detached from *pīti*.

231. Great King! Take the example of uppala, paduma and puṇḍarika lotuses in a pond where they grow in the water and thrive in it. Even when they are submerged, they thrive under water, soaked, drenched, permeated and suffused from root to apex with cool water. There is no spot in the whole plant of an uppala, paduma or puṇḍarika lotus not suffused with it.

Great King! In the same way, that bhikkhu soaks, drenches, permeates and suffuses his body with *sukha* detached from *pīti*; and there is no place in his body which is not suffused with *sukha* detached from *pīti*.

Great King! This also is an advantage of being a Samaṇa, personally experienced, which is more pleasing and higher than the advantages previously mentioned.

The Fourth Jhāna as an Advantage for a Samaṇa

232. And again, Great King, by dispelling both pain and pleasure, and by the previous disappearance of sadness and gladness, that bhikkhu achieves and remains in the fourth *Jhāna*, without pain and pleasure, a state of equanimity and absolute purity of mindfulness. That bhikkhu abides in the purity of mind suffused in his body. There is no place in his body which is not suffused with it.

233. Great King! Take the example of a man sitting wrapped up head to foot in a white cloth leaving no place on his whole body uncovered by it.[46]

---

46. The Commentary says that in this comparison, body warmth, generated by the body which is covered from head to foot, is meant.

Great King! In the same way, that bhikkhu abides in the purity of mind suffused in his body and there is no place in his body which is not suffused with it.

Great King! This also is an advantage of being a samaṇa, personally experienced, which is more pleasing and higher than the advantages previously mentioned.

(1) Insight-Knowledge
Vipassanā Ñāṇa

234. When the concentrated mind has thus become purified, pellucid, unblemished, undefiled, malleable, pliable, firm and imperturbable, that bhikkhu directs and inclines his mind to Insight-Knowledge (*vipassanā ñāṇa*). Then he understands thus:

> "This body of mine is corporeal. It is made up of four great primary elements. It is born of the union of mother and father. It is nurtured on rice and bread. It has the nature of impermanence, breaking up and disintegrating. It needs the tender care of rubbing and massaging. My consciousness too depends on it and is attached to it."

235. Great King! Take the example of a veḷuriya gem, brilliant, genuine, eight-faceted, well-cut, crystal-clear, transparent, flawless, and complete with all good characteristics. It is threaded with a dark-blue, or yellow, or red, or white, or light yellow string. A man of good eyesight, placing it on his palm, might reflect thus:

> "This gem is brilliant, genuine, eight-faceted, well-cut, crystal-clear, transparent, flawless, and complete with all good characteristics, I see that it is threaded with a dark-blue, or yellow, or red, or white, or light yellow string."

In the same way, Great King, when the concentrated mind has thus become purified, pellucid, unblemished, undefiled, malleable, pliable, firm and imperturbable, that bhikkhu directs and inclines his mind to Insight-Knowledge. Then he understands thus:

> "This body of mine is corporeal. It is made up of four great primary elements. It is born of the union of mother and father. It is nurtured on rice and bread. It has the nature of impermanence, breaking up and disintegrating. It needs the tender care of rubbing and massaging. My consciousness too depends on it and is attached to it."

Great King, this also is an advantage of being a Samaṇa, personally experienced, which is more pleasing and higher than the advantages previously mentioned.

(2) Power of Creation by Mind
Manomayiddhi Ñāṇa[47]

236. When the concentrated mind has thus become purified, pellucid, unblemished, undefiled, malleable, pliable, firm and imperturbable, that bhikkhu directs and inclines his mind to the power of creating a mentally-generated body. That bhikkhu produces another body out of his own and creates a mentally-generated form complete with all organs, major or minor, without any defective faculties.

237. Great King! Take the example of a man pulling out the core of a stalk of muñja grass from its sheath. It might occur to him thus:

> "This is the core and this, the sheath. The core is one thing and the sheath is another. It is from the sheath that the core has been pulled out."

Great King, take another example. A man might pull out a sword from its scabbard. It might occur to him thus:

> "This is the sword and this, the scabbard. The sword is one thing and the scabbard is another. It is from the scabbard that the sword has been pulled out."

Great King, take yet another example. A man might (mentally) take out a snake from its slough. It might occur to him thus:

> "This is the snake and this, its slough. The snake is one thing and its slough is another. It is from the slough that the snake has been pulled out."

In the same way, Great King, when the concentrated mind has thus become purified, pellucid, unblemished, undefiled, malleable, pliable, firm and imperturbable, that bhikkhu directs and inclines his mind to the power of creating a mentally-generated body. He produces another body out of his own and creates a mentally-generated form complete with all organs, major or minor, without any defective faculties.

Great King, this also is an advantage of being a Samaṇa, personally experienced, which is more pleasing and higher than the advantages previously mentioned.

---

47. *Ñāṇa*: lit., knowledge; here, it means power arising out of that knowledge.

(3) Psychic Powers
Iddhivida Ñāṇa

238. When the concentrated mind has thus become purified, pellucid, unblemished, undefiled, malleable, pliable, firm and imperturbable, that bhikkhu directs and inclines his mind to supernormal psychic powers. He wields the various kinds of supernormal powers: being one, he becomes many; and from being many, he becomes one; he makes himself visible or invisible; he passes unhindered through walls, enclosures, and mountains, as though going through space; he plunges into or out of the earth as though plunging into or out of water; he walks on water as though walking on earth; he travels in space cross-legged as if he were a winged bird; he touches and strokes the moon and the sun which are so mighty and powerful; and he gains mastery over his body (to reach) even up to the world of the Brahmās.

239. Great King! To give an example, it is as if a skilled potter or his apprentice could make out of well-kneaded clay various kinds of pots as desired.

Great King! To give another example, it is as if a skilled ivory carver or his apprentice could make out of duly-prepared elephant tusk various kinds of ivory-carvings as desired.

Great King! To give still another example, it is as if a skilled goldsmith or his apprentice could make out of duly-prepared gold, gold-ornaments as desired.

In the same way, Great King, when the concentrated mind has thus become purified, pellucid, unblemished, undefiled, malleable, pliable, firm and imperturbable, that bhikkhu directs and inclines his mind to supernormal psychic powers. He wields the various kinds of supernormal powers: being one, he becomes many; and from being many, he becomes one; he makes himself visible or invisible; he passes unhindered through walls, enclosures, and mountains, as though going through space; he plunges into or out of the earth as though plunging into or out of water; he walks on water as though walking on earth; he travels in space cross-legged as if he were a winged bird; he touches and strokes the moon and the sun which are so mighty and powerful; and he gains mastery over his body (to reach) even up to the world of the Brahmās.

Great King, this also is an advantage of being a Samaṇa, personally experienced, which is more pleasing and higher than the advantages previously mentioned.

(4) Divine Power of Hearing
Dibbasota Ñāṇa

240. When the concentrated mind has thus become purified, pellucid, unblemished, undefiled, malleable, pliable, firm and imperturbable, that bhikkhu directs and inclines his mind to (the gaining of) the hearing-power like the divine hearing-power. With the divine hearing-power which is extremely clear, surpassing the hearing-power of men, he hears both kinds of sounds, of devas and men, whether far or near.

241. Great King! Take the example of a man travelling on a highway who might hear the sounds of a big drum, a cylindrical drum, a conch, a small drum and a kettledrum. It might occur to him thus:

> "This is the sound of the big drum; this is the sound of the cylindrical drum; this is the sound of the conch; this is the sound of the small drum; and this is the sound of the kettledrum."

In the same way, Great King, when the concentrated mind has thus become purified, pellucid, unblemished, undefiled, malleable, pliable, firm and imperturbable, that bhikkhu directs and inclines his mind to (the gaining of) the hearing-power like the divine hearing-power. With the divine hearing-power which is extremely clear, surpassing the hearing-power of men, he hears both kinds of sounds, of devas and men, whether far or near.

Great King, this also is an advantage of being a Samaṇa, personally experienced, which is more pleasing and higher than the advantages previously mentioned.

(5) Knowledge of the Minds of Others
Cetopariya Ñāṇa

242. When the concentrated mind has thus become purified, pellucid, unblemished, undefiled, malleable, pliable, firm and imperturbable, that bhikkhu directs and inclines his mind to (discriminating) knowledge of the minds of others (*Cetopariya Ñāṇa*). He discriminatively knows with his own mind the minds of other beings or individuals. He knows the lustful mind as such, and he knows the mind devoid of lust as such; he knows the angry mind as such, and he knows the mind devoid of anger as such; he knows the bewildered mind[48] as such, and he knows the mind

48. Bewilderment consists of ignorance of, or misconception of, the Four Noble Truths.

devoid of bewilderment as such; he knows the constricted mind as such, and he knows the distracted mind as such; he knows the exalted mind (to be met with beyond the domain of sensual pleasure) as such, and he knows the unexalted mind (of the domain of sensual pleasure) as such; he knows the inferior mind (of the three mundane planes) as such, and he knows the superior mind (of the supra-mundane plane) as such; he knows the concentrated mind as such, and he knows the unconcentrated mind as such; he knows the mind liberated (from defilements) as such, and he knows the unliberated mind as such.

243. Great King! Take the example of a young lass or a young lad, who is wont to beautifying herself or himself, looking at herself or himself in a clear mirror or in a bowl of clear water. Then she or he would at once recognize in her or his face blemishes or, if they are absent, the absence of blemishes.

In the same way, Great King, when the concentrated mind has thus become purified, pellucid, unblemished, undefiled, malleable, pliable, firm and imperturbable, that bhikkhu directs and inclines his mind to (discriminating) knowledge of the minds of others. He discriminatively knows with his own mind the minds of other beings or individuals. He knows the lustful mind as such, and he knows the mind devoid of lust as such; he knows the angry mind as such, and he knows the mind devoid of anger as such; he knows the bewildered mind as such, and he knows the mind devoid of bewilderment as such; he knows the constricted mind as such, and he knows the distracted mind as such; he knows the exalted mind (to be met with beyond the domain of sensual pleasure) as such, and he knows the unexalted mind (of the domain of sensual pleasure) as such; he knows the inferior mind (of the three mundane planes) as such, and he knows the superior mind (of the supra-mundane plane) as such; he knows the concentrated mind as such, and he knows the unconcentrated mind as such; he knows the mind liberated (from defilements) as such, and he knows the unliberated mind as such.

Great King, this also is an advantage of being a samaṇa, personally experienced, which is more pleasing and higher than the advantages previously mentioned.

(6) Knowledge of Past Existences
Pubbenivāsānussati Ñāṇa

244. When the concentrated mind has thus become purified, pellucid, unblemished, undefiled, malleable, pliable, firm and imperturbable, that bhikkhu directs and inclines his mind to knowledge of past existences (*Pubbenivāsānussati Ñāṇa*). He recollects many and varied existences of the past. And what does he recollect?

> "He recollects one past existence, or two, or three, or four, or five, or ten, or twenty, or thirty, or forty, or fifty, or a hundred, a thousand, a hundred thousand existences, or many hundred, many thousand, many hundred thousand existences, or existences in many cycles of dissolution, or in many cycles of development, or in many cycles of the rounds of dissolution and development, in this way: 'In that past existence I was known by such a name. I was born into such a family. I was of such an appearance. I was thus nourished. I enjoyed pleasure thus. I suffered pain thus. My life-span was such. I died in that existence. Then I was born in another existence. In that (new) existence I was known by such a name. I was born into such a family. I was of such an appearance. I was thus nourished. I enjoyed pleasure thus. I suffered pain thus. My life-span was such. I died in that existence. Then I was born in this existence.' In this way he recollects many and varied past existences, together with their characteristics and related facts (such as names and clans)."

245. Great King! Take the example of a man travelling to another village, then to another village, and then returning home later. Then it might occur to him thus:

> "I went out from my village to such and such a village. In that village, I stood thus, I sat thus, I spoke thus, and I remained silent thus. Then I again set out from that village to still another village. In that (second) village, I stood thus, I sat thus, I spoke thus, and I remained silent thus. Then I returned to my own village."

In the same way, Great King, when the concentrated mind has thus become purified, pellucid, unblemished, undefiled, malleable, pliable, firm and imperturbable, that bhikkhu directs and inclines his mind to knowledge of past existences. He recollects his many and varied existences of the past. And what does he recollect?

> He recollects one past existence, or two, or three, or four, or five, or ten, or twenty, or thirty, or forty, or fifty, or a hundred, a thousand,

a hundred thousand existences, or many hundred, many thousand, many hundred thousand existences, or existences in many cycles of dissolution, or in many cycles of development, or in many cycles of the rounds of dissolution and development, in this way: 'In that past existence I was known by such a name. I was born into such a family. I was of such an appearance. I was thus nourished. I enjoyed pleasure thus. I suffered pain thus. My life-span was such. I died in that existence. Then I was born in another existence. In that (new) existence, I was known by such a name. I was born into such a family. I was of such an appearance. I was thus nourished. I enjoyed pleasure thus. I suffered pain thus. My life-span was such. I died in that existence. Then I was born in this existence.' In this way he recollects many and varied existences, together with their characteristics and related facts (such as names and clans).

Great King, this also is an advantage of being a samaṇa, personally experienced, which is more pleasing and higher than the advantages previously mentioned.

(7) Divine Power of Sight
Dibbacakkhu Ñāṇa

246. When the concentrated mind has thus become purified, pellucid, unblemished, undefiled, malleable, pliable, firm and imperturbable, that bhikkhu directs and inclines his mind to knowledge of the passing away and arising of beings (*cutūpapāta ñāṇa*). With the divine power of sight, which is extremely clear, surpassing the sight of men, he sees beings in the process of passing away and also of arising, inferior or superior beings, beautiful or ugly beings, beings with good or bad destinations. He knows beings arising according to their own kamma-actions.

"Friends! These beings were full of evil committed bodily, verbally and mentally. They maligned the Ariyas, held wrong views and performed actions according to these wrong views. After death and dissolution of their bodies, they reappeared in wretched destinations (*duggati*), in miserable existences (*apāya*), states of ruin (*vinipāta*), realms of continuous suffering (*niraya*). But, friends, there were also beings who were endowed with goodness done bodily, verbally and mentally. They did not malign the Ariyas, held right views and performed actions according to right views. After death and dissolution of their bodies, they reappeared in good destinations, the happy world of the devas."

Thus, with the divine power of sight which is extremely clear, surpassing the sight of men, the bhikkhu sees beings in the process of passing away and also of arising, inferior or superior beings, beautiful or ugly beings, beings with good or bad destinations and beings arising according to their own kamma-actions.

247. Great King! Take the example of a man with good eyesight, standing above, in a pinnacled mansion situated at a crossroads, who could see men entering a house, or coming out of a house, strolling about on the street or sitting at the crossroads. It might occur to him thus:

> "These men are entering a house. Those are coming out of a house. These men are strolling about on the street. Those are sitting at the crossroads."

In the same way, Great King, when the concentrated mind has thus become purified, pellucid, unblemished, undefiled, malleable, pliable, firm and imperturbable, that bhikkhu directs and inclines his mind to knowledge of the passing away and arising of beings. With the divine power of sight, which is extremely clear, surpassing the sight of men, he sees beings in the process of passing away and also of arising, inferior or superior beings, beautiful or ugly beings, beings with good or bad destinations, and beings arising according to their own kamma-actions.

"Friends! These beings were full of evil committed bodily, verbally and mentally. They maligned the Ariyas, held wrong views and performed actions according to these wrong views. After death and dissolution of their bodies, they reappeared in wretched destinations (*duggati*), in miserable existences (*apāya*), states of ruin (*vinipāta*), realms of continuous suffering (*niraya*). But friends, there were also beings who were endowed with goodness done bodily, verbally and mentally. They did not malign the Ariyas, held right views and performed actions according to these right views. After death and dissolution of their bodies, they reappeared in good destinations, the happy world of the devas."

Thus, with the divine power of sight which is extremely clear, surpassing the sight of men, the bhikkhu sees beings in the process of passing away and also of arising, inferior or superior beings, beautiful or ugly beings, beings with good or bad destinations and beings arising according to their own kamma-actions.

Great King, this also is an advantage of being a samaṇa, personally experienced, which is more pleasing and higher than the advantages previously mentioned.

(8) Knowledge of Extinction of Moral Intoxicants
Āsavakkhaya Ñāṇa

248. When the concentrated mind has thus become purified, pellucid, unblemished, undefiled, malleable, pliable, firm and imperturbable, that bhikkhu directs and inclines his mind to knowledge of the extinction of moral intoxicants (*āsavakkhaya ñāṇa*). Then he truly understands *dukkha*[49] as it really is, the cause of *dukkha* as it really is, the cessation of *dukkha* as it really is, and the way leading to the cessation of *dukkha* as it really is. He also truly understands the *āsavas* as they really are, the cause of the *āsavas* as it really is, the cessation of the *āsavas* as it really is, and the way leading to the cessation of the *āsavas* as it really is. The mind of the bhikkhu who thus knows and thus sees is liberated from the moral intoxicant of sensual pleasures and sensuous realms (*kāmāsava*), the moral intoxicant of hankering after (better) existence (*bhavāsava*), and the moral intoxicant of ignorance (of the Four Noble Truths) (*avijjāsava*). When thus liberated, the knowledge of liberation arises (in him). He knows that rebirth is no more (for him), that he has lived the Life of Purity, that what he has to do (for the realization of Magga) has been done, and that he has nothing more to do (for such realization).[50]

249. Great King! Take the example of a man, with good eyesight, standing at the edge of a clear and transparent lake in a mountain glen. He sees oysters, mussels, pebbles, broken pottery, and shoals of fish moving about or just lying still. It might occur to him thus:

> "This lake is clear and transparent. In it there are oysters, mussels, pebbles, broken pottery and shoals of fish either moving about or just lying still."

In the same way, Great King, when the concentrated mind has thus become purified, pellucid, unblemished, undefiled, malleable, pliable, firm and imperturbable, that bhikkhu directs and inclines his mind to the extinction of moral defilements. Then he truly understands *dukkha* as it really is, the cause of *dukkha* as it really is, the cessation of *dukkha* as it really is, and the way leading to the cessation of *dukkha* as it really is. He also truly understands the *āsavas* as they really are, the cause of the *āsavas* as it really is, the cessation of the *āsavas* as it really is, and the way leading to the cessation of the *āsavas* as it really is. The mind of

---

49. *Dukkha*: see Appendix A 7.

50. Another interpretation in the Commentary of this last phrase "*nā paraṃ itthattāya*" is that there will be no further existence.

the bhikkhu who thus knows and thus sees is liberated from the moral intoxicant of sensual pleasures and sensuous realms (*kāmāsava*), the moral intoxicant of hankering after (better) existence (*bhavāsava*), and the moral intoxicant of ignorance (of the Four Noble Truths) (*avijjāsava*). The knowledge of liberation arises in him who has become thus liberated. He now knows that rebirth is no more (for him), that he has lived the Life of Purity, that what he has to do (for the realization of Magga) has been done, and that he has nothing more to do for such realization.

Great King, this also is an advantage of being a samaṇa, personally experienced, which is more pleasing and higher than the advantages previously mentioned.

Great King, there is no other advantage of being a samaṇa, personally experienced, more pleasing and higher than this which one can see for oneself.

Ajātasattu Becomes a Lay Disciple

250. When the Bhagavā had thus spoken, King Ajātasattu of Magadha, the son of Queen Vedehī, addressed him thus:

"Venerable Sir! Excellent (is the dhamma)! Venerable Sir! Excellent (is the dhamma)! Just as, Venerable Sir, one turns up what lies upside down, just as one uncovers what lies covered, just as one shows the way to another who is lost, just as one holds up a lamp in the darkness for those with eyes to see visible objects, even so have you revealed the dhamma to me in various ways. Venerable Sir, I take refuge in the Buddha; I take refuge in the Dhamma and I take refuge in the Saṅgha. Please take me as a lay disciple, from now on till the end of my life. I was overwhelmed by (i.e., I have committed) a misdeed, being foolish, bewildered and unwise. For the sake of gaining sovereign power, I put my father to death, who ruled with righteousness and kingly virtue. Venerable Sir, I request the Bhagavā to accept this admission of my guilt so that I can restrain myself in the future."

251. Great King! True indeed that you were overwhelmed by a misdeed, being foolish, bewildered and unwise. You have put to death your father who ruled with righteousness and kingly virtue. But now, as you have realized your guilt and admitted it to make amends, we accept your admission. Great King! Realizing one's guilt, making amends and abstaining from such misdeeds in the future means enhancement according to the injunctions of the Ariyas.

252. After the Bhagavā had spoken, King Ajātasattu of Magadha, the son of Queen Vedehī, addressed him thus:

"Venerable Sir! Let me take leave of you. We have many things to do."

"Great King! You may go when you wish." (Lit., now you know the time.)

Then King Ajātasattu of Magadha, the son of Queen Vedehī, pleased and delighted with what the Bhagavā said, rose from his seat, paid obeisance to him and departed from his presence.

253. Soon after the departure of King Ajātasattu of Magadha, the son of Queen Vedehī, the Bhagavā said to the bhikkhus:

> "Bhikkhus! This king has ruined himself. He has destroyed himself (i.e., destroyed all his potentialities for the Path). Bhikkhus! Had not this king put his father to death, who ruled with righteousness and kingly virtue, there would have arisen in him, here and now, the clear and undefiled eye of the dhamma (*Sotāpatti magga*)" Thus said the Bhagavā. And the bhikkhus were delighted and they rejoiced in his words.

End of Sāmaññaphala Sutta, the second sutta from division one (Sīlakkhandha Vagga)

Namo tassa bhagavato arahato sammāsambuddhassa

POṬṬHAPĀDA SUTTA

IX. POṬṬHAPĀDA SUTTA

(Discourse on Poṭṭhapāda, the Wandering Ascetic)

406. Thus have I heard:

Once the Bhagavā was staying at the monastery of Anāthapiṇḍika in Jeta Park at Sāvatthi.

At that time Poṭṭhapāda, the wandering ascetic, with a following of three thousand wandering ascetics, was dwelling at the Ekasālaka Hall, where various views were debated, in Queen Mallikā's garden bordered by Tinduka (persimmon) trees.

Then the Bhagavā, having rearranged his robes and taking alms bowl and robe, set out early in the morning for Sāvatthi on his daily round for alms.

407. And the Bhagavā thought: "It is too early to go round for alms in Sāvatthi. I should go to the Ekasālaka Hall, where various views are debated, in Queen Mallikā's garden bordered by Tinduka trees, and meet Poṭṭhapāda, the wandering ascetic."

Then the Bhagavā visited the Ekasālaka Hall, where various views were debated, in Queen Mallikā's garden bordered by Tinduka trees.

408. At that time, Poṭṭhapāda, the wandering ascetic, was seated with his followers who were talking loudly and vociferously on unprofitable subjects (not conducive to moral conduct leading to the attainment of the deva world and Nibbāna). Such kinds of talk are:

> Talk about kings, thieves, ministers, armed forces, calamities, battles, food, drinks, clothing, beds, flowers, unguents, relatives, vehicles, villages, market-towns, cities, provinces, womenfolk, heroes, streets, waterfronts, the dead and the departed, trivialities, the universe, the oceans, prosperity, adversity and so on.

409. When Poṭṭhapāda, the wandering ascetic, caught sight of the Bhagavā approaching in the distance, he called his followers to order, saying: "Friends! Remain quiet and make no noise. Here comes Samaṇa Gotama.

That venerable one appreciates silence, praising its virtues. Perhaps he may think it fit to approach us if he knows that it is a quiet assembly." When thus called to order, the ascetics kept silent.

410. Then the Bhagavā approached Poṭṭhapāda, the wandering ascetic, who addressed him thus:

"Be pleased to come, Venerable Sir! Venerable Sir, your coming is good. You have taken quite a long time to visit us here. Here is a seat duly prepared. Venerable Sir, please take the seat."

And the Bhagavā took the prepared seat while Poṭṭhapāda, the wandering ascetic, took a low seat at a suitable place. The Bhagavā said to him:

"Poṭṭhapāda! What was the subject of your discussion as you were seated together here? What was the nature of the talk that has been interrupted?"

Cessation of Saññā

411. When the Bhagavā had thus spoken, Poṭṭhapāda, the wandering ascetic, addressed him thus:

"Venerable Sir! Let us put aside what we have been discussing in our assembly. Venerable Sir, it will not be difficult for the Bhagavā to hear about it afterwards. But, Venerable Sir, on many a previous day, when samaṇas and brāhmaṇas holding diverse views assembled here in this Hall, eager to listen to fresh views, the talk arose on the subject of cessation of *saññā*,[51] and it was asked, 'How is the cessation of *saññā* brought about?'

"Some of them said:

'Forms of *saññā* arise in a being without reason, without cause, just as they cease without reason, without cause. When forms of *saññā*, arise, there is *saññā* and when they cease, there is no *saññā*.'

"Thus did they explain the cessation of *saññā*. To him, another said:

'It will not be as you say, friend. *Saññā* is the *atta* of a being. That *saññā* goes into and leaves a being. When it goes into a being, there is *saññā*. When it leaves a being, there is no *saññā*.'

'Thus did they explain the cessation of *saññā*.' To him, still another said:

'It will not be as you say, friend. There are samaṇas and brāhmaṇas who possess psychic potency and power and who can implant *saññā* in that being or draw it out. When implanted, there is *saññā*; and when drawn out, there is no *saññā*.'

"Thus did they explain the cessation of *saññā*." To him, still another said:

51. *Saññā*: lit., perception. The Commentary says that 'cessation of *saññā*' is to be taken as cessation of *citta*, Mind or Consciousness.

'Friend! It will not be as you say. There are mighty and powerful devas who can implant *saññā* in that being or draw it out. When implanted, there is *saññā* and when drawn out, there is no *saññā*.'

"Thus did they explain the cessation of *saññā*."

"When, Venerable Sir, I heard such words, my mind turned towards the Bhagavā himself, and I thought: "Would that the Bhagavā were here! Would that the Sugata[52] were here! He is highly accomplished in such dhammas.' Venerable Sir, the Bhagavā is well-versed in the subject of the cessation of *saññā*. The Bhagavā knows the nature of the cessation of *saññā*. Venerable Sir, how does the cessation of *saññā* happen?"

Existence of Cause in the Arising and Cessation of Saññā

412. Poṭṭhapāda, among those, there are samaṇas and brāhmaṇas who maintain: 'Forms of *saññā* in a being arise and cease without reason, without cause.

Their assertion is wrong from the very beginning for, Poṭṭhapāda, it is through reason and cause that forms of *saññā* in a being arise and cease. A certain form of *saññā* arises through practice[53] and a certain form of *saññā* ceases through practice.

413. 'And what is that practice?' asked the Bhagavā (of himself).

Herein, Poṭṭhapāda, there arises in this world the Tathāgata who is worthy of special Veneration, who truly comprehends all dhammas by his own intellect and insight.

(Repeat as in paras 190 to 212, Samaññaphala Sutta)

Poṭṭhapāda! Thus is the bhikkhu endowed with morality.

(Repeat as in paras 213 to 224)

That bhikkhu who clearly sees that the five hindrances have been got rid of becomes gladdened. This gladness gives rise to *pīti* (delightful satisfaction) and the delighted mind of the bhikkhu generates calm. The bhikkhu who enjoys calmness experiences *sukha* (bliss). Being blissful, his mind gains concentration.

Being detached from pleasures of the senses and demeritorious factors, that bhikkhu achieves and remains in the first *jhāna* which has

---

52. *Sugata*: he who speaks only true and beneficial words.

53. **Practice**: of *Adhisīla Sikkhā*, High Morality; *Adhicitta Sikkhā*, Concentration Meditation or *samatha bhāvanā*; and *Adhipaññā Sikkha*, Vipassanā Insight and Magga Insight.

vitakka (initial application of the mind), *vicāra* (sustained application of the mind), (delightful satisfaction) and *sukha* (bliss), born of detachment from the hindrances (*nīvaraṇa*). His *saññā* of the pleasures of the senses that used to arise in him (before attainment of *jhāna*) ceases.[54] At that time there arises a delicate and really-existing *saññā* of *pīti* (delightful satisfaction) and *sukha* (bliss), born of detachment from the hindrances. At that time the bhikkhu becomes one who is endowed with the delicate and really-existing *saññā* of *pīti* and *sukha*, born of detachment from the hindrances. In this way, a certain form of *saññā* arises through practice, and a certain form of *saññā* ceases through practice. This is the practice, said the Bhagavā.

And again, Poṭṭhapāda, having got rid of *vitakka* and *vicāra*, that bhikkhu achieves and remains in the second *jhāna* with internal tranquillity, with enhancement of one-pointedness of Concentration, devoid of *vitakka* and *vicāra* but with *pīti* and *sukha* born of Concentration. His delicate and really-existing *saññā* of *pīti* and *sukha*, born of detachment from the hindrances, that used to arise in him (before the attainment of the second *jhāna*), ceases. At that time there arises a delicate and really-existing *saññā* of *pīti* and *sukha*, born of Concentration. At that time the bhikkhu becomes one who is endowed with the delicate and really-existing *saññā* of *pīti* and *sukha*, born of Concentration. In this way, a certain form of *saññā* arises through practice, and a certain form of *saññā* ceases through practice. This also is the practice, said the Bhagavā.

And again, Poṭṭhapāda, having been detached from *pīti*, that bhikkhu dwells in *upekkhā* (equanimity) with mindfulness and clear comprehension, and experiences *sukha* in mind and body. He achieves and remains in the third *jhāna* that which causes a person who attains it to be praised by the Ariyas as one who has *upekkhā* (equanimity) and mindfulness, one who abides in *sukha*. His delicate and really-existing *saññā* of *pīti* and *sukha*, born of Concentration, that used to arise in him (before the attainment of the third *jhāna*), ceases. At that time there arises a delicate and really-existing *saññā* of *upekkhā* and *sukha*. At that time the bhikkhu becomes one who is endowed with the delicate and really-existing *saññā* of *upekkhā* and *sukha*. In this way, a certain form

54. **Ceases**: *nirujjhati*: this word can have two implications: (i) entirely ceases after arising or existing; (ii) is absent because of lack of opportunity to arise. Here according to the Commentary the word 'ceases' has the second implication.

of *saññā* arises through practice, and a certain form of *saññā* ceases through practice. This also is the practice, said the Bhagavā.

And again, Poṭṭhapāda, by dispelling both pleasure and pain, and by the previous disappearance of gladness and sadness, that bhikkhu achieves and remains in the fourth *jhāna*, without pain and pleasure, a state of equanimity and absolute purity of mindfulness. His delicate and really-existing *saññā* of *upekkhā* and *sukha*, that used to arise in him (before the attainment of the fourth *jhāna*), ceases. At that time there arises a delicate and really-existing *saññā* without pain and pleasure. At that time the bhikkhu becomes one who is endowed with the delicate and really-existing *saññā* without pain and pleasure. In this way, a certain form of *saññā* arises through practice, and a certain form of *saññā* ceases through practice. This also is the practice, said the Bhagavā.

And again, Poṭṭhapāda, that bhikkhu concentrates on the concept 'Space is Infinite' and achieves and remains in the *ākāsānañcāyatana jhāna*, where all forms of *rūpa-saññā*[55] have been completely transcended, all forms of *paṭighasaññā*[56] have vanished and all forms of *nānatta-saññā*[57] are not paid attention to. His *saññā* of corporeality that used to arise in him (before the attainment of *ākāsānañcāyatana jhāna*) ceases. At that time there arises the delicate and really-existing *ākāsānañcāyatana jhāna saññā*. At that time the bhikkhu becomes one who is endowed with the delicate and really-existing *ākāsānañcāyatana jhāna saññā*. In this way, a certain form of *saññā* arises through practice, and a certain form of *saññā* ceases through practice. This also is the practice, said the Bhagavā.

And again, Poṭṭhapāda, completely passing beyond the *ākāsānañcāyatana jhāna*, that bhikkhu concentrates on the concept 'Consciousness is Infinite' and achieves and remains in the *viññānañcāyatana jhāna*. His delicate and really-existing *ākāsānañcāyatana jhāna saññā* that used to arise in him (before the attainment of *viññānañcāyatana jhāna*) ceases. At that time there arises the delicate and really-existing *viññānañcāyatana jhāna saññā*. At that time the bhikkhu becomes one who is endowed with the delicate and really-existing *viññānañcāyatana*

---

55. *Rūpasaññā: saññā* associated with *rūpa jhānas* (concentration meditation on a corporeal object).
56. *Paṭighasaññā*: *saññā* that occurs on contact of the five senses with their objects, also called *pañcaviññāṇa*, or mind conscious of the work of the five senses.
57. *Nānattasaññā:* All forms of *saññā* that take place in the *kāmāvacara* sphere, except *paṭighasaññā*.

jhāna saññā. In this way, a certain form of *saññā* arises through practice, and a certain form of *saññā* ceases through practice. This also is the practice, said the Bhagavā.

And again, Poṭṭhapāda, completely passing beyond the *viññānañcāyatana jhāna*, that bhikkhu concentrates on the Concept of Nothingness and achieves and remains in the *ākiñcaññāyatana jhāna*. His delicate and really-existing *viññānañcāyatana jhāna saññā* that used to arise in him (before the attainment of the ākiñcāññāyatana *jhāna*) ceases. At that time there arises the delicate and really-existing *ākiñcaññāyatana jhāna saññā.*

At that time the bhikkhu becomes one who is endowed with the delicate and really-existing *ākiñcaññāyatana jhāna saññā.* In this way, a certain form of *saññā* arises through practice, and a certain form of *saññā* ceases through practice. This also is the practice, said the Bhagavā.

414. In my Teaching, Poṭṭhapāda, that bhikkhu has (initially) *saññā* of his own (i.e., the first *jhāna saññā*). Then he progresses from one stage (i.e., the first *jhāna*) to the next (i.e., the second *jhāna*), and from that to the next (i.e., the third *jhāna*) and so on in sequence until he reaches the supreme form of *saññā* (i.e., *ākiñcaññayatana jhāna saññā*). As he reaches it, it occurs to him thus:

> 'It will not be proper for me to try to get absorbed (in further jhāna). It will be proper for me not to get absorbed in it. If I were to try to get absorbed in it and strive for the higher *nevasaññānāsaññāyatana jhāna*, this *ākiñcaññayatana jhāna saññā* might come to cessation and other forms of *saññā* which are gross[58] might arise. It would be better if I do not try to get absorbed in it and do not try to strive for the higher Jhāna.'

Then that bhikkhu stops trying to get absorbed in it and striving for the higher *jhāna*. And in that bhikkhu who neither tries to get absorbed in it nor strives for the higher *jhāna*, that (*nevasaññānāsaññāyatana jhāna*)[59] *saññā* ceases (after arising for one or two thought-moments), and no other forms of *saññā* which are gross arise. Then he achieves the cessation of all forms of *saññā*. In this way, Poṭṭhapāda, the cessation of *saññā* (*nirodha samāpatti*) is attained step by step by the bhikkhu who has Insight Knowledge (*sampajāna*).

---

58. Gross forms of *saññā*: by this is meant Bhavaṅga-saññā.
59. The Commentary merely states '*tā jhāna saññā*', the *saññā* of that *jhāna*; but the Sub-Commentary explains it to be specifically '*nevasaññānāsaññāyatana jhāna saññā*', the *saññā* of the *jhāna* of neither *saññā* nor non-*saññā*.

Now, Poṭṭhapāda, what do you think of this? Have you ever before heard of such attainment of cessation of *saññā*, step by step, by a bhikkhu who has Insight Knowledge?

"No, Venerable Sir! I have not. But I now understand what you say as follows:

In my Teaching, Poṭṭhapāda, that bhikkhu has (initially) *saññā* of his own (i.e., the first *jhāna saññā*). Then he progresses from one stage (i.e., the first *jhāna*) to the next (i.e., the second *jhāna*), and from that to the next (i.e., the third *jhāna*) and so on in sequence until he reaches the supreme form of *saññā* (i.e., ākiñcaññayatana *jhāna saññā*). As he reaches it, it occurs to him thus:

> 'It will not be proper for me to try to get absorbed (in further jhāna). It will be proper for me not to get absorbed in it. If I were to try to get absorbed in it and strive for the higher *nevasaññānāsaññāyatana* jhāna, this *ākiñcaññāyatana jhāna saññā* might come to cessation and other forms of *saññā* which are gross might arise. It would be better if I do not try to get absorbed in it and do not try to strive for the higher Jhāna.'

Then that bhikkhu stops trying to get absorbed in it and striving for the higher *jhāna*. And in that bhikkhu who neither tries to get absorbed in it nor strives for the higher *jhāna*, that (*nevasaññānāsaññāyatana jhāna*) *saññā* ceases (after arising for one or two thought-moments), and no other forms of *saññā* which are gross arise. Then he achieves the cessation of all forms of *saññā*. In this way, Poṭṭhapāda, the cessation of *saññā* (*nirodha samāpatti*) is attained step by step by the bhikkhu who has Insight Knowledge."

Poṭṭhapāda, that is right, said the Bhagavā.

415. Venerable Sir! Does the Bhagavā declare only one supreme form of *saññā* or many supreme forms of *saññā*?

Poṭṭhapāda! I declare one supreme form of *saññā* as well as many supreme forms of *saññā*.

But, Venerable Sir, how is it that the Bhagavā declares one supreme form of *saññā* as well as many supreme forms of *sanññā*.

Poṭṭhapāda! Whenever a *jhāna saññā* (is achieved and then) ceases, that I declare as the supreme form of *saññā*. Thus, I declare one supreme form of *saññā* as well as many supreme forms of *saññā*.

416. And, Venerable Sir, (after *nirodha samāpatti*), does *saññā* arise first and Knowledge afterwards? Or does Knowledge arise first and *saññā* afterwards? Or do *saññā* and Knowledge arise simultaneously?

Poṭṭhapāda! *Saññā* arises first and Knowledge[60] follows. Knowledge arises only because of the arising of *saññā.* That bhikkhu knows: 'Knowledge springs up in me depending on the arising of *saññā*'. Poṭṭhapāda! One should understand by this means that '*Saññā* arises first, and Knowledge follows: Knowledge arises only because of the arising of *saññā.*'

WHETHER SAÑÑĀ IS *ATTA* OR NOT

417. Venerable Sir! Is *saññā* the *atta* of a being? Or, is *saññā* one thing and *atta* another?

Poṭṭhapāda! What kind of *atta* do you believe in?

Venerable Sir! I believe in *atta* that is made up of four great primary elements, nourished by solid nutriments and having corporeality and substantiality.

Poṭṭhapāda! If (in) your (view) *atta* were made up of four great primary elements, nourished by solid nutriments, and having corporeality, and substantiality, then in this case, Poṭṭhapāda, (in) your (view) *saññā* would be one thing and *atta* another. Poṭṭhapāda! That will be evident also from what now follows.

Poṭṭhapāda! Though that *atta* (of your view), made up of four great primary elements, nourished by solid nutriments, and having corporeality and substantiality, remains constant, yet some forms of *saññā* in a being arise and other forms of *saññā* cease. In this way, Poṭṭhapāda, it should be understood that *saññā* is one thing and *atta* another.

418. Venerable Sir! I believe in *atta* that is made of *jhāna* mind and endowed completely with (all the minor and major) physical organs, and not deficient in any of the faculties of the senses.

Poṭṭhapāda! If (in) your (view) *atta* were made of *jhāna* mind, and endowed completely with (all the minor and major) physical organs, and not deficient in any of the faculties of the senses, then in this case also, Poṭṭhapāda, (in) your (view) *saññā* would be one thing and *atta* another. Poṭṭhapāda! That will be evident also from what now follows.

---

60. In the Buddha's answer '*saññā*' refers to the Anāgāmiphala Saññā or Arahattaphala Saññā; and 'Knowledge' refers to Paccavekkhaṇāñāṇa, which generally means reflection on Magga, Phala, Nibbāna, uprooted defilements and remnant defilements.

But, in this context, this term refers to reflection on Anāgāmiphala or Arahattaphala, as the case may be. Paccavekkhaṇāñāṇa on these phalas arises invariably and spontaneously after *Nirodha samāpatti.*

Poṭṭhapāda! Though that *atta* (of your view), made of *jhāna* mind and endowed completely with (all the minor and major) physical organs, and not deficient in any of the faculties of the senses, remains constant, yet some forms of *saññā* in a being arise and other forms of *saññā* cease. In this way, Poṭṭhapāda, it should be understood that *saññā* is one thing and *atta* another.

419. Venerable Sir! I believe in *atta* that is without corporeality and that is made of *saññā* (i.e., *jhāna saññā*).

Poṭṭhapāda! If (in) your (view) *atta* were made of *saññā* and is without corporeality, then in this case also, Poṭṭhapāda, (in) your (view) *saññā* would be one thing and *atta* another. Poṭṭhapāda, that will be evident also from what now follows.

Poṭṭhapāda! Though that *atta* (of your view), which is made of *saññā* and is without corporeality, remains constant, yet some forms of *saññā* in a being arise and other forms of *saññā* cease. In this way, Poṭṭhapāda, it should be understood that *saññā* is one thing and *atta* another.

420. Venerable Sir! Will it be possible for me to know whether *saññā* is the *atta* of a being, or whether *saññā* is one thing and *atta* another?

Poṭṭhapāda! Hard will it be for you to know whether *saññā* is the *atta* of a being, or whether *saññā* is one thing and *atta* another, as you hold a different view, belong to a different faith, have a different inclination (in belief), pursue a different practice and follow a teacher of another school of doctrine.

Venerable Sir! If it is hard for me to know whether *saññā* is the *atta* of a being, or whether *saññā* is one thing and *atta* another, since I hold a different view, belong to a different faith, have a different inclination in belief, pursue a different practice and follow a teacher of another school of doctrine, Venerable Sir, (may I know this): Is the world (i.e., *loka*) eternal? Is this view (of eternalism) true while any other view is false?

Poṭṭhapāda! I do not declare that the world is eternal, and that only this view (of eternalism) is true while any other view is false.

Then, Venerable Sir, is the world not eternal? Is this view (of non-eternity of the world) true while any other view is false?

Poṭṭhapāda! I do not declare also that the world is not eternal, and that only this view (of non-eternity of the world) is true while any other view is false.

Then, Venerable Sir, is the world finite? Is the world infinite? ... Is the soul (*jīva*) the same as the body, or the body the same as the soul? ... Or, is the soul one thing and the body another? ... Does a sentient being exist after death, or does a sentient being not exist after death? ... Or, is it that a sentient being does, as well as does not, exist after death? ... Or, is it that a sentient being neither does exist, nor does not exist after death? Is this view true while any other view is false?

Poṭṭhapāda! I do not declare also that it is that a sentient being neither does exist, nor does not exist after death and that only this view is true while any other view is false.

Venerable Sir! Why does the Bhagavā not make such a declaration?

Poṭṭhapāda! It is not in consonance with one's benefit. It is not in consonance with the dhamma (i.e, *Lokuttara dhamma*).[61] It is not even the beginning of the Noble Practice (*brahmacariya*). It is not conducive to the development of disillusionment with the five khandhas. It is not conducive to the abandonment of attachment. It is not conducive to the cessation of *dukkha*. It is not conducive to the extinction of defilements. It is not conducive to the attainment of Magga Insight (*abhiññā*). It is not conducive to the realization of the Four Noble Truths. It is not conducive to the realization of Nibbāna.

Therefore, I do not make such a declaration.

Venerable Sir! What, then, does the Bhagavā declare?

Poṭṭhapāda! I declare what *dukkha* is. Poṭṭhapāda! I declare what the cause of *dukkha* is. Poṭṭhapāda! I declare what the cessation of *dukkha* is. Poṭṭhapāda! I declare what the Path leading to the cessation of *dukkha* is.

Venerable Sir! Why does the Bhagavā make such a declaration?

Poṭṭhapāda! It is in consonance with one's benefit. It is in consonance with the dhamma (i.e., *Lokuttara dhamma*). It is the beginning of the Noble Practice (*brahmacariya*). It is conducive to the development of disillusionment with the five khandhas. It is conducive to the abandonment of attachment. It is conducive to the cessation of *dukkha*. It is conducive to the extinction of defilements. It is conducive to the attainment of Magga Insight (*abhiññā*). It is conducive to the realization of the Four Noble Truths. It is conducive to the realization of Nibbāna.

Hence, I make such a declaration.

That, indeed, is so, Bhagavā. That, indeed, is so, Sugata. Venerable Sir, the Bhagavā knows his own time when to leave.

Then, the Bhagavā rose from his seat and left.

421. Now, no sooner had the Bhagavā left the place than the ascetics all around censured Poṭṭhapāda, the wandering ascetic, acrimoniously from all sides, with these words:

---

61. *Lokuttara dhamma*: The dhamma of Magga, Phala and Nibbāna.

"This respected Poṭṭhapāda always has words of praise for whatever Samaṇa Gotama says, exclaiming 'That, indeed, is so, O Bhagavā! That, indeed, is so, O Sugata!'

"However, we fail to get to know what Samaṇa Gotama has expounded as matters of certainty in relation to the propositions: whether the world is eternal or not eternal; whether the world is finite or infinite; whether the soul is the same as the body; whether the soul is one thing and the body another; whether a sentient being does exist or does not exist after death; whether a sentient being does exist as well as does not exist after death; whether it is that a sentient being neither does exist nor does not exist after death."

When this was said, Poṭṭhapāda, the wandering ascetic, replied thus to those ascetics:

"I also do not know, friends, any matter of certainty that Samaṇa Gotama has expounded in relation to the propositions: Whether the world is eternal or not eternal ... whether it is that a sentient being neither does exist nor does not exist after death. But Samaṇa Gotama declares the practice which is true, real, correct, having the dhamma (i.e., *Lokuttara dhamma*) as its basis, and which is enduring according to the (*Lokuttara*) dhamma. Why should not I, appreciating what is well-spoken, praise the good words of Samaṇa Gotama who declares the practice which is true, real, correct, having the dhamma (i.e., *Lokuttara dhamma*) as its basis, and which is enduring according to the (*Lokuttara*) dhamma?"

About Citta, Son of an Elephant Trainer, and Poṭṭhapāda

422. Now, two or three days later, Citta, the son of an elephant trainer, and Poṭṭhapāda, the wandering ascetic, approached the Bhagavā. Having thus approached the Bhagavā, Citta, the son of an elephant trainer, did obeisance to the Bhagavā and took his seat in a suitable place. Poṭṭhapāda, the wandering ascetic, on the other hand, offered courteous greetings to the Bhagavā who replied fittingly, and having said memorable words of felicitation, he also took his seat. After taking the seat, Poṭṭhapāda, the wandering ascetic, said to the Bhagavā:

"Venerable Sir, no sooner had the Bhagavā left than the ascetics all around censured me acrimoniously from all sides, with these words:

'This respected Poṭṭhapāda always has words of praise for whatever Samaṇa Gotama says, exclaiming: That, indeed, is so, O Bhagavā! That, indeed, is so, O Sugata!

'However, we fail to get to know what Samaṇa Gotama has expounded as matters of certainty in relation to the propositions: Whether the world is eternal or not eternal; whether the world is finite or infinite; whether the soul is the same as the body; whether the soul is one thing and the body another; whether a sentient being does exist or does not exist after death; whether a sentient being does exist as well as does not exist after death; whether it is that a sentient being neither does exist nor does not exist after death.'

"Venerable Sir, when this was said, I replied thus to those ascetics:

I also do not know, friends, any matter of certainty that Samaṇa Gotama has expounded in relation to the propositions: Whether the world is eternal or not eternal ... whether it is that a sentient being neither does exist nor does not exist after death. But Samaṇa Gotama declares the practice which is true, real, correct, having the dhamma (i.e., *Lokuttara dhamma*) as its basis, and which is enduring according to the (*Lokuttara*) dhamma. Why should not I, appreciating what is well-spoken, praise the good words of Samaṇa Gotama who declares the practice which is true, real, correct, having the dhamma (i.e., *Lokuttara dhamma*) as its basis, and which is enduring according to the (*Lokuttara*) dhamma?"

423. Poṭṭhapāda! All those wandering ascetics are blind, without eyes (of wisdom). You alone possess eyes (of wisdom).

Poṭṭhapāda! I declare and lay down the dhammas that are certain (to lead to Nibbāna), as such.

Poṭṭhapāda! I declare and lay down the dhammas that are not certain (to lead to Nibbāna), as such.

Poṭṭhapāda! What are the dhammas that I declare and lay down as not certain (to lead to Nibbāna)?

Dhammas Not Certain (to Lead to Nibbāna)

Poṭṭhapāda! I declare and lay down as a dhamma that is not certain (to lead to Nibbāna) the proposition that the world is eternal. I declare and lay down as a dhamma that is not certain (to lead to Nibbāna) the proposition that the world is not eternal ... the proposition that the world is finite ... that the world infinite ... that the soul is the body ... that the body is the soul itself ... that the soul is one thing and the body another ... that a sentient being does exist after death ... that a sentient being does not exist after death ... that a sentient being does, as well as does not, exist after death ... Poṭṭhapāda! I declare and lay down as a dhamma that is not certain (to lead to Nibbāna) the proposition that a sentient being neither does nor does not exist after death.

Why, Poṭṭhapāda, do I declare and lay down that these propositions are not certain (to lead to Nibbāna)?

Poṭṭhapāda! They are not in consonance with one's benefit. They are not in consonance with the dhamma (i.e., *Lokuttara dhamma*). They are not even the beginning of the Noble Practice (*brahmacariya*). They are not conducive to the development of disillusionment with the five khandhas. They are not conducive to the abandonment of attachment. They are not conducive to the cessation of *dukkha*. They are not conducive to the extinction of defilements. They are not conducive to the attainment of Magga Insight (*abhiññā*). They are not conducive to the realization of the Four Noble Truths. They are not conducive to the realization of Nibbāna.

Therefore, I declare and lay them down as the dhammas not certain (to lead to Nibbāna).

Dhammas Certain (to Lead to Nibbāna)

424. Poṭṭhapāda! And what are the dhammas that I declare and lay down as certain (to lead to Nibbāna)?

Poṭṭhapāda! I declare and lay down that 'This is *dukkha*' as' a dhamma that is certain (to lead to Nibbāna). I declare and lay down that 'This is the cause of *dukkha*' as a dhamma that is certain (to lead to Nibbāna). I declare and lay down that 'This is the cessation of *dukkha*' as a dhamma that is certain (to lead to Nibbāna). I declare and lay down that 'This is the practice of the Path leading to the cessation of *dukkha*' as a dhamma that is certain (to lead to Nibbāna).

Poṭṭhapāda! Why do I declare and lay down these dhammas as certain (to lead to Nibbāna)?

Poṭṭhapāda! These dhammas are in consonance with one's benefit. They are in consonance with the dhamma (i.e., *Lokuttara dhamma*). They are the beginning of the Practice (*brahmacariya*). They are conducive to the development of disillusionment with the five khandhas. They are conducive to the abandonment of attachment. They are conducive to the cessation of *dukkha*. They are conducive to the extinction of defilements. They are conducive to the attainment of Magga Insight (*abhiññā*). They are conducive to the realization of the Four Noble Truths. They are conducive to the realization of Nibbāna.

Therefore, I declare and lay them down as dhammas certain (to lead to Nibbāna).

425. There are, Poṭṭhapāda, some samaṇas and brāhmaṇas who believe and declare '*Atta* is indeed eternal bliss. It does not perish after the death (of the body in which it had lived).' And I approached them and asked:

"Friends! Is it true you believe and declare that *atta* is indeed eternal bliss; it does not perish after the death (of the body in which it had lived)?"

When thus asked, they affirmed "Indeed so." And I asked them again, "If that be so, friends, do you know and perceive the eternally blissful world?"

When thus asked, they replied "No". Then I asked them again:

"Friends! If that be so, do you personally experience the eternally blissful *atta* for a night, or a day, or half a night or half a day?"

When thus asked, they replied "No." Then I asked them again:

"Friends! If that be so, do you know what the Path is and what the Practice is for the realization of the eternally blissful world?"

When thus asked, they replied "No". Then I asked them again:

"Friends! If that be so, do you hear devas who have been reborn in the eternally blissful world say: 'Friends! Engage in right and proper Practice for the realization of the eternally blissful world. We also have been reborn in the eternally blissful world because of such Practice'?"

When thus asked, they said "No".

Now, Poṭṭhapāda, what do you think of this? If that be so, does not what those samaṇas and brāhmaṇas say turn out to be without good ground?

"Venerable Sir! If that be so, what those samaṇas and brāhmaṇas say is certainly without good ground."

426. Poṭṭhapāda! Take this simile. Suppose there is a man who says 'How I long for and how I love the most beautiful woman in this land!' He might be asked thus:

'Friend, do you know whether this most beautiful woman whom you so love and long for belongs to the ruling class, or the brahmin class, or the mercantile class or the working class?'

When thus asked, he might answer 'No'.

Then he might again be asked:

'Friend, regarding this most beautiful woman you so love and long for, do you know her name, or her clan name; whether she be tall, or short, or of medium height; whether she be dark, or fair, or golden-brown; or whether she lives in a village, or in a market-town, or in a city?'

When thus asked, he might answer 'No'.

Then he might again be asked:

'Well, friend, do you love and long for this woman whom you neither know nor see?'

When thus asked, he might answer 'Yes'.

Now, Poṭṭhapāda, what do you think of this? If that be so, does not what that man says turn out to be without good ground?

"Venerable Sir! If that be so, what that man says is certainly without good ground."

Poṭṭhapāda! It is the same in this case. I approached those samaṇas and brāhmaṇas who believe and declare '*Atta* is indeed eternal bliss. It does not perish after the death (of the body in which it had lived)', and asked:

"Friends! Is it true you believe and declare that *atta* is indeed eternal bliss and that it does not perish after the death (of the body in which it had lived)?"

When thus asked, they affirmed "Indeed so". And I asked them again, "If that be so, friends, do you know and perceive the eternally blissful world?"

When thus asked, they replied "No". Then I asked them again:

"Friends! If that be so, do you personally experience the eternally blissful *atta* for a night, or a day, or half a night or half a day?"

When thus asked, they replied "No". Then I asked them again:

"Friends! If that be so, do you know what the Path is and what the Practice is for the realization of the eternally blissful world?"

When thus asked, they replied "No". Then I asked them again:

"Friends! If that be so, do you hear devas who have been reborn in the eternally blissful world say: 'Friends! Engage in right and proper

Practice for the realization of the eternally blissful world. We also have been reborn in the eternally blissful world because of such Practice'?"

When thus asked, they said "No."

Now, Poṭṭhapāda, what do you think of this? If that be so, does not what the samaṇas and brāhmaṇas say turn out to be without good ground?

"Venerable Sir! If that be so, what the samaṇas and brāhmaṇas say is certainly without good ground."

427. Poṭṭhapāda! Take another simile. Suppose there is a man making a stair case in order to go up the turreted mansion in a place where four roads meet. He might be asked thus:

Friend! Do you, in making a stair-case in order to go up a turreted mansion, know whether that mansion is in the East, or in the South, or in the West, or in the North; whether it is high or low, or of medium height?'

When thus asked, he might answer 'No'.

Then, he might again be asked:

'Friend! Are you making a stair-case in order to go up a turreted mansion that you neither know nor perceive?'

When thus asked, he might answer 'Yes'.

Now, Poṭṭhapāda, what do you think of this? If that be so, does not what that man says turn out to be without good ground?

"Venerable Sir! If that be so, what that man says is certainly without good ground."

Poṭṭhapāda! It is the same in this case. I approached those samaṇas and brāhmaṇas who believe and declare '*Atta* is indeed eternal bliss. It does not perish after the death (of the body in which it had lived)', and asked:

"Friends! Is it true you believe and declare that *atta* is indeed eternal bliss and that it does not perish after the death (of the body in which it had lived)?"

When thus asked, they affirmed "Indeed so '. And I asked them again, "If that be so, friends, do you know and perceive the eternally blissful world?"

When thus asked, they replied "No". Then I asked them again:

"Friends! If that be so, do you personally experience the eternally blissful *atta* for a night, or a day, or half a night or half a day?"

When thus asked, they replied "No". Then I asked them again:

"Friends! If that be so, do you know what the Path is and what the Practice is for the realization of the eternally blissful world?"

When thus asked, they replied "No". Then I asked them again:

"Friends! If that be so, do you hear devas who have been reborn in the eternally blissful world say: 'Friend! Engage in right and proper Practice for the realization of the eternally blissful world. We also have been reborn in the eternally blissful world because of such Practice'?"

When thus asked, they said "No."

Now, Poṭṭhapāda, what do you think of this? If that be so, does not what those samaṇas and brāhmaṇas say turn out to be without good ground?

"Venerable Sir! If that be so, what those samaṇas and brāhmaṇas say is certainly without good ground."

Arising of Three Forms of Attabhāva

428. Poṭṭhapāda, there are three forms of *attabhāva*[62] that can arise, namely, the gross form of *attabhāva*, the *attabāva* generated by *jhāna* mind, and the *attabhāva* without corporeality.

Poṭṭhapāda! What is that arising of the gross form of *attabhāva*?

There is the arising of the *attabhāva* made up of the four great primary elements, nourished by solid nutriments and having corporeality. This is the arising of the gross form of *attabhāva*.

Poṭṭhapāda! What is that arising of the *attabhāva* made of *jhāna* mind?

There is the arising of the *attabhāva* generated by *jhāna* mind, endowed completely with all its minor and major physical organs and not deficient in any of the faculties of the senses. This is the arising of the-*attabhāva* generated by *jhāna* mind:

Poṭṭhapāda! What is that arising of the *attabhāva* without corporeality?

There is the arising of the *attabhāva* which is made of *saññā* without corporeality. This is the arising of the *attabhāva* without corporeality.

429. Poṭṭhapāda! I teach the doctrine that renounces the arising of the gross form of *attabhāva*.

I declare: 'By the practice (of the dhamma I teach) you will be free from dispositions that defile, you will develop the states (of Tranquillity and Insight) that bring about purification (of mind) and you will

---

62. *Attabhāva:* The Pāḷi text has *attapaṭilābha*, which is explained in the Commentary as *attabhāvapaṭilābha*, lit., getting *attabhāva*. *Attabhāva* means the khandha aggregates, consisting of all the five khandhas in the eleven sensual and fifteen Rūpa Brahmā realms, of one khandha (i.e., the corporeal aggregate) in the Brahmā realm of only corporeality and of the other four khandhas (i.e., only the mental aggregates) in the Arūpa Brahmā realms devoid of corporeality. Therefore, *attabhāvapaṭilābha* means 'the arising of new khandhas'.

yourselves come to realize and achieve in this very life the expansion and perfection of Wisdom (i.e., Magga and Phala) through Magga Insight (*abhiññā*).

But then, Poṭṭhapāda, you might think:

> 'If the dhamma is practiced as taught, dispositions that defile will be discarded, the states (of Tranquillity and Insight) that bring about purification (of mind) will be developed, and the expansion and perfection of Wisdom, through Magga Insight, will come to be realized and achieved in this very life by oneself. To dwell thus (in that state) will be painful.'

Poṭṭhapāda! It should not be taken in that light. If the dhamma is practiced as taught, dispositions that defile will be discarded, the states (of Tranquillity and Insight) that bring about purification (of mind) will be developed, and the expansion and perfection of Wisdom, through Magga Insight, will come to be realized and achieved in this very life by oneself. To dwell thus (in that state) will bring about gladness, delightful satisfaction, calm, mindfulness, clear comprehension and bliss.

430. And, Poṭṭhapāda! I teach the doctrine that renounces the arising of the *attabhāva* made of *jhāna* mind.

I declare: 'By the practice (of the dhamma I teach) you will be free from dispositions that defile, you will develop the states (of Tranquillity and Insight) that bring about purification (of mind) and you will yourselves come to realize and achieve in this very life the expansion and perfection of Wisdom (i.e., Magga and Phala) through Magga Insight (*abhiññā*).'

But then, Poṭṭhapāda, you might think:

> 'If the dhamma is practiced as taught, dispositions that defile will be discarded, the states (of Tranquillity and Insight) that bring about purification (of mind) will be developed, and the expansion and perfection of Wisdom, through Magga Insight, will come to be realized and achieved in this very life by oneself. To dwell thus (in that state) will be painful.'

Poṭṭhapāda! It should not be taken in that light. If the dhamma is practiced as taught, dispositions that defile will be discarded, the states (of Tranquillity and Insight) that bring about purification (of mind) will be developed, and the expansion and perfection of Wisdom, through Magga Insight, will come to be realized and achieved in this very life by oneself. To dwell thus (in that state) will bring about gladness, delightful satisfaction, calm, mindfulness, clear comprehension and bliss.

431. Poṭṭhapāda! I teach the doctrine that renounces the arising of the *attabhāva* without corporeality.

I declare: 'By the practice (of the dhamma I teach) you will be free from dispositions that defile, you will develop the states (of Tranquillity and Insight) that bring about purification (of mind) and you will yourselves come to realize and achieve in this very life the expansion and perfection of Wisdom (i.e., Magga and Phala) through Magga Insight (*abhiññā*).'

But then, Poṭṭhapāda, you might think:

> 'If the dhamma is practiced as taught, dispositions that defile will be discarded, the states (of Tranquillity and Insight) that bring about purification (of mind) will be developed, and the expansion and perfection of Wisdom, through Magga Insight, will come to be realized and achieved in this very life by oneself. To dwell thus (in that state) will be painful.'

Poṭṭhapāda! It should not he taken in that light. If the dhamma is practiced as taught, dispositions that defile will be discarded, the states (of Tranquillity and Insight) that bring about purification (of mind) will be developed, and the expansion and perfection of Wisdom, through Magga Insight, will come to be realized and achieved in this very life by oneself. To dwell thus (in that state) will bring about gladness, delightful satisfaction, calm, mindfulness, clear comprehension and bliss.

432. Poṭṭhapāda! Others might question us thus:

> 'Friends, what is that arising of the gross form of *attabhāva*, the renunciation of which you teach, (saying) if the dhamma is practiced as taught, dispositions that defile will be discarded, the states (of Tranquillity and Insight) that bring about purification (of mind) will be developed, and the expansion and perfection of Wisdom, through Magga Insight, will come to be realized and achieved in this very life by oneself?'

To them, we would reply thus:

> 'Friends, this[63] is the arising of the gross form of *attabhāva*, the renunciation of which we teach, (saying) if the dhamma is practiced as taught, dispositions that defile will be discarded, the states (of Tranquillity and Insight) that bring about purification (of mind) will be developed, and the expansion and perfection of wisdom, through

63. The word "this" here, and in the replies in Paras 433, 434 and 435 stands in a very much abridged form for the definitions given in Para 428.

Magga Insight, will come to be realized and achieved in this very life by oneself.'

433. Poṭṭhapāda! Others might question us thus:

'Friends, what is that arising of the *attabhāva* made of jhāna mind, the renunciation of which you teach, (saying) if the dhamma is practiced as taught, dispositions that defile will be discarded, the states (of Tranquillity and Insight) that bring about purification (of mind) will be developed, and the expansion and perfection of Wisdom, through Magga Insight, will come to be realized and achieved in this very life by oneself.'

To them, we would reply thus:

'Friends, this is the arising of the *attabhāva* generated by jhāna mind, the renunciation of which we teach, (saying) if the dhamma is practiced as taught, dispositions that defile will be discarded, the states (of Tranquillity and Insight) that bring about purification (of mind) will be developed, and the expansion and perfection of Wisdom, through Magga Insight, will come to be realized and achieved in this very life by oneself.'

434. Poṭṭhapāda! Others might question us thus:

'Friends, what is that arising of the *attabhāva* without corporeality, the renunciation of which you teach, (saying) if the dhamma is practiced as taught, dispositions that defile will be discarded, the states (of Tranquillity and Insight) that bring about purification (of mind) will be developed, and the expansion and perfection of wisdom, through Magga Insight, will come to be realized and achieved in this very life by oneself.'

To them, we would reply thus:

'Friends, this is the arising of the *attabhāva* without corporeality, the renunciation of which we teach, (saying) if the dhamma is practiced as taught, dispositions that defile will be discarded, the states (of Tranquillity and Insight) that bring about purification (of mind) will be developed, and the expansion and perfection of Wisdom, through Magga Insight, will come to be realized and achieved in this very life by oneself.'

Now, Poṭṭhapāda, what do you think of this? That being so, are not our words based on good ground?

"Venerable Sir! That being so, your words are certainly based on good ground."

435. Poṭṭhapāda! Take this simile. A man, in order to go up a turreted mansion, might be making a stair-case below that very mansion. He might be asked thus:

'Friend! Do you, in making a stair-case to go up the turreted mansion, know whether that mansion is in the East, or in the South, or in the West, or in the North; whether it is high or low or of medium height?'

When asked thus, that man might answer:

'This, friend, is the turreted mansion; and I am making a stair-case below that very turreted mansion.'

What do you think of this, Poṭṭhapāda? If that be so, is not what that man said based on good ground?

"Venerable Sir! If that be so, what that man said is certainly based on good ground."

436. Similarly, Poṭṭhapāda, if others might question us thus:

'Friends, what is that arising of the gross form of *attabhāva*, ... by oneself?'

'Friends, what is that arising of the *attabhāva* generated by jhāna mind, ... by oneself?'

'Friends, what is that arising of the *attabhāva* without corporeality, the renunciation of which you teach, (saying) if the dhamma is practiced as taught, dispositions that defile will be discarded, the states (of Tranquillity and Insight) that bring about purification (of mind) will be developed, and the expansion and perfection of Wisdom, through Magga Insight, will come to be realized and achieved in this very life by oneself?'

To them, we would reply thus:

'Friends, this is the arising of the *attabhāva* without corporeality, the renunciation of which we teach, (saying) if the dhamma is practiced as taught, dispositions that defile will be discarded, the states (of Tranquillity and Insight) that bring about purification (of mind) will be developed, and the expansion and perfection of Wisdom, through Magga Insight, will come to be realized and achieved in this very life by oneself.'

What do you think of this, Poṭṭhapāda? If that be so, is not what we said based on good ground?

"Venerable Sir! If that be so, what you said is certainly based on good ground."

437. At the time when the Bhagavā had thus spoken, Citta, the son of the elephant trainer, said to him:

> "Venerable Sir! At the time when the gross form of *attabhāva* has arisen in one, the arising of the *attabhāva* generated by jhāna mind is non-existent; the arising of the *attabhāva* without corporeality is also non-existent. In him, at that time, only the arising of the gross form of *attabhāva* is real.
>
> "Venerable Sir! At the time when the *attabhāva* generated by jhāna mind has arisen in one, the arising of the gross form of *attabhāva* is non-existent; the arising of the *attabhāva* without corporeality is also non-existent. In him, at that time, only the arising of the *attabhāva* generated by jhāna mind is real.
>
> "Venerable Sir! At the time when the *attabhāva* without corporeality has, arisen in one, the arising of the gross form of *attabhāva* is non-existent; the arising of the *attabhāva* generated by jhāna mind is also non-existent. In him, at that time, only the arising of the *attabhāva* without corporeality is real."

Citta! At the time when there is the arising of the gross form of *attabhāva*, it should not be termed as the arising of the *attabhāva* generated by *jhāna* mind, nor the arising of the *attabhāva* without corporeality. It should only be termed as the arising of the gross form of *attabhāva.*

Citta! At the time when there is the arising of the *attabhāva* generated by *jhāna* mind, it should not be termed as the arising of the gross form of *attabhāva*, nor the arising of the *attabhāva* without corporeality. It should only be termed as the arising of the *attabhāva* generated by *jhāna* mind.

Citta! At the time when there is the arising of the *attabhāva* without corporeality, it should not be termed as the arising of the gross form of *attabhāva*, nor the arising of the *attabhāva* generated by *jhāna* mind. It should only be termed as the arising of the *attabhāva* without corporeality.

438. Citta! Suppose you were asked:

'Is it not that you existed in the past, and not that you did not exist? Is it not that you will exist in the future, and not that you will not exist? Is it not that you exist in the present, and not that you do not exist?'

How, then, Citta, would you answer that?

"Venerable Sir! Suppose I were asked:

'Is it not that you existed in the past, and not that you did not exist? Is it not that you will exist in the future, and not that you will not exist? Is it not that you exist in the present, and not that you do not exist?'

"Venerable Sir! I would answer thus:

'I did exist in the past; it is not that I did not exist. I shall exist in the future; it is not that I shall not exist. I exist in the present; it is not that I do not exist. Venerable Sir! Were I asked thus, I would answer in this way."

Citta! Suppose you were asked:

'When in the past, there was the arising of *attabhāva* in you, was only that arising of *attabhāva* real in you? Was the future arising of *attabhāva* non-existent? Was the present arising of *attabhāva*, too, nonexistent?

"When in the future, there will be the arising of *attabhāva* in you, will only that arising of *attabhāva* be real in you? Will the past arising *of attabhāva* be non-existent? Will the present arising of *attabhāva*, too, be non-existent?'

'When in the present, there is the arising of *attabhāva* in you, is only that arising of *attabhāva* real in you? Is the past arising of *attabhāva* non-existent? Is the future arising of *attabhāva*, too, non-existent? How, then, Citta, would you answer that?

"Venerable Sir! Suppose I were asked:

'When in the past, there was the arising of *attabhāva* in you, was only that arising of *attabhāva* real in you? Was the future arising of *attabhāva* non-existent? Was the present arising of *attabhāva*, too, non-existent?

'When in the future, there will be the arising of *attabhāva* in you, will only that arising of *attabhāva* be real in you? Will the past arising of *attabhāva* be nonexistent? Will the present arising of *attabhāva*, too, be non-existent?

'When in the present, there is the arising of *attabhāva* in you, is only that arising of *attabhāva* real in you? Is the past arising of *attabhāva* non-existent? Is the future arising of *attabhāva*, too, non-existent?'

"Venerable Sir! I would answer thus:

'When in the past, there was the arising of *attabhāva* in me, only that arising of *attabhāva* was real in me. The future arising of *attabhāva* was non-existent; the present arising of *attabhāva*, too, was non-existent.

'When in the future, there will be the arising of *attabhāva* in me, only that arising of *attabhāva* will be real in me. The past arising of *attabhāva* will be non-existent; the present arising of *attabhāva*, too, will be non-existent.'

'When in the present, there is the arising of *attabhāva* in me, only that arising of *attabhāva* is real in me. The past arising of *attabhāva* is nonexistent; the future arising of *attabhāva*, too, is non-existent.' Venerable Sir! Were I asked thus, I would answer in this way."

439. Similarly, Citta, at the time when there is the arising of the gross form of *attabhāva*, it should not be termed as the arising of the *attabhāva* generated by *jhāna* mind, nor as the arising of the *attabhāva* without corporeality. It should only be termed as the arising of the gross form of *attabhāva.*

Citta! At the time when there is the arising of the *attabhāva* generated by *jhāna* mind ...

Citta! At the time when there is the arising of the *attabhāva* without corporeality, it should not be termed as the arising of the gross form of *attabhāva*, nor as the arising of the *attabhāva* generated by *Jhāna* mind. It should only be termed as the arising of the *attabhāva* without corporeality.

440. Take this example, Citta. From a cow comes milk, and from the milk curds, and from the curds cream, and from the cream butter, and from the butter ghee; but when it is milk, it is not called curds, or cream, or butter, or ghee. At the time when it is milk, it is called milk.

But when it is curds, ... when it is cream, ... when it is butter, ... when it is ghee, it is not called milk, or curds, or cream, or butter. At the time when it is ghee, it is called ghee.

Similarly, Citta, at the time when there is the arising of the gross form of *attabhāva* ...

At the time when there is the arising of the *attabhāva* generated by *Jhāna* mind ...

At the time when there is the arising of the *attabhāva* without corporeality, it should not be termed as the arising of the gross form of *attabhāva*, nor as the arising of the *attabhāva* generated by *jhāna* mind. It should only be termed as the arising of the *attabhāva* without corporeality.

Citta! All these (such as the arising of *attabhāva*) *are* mere names, expressions, terms and designations in common use in the world. The Tathāgata uses these terms but does not consider them in a wrong way.

441. When that has been said, Poṭṭhapāda, the wandering ascetic, addressed the Bhagavā thus:

"Venerable Sir! Excellent (is the dhamma)! Venerable Sir! Excellent (is the dhamma)! Just as, Venerable Sir, one turns up what lies upside down, just as one uncovers what lies covered, just as one shows the way to another who is lost, just as one holds up a lamp in the darkness for those with eyes to see visible objects, even so have you revealed the dhamma to me in various ways. Venerable Sir! I take refuge in the Buddha; I take refuge in the Dhamma and I take refuge in the Saṅgha. Please take me as a lay disciple from now on till the end of my life."

Citta, Son of Elephant Trainer, Requests Admission into the Order

442. And, Citta, the son of the elephant trainer, addressed the Bhagavā thus:

"Venerable Sir! Excellent (is the dhamma)! Venerable Sir! Excellent (is the dhamma)! Just as, Venerable Sir, one has turned up what lies upside down, just as one has uncovered what lies covered, just as one shows the way to another who is lost, just as one holds up a lamp in the darkness for those with eyes to see visible objects, even so have you revealed the dhamma to me in various ways. Venerable Sir! I take refuge in the Buddha; I take refuge in the Dhamma and I take refuge in the Saṅgha. May I in the presence of the Bhagavā be permitted to go forth from the world; may I receive admission into the Order."

443. Citta, the son of the elephant trainer, was initiated into the Order in the presence of the Bhagavā and subsequently admitted as a bhikkhu. Not long after, Citta, the son of the elephant trainer, dwelling alone and in seclusion, vigilant and zealous, inclined his mind (to Nibbāna), and he soon attained, by himself, in this very life, by virtue of Magga Insight, the fruits of the noblest and the most supreme arahatship which is the ultimate goal for which men of good family renounce hearth and home to lead the homeless life.

Then he knew that rebirth was no more (for him); that he had lived the Life of Purity, that what he had to do (for the realization of Magga) had been done; and that he had nothing more to do (for such realization). And so the Venerable Citta, the son of the elephant trainer, became one of the arahats.

End of the Poṭṭhapāda Sutta, the ninth sutta from division one (*Sīlakkhandha Vagga*)

Ten Suttas from

Dīgha Nikāya

Collection of Long Discourses of the Buddha

THREE SUTTAS

FROM

MAHĀ VAGGA

Large Division

Mahānidāna Sutta
Mahāparinibbāna Sutta
Mahāsatipaṭṭhāna Sutta

Namo tassa bhagavato arahato sammāsambuddhassa

MAHĀNIDĀNA SUTTA

II. MAHĀNIDĀNA SUTTA

(Great Discourse on Causal Factors)

(A) PAṬICCA-SAMUPPĀDA
Doctrine of Dependent Origination

95. Thus have I heard:

At one time the Bhagavā was residing at the market-town of Kammāsadhamma in the country of Kuru. The Venerable Ānanda approached the Bhagavā, made obeisance to him, and seating himself on one side, addressed the Bhagavā thus:

"Venerable Sir, wonderful it is! Unprecedented it is! This doctrine of Paṭicca-samuppāda[1] is not only deep and profound, it also has the signs of being deep and profound. But to my mind it seems to be evident and fathomable."

Ānanda, say not so! Ānanda, say not so! This doctrine of Paṭicca-samuppāda is not only deep and profound, it also has the signs of being deep and profound.

Ānanda, because of lack of proper understanding and penetrative comprehension of this doctrine, (the minds of) these beings are in a state like that of a snarled skein of yarn, or that of a blighted, matted bird's nest or that of *muñja* grass or *pabbaja*[2] grass, and are unable to escape the miserable, ruinous realms of existence (*apāya*),[3] or to escape from the round of existences (*saṃsāra*).

96. Ānanda, should it be asked if there is a cause for (the occurrence of) ageing[4] and death (*jarā* and *maraṇa*), the answer has to be that there is.

---

1. *Paṭicca-samuppāda:* Dependent Origination. Some use the terms 'Conditioned Genesis', 'Law of Cause and Effect', 'Chain of Causation'.
2. *Muñja* and *pabbaja* grass: grass like fine thatch, which when processed like jute could be made into twine. When this twine was entangled, it became difficult to sort out the strands of twine. Similarly, people in the muñja-like state of mind could not know cause and effect.
3. *Apāya:* the four infra-human realms of existence, comprising the realm of intense continuous suffering (*niraya*), the realm of animals (*tiracchāna*), the realm of hungry beings (*peta*) and the realm of frightened beings (*asura*). *Apāya* is sometimes translated as the four Nether Worlds, a rather misleading term as it carries a spatial connotation.
4. **Ageing:** *jarā:* commonly translated as old age.

Again, if it be asked what the cause of ageing and death is, the answer has to be that ageing and death are due to *jāti*, new existence.[5]

Ānanda, should it be asked if there is a cause for (the occurrence of) *jāti*, coming into new existence, the answer has to be that there is.

Again, if it be asked what the cause of *jāti* is, the answer has to be that *jāti* is due to *bhava*,[6] the kammic causal process.

Ānanda, should it be asked if there is a cause for (the occurrence of) *bhava*, the answer has to be that there is.

Again, if it be asked what the cause of *bhava* is, the answer has to be that *bhava* is due to *upādāna*, clinging.

Ānanda, should it be asked if there is a cause for (the arising of) *upādāna*, clinging, the answer has to be that there is.

Again, if it be asked what the cause of clinging is, the answer has to be that clinging is due to *taṇhā*,[7] craving.

Ānanda, should it be asked if there is a cause for (the arising of) *taṇhā*, craving, the answer has to be that there is.

Again, if it be asked what the cause of *taṇhā* is, the answer has to be that *taṇhā* is due to *vedanā*, sensation.

Ānanda, should it be asked if there is a cause for (the arising of) *vedanā*, sensation, the answer has to be that there is.

Again, if it be asked what the cause of *vedanā* is, the answer has to be that *vedanā* is due to *phassa*,[8] contact.

Ānanda, should it be asked if there is a cause for (the occurrence of) *phassa*, contact, the answer has to be that there is.

Again, if it be asked what the cause of *phassa* is, the answer has to be that *phassa* is due to *nāmarūpa*,[9] mind-and-body.

---

5. **New existence:** *jāti:* commonly translated as birth.
6. *Bhava*, as the cause of *jāti*, is the causal process of *kamma* or volitional activities in the course of this life; *bhava* as the result of *upādāna* is existence.
7. *Taṇhā:* lit., "thirst", fig., mental thirst which becomes a craving, a fever of unsatisfied longing, for various kinds of objects or sensations. There are three aspects of *taṇhā*, viz., *kāmataṇhā*, craving for pleasures of the senses, *bhavataṇha*, craving for rebirth (especially rebirth in higher realms), and *vibhavataṇhā*, craving for annihilation (of Self). The six forms of the first aspect are listed in Para 101.
8. *Phassa* means the coming together of the sense-base, the sense-object, and consciousness.
9. *Nāmarūpa* is to be understood as the complex of mental and physical phenomena, it will be noticed that, here, *phassa*, contact, is conditioned by *nāmarūpa*, not mentioning *saḷāyatana*, the six fields of sense-perception (i.e.,

Ānanda, should it be asked if there is a cause for (the arising of) *nāmarūpa*, mind-and-body, the answer has to be that there is.

Again, if it be asked what the cause of *nāmarūpa* is, the answer has to be that *nāmarūpa* is due to *viññāṇa*, (birth-linking) consciousness.

Ānanda, should it be asked if there is a cause for (the arising of) *viññāṇa*, (birth-linking) consciousness, the answer has to be that there is.

Again, if it be asked what the cause of *viññāṇa*, (birth-linking) consciousnesses the answer has to be that *viññāṇa* is due to *nāmarūpa*.

97. Thus, Ānanda, *nāmarūpa* conditions the arising of *viññāṇa*, (birth-linking) consciousness.[10] *Viññāṇa* conditions the arising of *nāmarūpa*. *Nāmarūpa* conditions the arising of *phassa*. *Phassa* conditions the arising of *vedanā*. *Vedanā* conditions the arising of *taṇhā*. *Taṇhā* conditions the arising of *upādāna*. *Upādāna* conditions the arising of *bhava*. *Bhava* conditions the arising of *jāti*. *Jāti* conditions the arising of ageing, death, grief, lamentation, pain, distress and despair (*jarā-maraṇa*). In this way occurs the arising of that entire sum-total of *dukkha*, (the entire aggregate of suffering, pain, affliction, imperfection, impermanence, emptiness, insubstantiality, unsatisfactoriness, which are identified with the five khandha aggregates).

98. Ānanda, I have said that *jarā-maraṇa*, (ageing and death), are conditioned by *jāti*. This point, how *jarā-maraṇa* arise through *jāti*, can be understood by means of the following method (of reasoning):

Suppose, Ānanda, *jāti* does not occur at all or in any way to any being in any realm (of existence):[11]

(To amplify this, let us say) for instance, if *jāti* does not occur to devas to become devas, nor to Gandhabbas[12] to become Gandhabbas, nor to Yakkhas[13] to become Yakkhas, nor to beings (*bhūtā*) with visible forms

---

the six sense-bases). The Commentary explains that this is because the Buddha wanted to emphasize that *nāmarūpa* is the complete primary source of contact, and that the cause of contact is not restricted to the six sense-bases.

10. Another way of putting this, and the following sentences, would be "conditioned by (A), (B) arises".

11. That is, suppose there is no birth anywhere in any way. And the following paragraph may be roughly paraphrased as "If no devas, gandhabbas, yakkhas, bhūtās, human beings, etc., etc., are born in any realm ...", or "If there is no birth of devas, etc., etc., etc., at all".

12. *Gandhabbas*: devas who belong to the lowest (*cātumahārājika*) deva realm, and who are noted musicians and entertainers.

13. *Yakkhas:* sometimes roughly translated as "demons", "demon spirits", "genii", or (wrongly) "ogres", yakkhas are non-human beings. The term *yakkha*

to become such beings, nor to human beings to become human beings, nor to four-legged beings to become four-legged beings, nor to birds to become birds, nor to beings that creep and crawl to become beings that creep and crawl, — if, Ānanda, *jāti* does not occur to these various beings to become beings in their respective realms of existence, that is, if *jāti* altogether (i.e., absolutely) does not occur, — then due to the non-occurrence[14] of *jāti*, can *jarā-maraṇa* appear at all?

"Venerable Sir, they cannot appear at all."

Therefore, Ānanda, only this *jāti* is the cause of, the source of, the origin of, and the condition for, *jarā-maraṇa.*

99. Ānanda, I have said that *jāti* is conditioned by *bhava.* This point, how *jāti* arises through *bhava*, can be understood by means of the following method (of reasoning):

Suppose, Ānanda, *bhava* does not occur at all or in any way for any being in any realm (of existence):

(To amplify this, let us say) for instance, if *bhava* does not occur at all in any of the three states of existence, namely, *Kāmabhava*, *Rūpabhava*, and *Arūpabhava*[15] then due to the non-occurrence of *bhava*, can *jāti* appear at all?

"Venerable Sir, *jāti* cannot appear at all."

Therefore, Ānanda, only this *bhava* is the cause of, the source of, the origin of, and the condition for, *jāti.*

---

is used with widely varying attributes and connotations throughout the Pāḷi Canon, ranging from the pleasant to the hideous.

14. **Non-occurrence**, *nirodha* (i.e., cessation of the repeated phenomenon of birth).

15. The term *bhava* has two main meanings, besides a few supplementary others:

(1) *Kamma bhava*, i.e., the kammic process consisting of rebirth-producing volitions and the mental phenomena associated therewith;

(2) *Upapatti bhava*, the (kammic) resultant rebirth-process in three states of existence.

The three states of existence are:

(a) *Kāmabhava*, the state of sensual existence, comprising the eleven realms of sense-desire, a state of existence dominated by pleasures of the senses. This of course implies also corporeal existence;

(b) *Rūpabhava*, the state of existence with fine materiality, comprising sixteen of the realms of the Brahmās, the upper celestial beings;

(c) *Arūpabhava*, the state of non-corporeal (or formless, non-material existence, comprising four of the realms of the Upper Brahmās.

100. Ānanda, I have said that *bhava* is conditioned by *upādāna*, clinging. This point, how *bhava* arises through *upādāna*, can be understood by means of the following method (of reasoning):

Suppose, Ānanda, *upādāna* does not arise at all or in any way in any being in any realm (of existence) (i.e., if there is no clinging of any kind by anyone to anything):

(To amplify this, let us say) for instance, if *upādāna* does not arise at all in any of its forms, viz., clinging to sense-desires (i.e., sensuality), *kāmupādāna;* clinging to false doctrines of erroneous views and opinions, *diṭṭhupādāna;* clinging to practices of and belief in mere rules and rituals not leading to the right Path, *Sīlabbatupādāna;* and clinging to soul-theories, i.e., to theories that there is Self, Soul, Ego, *attavādupādāna,* — then, due to the non-occurrence of *upādāna*, can *bhava* appear at all?

"Venerable Sir, *bhava* cannot appear at all."

Therefore, Ānanda, only this *upādāna* is the cause of, the source of, the origin of, and the condition for, *bhava.*

101. Ānanda, I have said that *upādāna*, clinging, is conditioned by *taṇhā*, craving. This point, how *upādāna* arises through *taṇhā*, craving, can be understood by means of the following method (of reasoning):

Suppose, Ānanda, *taṇhā* does not arise at all or in any way in any being in any realm (of existence):

(To amplify this, let us say) for instance, if *taṇhā* does not arise at all in any of its six forms, namely, craving for (enjoyment of) visible objects, *rūpataṇhā;*[16] craving for (enjoyment of) sounds, *saddataṇhā;* craving for (enjoyment of) smells, *gandhataṇhā;* craving for (enjoyment of) tastes or flavors, *rasataṇhā*; craving for (enjoyment of) physical contact, *phoṭṭhabbataṇhā;* craving for (the pleasure of) ideas, thoughts, *dhammataṇhā,*[17] then, due to the non-occurrence of *taṇhā*, can *upādāna* appear at all?

"Venerable Sir, *upādāna* cannot appear at all."

Therefore, Ānanda, only this *taṇhā*, craving, is the cause of, the source of, the origin of, and the condition for, *upādāna*, clinging.

---

16. *Rūpataṇha*: craving for *rūpa*: *Rūpa* has many shades of meaning. Briefly, it may be rendered as materiality, material factor, matter, physical phenomenon, physical substance.

17. *Dhammataṇhā*: craving for *dhamma*, mind-objects; ideas, thoughts, concepts are sense-objects of the faculty of mind.

102. Ānanda, I have said that *taṇhā*, craving, is conditioned by *vedanā*,[18] sensation. This point, how *taṇhā* arises through *vedanā*, sensation, can be understood by means of the following method (of reasoning):

Suppose, Ānanda, *vedanā* does not arise at all or in any way in any being in any realm (of existence):

(To amplify this, let us say) for instance, if *vedanā* does not arise at all or in any way, either through contact by means of the eye, (i.e., by seeing), or through contact by means or the ear, (i.e., by hearing), or through contact by means of the nose, (i.e., by smelling), or through contact by means of the tongue, (i.e., by the sense of taste), or through contact by means of the body, (i.e., by touching), or through contact by means of the mind, (i.e., by the faculty of the mind having contact with mind-objects, such as thoughts, ideas), — then, due to the nonoccurrence of *vedanā*, can *taṇhā* appear at all?

"Venerable Sir, *taṇhā* cannot appear at all."

Therefore, Ānanda, only this *vedanā*, sensation, is the cause of, the source of, the origin of, and the condition for, *taṇhā*, craving.

103. Thus, Ānanda, because of *vedanā*, there arises *taṇhā*.[19] Because of *taṇhā*, there arises quest (for possessions, pleasures), (*pariyesana*). Because of quest, there arises getting, gaining, (*labha*). Because of getting, gaining, there arises (the process of) decision on how to use or enjoy (what has been got), (*vinicchaya*). Because of the decision on use and enjoyment (of what has been gained), there arises the excitement of passion and delight, (*chanda-rāga*).[20] Because of the excitement of passion and delight, there arises tenacious cleaving (to what has been got) as one's own, (*ajjhosāna*). Because of tenacious cleaving (to

---

18. *Vedanā*: has been rendered by some as "feeling".

19. *Taṇhā:* The Commentary says there are two kinds of *taṇhā*, craving:

(i) *vaṭṭamūla taṇhā*, craving leading to the round of existences; this is the general aspect of craving;

(ii) *samudācāra taṇhā*, craving in actual conduct and practice; this is the particular, applied aspect of craving.

From this Para 103 to Para 112, the successive effects of the particular aspect of craving are enlarged upon. The chain of causal factors interrupted here by these ten paragraphs is taken up again in Para 113.

20. *chanda-rāga: chanda* = impulse, excitement, desire for, wish for, delight in (something); *rāga* = passion, lust. Therefore, in this context, *chanda-rāga* means passion for and delight in (possessions etc.). *Chanda-rāga* is a weaker passion than tenacious cleaving (to possessions), *ajjhosāna*, rendered in the Burmese version as "firm determination that what has been gained is one's very own".

what has been got) as one's own, there arises selfish possessiveness, (*pariggaha*).[21] Because of selfish possessiveness, there arises meanness-and-stinginess, (*macchariya*).[22] Because of meanness-and-stinginess, there arises watchful guarding (of possessions), (*ārakkha*). And because of such watchful guarding, there arise many wicked demeritorious acts, such as hitting with sticks, wounding with weapons,[23] fighting, quarrelling,[24] contentiously disputing, using unbearable expressions, backbiting and telling lies.

104. Ānanda, I have said that because of watchful guarding (of possessions), there arise many wicked demeritorious acts, such as hitting with sticks, wounding with weapons, fighting, quarrelling, contentiously disputing, using unbearable expressions, backbiting and telling lies. This point, how these many wicked demeritorious acts such as hitting with sticks, wounding with weapons, fighting, quarrelling, contentiously disputing, using unbearable expressions, backbiting and telling lies, arise through watchful guarding of possessions, can be understood by this means:

Suppose, Ānanda, there is no watchful guarding (of possessions) at all or in any way by any being in any realm (of existence): If there is entirely no such watchful guarding, then due to the absence of such watchful guarding, can these many wicked demeritorious acts, such as hitting with sticks, wounding with weapons, fighting, quarrelling, contentiously disputing, using unbearable expressions, backbiting and telling lies, occur at all?

"Venerable Sir, they cannot occur at all."

Therefore, Ānanda, only this watchful guarding (of possessions) is the cause of, the source of, the origin of, and the condition for, the arising of these many wicked demeritorious acts, such as hitting with sticks, wounding with weapons, fighting, quarrelling, contentiously disputing, using unbearable expressions, backbiting and telling lies.

105. Ānanda, I have said that because of meanness-and-stinginess there arises watchful guarding (of possessions). This point, how

---

21. *Pariggaha:* holding on to, seizing, grasping on to, carefully keeping (possessions). "Acquisitiveness" or "Gloating over (what has been got)" are other possible renderings.

22. *Macchariya:* stinginess, selfishness, not wishing to share with others, thus jealously holding on to what one has.

23. Lit., carrying sticks, bearing weapons.

24. **Quarrelling**: *viggaha;* lit., going against (one another).

meanness-and-stinginess gives rise to watchful guarding of possessions, can be understood by this means:

Suppose, Ānanda, meanness-and-stinginess does not arise at all or in any way in any being in any realm (of existence): If there is entirely no meanness-and-stinginess, then due to the absence of meanness-and-stinginess, can watchful guarding of possessions appear at all?

"Venerable Sir, it cannot appear at all."

Therefore, Ānanda, only this meanness-and-stinginess is the cause of, the source of, the origin of, and the condition for, watchful guarding of possessions.

106. Ānanda, I have said that because of selfish possessiveness there arises meanness-and-stinginess. This point, how selfish possessiveness gives rise to meanness-and-stinginess, can be understood by this means:

Suppose, Ānanda, selfish possessiveness does not arise at all or in any way in any being in any realm (of existence): If there is entirely no selfish possessiveness, then due to the absence of selfish possessiveness, can meanness-and-stinginess appear at all?

"Venerable Sir, meanness-and-stinginess cannot appear at all."

Therefore, Ānanda, only this selfish possessiveness is the cause of, the source of, the origin of, and the condition for, meanness-and-stinginess.

107. Ānanda, I have said that because of tenacious cleaving (to what has been got, as one's own), there arises selfish possessiveness. This point, how tenacious cleaving gives rise to selfish possessiveness, can be understood by this means:

Suppose, Ānanda, tenacious cleaving (to what has been got, as one's own) does not arise at all or in any way in any being in any realm (of existence): If there is entirely no tenacious cleaving, then due to the absence of tenacious cleaving, can selfish possessiveness appear at all?

"Venerable Sir, it cannot appear at all."

Therefore, Ānanda, only this tenacious cleaving (to what has been got, as one's own) is the cause of, the source of, the origin of, and the condition for, selfish possessiveness.

108. Ānanda, I have said that because of the excitement of passion and delight, there arises tenacious cleaving (to what has been got, as one's own). This point, how the excitement of passion and delight gives rise to tenacious cleaving, can be understood by this means:

Suppose, Ānanda, the excitement of passion and delight does not arise at all or in any way in any being in any realm (of existence): If there is entirely no excitement of passion and delight, then due to the absence of the excitement of passion and delight, can tenacious cleaving to what one possesses appear at all?

"Venerable Sir, tenacious cleaving cannot appear at all."

Therefore, Ānanda, only this excitement of passion and delight (in what has been gained) is the cause of, the source of, the origin of, and the condition for, tenacious cleaving (to what has been got, as one's own).

109. Ānanda, I have said that because of (the process of) decision on how to use or enjoy (what one has got), there arises the excitement of passion and delight. This point, how (the process of) decision on use and enjoyment (of what has been gained) gives rise to the excitement of passion and delight, can be understood by this means:

Suppose, Ānanda, (the process of) decision on how to use or enjoy (what has been got) does not arise at all or in any way in any being in any realm (of existence): if there is entirely no (process of) decision on use and enjoyment, then due to the absence of such decision, can the excitement of passion and delight appear at all?

"Venerable Sir, it cannot appear at all."

Therefore, Ānanda, only this decision on how to use or enjoy (what has been got) is the cause of, the source of, the origin of, and the condition for, the excitement of passion and delight.

110. Ānanda, I have said that because of getting, gaining (things, property, etc.), there arises (the process of) decision on how to use or enjoy (what has been got). This point, how getting, gaining, gives rise to decision on use and enjoyment, can be understood by this means:

Suppose, Ānanda, getting or gaining does not occur at all or in any way to any being in any realm (of existence):[25] If there is entirely no getting, gaining (things etc.), then due to the absence of getting and gaining, can (the process of) decision on how to use and enjoy (what has been got) appear at all?

"Venerable Sir, it cannot appear at all."

Therefore, Ānanda, only this getting, gaining (things etc.) is the cause of, the source of, the origin of, and the condition for, decision on how to use and enjoy (what has been got).

111. Ānanda, I have said that because of quest (for possessions, pleasures), there arises getting, gaining. This point, how quest (for

25. That is, suppose there is no getting or gaining (of things) by any being in any realm of existence.

possessions etc.) gives rise to getting, gaining (things etc.), can be understood by this means:

Suppose, Ānanda, there is no quest (for possessions, pleasures) at all or in any way by any being in any realm (of existence): If there is entirely no quest for anything, anywhere, then due to the absence of quest, can getting or gaining occur at all?

"Venerable Sir, getting or gaining cannot occur at all."

Therefore, Ānanda, only this quest (for possessions, pleasures) is the cause of, the source of, the origin of, and the condition for, getting, gaining (things etc.).

112. Ānanda, I have said that because of *taṇhā*, craving, there arises quest (for possessions, pleasures). This point, how craving gives rise to quest, can be understood by this means:

Suppose, Ānanda, *taṇhā* does not arise at all or in any way in any being in any realm (of existence)?

(To amplify this, let us say) for instance, if *taṇhā*, craving, does not arise in any of those three forms,[26] namely, *kāmatanhā*, craving for pleasures of the senses, *bhavataṇhā*, craving for rebirth, (clinging to the view that there can be no ending to existence), and *vibhavataṇhā*, craving for annihilation (of Self) (clinging to the view that there is no existence after death)[27] — then, due to the absence of *taṇhā* can quest (for possessions, pleasures) appear at all?

"Venerable Sir, quest cannot appear at all."

Therefore, Ānanda, only this *taṇhā*, this craving, is the cause of, the source of, the origin of, and the condition for, quest (for possessions etc.).

Thus it is, Ānanda, that both these two kinds[28] of *taṇhā*, craving, arise from only one thing, namely, *vedanā*, sensation.

113. Ānanda, I have said that *vedanā* is conditioned by *phassa*, contact. This point, how *phassa* gives rise to *vedanā*, can be understood by means of the following method (of reasoning):

---

26. *Three forms of taṇhā:* see also footnote to *taṇhā* in Para 96.
27. As explained in the Commentary.
28. See footnote on *taṇhā* in Para 103. The two kinds of *taṇhā* are: (i) the *taṇhā* which gives rise to *upādāna*, clinging; i.e., the *taṇhā* which is the fundamental root cause, of the round of existences, and (ii) the *taṇhā* which gives rise to quest, as in this paragraph.

Suppose, Ānanda, there is no contact between sense-organs and sense-objects[29] at all or in any way in any being in any realm (of existence):

(To amplify this, let us say) for instance, if *phassa* does not occur at all in any of its six forms, namely, eye-contact (i.e., contact with the sense of vision), ear-contact (i.e., contact with the sense of hearing), nose-contact (i.e., contact with the sense of smell), tongue-contact (i.e., contact with the sense of taste), body-contact (i.e., contact with the sense of touch), mind-contact (i.e., contact of mind-object with the mind faculty), — then, due to the absence of *phassa*, can *vedanā* appear at all?

"Venerable Sir, *vedanā* cannot appear at all."

Therefore, Ānanda, only their *phassa*, this contact, is the cause of, the source of, the origin of, and the condition for, *vedanā*.

114. Ānanda, I have said that *phassa* is conditioned by *nāmarūpa*, mind-and-body. This point, how *phassa* arises through *nāmarūpa*, can be understood by this means:

Ānanda, the composite of mental phenomena, *nāma-kāya*, is manifested only through certain properties, features, signs and indications (such as sensation, perception,[30] volitional activities and consciousness); and the (various) mental phenomena (of that composite) are designated by terms (such as *vedanā*, sensation; *saññā*, perception; *saṅkhārā*, volitional activities; and *viññāṇa*, consciousness).[31] If these properties, features, signs and indications (in the form of sensation, perception, volitional activities and consciousness) do not exist, then can what is termed 'mind-contact', *adhivacanasamphassa*,[32] appear at all in the composite of (purely) physical phenomena, *rūpakāya*?

"Venerable Sir, it cannot appear at all."

---

29. Including the mind as sense-organ or faculty, and ideas, thoughts, imagery, or sometimes even physical phenomenon as sense-objects, (in short, cognizable objects). The sense-objects of the mind are called mind-objects (*dhammārammaṇa*).

30. **Perception:** *saññā*, perception, implying recognition by means of assimilation of sensations.

31. The words in the brackets are from the explanation in the Commentary.

32. *Adhivacanasaṃphassa*, (lit., contact which can be known only by its name), is explained in the Commentary as being the same as *manosaṃphassa*, contact of mind (see Para 113 above); i.e., contact of thoughts, ideas, imagery (mind-object) with the organ or faculty of mind.

Ānanda, the composite of physical phenomena, *rūpa-kāya*, is manifested only through certain properties, features, signs and indications (such as texture,[33] fluidity, temperature, extension); and the (various) physical phenomena are designated by terms (such as the element of solidity, *pathavī*, the element of fluidity and cohesion, *āpo;* the element of heat or cold, *tejo*; and the element of extension or motion, *vāyo*).[34] If these properties, features, signs and indications do not exist, then can the contact of sense-organs with sense-objects, *paṭi-ghasamphassa*, appear at all in the composite of (purely) mental phenomena, *nāmakāya*?

"Venerable Sir, it cannot appear at all."

Ānanda, the composite of mental phenomena, *nāmakāya*, and the composite of physical phenomena, *rūpa-kāya*, are manifested only through their respective properties, features, signs and indications. If such properties, features, signs and indications do not exist, then can contact of mind or contact of the five sense-organs appear at all?

"Venerable Sir, neither can appear at all."

Ānanda, *nāmarūpa*, mind-and-body, is manifested by those properties, features, signs and indications. If such properties, features, signs and indications do not exist, can contact appear at all?

"Venerable Sir, it cannot appear at all."

Therefore, Ānanda, only this *nāmarūpa* is the cause of, the origin of, and the condition for, contact, *phassa.*

115. Ānanda, I have said that *nāmarūpa*[35] is conditioned by *viññāṇa*, (birth-linking) consciousness. This point, how *nāmarūpa* arises through *viññāṇa*, can be understood by this means:

Ānanda, if (birth-linking) consciousness were not to appear in the mother's womb, could *nāmarūpa* arise simultaneously[36] with it in the mother's womb?

---

33. **Texture**: hardness, softness, roughness, smoothness.

34. The words in the brackets are from the Burmese version. They bring out what is meant by properties, etc. of the corporeal aggregate. Here, the Four Great Primary Elements, *cattāri mahābhūtāni*, which underline and characterize the Aggregate of Matter (*rūpakkhandha*) are referred to. They are *pathavī, āpo, tejo, vāyo.* Some render *āpo* as fluidity, some as cohesion. Some render *vāyo* as motion or mobility.

35. Here *nāma* in *nāmarūpa* connotes mental concomitants associated with (birth-linking) consciousness.

36. **Arise simultaneously**: (*samuccati*): The Commentary says "become united to form the first stage of the embryonic (*kalala*) cell". Conception can take place

"Venerable Sir, *nāmarūpa* cannot arise simultaneously without *viññāṇa* in the mother's womb."

Ānanda, if *viññāṇa*, consciousness, after appearing in the mother's womb, were to cease, could *nāmarūpa* result in the complete five khandha-aggregates?

"Venerable Sir, *nāmarūpa* cannot result or develop without *viññāṇa*."

Ānanda, if *viññāṇa*, consciousness, were to cease abruptly (lit., to be cut off) in one who is still young, either boy or girl, could *nāmarūpa* reach (lit., meet with, undergo) (the stage of) full growth, maturation and development (lit., expansion)?

"Venerable Sir, *nāmarūpa* cannot reach the stage of full growth, were *viññāṇa to cease abruptly.*"

Therefore, Ānanda, only this *viññāṇa*, this consciousness, is the cause of, the source of, the origin of, and the condition for, *nāmarūpa*, mind-and-body.

116. Ānanda, I have said that *viññāṇa*, consciousness, is conditioned by *nāmarūpa*. This point, how *viññāṇa* arises through *nāmarūpa*, can be understood by this means:

Ānanda, if consciousness were not to have *nāma-rūpa* as a supporting base, could the sum-total of *dukkha*, together with birth, ageing and death appear in future?

"Venerable Sir, these cannot appear in future."

Therefore, Ānanda, only this *nāmarūpa* is the cause of, the source of, the origin of, and the condition for, *viññāṇa*, consciousness.

Ānanda, through just these mutually conditioning *viññāṇa* and *nāmarūpa*, there is birth, there is ageing, there is death, there is recurrent passing from one state of existence to another, there is repeated coming into existence. Through just these mutually conditioning *viññāṇa* and *nāmarūpa*, there arises the basis (*patha*, i.e., the five khandhas) for arbitrary nomenclature (*Adhivacana*),[37] the basis for significant term (*Nirutti*), and the basis for honorific appellation (*Paññatti*). Through just these *viññāṇa* and *nāmarūpa*, there arises the sphere of the intellect. Through just these mutually conditioning *viññāṇa* and *nāmarūpa*, the cycle[38] of existences turns round and round. Through just these mutually

---

only with the simultaneous arising of *viññāṇa* and *nāmarūpa* in the womb.

37. The Commentary here indicates: *Adhivacana*, name without specific meaning; *Nirutti*, name with some specific meaning; *Paññatti*, name indicating some honour.

38. **Cycle of existences,** in the three aspects of round of defilements, round of

conditioning *viññāṇa* and *nāmarūpa*, there arises what is designated as the five khandha-aggregates.

(B) Definition of *Atta*

117. Ānanda, how does a person,[39] who believes in[40] *atta*, Self, Soul, Ego, define *atta*?

Ānanda, the person who believes in *atta* as having corporeality and limitedness would define it by saying "My *atta* is corporeal and limited".

Ānanda, the (second) person who believes in *atta* as having corporeality but no limitedness would define it by saying "My *atta* is corporeal and unlimited".

Ānanda, the (third) person who believes in *atta* as having no corporeality but having limitedness would define it by saying "My *atta* is incorporeal and is limited".

Ānanda, the (fourth) person who believes in *atta* as having no corporeality and no limitedness would define it by saying "My *atta* is incorporeal and is unlimited".[41]

118. Ānanda, of these (four persons), he who believes in *atta* as having corporeality and limitedness may be either one who defines a corporeal and limited *atta* only of this existence,[42] or one who defines a corporeal and limited *atta* of future existences also. Either of the two thinks "I shall put right the wrong view of the other"

---

actions and round of consequences of actions.

39. **A person**: The Buddha, in the following paragraphs, points out four kinds of persons who believe in the soul and who define it variously according to their conception of what the soul is.

40. **Who believes in**: *paññapento:* lit., who designates (something) as *atta.*

41. The Commentary says that these four definitions are deductions made by some persons who practise *kasiṇa* meditation.

42. **Only of this existence**: Here the Buddha is distinguishing between two kinds of wrong views regarding existence. One is the view that there is merely this existence; this is *uccheda diṭṭhi*, the doctrine of the annihilation of the soul; the other view is that the soul continues in other existences; this is *sassata diṭṭhi*, the doctrine of the eternal continuance of the soul after death. And the person who holds either view is firmly convinced that the person who has the other view is on the wrong track, believing what is untrue, and that it behoves him to put the other right, to make the other realize what is true. Both are wrong views.

Ānanda, this being so, it is proper to say that the wrong view termed *Rūpīparittattānudiṭṭhi*, the belief in *atta* with corporeality and limitedness, persists[43] in the mind of that person.

Ānanda, of these (four persons), he who believes in *atta* as having corporeality but no limitedness may be either one who defines a corporeal and unlimited *atta* only of this existence, or one who defines a corporeal and unlimited *atta* of future existences also. Either of the two thinks "I shall put right the wrong view of the other".

Ānanda, this being so, it is proper to say that the wrong view termed *Rūpīamntattānudiṭṭhi*, the belief in *atta* with corporeality and unlimitedness, persists in the mind of that person.

Ānanda, of these (four persons), he who believes in *atta* as having no corporeality but having limitedness may be either one who defines an incorporeal and limited *atta* only of this existence, or one who defines an incorporeal and limited *atta* of future existences also. Either of the two thinks "I shall put right the wrong view of the other".

Ānanda, this being so, it is proper to say that the wrong view termed *Arūpīparittattānudiṭṭhi*, the belief in *atta* with incorporeality and limitedness, persists in the mind of that person.

Ānanda, of these (four persons), he who believes in *atta* as having neither corporeality nor limitedness may be either one who defines an incorporeal and unlimited *atta* only of this existence, or one who defines an incorporeal and unlimited *atta* of future existences also. Either of the two thinks "I shall put right the wrong view of the other".

Ānanda, this being so, it is proper to say that the wrong view termed *Arūpīanantattānudiṭṭhi*, the belief in *atta* with incorporeality and unlimitedness, persists in the mind of that person.

Ānanda, this is how a person who believes in *atta* defines *atta.*

(C) Non-Definition of *Atta*

119. Ānanda, how does a person[44] who does not believe in *atta*, Self, Soul, Ego, refrain[45] from defining *atta.*?

Ānanda, the person who does not believe in *atta* as having corporeality and limitedness would make no such definition as "My *atta* is corporeal and limited".

---

43. **Persists:** *anuseti*: recurs again and again.

44. **A person:** here, the Buddha is describing persons who do not hold the *atta* theory.

45. **Refrain from:** lit., does not define or designate anything as *atta.*

Ānanda, the (second) person who does not believe in *atta* as having corporeality but no limitedness would make no such definition as "My *atta* is corporeal and unlimited".

Ānanda, the (third) person who does not believe in *atta* as having no corporeality but having limitedness would make no such definition as "My *atta* is incorporeal and is limited."

Ānanda, the (fourth) person who does not believe in *atta* as having no corporeality and no limitedness would make no such definition as "My *atta* is incorporeal and is unlimited".

120. Ānanda, of these (four persons), he who does not believe, in *atta* as having corporeality and limitedness may be either one who does not define a corporeal and limited *atta* only of this existence, or one who does not define a corporeal and limited *atta* of future existences also. Either of the two does not think "I shall put right the wrong view of the other".

Ānanda, this being so, it is proper to say that the wrong view termed *Rūpīparittattānudiṭṭhi*, the belief in a corporeal and limited *atta*, does not persist in the mind of that person.

Ānanda, of these (four persons), he who does not believe in *atta* as having corporeality but no limitedness may be either one who does not define a corporeal and unlimited *atta* only of this existence, or one who does not define a corporeal and unlimited *atta* of future existences also. Either of the two does not think "I shall put right the wrong view of the other".

Ānanda, this being so, it is proper to say that the wrong view termed *Rūpīanantattānudiṭṭhi*, the belief in a corporeal and unlimited *atta*, does not persist in the mind of that person.

Ānanda, of these (four persons), he who does not believe in *atta* as having no corporeality but having limitedness may be either one who does not define an incorporeal and limited *atta* only of this existence, or one who does not define an incorporeal and limited *atta* of future existence also. Either of the two does not think "I shall put right the wrong view of the other"

Ānanda, this being so it is proper to say that the wrong view termed *Arūpīparittattānudiṭṭhi*, the belief in an incorporeal and limited *atta*, does not persist in the mind of that person.

Ānanda, of these (four persons), he who does not believe in *atta* as having neither corporeality nor limitedness may be either one who does not define an incorporeal and unlimited *atta* only of this existence, or one who does not define an incorporeal and unlimited *atta* of future existences also. Either of the two does not think "I shall put right the wrong view of the other"

Ānanda, this being so, it is proper to say that the wrong view termed *Arūpīanantattānudiṭṭhi*, the belief in an incorporeal and unlimited *atta*, does not persist in the mind of that person.

Ānanda, this is how a person who does not believe in *atta* refrains from defining *atta.*

(D) CONSIDERATION OF *ATTA*

121. Ānanda, what does a person who considers *atta* take *atta* to be?

Ānanda, the person who considers *vedanā*, sensation, as *atta*, takes sensation as *atta* and believes: "Sensation is my *atta.*"

Ānanda, some other person, who considers *atta*, believes: "Sensation is not my *atta.* My *atta* cannot feel any mental phenomenon."[46]

Ānanda, still another person, who considers *atta*, believes: "Sensation is not my *atta.* And it is not that my *atta* cannot feel any mental phenomenon. My *atta* can feel a mental phenomenon. My *atta* has the property of feeling a mental phenomenon."[47]

122. Ānanda, of those (three persons), this should be said to the person who maintains that "Sensation is my *atta*":

"Friend, there are three kinds of sensation: pleasant sensation, unpleasant sensation, and neither pleasant nor unpleasant, neutral, sensation. Of these three kinds of sensation, which do you consider to be *atta*?"

Ānanda, when a pleasant sensation is felt, neither unpleasant sensation nor neutral sensation can be felt. At that time, only the pleasant sensation can be felt.

---

46. **Cannot feel any mental phenomenon**: here, *atta* is identified with *rūpa* or *rūpakkhandha*, the aggregate of physical phenomena, or roughly the body. If *atta* is the mere body it cannot expedience or feel any sensation or any other mental phenomenon.

47. Here, in the case of the third person, *atta* is identified with one or all of the three remaining Khandhas, namely, *saññākkhandha*, aggregate of perception, *saṅkhārakkhāndha*, aggregate of volitions or mental formations, and *viññānakkhandha*, aggregate of consciousness. The first person identifies *atta* with sensation, the second person with body, and the third person with one or all of the three factors of the mental make-up other than sensation, namely, perception, volitions, and consciousness. Thus, in the case of the third person, he believes that *atta* can experience these three mental phenomena.

Ānanda, when an unpleasant sensation is felt, neither pleasant sensation nor neutral sensation can be felt. At that time, only the unpleasant sensation can be felt.

Ānanda, when a neutral sensation is felt, neither pleasant sensation nor unpleasant sensation can be felt. At that time, only the neutral sensation can be felt.

123. Ānanda, a pleasant sensation is impermanent; it is a result produced by a combination of causes;[48] it arises due to being conditioned by causal factors; it has the nature of wasting away, of disintegrating, of disappearing, of ceasing.

Ānanda, an unpleasant sensation too is impermanent; it is a result produced by a combination of causes; it arises due to being conditioned by causal factors; it has the nature of wasting away, of disintegrating, of disappearing, of ceasing.

Ānanda, a neutral sensation, too, is impermanent; it is a result produced by a combination of causes; it arises due to being conditioned by causal factors; it has the nature of wasting away, of disintegrating, of disappearing, of ceasing.

While a person is having a pleasant sensation, he entertains the belief "This pleasant sensation is verily my *atta*". When that pleasant sensation disappears, he will have to say "My *atta* has perished". When he is having an unpleasant sensation, too, he again entertains the belief "This unpleasant sensation is verily my *atta*". When that unpleasant sensation disappears, he will have to say again "My *atta* has perished". When he is having a neutral sensation, too, he again entertains the belief "This neutral sensation is verily my *atta*". When that neutral sensation disappears, he will have to say again "My *atta* has perished".

Thus, the person who maintains that "Sensation is my *atta*" considers in effect that *atta* is in this very life impermanent, is imbued with pleasure and pain, and has the nature of arising (i.e., coming into existence) and wasting away (lit., decaying).

Therefore, Ānanda, the view that "Sensation is my *atta*" is not (by the above demonstration) fitting or proper.

124. Ānanda, of those (three persons), this should be said to the person who maintains that "Sensation is not my *atta*. My *atta* cannot feel any mental phenomenon":

---

48. **A result of causes:** *saṅkhata*; formed.

"Friend, is it possible to consider a purely physical thing which does not have the capacity for feeling any mental phenomenon as: 'This verily is Myself'?"

"Venerable Sir, it must be said that it is not possible."

Therefore, Ānanda, the view that "Sensation is not my *atta.* My *atta* cannot feel any mental phenomenon" is not (by the above demonstration) fitting or proper.

125. Ānanda, of those (three persons), this should be said to the person who maintains that "Sensation is not my *atta.* And it is not that my *atta* cannot feel any mental phenomenon. My *atta* can feel a mental phenomenon. My *atta* has the property of feeling a mental phenomenon":

"Friend, if sensation in any form or of any kind were to cease absolutely, then in the complete absence of sensation, would it be possible to consider the mental phenomena[49] entirely free of sensation, as: 'This verily is Myself'?"

"Venerable Sir, it must be said that it would not be possible."

Therefore, Ānanda, the view that "Sensation is not my *atta.* And it is not that my *atta* cannot feel any mental phenomenon. My *atta* can feel a mental phenomenon. My *atta* has the property of feeling a mental phenomenon" is not (by the above demonstration) fitting or proper.

126. Ānanda, because of this, the bhikkhu does not consider sensation is *atta*; nor does he consider that *atta* cannot feel any mental phenomenon; nor does he consider that 'My *atta* can feel a mental phenomenon; my *atta* has the property of feeling a mental phenomenon'. Not considering like this, that bhikkhu does not cling to any of the five khandhas. Because of this lack of clinging, he does not crave[50] for anything. Because he becomes devoid of craving, he by himself will finally and completely become liberated (from moral defilements). He knows: "Rebirth is no more for me; the noble practice of the Path (leading to liberation) has been carried out; what should be done has already been done; and for this purpose (i.e., attainment of Magga) there is nothing more to be done."

Ānanda, should anyone say of the bhikkhu with such an emancipated mind,[51] –

that "he holds the view that a sentient being exists after death",

---

49. I.e., the mental phenomena (of perception, volition, consciousness).

50. Entirely without sensation because of its postulated complete cessation. Crave: *paritassati*, lit., long after (something).

51. I.e., An arahat.

or that "he holds the view that a sentient being does not exist after death",

or that "he holds the view that a sentient being exists and yet does not exist after death",

or that "he holds the view that a sentient being neither does exist nor does not exist after death", — such saying would be improper.

And why would it be improper?

Ānanda, whatever the extent there is of arbitrary nomenclature and its basis (i.e., the five khandhas); of significant term and its basis (i.e., the five khandhas); of honorific appellation and its basis (i.e., the five khandhas); of knowledge and intellect, and its sphere of activity (i.e., the five khandhas); of the round of existences and its continual turning, — all that is completely and thoroughly known "by the bhikkhu (who is an arahat), being emancipated from all moral defilements.

To say of such a bhikkhu (who is an arahat, and) who has been emancipated from all moral defilements that "he does not know, he does not see, he holds such and such a view" is improper indeed.

(E) The Seven Areas of Consciousness

127. Ānanda, there are seven areas[52] of Consciousness (*viññāṇa*). Besides, there are two spheres (*āyatana*).[53]

The seven areas of *viññāṇa*, Consciousness, are these:

Ānanda, there are beings with diversity of bodily form and diversity of birth-linking Consciousness.[54] These are human beings, devas of the six sensual realms,[55] and some lower earth-bound spirits. This is the first area of *viññāṇa*.

---

52. **Area**: *ṭhiti:* "The place where *viññāṇa* is (or is sited)". The Commentary explains *ṭhiti* by *patiṭṭhāna*, support, base. Each area of consciousness covers one or more realms of existence, so that these seven areas together with the two "spheres" (*āyatana*) cover all the thirty-one realms of existence, (some, by implication, though not mentioned), which comprise the field of *saṃsāra*, the cycle of existences.

53. *Āyatana:* In this context, sphere, field, range. The Burmese version simply renders it as "place", the Commentary as "place or abode".

54. **Birth-linking Consciousness**: *saññā:* in this term, the semantic fields of perception and consciousness overlap. The Burmese version renders it as *paṭisandhi* (birth-linking) *saññā*, in effect equating it with birth-linking consciousness, *viññāṇa*.

55. I.e., not including the Brahmās. The text has "some devas" meaning devas who are not Brahmās.

Ānanda, there are beings with diversity of bodily form and uniformity of birth-linking Consciousness. These are Brahmās of the first *jhāna* realms. This is the second area of *viññāṇa.*

Ānanda, there are beings with uniformity of bodily form and diversity of birth-linking Consciousness. These are the Brahmās of the *Abhassara*[56] realm. This is the third area of *viññāṇa.*

Ānanda, there are beings with uniformity of bodily form and also uniformity of birth-linking Consciousness. These are the Brahmās of the *Subhakinha*[57] realm. This is the fourth area of *viññāṇa.*

Ānanda, there are the Brahmās who by concentrating on the concept 'Space is Infinite' have reached the *Ākāsānañcāyatana*[58] realm, where all forms of Consciousness that turn on corporeality (*rūpasaññā*) have been completely transcended, all forms of Consciousness arising out of contact between the senses and their objects (*paṭighasaññā*) have vanished, and other forms of Consciousness, many and varied (*nānattasaññā*), are not paid attention to. This is the fifth area of *viññāṇa.*

Ānanda, there are the Brahmās who have reached the *Viññāṇañcāyatana*[59] realm, by concentrating on the concept 'Consciousness is Infinite', having totally gone beyond the *Jhāna* of the Infinity of Space. This is the sixth area of *viññāṇa.*

Ānanda, there are the Brahmās who have reached the *Ākiñcaññāyatana*[60] realm, by concentrating on the concept 'Nothing is there', having totally gone beyond the *Jhāna* of the Infinity of Consciousness. This is the seventh area of *viññāṇa.*

(The above are the seven areas of *viññāṇa.*)

The two *āyatana* spheres are: the sphere (or place or realm) of beings devoid of *saññā*,[61] and the sphere (or place or realm) of beings with neither *saññā* nor non-*saññā* (*nevasaññānāsaññāyatana*).[62]

---

56. *Ābhassara:* radiant celestial beings. (For this and the following realms of existence, see also Appendix A5 to the Translation of Sīlakkhandha Vagga, Dīgha Nikāya.)
57. *Subhakiṇha:* lustrous.
58. *Ākāsānañcāyatana:* The realm of Infinite Space.
59. *Viññāṇañcāyatana:* The realm of Infinite Consciousness.
60. *Ākiñcaññāyatana:* The realm of Nothingness. Nothingness in this context means the vanishing of the Consciousness of the previous (*Viññānañcāyatana*) Jhāna.
61. This realm, *asaññasatta*, a state without consciousness, according to the Commentary is one of the sixteen *rūpa* realms.
62. *Nevasaññānāsaññāyatana:* The realm of neither Consciousness nor non-

128. Ānanda, of those seven areas of *viññāṇa*, Consciousness, there is the first area of *viññāṇa*, where there are beings with diversity of bodily form and diversity of birth-linking Consciousness, such as human beings, devas of the six sensual realms and some lower earth-bound spirits.

Ānanda, would it be proper for a person who knows that first area of *viññāṇa*, who also knows how it comes into being, also how it vanishes or disappears, also its attractiveness, also its danger,[63] and also how to get free of it, —for such a person, would it be proper to find pleasure in it?

"Venerable Sir, it would not be proper."[64] ... (p) ...

Ānanda, of those (two *āyatana* spheres), there is the sphere of beings devoid of *saññā*.

Ānanda, would it be proper for a person who knows that *āyatana* sphere, who also knows how it comes into being, also how it vanishes or disappears, also its attractiveness, also its danger, and also how to get free of it, — for such a person, would it be proper to find pleasure in it?

"Venerable Sir, it would not be proper."

Ānanda, of those (two *āyatana* spheres), there is the sphere of beings without (coarse or evident) *saññā*, but not without (refined, tenuous, scarcely discernible) *saññā*, (i.e., the realm of neither *saññā* nor non-*saññā*).

Ānanda, would it be proper for a person who knows that *āyatana* sphere, who also knows how it comes into being, also how it vanishes or disappears, also its attractiveness, also its danger, and also how to get free of it, — for such a person, would it be proper to find pleasure in it?

"Venerable Sir, it would not be proper."

Ānanda, because of this, the bhikkhu (who is an arahat) knows the origin, the coming into being of these seven areas of *viññāṇa* and these two *āyatana* spheres, also their disappearance, also their attractiveness, also their danger, and also how to get free of them, and knowing them as they really are, he is without attachment to them, and thus is emancipated (from *kilesas*, moral defilements).

Ānanda, such a bhikkhu is called *paññāvimutta*, one who has attained emancipation, (i.e., who has become an arahat), through Magga Insight.

Consciousness, that is without coarse or evident consciousness but not without excessively refined or tenuous consciousness, scarcely discernible.

63. **Danger**: *ādīnava:* also translated as fault, disadvantage. The danger inherent in it is due to its impermanence, changeableness and the concomitant *dukkha.*

64. What is said about the first area of *viññāṇa* applies to the remaining six areas.

(F) Eight Stages of Release

129. Ānanda, there are eight stages of Release (*Vimokkha*).[65] These are:

Contemplating the *kasiṇa* objects in one's own body, and having attained the *rūpajhāna*,[66] the mental absorption in form and matter, one contemplates (also external) forms and objects (such as *kasiṇa* objects). This is the first Release.

Not paying attention to the *kasiṇa* objects in one's own body, such as colour, form and corporeal features, one contemplates external (*kasiṇa*) forms. This is the second Release.

One applies oneself to the brightness and clarity (*subha*) of the object of intense contemplation.[67] This is the third Release.

By concentrating on the concept 'Space is Infinite' one achieves and remains in *Ākāsānañcāyatana jhāna*, where all forms of consciousness that turn on corporeality (*rūpasaññā*) have been completely transcended, all forms of consciousness arising out of contact between the senses and their objects (*paṭighasaññā*) have vanished, and other forms of consciousness, many and varied (*nānattasaññā*), are not paid attention to. This is the fourth Release.

By concentrating on the concept 'Consciousness is Infinite' one achieves and remains in the *Viññānañcāyatana jhāna*, having totally gone beyond the *jhāna* of the Infinity of Space. This is the fifth Release.

By concentrating on the concept 'Nothing is there' one achieves and remains in the *Ākiñcaññāyatana jhāna*, having totally gone beyond the *jhāna* of the Infinity of Consciousness. This is the sixth Release.

---

65. **Release**: *vimokkha*, freed of moral hindrances and defilements, but not completely rooting them out. Freedom or release through *jhāna*, mental absorption, not identical with the emancipation of an arahat as it is possible to fall from the *jhāna* state.

66. *Jhāna:* Jhāna is a kind of mental culture (usually translated Mental Absorption) in which the mind is concentrated on objects such as *kasiṇas*, and in which the hindrances (i.e., *nīvaraṇas*) are kept away from the mind (i.e., the mind is 'distanced' from hindrances). The *kasiṇa*-induced *jhāna* is mundane or worldly *jhāna*.

There are four *Rūpāvacara jhānas* and four *Arūpavacara jhānas*. The former can be practised to attain the sixteen Fine-material Realms of the Brahmās.

67. The object of intense contemplation (in the first two states) is a *kasiṇa*, whether it is a physical object (internal to the body, i.e., subjectively, or external, i.e., objectively), or an after-image resulting from prolonged fixation of consciousness on the actual *kasiṇa* object.

One achieves and remains in the *Nevasaññā-nāsaññāyatana jhāna*, the *jhāna* of neither *saññā* nor *non-saññā*, Having totally gone beyond the *jhāna* of Nothingness. This is the seventh Release.

One achieves and remains in the sustained attainment of Cessation, *Nirodha-samāpatti*, in which all forms of Consciousness cease, having totally gone beyond the *jhāna* of neither *saññā* nor *non-saññā.* This is the eighth Release.

Ānanda, these are the eight stages of Release.

130. Ānanda, the bhikkhu enters upon and attains these eight stages of Release in straightforward order, and also in reverse order, and also in straightforward and reverse order (i.e., forward and backward). He repeatedly enters upon and remains in any *jhāna* at will, anywhere at will, for any pre-determined length of time. He also rises out of the *jhāna* at will. Because of the complete destruction of the *āsavas*, moral intoxicants or taints, he realizes and attains by himself in the present life the taint-free emancipation of the mind (Arahattaphala Samādhi) as well as the Insight emancipation (Arahattaphala Paññā), through Magga Insight.

Ānanda, such a bhikkhu is called *ubhatobhāga vimutta,*[68] one who is emancipated (from all *kilesas*, moral defilements) and attains Arahatship, being free in both ways.[69]

Ānanda, there is no other emancipation (from moral defilements) in both ways that is loftier and more excellent than this emancipation (from moral defilements) in both ways.

The Bhagavā gave this discourse. Ānanda, being delighted with the discourse, received it rejoicingly.

End of the Mahānidāna Sutta, the second sutta from division two (Mahā Vagga)

---

68. *Ubhatobhāga vimutta:* one who is emancipated in both ways. There are five kinds of emancipation in both ways. Of these, emancipation in both ways after the attainment of *Nirodha samāpatti* is the loftiest and the most excellent.

69. **In both ways**: *ubhatobhāga:* (lit., in both parts) i.e., free both by the discipline of the eight stages of Release and by Insight Wisdom. The Commentary says: "both ways" means emancipation from material composite (*rūpakāya*) is attained through the repeated *arūpa jhānas;* and from mental aggregates (*nāmakāya*) through Magga Insight.

Namo tassa bhagavato arahato sammāsambuddhassa

MAHĀPARINIBBĀNA SUTTA

III. MAHĀPARINIBBĀNA SUTTA

(Discourse on the Great Event of the Passing Away of the Buddha)

131. Thus have I heard:

At one time the Bhagavā was residing at Rājagaha, on the Gijjhakūṭa[70] hill. During that time the king of Magadha, Ajātasattu, son of Queen Vedehī, wanted to attack the Vajjī princes, and declared thus: "I shall annihilate these Vajjī princes, powerful and mighty[71] as they are. I shall destroy them, bring them to utter rack and ruin."

132. Then King Ajātasattu of Magadha, son of Queen Vedehī, called to him the Chief Minister of Magadha, the brahmin Vassakāra, and said to him:

"Come, brahmin, go to the Bhagavā, and pay homage at his feet, carrying my words. Enquire whether the Bhagavā is free from illness and affliction, whether he is enjoying bodily vigour, strength, ease and comfort. Say to the Bhagavā 'Venerable Sir, King Ajātasattu of Magadha, son of Queen Vedehī, pays homage at your feet. He enquires by me whether the Bhagavā is free from illness and affliction, whether he is enjoying bodily vigour, strength, ease and comfort'. And say thus to him, 'He wishes to attack the Vajjī princes and has declared that he will annihilate the Vajjī princes, powerful and mighty as they are, and that he will destroy them and bring them to utter rack and ruin.' And carefully noting what the Bhagavā says, repeat to me his remarks. The Tathāgatas never speak what is untrue."

133. The brahmin Vassakāra, Chief Minister of Magadha, said "Very well, Your Majesty", in assent to King Ajātasattu of Magadha, son of Queen Vedehī. And he had excellent and elegant carriages harnessed, and mounting an excellent carriage, left Rājagaha for the Gijjhakūṭa hill, accompanied by other excellent carriages. After proceeding as far as the carriage might properly go, he dismounted from the carriage, and approached the Bhagavā on foot. After offering courteous greetings to the Bhagavā and having said memorable words of felicitation, the Chief Minister, the brahmin Vassakāra, seated himself on one side, and thus addressed the Bhagavā:

---

70. **Gijjhakūṭa**: mount of vultures.

71. **Powerful and mighty**, through harmonious union and military preparedness.

"Venerable Gotama, King Ajātasattu of Magadha, son of Queen Vedehī, pays homage at your feet. He enquires after (the state of) your health, your vigour, strength, ease and comfort. He wishes to attack the Vajjī princes, and has declared that he will annihilate them, powerful and mighty as they are, and that he will destroy them and bring them to utter rack and ruin."

Seven Factors of Non-Decline[72] of Kings and Princes

134. At that time the Venerable Ānanda was at the back of the Bhagavā, fanning him.

The Bhagavā said to the Venerable Ānanda:

Ānanda, do the Vajjī princes meet in assembly frequently? Do they have meetings many times? What have you heard?

"Venerable Sir, I have heard that the Vajjī princes meet in assembly frequently, and that they have meetings many times."

Ānanda, so long as the Vajjī princes assemble frequently and have many meetings, the furtherance of their welfare and prosperity is to be expected, not their decline. (1)

Ānanda, do the Vajjī princes assemble in harmony and unity and do they leave the assemblies in harmony and unity? And do they carry out the affairs of the Vajjī country in harmony and unity? What have you heard?

"Venerable Sir, I have heard that the Vajjī princes assemble in harmony and unity, that they leave the assemblies in harmony and unity, and that they carry out the affairs of the Vajjī country in harmony and unity."

Ānanda, so long as the Vajjī princes assemble and disperse in harmony and unity, and carry out in harmony and unity the affairs of the Vajjī country, the furtherance of their welfare and prosperity is to be expected, not their decline. (2)

Ānanda, do the Vajjī princes refrain from ordaining what has not been ordained before, and do they refrain from abolishing what has been ordained before, and do they act in conformity with the ancient, established Vajjī practices, customs and institutions? What have you heard?

---

72. Non-Decline or Non-Diminution: *aparihāna* from *parihāna*, lessening, decline, deterioration. The opposite is *vuddhi*, increase, growth, prosperity, furtherance.

"Venerable Sir, I have heard that the Vajjī princes refrain from ordaining what has not been ordained before, that they refrain from abolishing what has been ordained before, and that they act in conformity with the ancient, established Vajjī practices, customs and institutions."

Ānanda, so long as the Vajjī princes refrain from ordaining what has not been ordained before, refrain from abolishing what has been ordained before, and act in conformity with the ancient, established Vajjī practices, customs and institutions, the furtherance of their welfare and prosperity is to be expected, not their decline. (3)

Ānanda, do the Vajjī princes treat their elders with respect, esteem, veneration and reverence, and do they consider that those elders ought to be listened to? What have you heard?

"Venerable Sir, I have heard that the Vajjī princes treat their elders with respect, esteem, veneration and reverence, and consider that those elders ought to be listened to."

Ānanda, so long as the Vajjī princes treat their elders with respect, esteem, veneration and reverence, and consider that those elders ought to be listened to, the furtherance of their welfare and prosperity is to be expected, not their decline. (4)

Ānanda, do the Vajjī princes refrain from forcibly abducting women and maidens and detaining them? What have you heard?

"Venerable Sir, I have heard that the Vajjī princes refrain from forcibly abducting women and maidens and detaining them."

Ānanda, so long as the Vajjī princes refrain from forcibly abducting women and maidens and detaining them, the furtherance of their welfare and prosperity is to be expected, not their decline. (5)

Ānanda, do the Vajjī princes show respect, esteem, veneration and reverence towards their shrines, within and without the city, and do they cause appropriate offerings and oblations to be made to those shrines as formerly, without neglect or omission? What have you heard?

"Venerable Sir, I have heard that the Vajjī princes show respect, esteem, veneration and reverence towards their shrines, within and without the city, and that they cause appropriate offerings and oblations to be made to those shrines as formerly, without neglect or omission."

Ānanda, so long as the Vajjī princes show respect, esteem, veneration and reverence towards their shrines, within and without the city, and cause appropriate offerings and oblations to be made to those shrines as formerly, without neglect or omission, the furtherance of their welfare and prosperity is to be expected, not their decline. (6)

Ānanda, do the Vajjī princes take appropriate measures to afford proper care, protection and security to the arahats[73] so that those arahats who have not yet come to the Vajjī country may come, and so that those who have already come may live in the Vajjī country in ease and comfort? What have you heard?

"Venerable Sir, I have heard that the Vajjī princes take appropriate measures to afford proper care, protection and security to the arahats so that those arahats who have not yet come to the Vajjī country may come, and so that those who have already come may live in the Vajjī country in ease and comfort."

Ānanda, so long as the Vajjī princes take appropriate measures to afford proper care, protection and security to the arahats so that those arahats who have not yet come to the Vajjī country may come, and so that those who have already come may live in the Vajjī country in ease and comfort, the furtherance of their welfare and prosperity is to be expected, not their decline. (7)

135. Then, the Bhagavā said to the brāhmin Vassakāra, Chief Minister of Magadha:

Brahmin, at one time I was staying at the shrine called Sārandada in Vesalī. At that time I taught, the Vajjī princes these seven *aparihāniya* factors of Non-Decline.

Brahmin, so long as these seven factors of Non-Decline endure among the Vajjī princes, and so long as the Vajjī princes observe and apply these seven factors thoroughly, the furtherance of their prosperity, their welfare, is to be expected, not their decline.

Then the brahmin Vassakāra, Chief Minister of Magadha, replied thus to the Bhagavā:

"Venerable Gotama, if the Vajjī princes are endowed with even a single one of these factors of Non-Decline, the furtherance of their prosperity is to be expected, not their decline; how much more so if they should be endowed with all the seven factors!

"Venerable Gotama, there is no possibility of King Ajātasattu of Magadha, son of Queen Vedehī, overcoming the Vajjī princes in battle, unless means of cunning persuasion or of causing discord (by breaking up their unity) are employed.

"Now, Venerable Gotama, we shall depart. We have many affairs (to attend to), much to do."

---

73. **The arahats**: the Commentary implies that here the term *Arahanto* (*Arahats*) includes all ascetics who have left the home life.

Brahmin, go when you wish (lit., you know the time to go), the Bhagavā said.

Then the Chief Minister of Magadha, the brahmin Vassakāra, delighted and pleased with the Bhagavā's discourse, rose from his seat and departed.

Seven Factors of Non-Decline of Bhikkhus

136. The Bhagavā, soon after the brahmin Vassakāra, Chief Minister of Magadha, had left, said to the Venerable Ānanda, "Go, Ānanda, and let all the bhikkhus who live around Rājagaha gather in the assembly hall."

Ānanda, saying "Very well, Venerable Sir", by way of assent, caused all the bhikkhus living around Rājagaha to gather in the assembly hall, and approaching the Bhagavā and making obeisance to him stood on one side. Then Ānanda said to the Bhagavā:

"Venerable Sir, the community of bhikkhus is assembled. It is for the Bhagavā to go as and when he wishes."

Then the Bhagavā arose from where he was sitting, and going to the assembly hall and taking the seat prepared for him, addressed the bhikkhus thus:

Bhikkhus, I shall expound to you the seven factors of Non-Decline. Listen attentively and bear it well in mind. I shall speak.

The bhikkhus assenting respectfully, the Bhagavā gave this discourse:

Bhikkhus, so long as the bhikkhus meet in assembly frequently, and have meetings many times, the furtherance of their (spiritual) progress is to be expected, not its decline. (1)

Bhikkhus, so long as the bhikkhus assemble and disperse from assembly in harmony and unity, and attend to the affairs of the Saṅgha (the community of bhikkhus) in harmony and unity, the furtherance of their (spiritual) progress is to be expected, not its decline. (2)

Bhikkhus, so long as the bhikkhus do not prescribe that (viz., rules) which has not been prescribed, and do not abolish what has been prescribed, and observe well the prescribed rules (of the Discipline of Bhikkhus), conducting themselves accordingly, the furtherance of their (spiritual) progress is to be expected, not its decline. (3)

Bhikkhus, so long as the bhikkhus respect, esteem, venerate and revere the bhikkhu elders who are of long standing (in their bhikkhuhood) who had long since become bhikkhus, who are the fathers and leaders of the Saṅgha, and consider that those bhikkhu elders ought to be listened to, the furtherance of the bhikkhus' (spiritual) progress is to be expected, not its decline. (4)

Bhikkhus, so long as the bhikkhus do not fall under the power, the influence of that *taṇhā*, craving, which arises (within them) and which leads to rebirth, the furtherance of their (spiritual) progress is to be expected, not its decline. (5)

Bhikkhus, so long as the bhikkhus desire a sequestered life in remote forest dwellings, the furtherance of their (spiritual) progress is to be expected, not its decline. (6)

Bhikkhus, so long as the bhikkhus maintain mindfulness in themselves, in order that those fellow-practitioners of the life of purity who cherish virtue and who have not yet come might come, and those (of the same nature) who have come might live in comfort and ease, the furtherance of their (spiritual) progress is to be expected, not its decline. (7)

Bhikkhus, so long as these seven factors of Non-Decline endure among the bhikkhus, and so long as the bhikkhus observe and apply these seven factors thoroughly, the furtherance of the (spiritual) progress of the bhikkhus is to be expected, not its decline.

A Second Set of Seven Factors of Non-Decline

137. Bhikkhus, I shall further expound to you another set of seven factors of Non-Decline. Listen attentively to this exposition and bear it well in mind.

The bhikkhus assenting respectfully, the Bhagavā gave this discourse:

Bhikkhus, so long as the bhikkhus do not delight in, are not given to pleasure in, and make no endeavour to derive enjoyment from (mundane) activities or transactions, the furtherance of their (Spiritual) progress is to be expected, not its decline. (1)

Bhikkhus, so long as the bhikkhus do not delight in, are not given to pleasure in, and make no endeavour to enjoy idle talk, the furtherance of their (spiritual) progress is to be expected, not its decline. (2)

Bhikkhus, so long as the bhikkhus do not delight in, are not given to pleasure in, and make no endeavour to enjoy (slothfulness and) sleeping, the furtherance of their (spiritual) progress is to be expected, not its decline. (3)

Bhikkhus, so long as the bhikkhus do not delight in, are not given to pleasure in, and make no endeavour to enjoy the company of associates, the furtherance of their (spiritual) progress is to be expected, not its decline. (4)

Bhikkhus, so long as the bhikkhus are without evil desires (such as the desire to boast of non-existent attainments or achievements), and so long as they do not fall under the influence of evil desires, the furtherance of their (spiritual) progress is to be expected, not its decline. (5)

Bhikkhus, so long as the bhikkhus do not associate with evil friends or evil companions, and are not inclined towards evil companionship, the furtherance of their (spiritual) progress is to be expected, not its decline. (6)

Bhikkhus, so long as the bhikkhus do not stop halfway (before attainment of Arahatship), through achieving some small spiritual attainment, the furtherance of their (spiritual) progress is to be expected, not its decline. (7)

Bhikkhus, so long as these seven factors of Non-Decline endure among the bhikkhus, and so long as the bhikkhus observe and apply these seven factors thoroughly, the furtherance of the (spiritual) progress of the bhikkhus is to be expected, not its decline.

A Third Set of Seven Factors of Non-Decline

138. Bhikkhus, I shall further expound to you another set[74] of seven factors of Non-Decline. Listen attentively to this exposition and bear it well in mind.

The bhikkhus assenting respectfully, the Bhagavā gave this discourse:

Bhikkhus, so long as the bhikkhus are endowed with confidence based on conviction, *saddhā*,[75] the furtherance of the (spiritual) progress of the bhikkhus is to be expected, not its decline. (1)

Bhikkhus, so long as the bhikkhus have a sense of moral shame, *hiri*,[76] the furtherance of the (spiritual) progress of the bhikkhus is to be expected, not its decline.

Bhikkhus, so long as the bhikkhus have fear of wrong-doing, *ottappa*,[77] the furtherance of the (spiritual) progress of the bhikkhus is to be expected, not its decline. (3)

---

74. **Another set**: the third set consists of seven good qualities (*satta saddhammā*).
75. *Saddhā*: usually rendered 'faith' which might, however, be confused with blind faith.
76. *Hiri*: loathing of, or aversion to, immoral deeds, hence an inner sense of decency.
77. *Ottappa*: fear of committing immoral deeds, hence reflected in decent conduct.

Bhikkhus, so long as the bhikkhus have wide learning and knowledge, the furtherance of the (spiritual) progress of the bhikkhus is to be expected, not its decline. (4)

Bhikkhus, so long as the bhikkhus are firmly energetic and industrious, the furtherance of the (spiritual) progress of the bhikkhus is to be expected, not its decline. (5)

Bhikkhus, so long as the bhikkhus have sustained mindfulness, the furtherance of the (spiritual) progress of the bhikkhus is to be expected, not its decline. (6)

Bhikkhus, so long as the bhikkhus are possessed of insight and wisdom,[78] the furtherance of their (spiritual) progress is to be expected, and not its decline. (7)

Bhikkhus, so long as these seven factors of Non-Decline endure among the bhikkhus, and so long as the bhikkhus observe and apply these seven factors thoroughly, the furtherance of their (spiritual) progress is to be expected, not its decline.

A Fourth Set of Seven Factors of Non-Decline

139. Bhikkhus, I shall further expound to you another set[79] of seven factors of Non-Decline. Listen attentively to this exposition and bear it well in mind.

The bhikkhus assenting respectfully, the Bhagavā gave this discourse:

Bhikkhus, so long as the bhikkhus cultivate Mindfulness, *sati*, a factor which leads to Enlightenment, the furtherance of the (spiritual) progress of the bhikkhus is to be expected, not its decline. (1)

Bhikkhus, so long as the bhikkhus cultivate investigative knowledge of phenomena, *dhammavicaya*,[80] leading to Enlightenment, the furtherance of the (spiritual) progress of the bhikkhus is to be expected, not its decline. (2)

Bhikkhus, so long as the bhikkhus cultivate effort, *vīriya*,[81] leading to Enlightenment, the furtherance of the (spiritual) progress of the bhikkhus is to be expected, not its decline. (3)

---

78. **Insight and wisdom**: *paññāvanto*: The Commentary has "*vipassanā paññā*" i.e, Wisdom gained from Insight Meditation, not ordinary wisdom.

79. The fourth set is of the Seven Factors of Enlightenment, *satta bojjhaṅga; Bodhi*, Enlightenment, Insight into the Four Noble Truths + aṅga, factor or limb.

80. *dhammavicaya*: *dhamma*, (phenomena) here means mind and matter (*nāmarūpa*).

81. *Viriya*: same as *sammā vāyama* (Right Effort).

Bhikkhus, so long as the bhikkhus cultivate delightful satisfaction, *pīti*, leading to Enlightenment, the furtherance of the (spiritual) progress of the bhikkhus is to be expected, not its decline. (4)

Bhikkhus, so long as the bhikkhus cultivate serenity, *passaddhi*, leading to Enlightenment, the furtherance of the (spiritual) progress of the bhikkhus is to be expected, not its decline. (5)

Bhikkhus, so long as the bhikkhus cultivate Concentration, *samādhi*, leading to Enlightenment, the furtherance of the (spiritual) progress of the bhikkhus is to be expected, not its decline. (6)

Bhikkhus, so long as the bhikkhus cultivate equanimity, *upekkhā*,[82] leading to Enlightenment, the furtherance of the (spiritual) progress of the bhikkhus is to be expected, not its decline. (7)

Bhikkhus, so long as these seven factors of Non-Decline endure among the bhikkhus, and so long as the bhikkhus observe and apply these seven factors thoroughly, the furtherance of their (spiritual) progress is to be expected, not its decline.

A Fifth Set of Seven Factors of Non-Decline

140. Bhikkhus, I shall further expound to you another set[83] of seven factors of Non-Decline. Listen attentively to this exposition and bear it well in mind.

The bhikkhus assenting respectfully, the Bhagavā gave this discourse:

Bhikkhus, so long as the bhikkhus cultivate the perception of Impermanence, *anicca*, the furtherance of the (spiritual) progress of the bhikkhus is to be expected, not its decline. (1)

Bhikkhus, so long as the bhikkhus cultivate the perception of Non-Soul, Non-Ego, Non-Self, *anattā*, the furtherance of the (spiritual) progress of the bhikkhus is to be expected, not its decline. (2)

Bhikkhus, so long as the bhikkhus cultivate the perception of the corruptness, the impurity (of the body), *asubha*, the furtherance of the (spiritual) progress of the bhikkhus is to be expected, not its decline. (3)

Bhikkhus, so long as the bhikkhus cultivate the perception of the danger of all formations of existence, *ādīnava*, the furtherance of the (spiritual) progress of the bhikkhus is to be expected, not its decline. (4)

---

82. *Upekkhā*: equanimity is mental equipoise, not mere indifference. It is the result of a calm concentrative mind, a quiet mind.

83. The fifth set is a set of seven perceptions.

Bhikkhus, so long as the bhikkhus cultivate the perception of abandonment, *pahāna*,[84] the furtherance of the (spiritual) progress of the bhikkhus is to be expected not its decline. (5)

Bhikkhus, so long as the bhikkhus cultivate the perception of detachment from desire, *virāga*, the furtherance of the (spiritual) progress of the bhikkhus is to be expected, not its decline. (6)

Bhikkhus, so long as the bhikkhus cultivate the perception of cessation, *nirodha*,[85] the furtherance of the (spiritual) progress of the bhikkhus is to be expected, not its decline. (7)

Bhikkhus, so long as these seven factors of Non-Decline endure among the bhikkhus, and so long as the bhikkhus observe and apply these seven factors thoroughly, the furtherance of their (spiritual) progress is to be expected, not its decline.

Six Factors of Non-Decline of Bhikkhus

141. Bhikkhus, I shall expound to you six factors[86] of Non-Decline. Listen attentively to this exposition and bear it well in mind.

The bhikkhus assenting respectfully, the Bhagavā gave this discourse:

Bhikkhus, so long as the bhikkhus minister to fellow-disciples[87] with loving-kindness in deed and action, both openly and in private, the furtherance of their (spiritual) progress is to be expected, not its decline. (1)

Bhikkhus, so long as the bhikkhus minister to fellow-disciples with loving-kindness in speech, both openly and in private, the furtherance of their (spiritual) progress is to be expected, not its decline. (2)

Bhikkhus, so long as the bhikkhus minister to fellow-disciples with loving-kindness in thought, both openly and in private, the furtherance of their (spiritual) progress is to be expected, not its decline. (3)

Bhikkhus, so long as the bhikkhus share with virtuous fellow-disciples such offerings and gifts as they receive in accordance with the rules and prescriptions of the Order of Bhikkhus, including, to say the least, even the contents of their alms-bowl, without making use of them apart from the others, the furtherance of their (spiritual) progress is to be expected, not its decline. (4)

---

84. *Pahana*: abandonment or discarding (of *kilesas*, moral defilements).
85. *Nirodha*: cessation (of *kilesas*, moral defilements).
86. **Six factors**: *sāranīyā dhammā*, (six) conditions for happy fraternal living.
87. **Fellow-disciples**: *sabrahmacārī*: fellow practitioners of the life of purity, rendered here as fellow-disciples.

Bhikkhus, so long as the bhikkhus, both openly and in private, together with fellow-disciples in equal observance, abide by those precepts of *sīla*,[88] morality, which lead to liberation (from slavery to *taṇhā*, craving), which are praised by the wise, which are not subject to *taṇhā* and *diṭṭhi*, craving and wrong views, which are conducive to concentration of mind, and which are unbroken, intact, unblemished and unspotted, (thus complete, perfect and pure), the furtherance of the (spiritual) progress of the bhikkhus is to be expected, not its decline. (5)

Bhikkhus, so long as the bhikkhus, both openly and in private, together with fellow-disciples in equal insight, abide in that faultless and pure insight[89] which leads to Nibbāna, and which truly leads him who acts upon it to the utter destruction of *dukkha*, the furtherance of the (spiritual) progress of the bhikkhus is to be expected, not its decline. (6)

Bhikkhus, so long as these six factors of Non-Decline endure among the bhikkhus, and so long as the bhikkhus observe and apply these six factors thoroughly, the furtherance of their (spiritual) progress is to be expected, not its decline.

142. While the Bhagavā was sojourning there at the Gijjhakūṭa hill in Rājagaha, he repeatedly expounded this discourse:

"Such is *sīla*, morality; such is *samādhi*, concentration of mind; such is *paññā*, wisdom. *Samādhi*, when based upon[90] *sīla*, is rich in result and of great effect. *Paññā*, when based upon *samādhi*, is rich in result and of great effect. The mind, when developed through *paññā*, is thoroughly liberated from the *āsavas*, taints, moral intoxicants, namely, *kāmāsava*, the taint of sensuous desire, *bhavāsava*, the taint of hankering after repeated existence, and *avijjāsava*, the taint of ignorance of the true nature of existence as set out in the Four Noble Truths."

143. Then the Bhagavā, after staying at Rājagaha as long as he wished, said to the Venerable Ānanda, "Come, Ānanda, let us go to the Ambalaṭṭhikā garden."

The Venerable Ānanda assented, saying "Very well, Venerable Sir".

Then the Bhagavā, accompanied by many bhikkhus, went to the Ambalaṭṭhikā garden and stayed at the king's rest house. While there also, the Bhagavā repeatedly expounded this very discourse:

---

88. *Sīla*: in the Pāḷi text, in plural form. Forms of right conduct.

89. **Insight**: *diṭṭhi ariyā*: rendered by the Burmese version, as *ariya paññā*, faultless or pure knowledge, wisdom, insight.

diṭṭhi = *sammādiṭṭhi*, right view; *paññā* = *maggapaññā*, Magga-Insight.

90. **Based upon: developed through**: *paribhāvito*, lit., set around with.

"Such is *sīla*, morality; such is *samādhi*, concentration of mind; such is *paññā*, wisdom. *Samādhi*, when based upon *sīla*, is rich in result and of great effect. *Paññā*, when based upon *samādhi*, is rich in result and of great effect. The mind, when developed through *paññā*, is thoroughly liberated from the *āsāvas*, taints, namely, *kāmāsava*, *bhavāsava*, and *avijjāsava*."

144. Then the Bhagavā, after staying at the Ambalaṭṭhikā garden as long as he wished, said to the Venerable Ānanda, "Come, Ānanda, let us go to the town of Nāḷandā".

The Venerable Ānanda assented, saying "Very well, Venerable Sir".

Then the Bhagavā, accompanied by many bhikkhus, went to the town of Nāḷandā and stayed at the mango orchard of (the rich man) Pāvārika.

The Venerable Sāriputta's Brave Utterance[91]

145. At that time, the Venerable Sāriputta approached the Bhagavā, and having made obeisance, seated himself on one side. He said to the Bhagavā thus:

"Venerable Sir, I have this faith in the Bhagavā that there has never been, nor there is, nor there will be, any samaṇa (recluse) or brāhmaṇa (one leading a religious life), who can excel the Bhagavā in Enlightenment."

Indeed, Sāriputta, you proclaim in lofty, majestic, precise words, sounding bravely like a lion's roar, that you have this faith in the Bhagavā that there never has been, nor there is, nor there will be any samaṇa or brāhmaṇa who can excel the Bhagavā in Enlightenment.

How is it, Sāriputta; do you know definitely in your mind the minds of those Homage-Worthy, Perfectly Self-Enlightened Bhagavās of the past, to be able to say[92] "Such was their *sīla*, practice of morality, such was their mental discipline,[93] such was their *paññā*, wisdom, such was their way of living,[94] and such was their emancipation"?

---

91. **Brave Utterance**: *Sīhanāda*: The lion's roar.

92. **To be able to say**: a free rendering of *itipi:* "thus (it was)."

93. **Mental discipline**: the Pāḷi text has dhamma, which is explained by the Commentary as here referring to concentration and to the mental qualities, such as energy, mindfulness, pertaining to concentration (*samādhipakkhiyā dhammā*).

94. **Way of living**: the Commentary says this means 'the abiding in the sustained attainment of Cessation (*nirodhasamāpattivihāra*).

"I have no such knowledge, Venerable Sir."

How is it, Sāriputta; do you know definitely in your mind the minds of those Homage-Worthy, Perfectly Self-Enlightened Bhagavās of the future, to be able to say "Such will be their *sīla*, practice of morality, such will be their mental discipline, such will be their *paññā*, wisdom, such will be their way of living, and such will be their emancipation"?

"I have no such knowledge, Venerable Sir."

How is it, Sāriputta; do you by means of your mind know definitely the mind of myself, the present Buddha, the Homage-Worthy, the Perfectly Self-Enlightened, to be able to say "Such is the Bhagavā's *sīla*, such is his mental discipline, such is his *paññā*, such is his way of living, and such is his emancipation"?

"I have no such knowledge, Venerable Sir."

Sāriputta, if you do not have the *cetopariya ñāṇa*,[95] the faculty by which you can know definitely the minds of the Homage-Worthy, the Perfectly Self-Enlightened Bhagavās of the past, the future and the present, how can you proclaim in lofty, majestic, precise words, sounding like a lion's roar, to the effect that you have this faith in the Bhagavā, that there has never been, nor there is, nor there will be any samaṇa or brāhmaṇa who can excel the Bhagavā in Enlightenment?

146. "Venerable Sir, I do not have the *cetopariya ñāṇa*, the faculty by which I can know definitely the minds of the Homage-Worthy, the Perfectly Self-Enlightened Bhagavās of the past, the future and the present. But I do have the *dhammanvaya ñāṇa*, knowledge by inference from personal experience.

"Venerable Sir, if I may give an example, let us say that far away from the royal city there is a border town with firm foundations, solid walls, and a single arched gateway, and that there is a gate-keeper, wise, prudent and intelligent, who would keep out strangers and would admit only known persons.

"When that gate-keeper on his rounds along the roadway circling the town sees no breaks, no holes in the walls, not even a hole by which a cat can get through, he will come to the conclusion that all big living things who or which enter or leave the town do so only by that single gateway.

"In the same way, Venerable Sir, I am in possession of the *dhamman-vaya ñāṇa*, knowledge by inference from personal experience.

---

95. *Cetopariya ñāṇa*: knowledge of the working of another person's mind.

"Venerable Sir, (thus I know that) all the Homage-Worthy, the Perfectly Self-Enlightened Bhagavās who had arisen in the past had abandoned the five Hindrances, *nīvaraṇa*[96] which defile the mind and weaken the intellect; had well established their minds in the practice of the four Methods of Steadfast Mindfulness, *satipaṭṭhāna*;[97] had correctly cultivated the seven Factors of Enlightenment, *bojjhaṅga*;[98] and had fully attained unsurpassed, supreme Enlightenment.

"Venerable Sir, (thus I know that) all the Homage-Worthy, the Perfectly Self-Enlightened Bhagavās who will arise in the future, will abandon the five Hindrances *nīvaraṇa*, which defile the mind and weaken the intellect; will well establish their minds in the four Methods of Steadfast Mindfulness, *satipaṭṭhāna*; will correctly cultivate the seven Factors of Enlightenment, *bojjhaṅga* and will fully attain unsurpassed, supreme Enlightenment.

"Venerable Sir, (thus I know that) the Homage-Worthy, the Perfectly Self-Enlightened Bhagavā also, who has now arisen in this world, has abandoned the five Hindrances which defile the mind and weaken the intellect; has well established the Bhagavā's mind in the four Methods of Steadfast Mindfulness; has correctly cultivated the seven Factors of Enlightenment: and has fully attained unsurpassed, supreme Enlightenment."

147. While the Bhagavā was staying at the mango orchard of (the rich man) Pāvārika in the town of Nāḷandā, there, too, he gave this very discourse repeatedly, thus:

"Such is *sīla*, morality; such is *samādhi*, concentration of mind; such is *paññā*, wisdom. *Samādhi*, when based upon *sīla*, is rich in

---

96. **The five Hindrances**, *nīvaraṇa*, which obstruct or hinder the way to liberation are (1) *kāmacchanda*, sensual desires; (2) *byāpāda*, ill will, hatred or anger; (3) *thīna middha*, torpor and languor, sloth, drowsiness, stolidity, (also translated as obduracy of mind and mental factors); (4) *uddhacca-kukkucca*, restlessness and worry; and (5) *vicikicchā*, doubt, wavering.

97. **Methods of Steadfast Mindfulness**: *satipaṭṭhāna*, (*the* setting up of mindfulness). This means the cultivation of mindfulness or awareness of (1) the body, *kāya*; (2) sensations and feelings, *vedanā;* (3) mind or consciousness, *citta;* and (4) *dhamma.* This last involves various moral and intellectual subjects, such as the five Hindrances, the five Aggregates of Clinging, the twelve sense-bases, the seven Factors of Enlightenment and the Four Noble Truths.

98. **Seven Factors of Enlightenment**, *satta bojjhaṅga*: (1) mindfulness; (2) investigative knowledge of phenomena; (3) effort; (4) delightful satisfaction; (5) serenity; (6) concentration; and (7) equanimity.

result and of great effect. *Paññā*, when based upon *samādhi*, is rich in result and of great effect. The mind, when developed through *paññā*, is thoroughly liberated from the *āsavas*, taints, namely, *kāmāsava*, *bhavāsava*, and *avijjāsava*."

The Disadvantages to an Immoral Man

148. Then the Bhagavā after staying at the town of Nāḷandā as long as he wished, said to the Venerable Ānanda, "Come, Ānanda, let us go to Pāṭali village."

The Venerable Ānanda assented, saying "Very well, Venerable Sir."

Then the Bhagavā, accompanied by many bhikkhus, went to Pāṭali village.

When the lay devotees of Pāṭali village heard that the Bhagavā had arrived at their village, they approached the Bhagavā, made obeisance to him, and seated themselves on one side. They said to him, "May it please the Bhagavā to consent to sojourn in our guest-house." And by his silence the Bhagavā consented.

The lay devotees of Pāṭali village, on receiving the Bhagavā's consent, rose from their seats, made obeisance to him and respectfully departed (by keeping their right side to him) and went to their guest-house. They prepared the guest-house by covering the floor all over with floor-coverings, arranging seats, placing big water-filled pots, and setting up oil-lamps in their holders. Then they approached the Bhagavā, made obeisance to him, and standing on one side, said to him:

"Venerable Sir, at the guest-house, the floor has been fully covered with floor-coverings, the seats have been arranged, the big water-filled pots have been placed, and the oil-lamps have been set up in their holders. It is for the Bhagavā to proceed there when he wishes, (lit., The Exalted One knows the time to proceed there.)

Then the Bhagavā, at evening time, re-arranged his robes, took his alms-bowl and great robe, and proceeded to the guest-house accompanied by the bhikkhus. He entered the guest-house after washing his feet, and sat against the middle post, facing east.

The bhikkhus also washed their feet and entered the guest-house, and sat against the west wall, facing east, with the Bhagavā in front of them. The lay devotees of Pāṭali village also washed their feet and entered the guest-house, and sat against the east wall facing west, with the Bhagavā in front of them.

149. Then Bhagavā addressed the devotees of Pāṭali village thus:

Householders, the immoral man lacking moral virtue faces five disadvantages.[99] What are these five (disadvantages)?

Householders, in this world, the immoral man lacking moral virtue encounters through heedlessness great loss of wealth. This is the first disadvantage befalling the immoral man who lacks moral virtue.

Householders, in addition, the ill repute of an immoral man lacking moral virtue spreads far and wide. This is the second disadvantage befalling the immoral man who lacks moral virtue.

Householders, in addition, when the immoral man lacking moral virtue goes into any kind of society, whether it be the society of the ruling class, or of brahmins, or of well-to-do people, or of recluses, he does so with timidity and troubled demeanour. This is the third disadvantage befalling the immoral man who lacks moral virtue.

Householders, in addition, the immoral man lacking moral virtue dies in bewilderment.[100] This is the fourth disadvantage befalling the immoral man who lacks moral virtue.

Householders, in addition, the immoral man, after death and dissolution of the body, reaches (i.e., is reborn in) one of four undesirable, sub-human realms, a miserable destination, a ruinous existence, (such as) the realm of continuous intense suffering, through lacking moral virtue. This is the fifth disadvantage befalling the immoral man who lacks moral virtue.

Householders, these are the five disadvantages befalling the immoral man, through lacking moral virtue.

Advantages Accruing to a Man of Virtue

150. Householders, five advantages accrue to the man of moral virtue, through his ethical conduct. What are these five (advantages)?

Householders, in this world, the man of moral virtue, through his ethical conduct, by being heedful, gains a great mass of wealth. This is the first advantage accruing to the man of virtue, through his ethical conduct.

Householders, in addition, the good reputation of a man of virtue, through his ethical conduct, spreads far and wide. This is the second advantage accruing to the man of virtue, through his ethical conduct.

---

99. **Disadvantages:** *ādīnavā*; singular form *ādīnava*, sometimes translated as danger, fault.

100. **Bewilderment:** *sammūḷha*. The Commentary explains this as delirium.

Householders, in addition, the man of virtue, through his ethical conduct, can go into any kind of society, whether it be the society of the ruling class, or of brahmans, or of well-to-do people, or of recluses, with confidence and untroubled demeanour. This is the third advantage accruing to the man of virtue, through his ethical conduct.

Householders, in addition, the man of virtue, through his ethical conduct, dies without any bewilderment. This is the fourth advantage accruing to the man of virtue, through his ethical conduct.

Householders, in addition, the man of virtue, through his ethical conduct, after death and dissolution of the body, reaches (i.e., is reborn in) the realms of the devas, (celestial beings), a happy destination. This is the fifth advantage accruing to the man of virtue, through his ethical conduct.

151. And the Bhagavā spent the greater part of the night instructing the devotees of Pāṭali village in the Teaching, causing them to realize (the benefits of) the Dhamma, to become established in (the observance of) the Teaching, and to be filled with gladness and enthusiasm for (the practice of) the Teaching. Then he sent them away, saying "The night is far advanced, householders; it is for you to leave when you wish."

The devotees of Pāṭali village assented, saying "Very well, Venerable Sir", and arising from their seats, made obeisance to the Bhagavā and departed respectfully. Then the Bhagavā, not long after the departure of the devotees of Pāṭali village, retired in seclusion.

Founding of the (Fortified) City of Pāṭaliputta

152. At that time, (the brahmins) Sunidha and Vassakāra, chief ministers of Magadha Kingdom, were building a (fortified) city at the (site of) Pāṭali village to keep out the Vajjī princes.

During that period, many devas, in groups of a thousand each, were taking possession of plots of land at the Pāṭali village.

In the locations where the devas of great power had taken possession of plots of land, there princes and king's ministers of great power were inclined to build (lit., their minds were bent towards building) houses. And where the devas of medium power had taken possession of plots of land, there princes and king's ministers of medium power were inclined to build houses. And where the devas of lesser power had taken possession of plots of land, there princes and king's ministers of lesser power were inclined to build houses.

The Bhagavā saw by means of *dibba-cakkhu*, (the extremely clear and divine power of vision, comparable to the vision-faculty of the devas and surpassing the seeing ability of men), those devas who were gathered in groups of a thousand each and who were taking possession of plots of land in the Pāṭali village. Then the Bhagavā arose at dawn and asked the Venerable Ānanda, "Ānanda, who are building a (fortified) city at the (site of) Pāṭali village?"

"Venerable Sir, (the brahmins) Sunidha and Vassakāra, chief ministers of Magadha Kingdom, are building a (fortified) city at the (site of) Pāṭali village, to hold back the Vajjī princes."

Ānanda, it is as if they are building the fortified city in consultation with the devas of the Tāvatiṃsa realm.

Ānanda, I have seen by means of *dibba-cakkhu* many devas who are gathered in groups of a thousand each and who are taking possession of plots of land in the Pāṭali village.

Ānanda, in the locations where devas of great power have taken possession of plots of land, princes and king's ministers of great power are inclined to build (their) houses. And where devas of medium power have taken possession of plots of land, princes and king's ministers of medium power are inclined to build (their) houses. And where devas of lesser power have taken possession of plots of land, princes and king's ministers of lesser power are inclined to build (their) houses.

Ānanda, among the towns and cities which are centres of congregation and commerce of people of the Aryan race, this new town will become the greatest city, called Pāṭaliputta, a place where goods are unpacked and sold and distributed.

Ānanda, three misfortunes will befall the city of Pāṭaliputta, through fire, through flood, through internal dissension.

153. Then, the chief ministers of Magadha, (the brahmins) Sunidha and Vassakāra, went to the Bhagavā. After offering courteous greetings to the Bhagavā and having said memorable words of felicitation, the chief ministers stood on one side, and said, "Venerable Sir, may it please the Venerable Gotama to accept our offering of food for today, together with the company of bhikkhus." The Bhagavā, by silence, signified his acceptance.

Then, the Magadha chief ministers, Sunidha and Vassakāra, knowing that the Bhagavā had accepted their request, went to their house and having prepared at their house choice food and eatables, both hard and soft kinds, they informed the Bhagavā that it was time, by the message, "Venerable Gotama, it is time (to proceed), the food-offering is ready."

Then in the morning time the Bhagavā re-arranged his robes, and taking alms-bowl and great robe, went to the house of the Magadha chief ministers, Sunidha and Vassakāra, in the company of the bhikkhus, and took the seat prepared for him.

And the Magadha chief ministers, Sunidha and Vassakāra, personally attended on the Bhagavā and the bhikkhus, offering the choice food and eatables with their own hands till the Bhagavā and the bhikkhus caused them to stop, signifying they had had enough.

When the Bhagavā had finished his meal and had removed his hand from his alms-bowl, the Magadha chief ministers, Sunidha and Vassakāra, took low seats and sat down on one side.

To the Magadha chief ministers, Sunidha and Vassakāra, who were thus seated, the Bhagavā signified his pleasure and appreciation by these verses (rendered below in prose):

> "Brahmins, when the wise man offers food to those endowed with moral conduct, self-control, and purity of life, at the place where he has made his home, he should share the merit of the almsgiving with the devas of that place. (When merit is thus shared with them), the devas being honoured, honour him (the sharer of merit) in return; being revered, revere him in return. Therefore, just as a mother safeguards her own son, the devas safeguard the sharer of merit. And the person who is under the protection of the devas meets with only good fortune at all times."

After signifying his pleasure and appreciation by these verses to the Magadha chief ministers, Sunidha and Vassakāra, the Bhagavā arose from his seat and left.

154. Then, the Magadha chief ministers, Sunidha and Vassakāra, thinking "We shall call the gateway by which the Venerable Gotama leaves today the Gotama Gateway, and the landing place by which the Venerable Gotama crosses the river Ganges the Gotama Landing Place," followed the Bhagavā all along the route.

The gateway by which the Bhagavā then left came to be known as the Gotama Gateway. When the Bhagavā approached the river Ganges, the river was full to the brim so that a crow on the bank might easily drink from it.

Some people, who wanted to cross from one shore to the other, looked for boats. Others looked for log rafts. Still others built bamboo rafts.

Then, as instantaneously as a strong man stretches his bent arm or bends his outstretched arm, even so the Bhagavā vanished from this side of the Ganges and reappeared on the other shore together with the company of bhikkhus.

The Bhagavā saw the people who wanted to cross from one shore to the other looking for boats, for log rafts, or making bamboo rafts. Then, the Bhagavā, seeing them thus, uttered these exultant words:

> "The (*ariya*) persons have crossed the deep and wide river of *taṇhā*, craving, by building the bridge of *ariyāmaggañāṇa*, Noble Magga Insight, leaving behind the marshy grounds of moral defilements. As for the (non-*ariya*) persons, they have to build rafts (to cross the river). However, the wise *ariya* persons, who have crossed (the river of craving), have no more need to make rafts."

End of the first portion for recitation

The Four Noble Truths

155. Then the Bhagavā said to the Venerable Ānanda, "Come, Ānanda, let us go to Koṭi village."

The Venerable Ānanda respectfully assenting, the Bhagavā, accompanied by a large number of bhikkhus, went to Koṭi village and dwelt there. During that time, the Bhagavā addressed the bhikkhus thus:

Bhikkhus, it is through not having proper understanding and penetrative comprehension of the Four Noble Truths[101] that I as well as yourselves have had to go incessantly through this long stretch (of *saṃsāra*, round of existences), that we have had to go through one life after another continuously.

What are the Four Noble Truths that are not known properly, penetratingly? Bhikkhus, it is through not having proper understanding and penetrating comprehension of the Noble Truth of Dukkha, (*Dukkha Ariya Sacca*), that I as well as yourselves have had to go incessantly through this long stretch (of *saṃsāra*, round of existences), that we have had to go through one life after another continuously.

Bhikkhus, it is through not having proper understanding and penetrating comprehension of the Noble Truth of the Origin of Dukkha, (*Dukkha Samudaya Ariya Sacca*), that I as well as yourselves have had to go

---

101. **The Four Noble Truths**: *Dukkha Ariya Sacca, Samudaya Ariya Sacca, Nirodha Ariya Sacca*, and *Magga Ariya Sacca*.

incessantly through this long stretch of *saṃsāra*, that we have had to go through one life after another continuously.

Bhikkhus, it is through not having proper understanding and penetrating comprehension of the Noble Truth of the Cessation of Dukkha, (*Dukkha Nirodha Ariya Sacca*), that I as well as yourselves have had to go incessantly through this long stretch of *saṃsāra*, that we have had to go through one life after another continuously.

Bhikkhus, it is through not having proper understanding and penetrating comprehension of the Noble Truth of the Way to the Cessation of Dukkha, (*Dukkha Nirodha Gāmini Paṭipadā Ariya Sacca*), that I as well as yourselves have had to go incessantly through this long stretch of *saṃsāra*, that we have gone through one life after another continuously.

Bhikkhus, I have properly understood and penetratingly comprehended the Noble Truth of Dukkha. I have properly understood and penetratingly comprehended the Noble Truth of the Origin of Dukkha. I have properly understood and penetratingly comprehended the Noble Truth of the Cessation of Dukkha. I have properly understood and penetratingly comprehended the Noble Truth of the Way to the Cessation of Dukkha. The craving for existence, *bhavataṇhā*, has been cut off without any vestige remaining. The *bhavataṇhā*, which is like a rope that drags one to renewed existence, is exhausted. Now, there will be no more rebirth.

After the Bhagavā had spoken the above words, he further said these verses:

> "Existence after existence has had to be gone through in this long stretch of *saṃsāra* because of lack of understanding of the Four Noble Truths as they really are. I have now perceived the Noble Truths. The *bhavataṇhā*, craving for existence, which is like a rope dragging one to renewed existence, has been rooted out. The root of *dukkha* has been cut off without any vestige remaining. Now, there will be no more rebirth."

While the Bhagavā was thus sojourning at that Koṭi village, he repeatedly expounded to the bhikkhus this very discourse;

"Such is *sīla*, morality; such is *samādhi*, concentration of mind; such is *paññā*, wisdom. *Samādhi*, when based upon *sīla*, is rich in result and of great effect. *Paññā*, when based upon *samādhi*, is rich in result and of great effect. The mind, when developed through *paññā*, is thoroughly liberated from the *āsavas*, taints, namely, *kāmāsava*, *bhavāsava* and *avijjāsava*."

Those Who Will Reach the Higher Levels of Magga Insight without the Possibility of Returning

156. Then the Bhagavā, after staying at Koṭi village as long as he wished, said to the Venerable Ānanda, "Come, Ānanda, let us go to Nātika village."

The Venerable Ānanda respectfully assented. The Bhagavā, accompanied by a large number of bhikkhus, went to Nātika village and stayed at a brick building.

At that time the Venerable Ānanda approached the Bhagavā and after making obeisance to him, sat on one side and asked the Bhagavā these questions:

"Venerable Sir, at Nātika village a bhikkhu by the name of Sāḷha has passed away. What is his destination, *gati*?[102] What is his next existence?

"Venerable Sir, at (this same) Nātika village, a bhikkhunī[103] named Nandā has passed away. What is her destination, *gati*? What is her next existence?

"Venerable Sir, at (this same) Nātika village, a devotee named Sudatta has passed away. What is his destination? What is his next existence?

"Venerable Sir, at (this same) Nātika village, a female devotee named Sujātā has passed away. What is her destination? What is her next existence?

"Venerable Sir, at (this same) Nātika village, a devotee named Kukkuṭa has passed away. What is his destination? What is his next existence?

"Venerable Sir, at (this same) Nātika village, a devotee named Kāḷimba has passed away. What is his destination? What is his next existence?

"Venerable Sir, at (this same) Nātika village, a devotee named Nikaṭa has passed away. What is his destination? What is his next existence?

"Venerable Sir, at (this same) Nātika village, a devotee named Kaṭissaha has passed away. What is his destination? What is his next existence?

"Venerable Sir, at (this same) Nātika village, a devotee named Tuṭṭha has passed away. What is his destination? What is his next existence?

---

102. *Gati*: in this context, course after death. *Gati* means literally 'going', that is, going from life to life, by way of rebirth.

103. *Bhikkhunī*: a female bhikkhu.

"Venerable Sir, at (this same) Nātika village, a devotee named Santuṭṭha has passed away. What is his destination? What is his next existence?

"Venerable Sir, at (this same) Nātika village, a devotee named Bhadda has passed away. What is his destination? What is his next existence?

"Venerable Sir, at (this same) Nātika village, a devotee named Subhadda has passed away. What is his destination? What is his next existence?"

157. Ānanda, the bhikkhu Sāḷha, due to the extinction of the *āsavas*,[104] moral intoxicants, taints, was an arahat, who in this very life had attained to the taint-free emancipation of the mind (*Arahattaphala Samādhi*), and to the Insight emancipation (*Arahattaphala Paññā*), having realized this emancipation for himself through Magga Insight.

Ānanda, the bhikkhunī Nandā, through the complete destruction of the five Fetters, *samyojana*,[105] which lead to rebirth in the lower sensuous realms, is an Anāgāmi. She has arisen spontaneously[106] in the Brahmā realm, and being an Anāgāmi. a Never-Returner, with no possibility of returning from that realm to existence in any form or in any other realm, will finally pass away in the realization of Nibbāna in that very realm.

Ānanda, the devotee named Sudatta, through the complete destruction of three Fetters, *samyojana*, and the lessening of *rāga* (passion), *dosa* (hatred), and *moha* (bewilderment), is a Sakadāgāmī, a Once-Returner, who will make an end of *dukkha*, after returning to this realm of human beings only once.

Ānanda, the woman devotee named Sujātā, through the complete destruction of three Fetters, is a Sotāpanna, a Stream-Winner, who is not liable to fall into realms of misery and suffering (*apāya*) assured of a good destination and of attaining (the three higher levels of Insight, culminating in) Enlightenment.

Ānanda, the devotee named Kukkuṭa, through the complete destruction of the five Fetters which lead to (rebirth in) the lower sensuous realms, is an Anāgāmī. He has arisen spontaneously in the Brahmā realm, and being an Anāgāmi, a Never-Returner, with no possibility of returning from that realm to existence in any form or in any other realm, will finally pass away in the realization of Nibbāna in that very realm.

---

104. *Āsavas*: see para 249 of Sāmaññaphala Sutta.

105. *Samyojana*: fetter. See Appendix B 1.

106. **Spontaneously**: *opapātika:* arisen or reborn without being conceived in or issuing from a womb, appearing suddenly in complete mature form.

Ānanda, the devotee named Kāḷimba, the devotee named Nikaṭa, the devotee named Kaṭissaha, the devotee named Tuṭṭha, the devotee named Santuṭṭha, the devotee named Bhadda, the devotee named Subhadda, each, through the complete destruction of the five Fetters which lead to (rebirth in) the lower sensuous realms, is an Anāgāmi. Each (of them) has arisen spontaneously in the Brahmā realm and being an Anāgāmi, a Never-Returner, with no possibility of returning from that realm to existence in any form or in any other realm, will finally pass away in the realization of Nibbāna in that very realm.

Ānanda, over fifty devotees from Nātika village who have died are Anāgāmis through the complete destruction of the five Fetters which lead to (rebirth in) the lower sensuous realms. They have arisen spontaneously in the Brahmā realm and being Anāgāmis, Never-Returners, with no possibility of returning from that realm to existence in any form or in any other realm, will finally pass away in the realization of Nibbāna in that very realm.

Ānanda, over ninety devotees from Nātika village who have died are Sakadāgāmis, Once-Returners, through the complete destruction of the three lower Fetters, and the lessening of passion, hatred and bewilderment (*moha*). They will make an end of *dukkha* after returning to this realm of human beings only once.

Ānanda, over five hundred devotees from Nātika village who have died are Sotāpannas, Stream-Winners, through the complete destruction of the three lower Fetters. They are not liable to fall into realms of misery and suffering, and are assured of a good destination and of attaining (the three higher levels of Insight, culminating in) Enlightenment.

Exposition of the 'Mirror of Wisdom'

158. Ānanda, there is nothing strange in this. Ānanda, if the Tathāgata were to be approached every time a person dies, and asked about this matter (i.e., the destination or next existence of that person), it would only be tiresome for him.

Therefore, Ānanda, I shall expound this discourse on the Mirror of Wisdom, (i.e., Mirror of Magga Insight).

An *ariya* disciple who is fully endowed with this Mirror of Wisdom, can, if he wishes to, say of himself, "For me there is no possibility of being reborn in the realm of continuous suffering (*niraya*), or in the realm of animals, or in the realm of famished spirits (*peta*), or of falling to ruin in (any of) the sub-human, miserable realms (*apāya*). I have become a

Sotāpanna, not liable to fall into realms of misery and suffering; assured am I of a good destination and of attaining (the three higher levels of Insight, culminating in) Enlightenment."

159. Now, Ānanda. what is this Mirror of Wisdom, possessing which the *ariya* disciple can, if he wishes to, say of himself, "For me there is no possibility of being reborn in the realm of continuous suffering (*niraya*), or in the realm of animals, or in the ream of famished spirits (*peta*), or of filling to ruin in (any of) the subhuman, miserable realms (*apāya*). I have become a Sotāpanna, not liable to fall into realms of misery and suffering; assured am I of a good destination and of attaining (the three higher levels of Insight, culminating in) Enlightenment."

In this matter, Ānanda, the *ariya* disciple has unshakable perfect faith[107] in the Bhagavā, (and reflects on the attributes of the Bhagavā thus:)

"The Bhagavā is worthy of special veneration (*Arahaṃ*); he truly comprehends all the dhammas by his own intellect and insight (*Sammāsambuddha*);[108] he possesses supreme knowledge and perfect practice of morality (*Vijjācaraṇa- saṃpanna*); he speaks only what is beneficial and true (*Sugata*); he knows all the three *lokas* (*Lokavidū*); he is incomparable in taming those who deserve to be tamed (*Anuttaro purisa dammasārathi*); he is the Teacher of devas and men (*Satthā devamanussānaṃ*); he is the Enlightened One, knowing and teaching the Four Noble Truths (*Buddha*); and he is the Most Exalted (*Bhagavā*)."

The Ariya disciple has unshakable perfect faith in the *Dhamma*, (and reflects on the attributes of the *Dhamma* thus:)

"The Teaching of the Bhagavā, the *Dhamma*, is well-expounded, *Svākkhata*, (because it is the exposition of the Four Noble Truths which lead to the realization of Nibbāna). Its truths are personally apperceivable, *Sandiṭṭhika*, (because they can actually be experienced and comprehended by anyone through adequate practice of Insight development). It is not delayed in its results, *Akālika*, (because it

---

107. **Faith**: *aveccappasādena*, with 'perfect, absolute' (*avecca*) (ava+i+tva); 'serene satisfaction in, confidence in, inclination of the heart towards' (*pasāda*). Although this term is rendered here as 'faith', for the sake of readability of the text, it is not blind faith, unquestioning acceptance on trust, but rather 'confidence based on conviction, on reason'.

108. *Sammāsambuddha*: He who has attained *Sabbaññutaññāṇa*, Perfect Wisdom through self-enlightenment. An abridged rendering is "The Perfectly Self-Enlightened".

immediately yields the benefit of realization of Nibbāna, i.e., achieving *phala* immediately after *magga*, to anyone who adequately practices Insight development). It can stand investigation, *Ehipassika*, (lit., come and see), (because its truths can be tested by anyone). It is worthy of being perpetually borne in mind *Opāneyyika.* And its truths can be realized and experienced by the *ariyas* individually, by their own effort and practice, *Paccattaṃ Veditabba Viññūhi.*

The Ariya disciple has unshakable perfect faith in the Saṅgha, (and reflects on the attributes of the Saṅgha thus:)

"The disciples of the Bhagavā, the Saṅgha, are endowed with right practice, *Suppaṭipanna*, (because the Saṅgha practice the right practice, i.e., the development of the Noble Path of Eight Constituents). They are endowed with straightforward uprightness, *Ujuppaṭipanna*, (because the Saṅgha diligently and unswervingly follow the Straight Middle Way, i.e., the Noble Path of Eight Constituents). They are endowed with right conduct, *Ñāyappaṭipanna*, (because the practice of the Saṅgha is solely directed to the realization of Nibbāna). They are endowed with correctness in practice, *Sāmīcippaṭipanna*, (because the Saṅgha devotedly cultivate the development of the Noble Path of Eight Constitucnts).Thc disciples of the Bhagavā, the Saṅgha, consisting of eight categories or four pairs[109] of disciples of the Bhagavā, are worthy of receiving offerings brought even from afar, *Āhuneyya.* They are worthy of receiving offerings specially set aside for guests, *Pāhuneyya.* They are worthy of receiving offerings donated for well-being in the next existence. *Dakkhiṇeyya*; and are worthy of receiving obeisance, *Añjalikaraṇiya.* They are the incomparably fertile field for all to sow the seed of merit, *Anuttaraṃ puññakkhettaṃ lokassa.*"

The *ariya* disciple is endowed with *sīla*, morality, which leads to liberation from slavery *to taṇhā*, craving; which is praised by the wise; which is untarnished (by *taṇhā* and *diṭṭhi*, craving and wrong view); which is conducive to concentration of mind; which is unbroken, intact, unblemished and unspotted and which is cherished by the *ariyas.*

Ānanda, a noble (*ariya*) disciple who is fully endowed with (lit., who completely possesses) this Mirror of Wisdom, can, if he wishes to, say of

109. **Four pairs**: there are eight categories of disciples, namely: four attainers of Magga-ñāṇa, and four attainers of Phala-ñāṇa. Magga-ñāṇa is the flash of Insight into Nibbāna, and Phala-ñāṇa is the Fruition or repeated Insight into Nibbāna; and so attainers of Magga-ñāṇa and Phala-ñāṇa come in pairs. Hence four pairs.

himself, "For me there is no possibility of being reborn in the realm of continuous suffering (*niraya*), or in the realm of animals, or in the realm of famished spirits (*peta*), or of falling to ruin (in any) of the sub-human, miserable realms (*apāya*). I have become a Sotāpanna, not liable to fall into realms of misery and suffering; assured am I of a good destination and of attaining (the three higher levels of Insight, culminating in) Enlightenment." This is the exposition of the Mirror of Wisdom.

While the Bhagavā was sojourning at the brick building at that Nātika village, too, he repeatedly expounded this very discourse:

"Such is *sīla*, morality; such is *samādhi*, concentration of mind; such is *paññā*, wisdom. *Samādhi*, when based upon *sīla*, is rich in result and of great effect. *Paññā*, when based upon *samādhi*, is rich in result and of great effect. The mind, when developed through *paññā*, is thoroughly liberated from the *āsavas*, moral intoxicants, taints, namely, *kāmāsava*, the taint of sensuous desire, *bhavāsava*, the taint of hankering after repeated existence, and *avijjāsava*, the taint of ignorance of the true nature of existence as set out in the Four Noble Truths."

160. Then the Bhagavā, after staying at Nātika village as long as he wished, said to the Venerable Ānanda, "Come, Ānanda, let us go to Vesālī."

The Venerable Ānanda assented, saying "Very well, Venerable Sir."

Then the Bhagavā, accompanied by many bhikkhus, went to Vesālī, and stayed at Ambapālī's grove. At that time the Bhagavā addressed the bhikkhus thus:

Bhikkhus, a bhikkhu should live with mindfulness and clear comprehension. This is our exhortation to you. How is the bhikkhu to be mindful? Bhikkhus, the bhikkhu (i.e., the disciple) following the practice of my Teaching keeps his mind steadfastly on the body (*kāya*), with diligence, comprehension and mindfulness, (and perceives its impermanent, insecure, soulless and unpleasant nature), thus keeping away covetousness and distress (which will appear if he is not mindful of the five khandhas). He keeps his mind steadfastly on sensation (*vedanā*), ... (p) ... (and perceives its impermanent, insecure, and soulless nature). He concentrates steadfastly on the mind (*citta*), ... (p) ... He keeps his mind steadfastly on the dhamma[110] with diligence, comprehension and mindfulness, (and perceives their impermanent, insecure, and soulless

---

110. *Dhammā*: The five *dhammas* consisting of (1) five *nīvaraṇas*; (2) five *khandhas*; (3) twelve *āyatanas*; (4) seven *bojjhaṅgas*; and (5) four *ariya saccas*. See Mahāsatipaṭṭhāna Sutta.

nature), thus keeping away covetousness and distress (which will appear if he is not mindful of the five khandhas). Bhikkhus, this is how the bhikkhu is to be mindful.

Bhikkhus, how does a bhikkhu exercise clear comprehension? Bhikkhus, the bhikkhu following the practice of my Teaching exercises clear comprehension in moving forward or back; in looking straight ahead or sideways; in bending or stretching; in carrying or wearing the double-layered robe, alms-bowl and the other two robes; in eating, drinking, chewing, savouring (food and beverages); in defecating and urinating; in walking, standing, sitting, falling asleep, waking, speaking, or in keeping silent. Bhikkhus, this is how the bhikkhu exercises clear comprehension. Bhikkhus, the bhikkhu should remain in mindfulness and clear comprehension. This is our exhortation to you.

Ambapālī, the Courtesan

161. Ambapālī, the courtesan, heard that the Bhagavā had arrived at Vesālī and that the Bhagavā was staying at her mango grove. Then Ambapālī, the courtesan, caused excellent and elegant carriages to be harnessed, and mounting an excellent carriage, left Vesālī for her mango grove, accompanied by other excellent carriages. After going in the carriage as far as carriages should properly go, she dismounted from her carriage and approached the Bhagavā on foot. She made obeisance to the Bhagavā and sat on one side.

And the Bhagavā, by his discourse to Ambapālī sitting on one side, caused her to realize (the benefits of) the Dhamma, to become established in (the observance of) the Teaching, and to be filled with gladness and enthusiasm for (the practice of) the Teaching.

After the Bhagavā had caused her to realize (the benefits of) the Teaching, to become established in (the observance of) the Teaching, and to be filled with gladness and enthusiasm for (the practice of) the Teaching, Ambapālī, the courtesan, said to the Bhagavā, "Venerable Sir, may it please the Bhagavā to accept my offering of food for tomorrow, together with the company of bhikkhus." The Bhagavā, by silence, signified his acceptance.

Then, Ambapālī, the courtesan, knowing that the Bhagavā had accepted her request, rose from her seat, made obeisance to the Bhagavā, and left respectfully.

The Licchavī princes who were at Vesālī heard that the Bhagavā had reached Vesālī and was staying at the orchard of Ambapālī. Then the

Licchavī princes caused excellent and elegant carriages to be harnessed, mounted them, and accompanied by other elegant carriages, left Vesālī.

Of these (Licchavī princes) some princes were dressed in dark-blue clothes, with dark-blue ornaments, presenting a dark-blue appearance.

Some princes were dressed in yellow clothes, with yellow ornaments, presenting a yellow appearance.

Some princes were dressed in red clothes, with red ornaments, presenting a red appearance.

Some princes were dressed in white clothes, with white ornaments, presenting a white appearance.

Then, Ambapālī, the courtesan, let her carriage strike against the carriages of the young Licchavī princes, axle against axle, wheel against wheel, yoke against yoke.

Then the Licchavī princes said to Ambapālī the courtesan, "Now then, Ambapālī! Why do you let your carriage strike against the carriages of the young Licchavī princes, axle against axle, wheel against wheel, yoke against yoke?"

"It is indeed this way, O my Princes. It is because I have invited the Bhagavā to a meal tomorrow, together with the company of bhikkhus."

"Now then, Ambapālī! Give us (in exchange) for a hundred thousand (the opportunity to offer) this meal (to the Bhagavā)."

"O my Princes, even if you were to give me Vesālī together with its (subject) territories, I could not give up (the opportunity to offer) this meal."

Then the Licchavī princes, fluttering their fingers (in admiration), exclaimed "O Sirs, we have been defeated by a woman! We have been outdone by a woman!"

Then the Licchavī princes went to the orchard of Ambapālī. The Bhagavā saw the Licchavī princes coming, from a distance, and said to the bhikkhus:

"O Bhikkhus, let those bhikkhus who have never seen the Tāvatiṃsa devas,[111] have a good look at the gathering of the Licchavīs; let them take a long look at the assembly of the Licchavis; let the bhikkhus gaze on them as if they were the Tāvatiṃsa devas."

Then the Licchavī princes went in their carriages as far as carriages should properly proceed, and then alighting from their carriages, went

111. The Tāvatiṃsa realm is the second, in ascending order, of the six realms of the devas, the lower celestial beings (the Brahmās being the higher celestial beings).

on foot to where the Bhagavā was. They made obeisance to the Bhagavā and seated themselves at a suitable place.

The Bhagavā, by his discourse to the Licchavī princes, caused them to realize (the benefits of) the Teaching, to become established in (the observance of) the Teaching, and to be filled with gladness and enthusiasm for (the practice of) the Teaching.

After the Bhagavā had caused them to realize (the benefits of) the Teaching, to become established in (the observance of) the Teaching, and to be filled with gladness and enthusiasm for (the practice of) the Teaching, the Licchavī princes said to the Bhagavā, "Venerable Sir, may it please the Bhagavā to accept our offering of food for tomorrow, together with the company of bhikkhus." Then the Bhagavā said to them, "O Licchavī princes, I have already accepted the offering of food for tomorrow by Ambapālī, the courtesan."

Then the Licchavī princes fluttered their fingers, exclaiming "O Sirs, we have been defeated by a woman! We have been outdone by a woman!"

After that, the Licchavī princes, being delighted with and showing appreciation of the Bhagavā's discourse, rose from their seats, made obeisance to the Bhagavā, and departed respectfully.

162. Then Ambapālī, the courtesan, after that night had passed, caused choice food and eatables of both hard and soft kinds to be prepared in her orchard, and then informed the Bhagavā that it was time for the meal by sending the message, "Venerable Sir, it is time; the food-offering is ready." Then the Bhagavā rearranged his robes suitably, and taking alms-bowl and great robe went in the forenoon to the house of Ambapālī, the courtesan, accompanied by the company of bhikkhus, and (on arriving there) took the seat prepared for him.

And Ambapālī, the courtesan, personally attended on the bhikkhus headed by the Bhagavā, offering choice hard and soft food with her own hands till the Bhagavā and the bhikkhus caused her to stop, signifying they had had enough.

When the Bhagavā had finished his meal and had removed his hand from his alms-bowl Ambapālī, the courtesan, took a low seat and sat down on one side. Then she said to the Bhagavā, "Venerable Sir, I give this orchard in donation to the community of bhikkhus headed by the Buddha." The Bhagavā accepted the donation of the orchard.

Then, after causing Ambapālī, the courtesan, by his discourse to realize (the benefits of) the Teaching, to become established in (the observance of) the Teaching, and to be filled with gladness and enthusiasm for (the practice of) the Teaching, the Bhagavā arose from his seat and departed.

While the Bhagavā was sojourning at the orchard of Ambapālī, the courtesan, in Vesālī, there too he repeatedly expounded this very discourse:

"Such is *sīla*, morality; such is *samādhi*, concentration of mind; such is *paññā*, wisdom. *Samādhi*, when based upon *sīla*, is rich in result and of great effect. *Paññā*, when based upon *samādhi*, is rich in result and of great effect. The mind, when developed through *paññā*, is thoroughly liberated from the *āsāvas*, moral intoxicants, taints, namely, *kāmāsava*, the taint of sensuous desire, *bhavāsava*, the taint of hankering after (repeated) existence, and *avijjāsava*, the taint of ignorance (of the true nature of existence as set out in the Four Noble Truths)."

Spending the Vassa at Veḷuva Village

163. The Bhagavā, after staying at the orchard of Ambapālī, the courtesan, as long as he wished, said to the Venerable Ānanda, "Come, Ānanda, let us go to the village called Veḷuva."

The Venerable Ānanda respectfully assented, saying "Very well, Venerable Sir."

Then the Bhagavā went to Veḷuva village with a great many bhikkhus, and while there, said to the bhikkhus:

"Come, bhikkhus, enter upon the residence period of the reins (*vassa*) in places where you have friends, acquaintances and intimates in the neighbourhood of Vesālī.

"As for me, I shall enter upon the residence period of the rains in this Veḷuva village itself."

The bhikkhus assented respectfully, saying "Very well, Venerable Sir", and entered upon the residence period of the rains in places where they had friends, acquaintances and intimates in the neighbourhood of Vesālī. The Bhagavā himself entered upon the residence period of the rains in Veḷuva village itself.[112]

164. Some time after the Bhagavā had entered upon the residence period of the rains, there arose in him a severe illness and he suffered excessive pain, near unto death. This the Bhagavā endured, with mindfulness and clear comprehension, and without being perturbed.

---

112. According to the Commentary, the Buddha made this arrangement because he realized that he would pass away into *parinibbāna* in ten months' time.

Then the Bhagavā had this thought: "It would not be proper for me to pass away in the realization of Nibbāna without letting the attendant bhikkhus know, without taking leave of the community of bhikkhus. (Therefore) I should ward off this illness by effort (of Insight meditation, *vipassanā bhāvanā*) and abide in the life-maintaining *phala samāpatti* (sustained absorption in Fruition attainment)."[113] Then the Bhagavā warded off his illness by effort (of *vipassanā bhāvanā*) and abided in the life-maintaining *phala samāpatti.* The Bhagavā's illness subsided.

Then the Bhagavā, having recovered from his illness, came out from his monastery soon after his recovery, and sat in the shade of the monastery on the seat prepared for him.

Then the Venerable Ānanda approached the Bhagavā, made obeisance, and having seated himself on one side, said thus to the Bhagavā:

"Venerable Sir, I see the Bhagavā now at ease. I find the Bhagavā now in good health. Though I now see the Bhagavā thus, when the Bhagavā was ill my body felt heavy and stiff; my sight in all directions became dim; I became bewildered, unable to grasp doctrines (such as on the methods of steadfast mindfulness). However, I took some small comfort from the thought that the Bhagavā would not pass away into *parinibbāna* so long as he had not left any instructions concerning the community of bhikkhus."

165. Ānanda, what does the community of bhikkhus still expect from me? Ānanda, I have set forth the Teaching without any distinction of inner or outer doctrine. The *Tathāgatas*, Ānanda, in (the matter of) their Teaching do not hold anything secret in the closed fist of a teacher, (i.e., do not keep back anything).

Ānanda, if a person should desire that he alone should lead the community of bhikkhus, or that the community of bhikkhus should depend on him alone, then it is that person who should lay down instructions concerning the community of bhikkhus.

But Ānanda, the *Tathāgata* has no such thought or desire that he alone should lead the community of bhikkhus, or that the community of bhikkhus should depend on him alone. Having no such thought or desire, why should the *Tathāgata* leave any instructions concerning the community of bhikkhus?

---

113. Just before entering into the *phala samāpatti*, the Buddha made the resolution that he would live for the next ten months free of severe illness which would result in death. (The Commentary) He thereby postponed for ten months the time of his final passing away (*parinibbāna*).

Ānanda, I am now frail, old, aged, far gone in years, and in the last stage of life. I have reached the eightieth year. Just as, Ānanda, a worn-out old cart is held together merely by bindings and repairs, so the body of the *Tathāgata* is held together merely by (the force of) the *phala-samāpatti.*

Ānanda, it is (only) when the *Tathāgata* attains and is abiding in the *animitta*[114] Concentration of Mind (in the *Arahatta phala samāpatti*), through not paying attention to any phenomenal image[115] and through the cessation of some sensations (i.e., mundane sensations) that the Tathāgata's body is at real ease and comfort (lit., at greater ease).

Therefore, Ānanda, let yourselves be[116] your own firm support,[117] and let yourselves, and not anyone or anything else, be your refuge; let the *Dhamma*, the Teaching, be your firm support, and let the *Dhamma*, and not anything else, be your refuge.

Ānanda, how is the bhikkhu to make himself his own firm support, and to make himself, and not anyone or anything else, his refuge; (how is he) to make the *Dhamma* his firm support, and to make the *Dhamma*, and not anything else, his refuge?

Ānanda, the bhikkhu (i.e., the disciple) following the practice of my Teaching keeps his mind steadfastly on the body (*kāya*), with diligence, comprehension and mindfulness, (and perceives its impermanent, insecure, soulless and unpleasant nature), thus keeping away covetousness and distress (which will appear if he is not mindful of the five khandhas). He keeps his mind steadfastly on sensation (*vedanā*), (and perceives its impermanent, insecure and soulless nature). He concentrates steadfastly on the mind (*citta*). He keeps his mind steadfastly on the dhamma[118] with diligence, comprehension, and mindfulness, (and perceives their impermanent, insecure and soulless nature), thus keeping away covetousness and distress (which will appear if he is not mindful of the five khandhas).

---

114. *Animitta*: disregarding signs or attributes of phenomena.

115. **Phenomenal image**: all signs, i.e., objects or ideas pertaining to the five khandhas.

116. **Let yourselves be**: *vihāratha*: lit., dwell (making yourselves your own firm base).

117. **Firm support**: *attadīpa:* be yourselves your island, support. An island in an ocean offers firm ground for standing on. (The Commentary)

118. See footnotes to Para 160.

Ānanda, thus the bhikkhu makes himself his own firm support and makes himself, and not anyone or anything else, his refuge; thus the bhikkhus makes the *Dhamma*, the Teaching, his firm support, and makes the *Dhamma*, and not anything else, his refuge.

Ānanda, those bhikkhus who, either now or after my passing away, make themselves their own firm support, and make themselves, and not anyone or anything else, their refuge; who make the *Dhamma* their firm support and make the *Dhamma*, and not anything else, their refuge, — all such bhikkhus, among all the bhikkhus who are desirous of (keeping to) right practice, shall reach the highest, noblest state.[119]

End of the second portion for recitation

Spoken Signs and Intimations

166. Then the Bhagavā, rearranging his robes in the morning time, took alms-bowl and great robe and went into Vesālī on his alms-round.

After his alms-round and after his meal, leaving the place of eating, the Bhagavā said to the Venerable Ānanda, "Ānanda, bring a leather rug (lit., thing to sit on); let us go to the Cāpāla shrine to spend the day (there)."

The Venerable Ānanda respectfully assented, and taking a leather rug, followed closely behind the Bhagavā.

Then the Bhagavā approached the Cāpāla shrine and seated himself on the seat placed for him. The Venerable Ānanda, making obeisance to the Bhagavā, seated himself at a suitable place.

167. To the Venerable Ānanda, who was seated on one side, the Bhagavā said thus:

Ānanda, pleasant is the country of Vesālī. Pleasant are the shrines of Udena, Gotamaka, Sattamba, Bahuputta, Sārandada, Cāpāla.

Ānanda, whosoever has cultivated, practiced, used as a means (lit., a vehicle), based himself on, maintained, mastered (lit., studied well), and perfectly developed the four Bases of Psychic Power,[120]

---

119. **The highest, noblest state**: *tamatagge*: According to the Commentary, *tamatagge* = *tama agge*, = *aggatamā*, the highest, the most eminent state reached by practising the *Satipaṭṭhāna*, the four Methods of Steadfast Mindfulness.

120. **The four Bases of Psychic Power**: *cattāro* (four) *iddhi* (Psychic Power or Potency) *pādā* (bases). These four are concentration, coupled with determination, on purpose, on will, on thoughts, and on investigative knowledge.

could, if he so desired, live the maximum life-span[121] or even beyond the maximum life-span.

Ānanda, the Tathāgata has cultivated, practiced, used as a means (lit., a vehicle), based himself on, maintained, mastered (lit., studied well), and perfectly developed the four Bases of Psychic Power. Therefore, Ānanda, the Tathāgata could, if he so desired, live the maximum life-span or even beyond the maximum life-span.

Although the Bhagavā thus gave plain intimations and hints, the Venerable Ānanda was unable to understand their significance, and failed to appeal to the Bhagavā in this way:

"Venerable Sir, may the Bhagavā live the maximum life-span! May the Sugata live the maximum life-span, for the welfare and happiness of mankind, out of compassion for the world, for the benefit, well-being and happiness of devas and men!" It was as if his mind was possessed by Māra.

For a second time, the Bhagavā said thus: ... (p) ...

For a third time, the Bhagavā said thus: Ānanda, pleasant is the country of Vesālī. Pleasant are the shrines of Udena, Gotamaka, Sattamba, Bahuputta, Sārandada, Cāpāla.

Ānanda, whosoever has cultivated, practiced, used as a means (lit., a vehicle), based himself on, maintained, mastered (lit., studied well), and perfectly developed the four Bases of Psychic Power, could, if he so desired, live the maximum life-span or even beyond the maximum life-span.

Ānanda, the Tathāgata has cultivated, practiced, used as a means (lit., a vehicle), based himself on, maintained, mastered (lit., studied well), and perfectly developed the four Bases of Psychic Power. Therefore, Ānanda, the Tathāgata could, if he so desired, live the maximum life-span or even beyond the maximum life-span.

Although the Bhagavā thus gave plain intimations and hints, the Venerable Ānanda was unable to understand their significance, and failed to appeal to the Bhagavā in this way:

"Venerable Sir, may the Bhagavā live the maximum life-span! May the Sugata live the maximum life-span, for the welfare and happiness of mankind, out of compassion for the world, for the benefit, well-being and happiness of devas and men!" It was as if his mind was possessed by Māra.

---

121. The maximum life-spin: (āyu*kappa*): the Commentary's rendering of *kappa*, which in some other context means 'world-cycle'or 'aeon'.

Then the Bhagavā said to the Venerable Ānanda, "Go now. Ānanda. Now you know the time to go."

The Venerable Ānanda respectfully assented, saying "Very well, Venerable Sir," arose from his seat, made obeisance to the Bhagavā, and left respectfully. He went and sat at the foot of a certain tree not very far away.

Māra's Request

168. Soon after the Venerable Ānanda had left the Bhagavā, the evil Māra approached the Bhagavā, and standing at a certain place, thus said to the Bhagavā:

"Venerable Sir, let the Bhagavā realize parinibbāna now by passing away! Let the Sugata realize parinibbāna! It is time now for the Bhagavā to pass away and realize parinibbāna.

"Venerable Sir, (at one time) the Bhagavā had indeed said (to me) these words: 'O Evil One, I shall not pass away so long as my disciples, the bhikkhus, are not yet accomplished in learning, not yet well-schooled (in control of deed, word and thought), not yet confident, not yet endowed with wide knowledge and learning, not yet able to remember or memorize the Teaching (lit., to carry the Teaching), not yet able to practice fully according to the Teaching (by means of Vipassanā, Insight Meditation leading to the attainment of Magga), not yet endowed with correctness in practice, not yet able to live (lit., walk) in perfect conformity with righteousness and truth,[122] not yet able to expound, to set forth, to make known, to establish, to make clear, to analyse or explain in detail, and to make manifest or evident their Teacher's doctrine or teaching, not yet able to refute by means of correct or proper reasons other doctrines, views or beliefs that may arise, and are not yet able to expound, to set forth the wonderful, sublime Teaching.'

"Venerable Sir, the Bhagavā's disciples, the bhikkhus, are now accomplished in learning, are well-schooled (in control of deed, word and thought), are confident, are endowed with wide knowledge and learning, are able to memorize the Teaching, are able to practice fully according to the Teaching, are endowed with correctness in practice, are able to live in perfect conformity with righteousness and truth, are able to expound, to set forth, to make known, to establish, to make clear,

---

122. **To live in ... truth**: *anudhammacārino*; *anudhamma* = in conformity with the highest stage of *vipassanā* meditation leading to *magga*; *cārino* = in the habit of practicing.

to analyse or explain in detail, and to make manifest or evident their Teacher's doctrine or teaching, are able to refute by means of correct reasons other doctrines, views or beliefs that may arise, and are able to expound the wonderful, sublime Teaching.

"Venerable Sir, (therefore) let the Bhagavā realize parinibbāna now by passing away! Let the Sugata realize parinibbāna! It is time now for the Bhagavā to pass away and realize parinibbāna.

"Venerable Sir, (at one time) the Bhagavā had indeed said (to me) these words: O Evil One, I shall not pass away so long as my female disciples, the bhikkhunīs, are not yet accomplished in learning, not yet well-schooled (in control of deed, word and thought), not yet confident, not yet endowed with wide knowledge and learning, not yet able to remember or memorize the Teaching (lit., to carry the Teaching), not yet able to practice fully according to the Teaching, not yet endowed with correctness in practice, not yet able to live (lit., walk) in perfect conformity with righteousness and truth, not yet able to expound, to set forth, to make known, to establish, to make clear, to analyse or explain in detail, and to make manifest or evident their Teacher's doctrine or teaching, not yet able to refute by means of correct or proper reasons other doctrines, views or beliefs that may arise, and are not yet able to expound, to set forth the wonderful, sublime Teaching.

"Venerable Sir, the Bhagavā's female disciples, the bhikkhunīs, are now accomplished in learning, are well-schooled (in control of deed, word and thought), are confident, are endowed with wide knowledge and learning, are able to memorize the Teaching, are able to practice fully according to the Teaching, are endowed with correctness in practice, are able to live in perfect. conformity with righteousness and truth, are able to expound, to set forth, to make known, to establish, to make clear, to analyse or explain in detail, and to make manifest or evident their Teacher's doctrine or teaching, are able to refute by means of correct reasons other doctrines, views or beliefs that may arise, and are able to expound the wonderful, sublime Teaching.

"Venerable Sir, (therefore) let the Bhagavā realize parinibbāna now by passing away! Let the Sugata realize parinibbāna! It is time now for the Bhagavā to pass away and realize parinibbāna.

"Venerable Sir, (at one time) the Bhagavā had indeed said (to me) these words: 'O Evil One, I shall not pass away so long as my lay-disciples are not yet accomplished in learning, not yet well-schooled (in control of deed, word and thought), not yet confident, not yet endowed with wide knowledge and learning, not yet able to remember or memorize the Teaching (lit., to carry the Teaching), not yet able to practice fully according to the Teaching, not yet endowed with correctness in practice, not yet able to live (lit., walk) in perfect conformity with righteousness and truth, not yet able to expound, to set forth, to make known, to establish, to make clear, to analyse or explain in detail, and to make manifest or evident their Teacher's doctrine or teaching, not yet able to refute by means of correct or proper reasons other doctrines, views or beliefs that may arise, and are not able to expound, to set forth the wonderful, sublime Teaching.'

"Venerable Sir, the Bhagavā's lay-disciples are now accomplished in learning, are well-schooled (in control of deed, word and thought), are confident, are endowed with wide knowledge and learning, are able to memorize the Teaching, are able to practice fully according to the Teaching, are endowed with correctness in practice, are able to live in perfect conformity with righteousness and truth, are able to expound, to set forth, to make known, to establish, to make clear, to analyse or explain in detail, and to make manifest or evident their Teacher's doctrine or teaching, are able to refute by means of correct reasons other doctrines, views or beliefs that may arise, and are able to expound the wonderful, sublime Teaching.

"Venerable Sir, (therefore) let the Bhagavā realize parinibbāna now by passing away! Let the Sugata realize parinibbāna! It is time now for the Bhagavā to pass away and realize parinibbāna.

"Venerable Sir, (at one time) the Bhagavā had indeed said (to me) these words: 'O Evil One, I shall not pass away so long as my female lay-disciples are not yet accomplished in learning, not yet well-schooled (in control of deed, word and thought), not yet confident, not yet endowed with knowledge and learning, not yet able to remember or memorize the Teaching (lit., to carry the Teaching), not yet able to practice fully according to the Teaching, not yet endowed with correctness in practice, not yet able to live (lit., walk) in perfect conformity with righteousness and truth, not yet able to expound, to set forth, to make known, to establish, to make clear, to analyse or explain in detail, and to make manifest or evident their Teacher's doctrine or teaching, not yet able to refute by means of correct or proper reasons other doctrines, views or beliefs that may arise, and are not yet able to expound, to set forth the wonderful, sublime Teaching.'

"Venerable Sir, the Bhagavā's female lay-disciples are now accomplished in learning, are well-schooled (in control of deed, word and thought), are confident, are endowed with wide knowledge and learning, are able to memorize the Teaching, are able to practice fully according to the Teaching, are endowed with correctness in practice, are able to live in perfect conformity with righteousness and truth, are able to expound, to set forth, to make known, to establish, to make clear, to analyse or explain in detail, and to make manifest Or evident their Teacher's doctrine or teaching, are able to refute by means of correct reasons other doctrines, views or beliefs that may arise, and are able to expound the wonderful, sublime Teaching.

"Venerable Sir, (therefore) let the Bhagavā realize parinibbāna now by passing away! Let the Sugata realize parinibbāna! It is time now for the Bhagavā to pass away and realize parinibbāna.

"Venerable Sir, (at one time) the Bhagavā had indeed said (to me) these words: 'O Evil One, I shall not pass away so long as this (Teaching of mine which should be termed the) Practice of Purity is not yet complete in effectiveness, not yet prosperous, renowned, prevalent among people, and widespread, to the extent that it can be thoroughly manifested, explained or made known by (wise) devas and men.'

"Venerable Sir, the Bhagavā's Teaching, fit to be termed the Practice of Purity, is now complete in effectiveness, is now prosperous, renowned, prevalent among people, and widespread, to the extent that it can be thoroughly manifested, explained or made known by (wise) devas and men.

"Venerable Sir, (therefore) let the Bhagavā realize parinibbāna now by passing away! Let the Sugata realize parinibbāna! It is time now for the Bhagavā to pass away and realize parinibbāna."

When this was said, the Bhagavā said to Māra, the Evil One, "You, Evil One, do not be anxious. Before long the parinibbāna of the Tathāgata will take place. Three months from today, the Tathāgata will realize parinibbāna."

Renunciation of the Life-Sustaining Mental Process

169. Then the Bhagavā, while at the Cāpāla shrine, decided mindfully and deliberately to give up[123] the life-sustaining mental process by not re-entering into *phalasamāpatti* (after three months). When the Bhagavā renounced the life-sustaining mental process, there

123. **Decided ... to give up**: In the Pāḷi Text 'gave up': *ossaji*, p.t. of *ossajati*: to let loose, give up, release; hence, by implication renounce.

occurred a great earthquake, terrible, hair-raising and goosefleshcausing in its dreadfulness. Also, rolls of thunder burst forth continuously.

Then the Bhagavā, perceiving this occurrence, uttered at that instant these exultant verses:

"The Buddha,[124] considering and weighing repeated existence against the incomparable and immeasurable Nibbāna, has renounced the existence-producing kammic volitions.[125] With delight in Insight Meditation and with absolute calm of mind, he has destroyed the network of *kilesas*, moral defilements, covering him like a coat of chain-mail."

Causes of Earthquakes

170. Then, this thought occurred to the Venerable Ānanda:

"O Sirs, wonderful it is! O Sirs, unprecedentedly marvellous it is! This dreadful and hair-raising earthquake is indeed a great earthquake. It is stupendous. Also, rolls of thunder burst forth continuously. What is the cause of great earthquakes? What is the condition leading to great earthquakes?"

The Venerable Ānanda then approached the Bhagavā, and after paying obeisance to him, and seating himself on one side, said to the Bhagavā thus:

"Venerable Sir, wonderful it is! Venerable Sir, unprecedentedly marvellous it is! This dreadful and hair-raising earthquake is indeed a great earthquake. It is stupendous. Also, rolls of thunder burst forth continuously. What is the cause of great earthquakes? What is the condition leading to great earthquakes?"

171. Ānanda, there are eight causes of, or conditions leading to, great earthquakes. What are the eight (causes)?

Ānanda, this great earth is supported by water, the water by air, the air by space. At times great winds blow strongly. When great winds blow strongly, the water is shaken. When the water is shaken, the earth is shaken. This is the first cause of, the first condition leading to, the occurrence of great earthquakes. (1)

Again, Ānanda, a samaṇa (recluse, ascetic) or a brāhmaṇa[126] (a man of religious pursuit), who has great (mental) power, and who is proficient

---

124. **The Buddha**: the term used here is *Muni*, one who has attained perfection in self-restraint and insight.

125. **Existence-producing kammic volitions**: *bhava-saṅkhāra*: the volitional activities leading to new existence.

126. *Brāhmaṇa*: a man leading a pure, ascetic life, free from demeritorious acts.

in the supernormal powers of the mind,[127] or a deva of great power and psychic potency, by developing intense concentration on the limited image of the earth-element[128] and on the unlimited image of the water-element, causes this earth to quake, to sway violently, to rock up and down and to convulse. This is the second cause of, the second condition leading to, the occurrence of great earthquakes. (2)

Again, Ānanda, when a Future Buddha, mindfully and deliberately, passes away in the Tusitā deva realm and is conceived in his mother's womb, this earth quakes, sways violently, rocks up and down, and is convulsed. This is the third cause of, the third condition leading to, the occurrence of great earthquakes. (3)

Again, Ānanda, when a Future Buddha, mindfully and deliberately, issues from the mother's womb, this earth quakes, sways violently, rocks up and down, and is convulsed. This is the fourth cause of, the fourth condition leading to, the occurrence of great earthquakes. (4)

Again, Ānanda, when a Tathāgata attains the most supreme Perfect Enlightenment, this earth quakes, sways violently, rocks up and down, and is convulsed. This is the fifth cause of, the fifth condition leading to, the occurrence of great earthquakes. (5)

Again, Ānanda, when a Tathāgata sets the noblest Wheel of the Dhamma in motion (by expounding the first discourse, on the Four Noble Truths), this earth quakes, sways violently, rocks up and down, and is convulsed. This is the sixth cause of, the sixth condition leading to, the occurrence of great earthquakes. (6)

Again, Ānanda, when a Tathāgata, mindfully and deliberately, decides to give up the life-sustaining mental process, *āyusaṅkhāra*, this earth quakes, sways violently, rocks up and down, and is convulsed. This is the seventh cause of, the seventh condition leading to, the occurrence of great earth-quakes. (7)

Again, Ānanda, when a Buddha passes away and enters upon parinibbāna, by experiencing the ultimate peace, *nibbānadhātu*, with

---

Here, a brahmin (of the brahmin religion or caste) is not meant.

127. **Proficient ... mind**: *cetovasippata*: lit., with mastery over one's mind. The Commentary explains this as "having cultivated and exercised the *abhiññā* (super-normal mental power)".

128. **Intense concentration on the earth**-element: *pathavīsaññā* is paraphrased as "developing earth-consciousness, that is, the *kasiṇa jhāna* (mental cultivation or mental absorption) with the earth-element as the object (*kasiṇa*) of the meditation."

complete extinction of the five khandhas, *anupādisesa*, this earth quakes, sways violently, rocks up and down, and is convulsed. This is the eighth cause of, the eighth condition leading to, the occurrence of great earthquakes. (8)

Ānanda, these are the eight causes of, the eight conditions leading to, the occurrence of great earthquakes.

Eight Categories of Assemblies

172. Ānanda, there are eight categories of assemblies. These are: assembly of nobles, assembly of brahmins, assembly of householders, assembly of recluses, assembly of the devas of the Cātumahārājika[129] deva realm, assembly of the devas of the Tavatiṃsa[130] deva realm, assembly of the devas led by Māra,[131] and assembly of the Brahmās.

Ānanda, I remember having attended hundreds of assemblies of nobles. In these assemblies I sat together with them, conversed with them, and had discussions with them. My appearance was like their appearance, and my voice was like their voice.[132] By religious discourse I caused them to realize (the benefits of) the Teaching, to become established in (the observance of) the Teaching and to be filled with gladness and enthusiasm for (the practice of) the Teaching. While I was thus discoursing, they did not know me, wondering "Who is this discoursing? Is he deva or man?" After I had caused them to realize (the benefits of) the Teaching, to become established in (the observance of) the Teaching and to be filled with gladness and enthusiasm for (the practice of) the Teaching, I vanished from there. Also when I vanished thus, they did not know me, wondering "Who was he that vanished thus? Was he deva or man?"

Ānanda, I remember having attended hundreds of assemblies of brahmins ... (p) ... (repeated as above). Ānanda, I remember having attended hundreds of assemblies of householders ... (p) ... (repeated as above). Ānanda, I remember having attended hundreds of assemblies of

129. **Cātumahārājika**: the lowest of the six deva realms, ruled by four Great Deva Kings.

130. **Tāvatimsa**: the second deva realm, next to the above.

131. There is only one Māra, a leader of the sixth and highest deva realm. He is symbolic of sensual pleasures.

132. Because of the supernormal powers of the Buddha, his form and his voice appeared to the nobles, etc., as those of one of them.

recluses; ... (p) ... of the Cātumahārājika devas; ... (p) ... of the Tāvatimsa devas; ... (p) ... of the devas led by Mara; ... (p) ... of the Brahmās.

In these assemblies also, I sat together with them, conversed with them and had discussions with them. My appearance was like their appearance, and my voice was like their voice. By religious discourse I caused them to realize (the benefits of) the Teaching, to become established in (the observance of) the Teaching and to be filled with gladness and enthusiasm for (the practice of) the Teaching. While I was thus discoursing, they did not know me, wondering "Who is this discoursing? Is he deva or man?" After I had caused them to realize (the benefits of) the Teaching, to become established in (the observance of) the Teaching, and to be filled with gladness and enthusiasm for (the practice of) the Teaching, I vanished from there. Also when I vanished thus, they did not know me, wondering, "Who was he that vanished thus? Was he deva or man?"

Ānanda, these are the eight categories of assemblies.

Eight Ways of Mastery

173. Ānanda, there are eight ways of overcoming the opposite phenomena and sense-objects,[133] *abhibhāyatana jhāna.* What are these eight? These are (as follows):

A person[134] concentrates on colour on (parts of) his own body, (such as colour of hair, eye, skin), and on finite external forms (such as *kasiṇa*[135] forms), unblemished or blemished (lit., with good or bad colour). He is thus aware that he knows and sees these (*kasiṇa*) forms[136] with mastery[137] over them. This is the first *abhibhāyatana jhāna.* (1)

---

133. **Sense-objects**: i.e., objects of kasiṇa meditation, including object of consciousness; opposite phenomena: i.e., hindrances, *nīvaraṇas.*

134. **A person**: one who has an extremely sharp intellect, among those who can quickly attain the desired *jhāna.*

135. *Kasiṇa*: objects of intense meditation. What is perceived in the mind's eye are the after-images arising through concentration.

136. The awareness of these forms expressed by the words 'knows and sees', takes place before or after a *jhāna.*

137. **With mastery**: *abhibuyya,* (lit., overcoming); i.e., with great facility, enabling the yogi who practises this meditation to enter into a *jhāna* immediately after achieving the umblemished mental image of a particular *kasiṇa* object (*paṭibhāga nimitta*).

A person concentrates on colour on (parts of) his own body (such as colour of hair, eye, skin), and on infinite external forms, (such as *kasiṇa* forms), umblemished or blemished. He is thus aware that he knows and sees these (*kasiṇa*) forms with mastery over them. This is the second *abhibhāyatana jhāna.* (2)

A person, without concentrating on colour on (parts of) his own body, concentrates on finite external forms (such as *kasiṇa* forms), umblemished or blemished. He is thus aware that he knows and sees these (*kasiṇa*) forms with mastery over them. This is the third *abhibhāyatana jhāna.* (3)

A person, without concentrating on colour on (parts of) his own body, concentrates on infinite external forms (such as *kasiṇa* forms), umblemished or blemished. He is thus aware that he knows and sees these (*kasiṇa*) forms with mastery over them. This is the fourth *abhibhāyatana Jhāna.* (4)

A person, without concentrating on colour on (parts of) his own body, concentrates on external (*kasiṇa*) forms that "are dark-blue, with a dark-blue colour, dark-blue hue, and dark-blue lustre, like the *ummāpuppha*[138] flower which is dark-blue, and has a dark-blue colour, dark-blue hue, dark-blue lustre, or like fine cloth made in Bārāṇasī, with a smooth finish on both sides, which is dark-blue, and has a dark-blue colour, dark-blue hue, dark-blue lustre. In this way, a person, without concentrating on colour on (parts of) his own body, concentrates on external (*kasiṇa*) forms that are dark-blue, with a dark-blue colour, dark-blue hue, and dark-blue lustre. He is thus aware that he knows and sees these (*kasiṇa*) forms with mastery over them. This is the fifth *abhibhāyatana jhāna.* (5)

A person, without concentrating on colour on (parts of) his own body, concentrates on external (*kasiṇa*) forms that are yellow, with a yellow colour, yellow hue, and yellow lustre, like the *kaṇikārapuppha*[139] flower which is yellow and has a yellow colour, yellow hue, yellow lustre, or like fine cloth made in Bārāṇasī, with a smooth finish on both sides, which is yellow, and has a yellow colour, yellow hue, yellow lustre. In this way, a person, without concentrating on colour on (parts of) his own body, concentrates on external (*kasiṇa*) forms that are yellow, with a yellow colour, yellow hue, and yellow lustre. He is thus aware that he

138. **Ummāpupphā**: flax blossom. Another interpretation is the flower of the butterfly pea.

139. **Kaṇikārapuppha**: the wild champak flower.

knows and sees these (*kasiṇa*) forms with mastery over them. This is the sixth *abhibhāyatana jhāna.* (6)

A person, without concentrating on colour on (parts of) his own body, concentrates on external (*kasiṇa*) froms that are red, with a red colour, red hue, and red lustre, like the *bandhujīvakapuppha*[140] flower which is red, and has a red colour, red hue, red lustre, or like fine cloth made in Bārāṇasī, with a smooth finish on both sides, which is red, and has a red colour, red hue, red lustre. In this way, a person, without concentrating on colour on (parts of) his own body, concentrates on external (*kasiṇa*) forms that are red, with a red colour, red hue, and red lustre. He is thus aware that he knows and sees these (*kasiṇa*) forms with mastery over them. This is the seventh *abhibhāyatana jhāna.* (7)

A person, without concentrating on colour on (parts of) his own body, concentrates on external (*kasiṇa*) forms that are white, with a white colour, white hue, and white lustre, like the Morning Star which is white, and has a white colour, white hue, white lustre, or like fine cloth made in Bārāṇasī, with a smooth finish on both sides, which is white, and has a white colour, white hue, white lustre. In this way, a person, without concentrating on colour on (parts of) his own body, concentrates on external (*kasiṇa*) forms that are white, with a white colour, white hue, and white lustre. He is thus aware that he knows and sees these (*kasiṇa*) forms with mastery over them. This is the eighth *abhibhāyatana jhāna.* (8)

Ānanda, these are the eight ways of overcoming the opposite phenomena and sense-objects, *abhibhāyatana jhāna.*[141]

---

140. **Bandhujīvakapuppha**: flower of the tree Pentapetes phoenicea.

141. This *abhibhāyatana jhāna* is not a separate *jhāna.* It is one of the *rūpa jhānas.* The distinctive feature of the *abhibhāyatana jhāna* is that it takes as its *kasiṇa* objects only the four colours of dark-blue, yellow, red and white, from amongst the forty kinds of objects of meditation. In abhidhamma, the four primary elements, namely, *pathavī, āpo, tejo, vāyo,* are also considered to be objects of meditation for this *abhibhāyatana jhāna.* This *abhibhāyatana jhāna* can be achieved only by those who can quickly attain the desired *jhāna,* and even from amongst them only by those with the sharpest intellect.

Abhibhāyatana jhāna is a special term employed when the attainment of *jhāna* immediately follows the achievement of the unblemished mental image of a particular *kasiṇa* object (*paṭibhāga nimitta*).

Of these eight ways of *abhibhāyatana jhāna,* the first four exercise mastery over the finite or infinite objects of *kasiṇa* meditation, both internal and external. The last four exercise mastery over the unblemished mental image

Eight Stages of Release

174. Ānanda, there are eight stages of Release (*Vimokkha*).[142] These are:

Contemplating the *kasiṇa* objects in one's own body, and having attained the *rūpa jhāna*,[143] the mental absorption in form and matter, one contemplates (also external) forms and objects (such as *kasiṇa* objects). This is the first Release. (1)

Not paying attention to the *kasiṇa* objects in one's own body, such as colour, form and corporeal features, one contemplates external (*kasiṇa*) forms. This is the second Release. (2)

One applies oneself to the brightness and clarity (*subha*) of the object of intense contemplation.[144] This is the third Release (3)

By concentrating on the concept, 'Space is Infinite' one achieves and remains in *Ākāsānañcāyatana jhāna* where all forms of consciousness that turn on corporeality (*rūpasaññā*) have been completely transcended, all forms of consciousness arising out of contact between the senses and their objects (*paṭighasaññā*) have vanished, and other forms of consciousness, many and varied (*nānattasaññā*), are not paid attention to. This is the fourth Release. (4)

By concentration on the concept 'Consciousness is Infinite' one achieves and remains in the *Viññāṇañcāyatana jhāna*, having totally gone beyond the *jhāna* of the Infinity of Space. This is the fifth Release. (5)

---

derived from a particular *kasiṇa* object. Their object of concentration is an external *kasiṇa* form, and the unblemished mental image is derived also from an external *kasiṇa* object. (See also Appendix B 2.)

142. **Release**: *vimokkha*, release through being freed of moral hindrances and defilements but not completely rooting them out; freedom or release through *jhāna*, mental absorption, not identical with the emancipation of an arahat as it is possible to fall from the *jhāna* stage. (See also Appendix B 3.)

143. *Jhāna* is a kind of mental culture (usually translated Mental Absorption) in which the mind is concentrated on objects such as *kasiṇas*, and in which the hindrances (i.e., *nīvaraṇas*) are kept away from the mind (i.e., the mind is 'distanced' from hindrances). The *kasiṇa*-induced *jhāna* is mundane or worldly *jhāna*.

There are four *Rūpavacara jhānas* and four *Arūpavacara jhānas*. The former can be practised to attain the sixteen Fine-material Realms of the Brahmās.

144. The object of intense contemplation (in the first two stages) is a *kasiṇa*, whether it is a physical object (internal to the body, i.e., subjectively, or external, i.e., objectively), or an after-image resulting from prolonged fixation of consciousness on the actual *kasiṇa* object.

By concentrating on the concept 'Nothing is there' one achieves and remains in the *Ākiñcaññāyatana jhāna*, having totally gone beyond the *jhāna* of the Infinity of Consciousness. This is the sixth Release. (6)

One achieves and remains in the *Nevasaññānāsaññāyatana jhāna*, the *jhāna* of neither *saññā* nor *non-saññā* having totally gone beyond the *jhāna* of Nothingness. This is the seventh Release. (7)

One achieves and remains in sustained attainment of Cessation, *Nirodha-samāpatti*, in which all forms of Consciousness cease, having totally gone beyond the *jhāna* of neither *saññā* nor non-*saññā*. This is the eighth Release. (8)

Ānanda, these are the eight stages of Release.

175. Ānanda, at one time, soon after I attained Enlightenment, (in the eighth week after Enlightenment),[145] I was staying at the foot of the goatherd's banyan tree near the bank of the Nerañjarā River, in Uruvela wood. While I was there the Evil Māra approached me, and standing at a certain place, said to me thus:

"Venerable Sir, let the Bhagavā realize parinibbāna now by passing away! Let the Sugata realize parinibbāna! It is time now for the Bhagavā to pass away and realize parinibbāna."

Ānanda, I replied thus to the Evil Māra:

"O Evil One, I shall not pass away so long as my disciples, the bhikkhus, are not yet accomplished in learning, not yet well-schooled (in control of deed, word and thought), not yet confident, not yet endowed with wide knowledge and learning, not yet able to remember or memorize the Teaching (lit., to carry the Teaching), not yet able to practice fully according to the Teaching, not yet endowed with correctness in practice, not yet able to live (lit., walk) in perfect conformity with righteousness and truth,[146] not yet able to expound, to set forth, to make known, to establish, to make clear, to analyse or explain in detail, and to make manifest or evident their Teacher's doctrine or teaching, not yet able to refute by means of correct or proper reasons other doctrines, views or beliefs that may arise, and are not yet able to expound, to set forth the wonderful, sublime Teaching.

"O Evil One, I shall not pass away so long as my female disciples, the bhikkhunīs, are not yet accomplished in learning, not yet well-schooled (in control of deed, word and thought), not yet confident, not yet endowed with wide knowledge and learning, not yet able to

145. As explained in the Commentary.

146. See footnote to Para 168.

remember or memorize the Teaching (lit., to carry the Teaching), not yet able to practice fully according to the Teaching, not yet endowed with correctness in practice, not yet able to live (lit., walk) in perfect conformity with righteousness and truth, not yet able to expound, to set forth, to make known, to establish, to make clear, to analyse or explain in detail, and to make manifest or evident their Teacher's doctrine or teaching, not yet able to refute by means of correct or proper reasons other doctrines, views or beliefs that may arise, and are not yet able to expound, to set forth the wonderful, sublime Teaching.

"O Evil One. I shall not pass away so long as my lay-disciples are not yet accomplished in learning, not yet well-schooled (in control of deed, word and thought), not yet confident, not yet endowed with wide knowledge and learning, not yet able to remember or memorize the Teaching (lit., to carry the Teaching), not yet able to practice fully according to the Teaching, not yet endowed with correctness in practice, not yet able to live (lit., walk) in perfect conformity with righteousness and truth, not yet able to expound, to set forth, to make known, to establish, to make clear, to analyse or explain in detail, and to make manifest or evident their Teacher's doctrine or teaching, not yet able to refute by means of correct or proper reasons other doctrines, views or beliefs that may arise, and are not yet able to expound, to set forth the wonderful, sublime Teaching.

"O Evil One, I shall not pass away so long as my female lay-disciples are not yet accomplished in learning, not yet well-schooled (in control of deed, word and thought), not yet confident, not yet endowed with wide knowledge and learning, not yet able to remember or memorize the Teaching (lit., to carry the Teaching), not yet able to practice fully according to the Teaching, not yet endowed with correctness in practice, not yet able to live (lit., walk) in perfect conformity with righteousness and truth; not yet able to expound, to set forth, to make known, to establish, to make clear, to analyse or explain in detail, and to make manifest or evident their Teacher's doctrine or teaching, not yet able to refute by means of correct or proper reasons other doctrines, views or beliefs that may arise, and are not yet able to expound, to set forth the wonderful, sublime Teaching.

"O Evil One, I shall not pass away so long as this (Teaching of mine which should be termed the) Practice of Purity is not yet complete in effectiveness, not yet prosperous, renowned, prevalent among people, and widespread, to the extent that it can be thoroughly manifested, explained or made known by (wise) devas and men."

176. Ānanda, the Evil Māra just now this day came to me at the Cāpāla shrine, and standing at a certain place, again said to me:

"Venerable Sir, let the Bhagavā realize parinibbāna now by passing away! Let the Sugata realize parinibbāna! It is now time for the Bhagavā to pass away and realize parinibbāna.

"Venerable Sir, (at one time) the Bhagavā had said (to me) these words: 'O Evil One, I shall not pass away so long as my disciples, the bhikkhus, ... (p) ... (repeated, as in Para 168); my female disciples, the bhikkhunīs, ... (p) ... (repeated); my lay-disciples ... (p) ... (repeated); my female lay-disciples ... (p) ... the wonderful, sublime Teaching.

O Evil One, I shall not pass away so long as this (Teaching of mine which should be termed the) Practice of Purity is not yet complete in effectiveness, not yet prosperous, renowned, prevalent among people, and widespread, to the extent that it can be thoroughly manifested, explained or made known by (wise) devas arid men.'

"Venerable Sir, the Bhagavā's Teaching, fit to be termed the Practice of Purity, is now complete in effectivenesses now prosperous, renowned, prevalent among people, and widespread, to the extent that it can be thoroughly manifested, explained or made known by (wise) devas and men. Venerable Sir, (therefore) let the Bhagavā realize parinibbāna now by passing away! Let the Sugata realize parinibbāna! It is time now for the Bhagavā to pass away and realize parinibbāna."

177. Ānanda, when this was said to me by the Evil Māra, I replied thus:

"You, Evil One, do not be anxious. Before long the parinibbāna of the Tathāgata will take place. Three months from today, the Tathāgata will realize parinibbāna."

Ānanda, now the Tathāgata, while at the Cāpāla shrine today, has decided, mindfully and deliberately, to give up the life-sustaining mental process (three months from now).

The Venerable Ānanda's Appeal

178. When the Bhagavā said this, the Venerable Ānanda appealed to the Bhagavā thus:

"Venerable Sir, for the welfare and happiness of mankind, out of compassion for the world and for the benefit, well-being and happiness of devas and men, may the Bhagavā live the maximum life-span! May the Sugata live the maximum life-span!"

And the Bhagavā answered: "Enough, Ānanda. Do not implore the Tathāgata (only) now. The time is past, Ānanda, for such entreaty."

For a second time and a third time, the Venerable Ānanda repeated his entreaty, thus: "Venerable Sir, for the welfare and happiness of mankind, out of compassion for the world, and for the benefit, well-being and happiness of devas and men, may the Bhagavā live the maximum life-span! May the Sugata live the maximum life-span!"

Ānanda, do you have faith in the enlightenment-wisdom[147] of the Tathāgata?

"I do, Venerable Sir."

Then, in spite of your belief, Ānanda, why do you harass the Tathāgata (by insisting) up to three times?

"Venerable Sir, I have heard these words of the Bhagavā from the Bhagavā himself; I have listened to (lit., received) these words from the Bhagavā himself:

'Ānanda, whosoever has cultivated, practiced, used as a means (lit., a vehicle), based himself on, maintained, mastered (lit., studied well), and perfectly developed the four Bases of Psychic Power, could if he so desired live the maximum life-span or even beyond the maximum life-span. Ānanda, the Tathāgata has cultivated, practiced, used as a means, based himself on, maintained, mastered, and perfectly developed the four Bases of Psychic Power. Therefore, the Tathāgata could if he so desired live the maximum life-span or even beyond the maximum life-span.' (Thus I have heard.)"

Do you believe this, Ānanda?

"I believe it, Venerable Sir."

Ānanda, though the Tathāgata thus gave plain hints and intimations, you were unable to grasp their significance. You did not beseech the Tathāgata (in such words as) 'Venerable Sir, for the welfare and happiness of mankind, out of compassion for the world, and for the benefit, well-being and happiness of devas and men, may the Bhagavā live the maximum life-span, may the Sugata live the maximum life-span.'

Therefore, Ānanda, this failure to entreat me (to continue to live) is your own fault, your own remissness.

Ānanda, if you had entreated me (thus) at that time, the Tathāgata might have refused the entreaty twice but might have acceded to the entreaty on the third time. Therefore, Ānanda, this (failure to entreat me) is your own fault, your own remissness,

---

147. Enlightenment-wisdom: *bodhi*, the Magga Insight possessed by a Buddha, as explained here by the Commentary. The Sub-Commentary explains this as Sabbaññuta Ñāṇa, Perfect Wisdom.

179. Ānanda, at one time I was dwelling on the Gijjhakūṭa hill in Rājagaha. While there, too, Ānanda, I had spoken these words to you: 'Pleasant, Ānanda, is Rājagaha; pleasant, Ānanda, is the Gijjhakūṭa hill. Ānanda, whosoever has cultivated, practiced, used as a means, based himself on, maintained, mastered and perfectly-developed the four Bases of Psychic Power, could if he so desired live the maximum life-span or even beyond the maximum life-span. Ānanda, the Tathāgata has cultivated, practiced, used as a means, based himself on, maintained, mastered and perfectly developed the four Bases of Psychic Power. Therefore, the Tathāgata could if he so desired live the maximum life-span or even beyond the maximum life-span.

Ānanda, though the Tathāgata thus gave plain hints and intimations, you were unable to grasp their significance. You did not beseech the Tathāgata (in such words as) 'Venerable Sir, for the welfare and happiness of mankind, out of compassion for the world, and for the benefit, well-being and happiness of devas and men, may the Bhagavā live the maximum life-span, may the Sugata live the maximum life-span."

Ānanda, if you had entreated me (thus) at that time, the Tathāgata might have refused the entreaty twice but might have acceded to the entreaty on the third time. Therefore, Ānanda, this (failure to entreat me) is your own fault, your own remissness

180. Ānanda, at one time, I dwelt at (the foot of) the Gotama peepul tree in Rājagaha ... (p) ... In that same Rājagaha, I dwelt at the Corapapāta cliff; at the Sattapaṇṇi cave in the side of the Vebhāra mountain; at Kāḷasīlā at the side of the Isigili mountain: at the ebony grove in the Sappasoṇḍika mountain range; at the Tapodā Grove monastery; at the place where black squirrels are fed in Veḷuvana Grove; at the mango grove of Jīvaka; and at the Migadāya Wood of the Maddakucchi locality

Ānanda, while I was dwelling at these places, too, I had spoken these words to you:

Ānanda, Rājagaha is pleasant. The Gijjhakūṭa hill is pleasant.[148] The Gotama peepul tree is pleasant. The Corapapāta cliff is pleasant. The Sattapaṇṇi Cave in the side of the Vebhāra mountain is pleasant. The Kāḷasīlā at the side of the Isigili mountain is pleasant. The ebony grove in the Sappasoṇḍika mountain range is pleasant. The Tapodā Grove monastery is pleasant. The black squirrels' feeding ground in the Veḷuvana Grove is pleasant. The mango grove of Jīvaka is pleasant.

---

148. This (mention of Gijjhakūṭa hill) seems to be redundant, as it has been mentioned in para 179.

The Migadāya Wood of the Maddakucchi locality is pleasant. Ānanda whosoever has cultivated, practiced, used as a means, based himself on, maintained, mastered and perfectly developed the four Bases of. Psychic Power Ānanda, therefore, the Tathāgata could if he so desired live the maximum life-span or even beyond the maximum life-span.'

Ānanda, though the Tathāgata thus gave plain hints and intimations, you were unable to grasp their significance. You did not beseech the Tathāgata (in such words as) 'Venerable Sir, for the welfare and happiness of mankind, out of compassion for the world, for the benefit, well-being and happiness of devas and men, may the Bhagavā live the maximum life-span, may the Sugata live the maximum life-span.'

Ānanda, if you had entreated me (thus) at that time, the Tathāgata might have refused the entreaty twice but might have acceded to the entreaty on the third time. Therefore, Ānanda, this (failure to entreat me) is your own fault, your own remissness.

181. Ānanda, at one time, I dwelt at the Udena shrine in this very city of Vesālī. While I was there, too, I had said to you, 'Pleasant is Vesālī. Pleasant is the Udena shrine. Ānanda, whosoever has cultivated, practiced, used as a means, based himself on, maintained, mastered and perfectly developed the four Bases of Psychic Power, could if he so desired live the maximum life-span, or even beyond the maximum life-span.' Ānanda, the Tathāgata has cultivated, practiced, used as a means, based himself on, maintained, mastered and perfectly developed the four Bases of Psychic Power. Therefore, the Tathāgata could if he so desired live the maximum life –span or evenbeyond the maximum life-span.'

Ānanda though the Tathāgata thus gave plain hints and intimations, you were unable to grasp their significance. You did not beseech the Tathāgata (in such words as) 'Venerable Sir, for the welfare and happiness of mankind, out of compassion for the world, for the benefit, well-being and happiness of devas and men, may the Bhagavā live the maximum life-span, may the Sugata live the maximum life-span.'

Ānanda, if you had entreated me (thus) at that time, the Tathāgata might have refused the entreaty twice but might have acceded to the entreaty on the third time. Therefore, Ānanda, this (failure to entreat me) is your own fault, your own remissness.

182. Ānanda, at one time, I dwelt at the Gotamaka shrine in this same Vesālī City ... (p) ... In this same Vesālī City I dwelt at the Sattamba shrine; at the Bahuputta shrine; at the Sarandada shrine.

Ānanda, at the Cāpāla shrine today, I had said to you, 'Ānanda, pleasant is this Vesālī. Pleasant are the shrines of Udena, Gotamaka, Sattamba, Bahuputta, Sārandada, Cāpāla. Ānanda, whosoever has cultivated, practiced, used as a means, based himself on, maintained, mastered and perfectly developed the four Bases of Psychic Power, could if he so desired live the maximum life-span or even beyond the maximum life-span.

Ānanda the Tathāgata has cultivated, practiced, used as a means, based himself on, maintained, mastered and perfectly developed the four Bases of Psychic Power. Therefore, the Tathāgata could if he so desired live the maximum life-span or even beyond the maximum life-span.'

Ānanda, though the Tathāgata thus gave plain hints and intimations, you were unable to grasp their significance. You did not beseech the Tathāgata (in such words as) 'Venerable Sir, for the welfare and happiness of mankind, out of compassion for the world, for the benefit, well-being and happiness of devas and men, may the Bhagavā live the maximum life-span; may the Sugata live the maximum life-span.'

Ānanda, if you had entreated me (thus) at that time, the Tathāgata might have refused the entreaty twice but might have acceded to the entreaty on the third time. Therefore. Ānanda, this (failure to entreat me) is your own fault, your own remissness.

183. Ānanda, have I not from former times proclaimed that there must be separation (while living), severance (through death) and sundering (through being in different states of existence) from all that are dear and beloved. Ānanda, in this matter, how can the wish be realized that anything which has the nature of arising, of appearing, of being compounded, and of decay and dissolution, should not disintegrate and disappear? There can be no such possibility.

Ānanda, the Tathāgata has abandoned, thrown up, let go, relinquished, thrown away and renounced the life-sustaining mental process, *āyusaṅkhāra.* And the Tathāgata has affirmed definitely that 'the *parinibbāna* of the Tathāgata will take place before long; three months from this day the Tathāgata will realize *parinibbāna.*' There is no possibility of the Tathāgata going back on that affirmation, just to live longer.

Ānanda, come, let us go to the pinnacled hall at the Mahāvana forest.

The Venerable Ānanda assented respectfully, saying "Very well, Venerable Sir." Then the Bhagavā, with the Venerable Ānanda, reached the pinnacled hall of the Mahāvana forest, and said to the Venerable Ānanda:

Ānanda, go and summon all the bhikkhus living in Vesālī to come and assemble in the assembly hall.

The Venerable Ānanda said "Very well, Venerable Sir," and caused all the bhikkhus living in Vesālī to gather in the assembly hall. Then he went to the Bhagavā and making obeisance to him stood in a certain place. Standing in a certain place, Ānanda said to the Bhagavā, "Venerable Sir, the bhikkhus are assembled. Now the Bhagavā may go to them when he wishes."

Thirty-Seven Elements of the Perpetuation of the Teaching

184. Then the Bhagavā went to the assembly hall and seating himself on the seat prepared for him, said to the bhikkhus:

Bhikkhus, you should thoroughly learn, pursue, cultivate and continually practice the doctrines which I have perceived through Magga Insight and which I have expounded to you. If you thus learn, pursue, cultivate and continually practice these doctrines, (this Teaching which is) the Noble Practice of Purity,[149] will endure long and will remain established for a long time, for the welfare and happiness of mankind, for the sake of the world, for the benefit, well-being and happiness of devas and men.

Bhikkhus, what are those doctrines which I have perceived through Magga Insight and which I have expounded to you, and which you should thoroughly learn, pursue, cultivate and continually practice? If you thus learn, pursue, cultivate and continually practice these doctrines, (this Teaching which is) the Noble Practice of Purity will endure long and will remain established for a long time for the welfare and happiness of mankind, for the sake of the world, for the benefit, well-being and happiness of devas and men.

These (doctrines) are the four Methods of Steadfast Mindfulness (*Satipaṭṭhāna*),[150] the four Supreme Efforts (*Sammappadhāna*),[151] the

---

149. **The Noble Practice of Purity**: (*brahmacariya*), i.e., the Teaching, *Sāsanā.*

150. *Satipaṭṭhāna*: See footnote 2 of Para 146 and Mahāsatipaṭṭhāna Sutta.

151. *Sammappadhāna*: *Samma = good*, thorough, proper, right, perfect; and *padhāna = exertion*, energetic effort, striving, concentration of mind.

The four Supreme Efforts are:

(i) The endeavour to prevent the arising of evil which has not yet arisen;

(ii) The endeavour to put away evil that has arisen;

(iii) The endeavour to bring about the arising of good which has not yet arisen; and

four Bases of Psychic Potency (*Iddhipāda*),[152] the five Controlling Faculties (*Indriya*),[153] the five Powers (*Bala*)[154] the Seven Factors of Enlightenment (*Bojjhaṅga*)[155] and the Noble Path of Eight Constituents (*Ariya Aṭṭhaṅgika Magga*).[156]

Bhikkhus, you should thoroughly learn, pursue, cultivate and continually practice these doctrines which I have perceived through Magga Insight and which I have expounded to you. If you thus learn, pursue, cultivate and continually practice these doctrines, (this Teaching which is) the Noble Practice of Purity will endure long and will remain established for a long time for the welfare and happiness of mankind, for the sake of the world, for the benefit, well-being and happiness of devas and men.

185. Then the Bhagavā further addressed the bhikkhus thus: O Bhikkhus, I now say this to you: All conditioned and compounded things, *saṅkhāra*, have the nature of decay and disintegration. With mindfulness[157] endeavour diligently (to complete the task).[158] The parinibbāna of the Tathāgata will take place before long. Three months from this day the Tathāgata will realize parinibbāna (i.e., will finally pass away).

Having said this, the Bhagavā, the Sugata, the Teacher made this further utterance (in verse):

"I am now quite ripe in age. Only a little of my life remains. I shall have to depart, forsaking you. I have made myself my own refuge.

(iv) The endeavour to further develop the good that has arisen.

152. *Iddhipāda*: See footnote (1) to Para 167.

153. *Indriya*: the five Controlling Faculties here meant are:
   (i) *Saddhindriya*, the faculty of Confidence based on Conviction;
   (ii) *Vīriyindriya*, the faculty of Effort;
   (iii) *Satindriya*, the faculty of Mindfulness;
   (iv) *Samādhindriya*, the faculty of Concentration; and
   (v) *Paññindriya*, the faculty of Wisdom.

154. *Bala*: the five Powers or Forces are Powers of Confidence based on Conviction, Effort, Mindfulness, Concentration and Wisdom.

155. *Bojjhaṅga*: See para 139 and footnote to Para 146.

156. *Aṭṭhaṅgika Magga*: See later portion of Mahāsatipaṭṭhāna Sutta.

157. **Mindfulness** in cultivating tranquillity and insight development meditation, *samatha vipassanā bhāvanā*.

158. **To complete the task**: i.e., to be liberated from the round of rebirths, *saṃsāra*, by achieving *Arahatta Magga* and *Phala*.

"Bhikkhus, vigilantly and with mindfulness, be of pure virtue.[159] Being composed and collected of mind, thinking right, watch over (i.e., control) your own mind.

"Bhikkhus, in this Teaching, this Doctrine and Discipline, he who is heedfully vigilant will be able to escape from the round of repeated rebirths and make an end of *dukkha*."

End of third portion for recitation

Looking Back Like a Noble Tusker

186. Then the Bhagavā, rearranging his robes in the morning-time, took alms-bowl and great robe and went into Vesālī for alms-food.

After the alms-round and after the meal, when he left (the place of the meal), the Bhagavā (turned around bodily and) looked back towards Vesālī, like an elephant looking back.[160] He said to Venerable Ānanda, "Ānanda, this will be the last time the Tathāgata looks on Vesālī. Come, Ānanda, let us go to Bhaṇḍa village."

The Venerable Ānanda, saying "Very well, Venerable Sir," respectfully assented. Then the Bhagavā, with a large company of bhikkhus, (went to and) reached Bhaṇḍa village, and took up his residence there.

While there, the Bhagavā said to the bhikkhus:

O Bhikkhus, it is through not having proper understanding and penetrating comprehension of four Principles that I as well as yourselves have had to go incessantly through this long stretch (of *saṃsāra*, round of existences), that we have had to go through one life after another continuously.

What are these four? (They are as follows:)

O Bhikkhus, it is through not having proper understanding and penetrating comprehension of Noble Morality, *Ariya sīla*, that I as well as yourselves have had to go incessantly through this long stretch (of *saṃsāra*, round of existence), that we have had to go through one life after another continuously.

O Bhikkhus, it is through not having proper understanding and penetrating comprehension of Noble Concentration, *Ariya samādhi*, that I as well as yourselves have had to go incessantly through this long

159. **Pure virtue**: *susīla*: endowed with pure conduct, character.
160. The Commentary says that the Buddhas, when looking back, 'turn the whole body round, as an elephant does'.

stretch (of *saṃsāra*, round of existences), that we have had to go through one life after another continuously.

O Bhikkhus, it is through not having proper understanding and penetrating comprehension of Noble Wisdom, *Ariya paññā*, that I as well as yourselves have had to go incessantly through this long stretch (of *saṃsāra*. round of existences), that we have had to go through one life after another continuously.

O Bhikkhus, it is through not having proper understanding and penetrating comprehension of Noble Emancipation, *Ariya vimutti*, that I as well as yourselves have had to go incessantly through this long stretch (of *saṃsāra*, round of existences), that we have had to go through one life after another continuously.

O Bhikkhus, I have properly understood and penetratingly comprehended (i.e., thoroughly realized) that Noble Morality; I have properly understood and penetratingly comprehended that Noble Concentration; I have properly understood and penetratingly comprehended that Noble Wisdom; I have properly understood and penetratingly comprehended that Noble Emancipation. The craving for existence, *bhavataṇhā*, has been cut off without any vestige remaining. The *bhavataṇhā*, which is like a rope that drags one to renewed existence, is exhausted (i.e., destroyed). Now, there will be no more rebirth.

Having said this, the Bhagavā, the Sugata, the Teacher again made this further (lit., other) utterance (in verse):

"Gotama Buddha, of glorious fame, has perfectly understood these Principles of highest Morality, Concentration, Wisdom and Emancipation, *Sīla*, *Samādhi*, *Paññā* and *Vimutti*.

Having perfectly understood them through Magga Insight, he has expounded them to the bhikkhus.

The Possessor of the Eye of Wisdom,[161] the Teacher (of devas and men), having put out the fires of *kilesā*, moral defilements, and being serenely at peace, has made an end of *dukkha*."

---

161. **Eye of Wisdom**: *cakkhu*: The Commentary explains that this is fivefold.
The Sub-Commentary lists them as:

(i) *Buddha-cakkhu*, the Buddha-Eye, complete intuition of another's inclinations, intentions, hopes, hankerings, will, disposition, proclivities, moral state;

(ii) *Samanta-cakkhu*, the Eye of all-round knowledge, the Eye of a Being perfected in wisdom;

(iii) *Dhamma-cakkhu* (or *ñāṇa-cakkhu*), the Eye of Truth, apperception of the attainment of the first three Maggas which leads to the fourth and final Magga, Arahatship;

While the Bhagavā was thus sojourning at that Bhaṇḍa village, there, too, he repeatedly expounded to the bhikkhus this very discourse:

"Such is *sīla*, morality; such is *samādhi*, concentration of mind; such is *paññā*, wisdom. *Samādhi*, when based upon *sīla*, is rich in result and of great effect. *Paññā*, when based upon *samādhi*, is rich in result and of great effect. The mind, when developed through *paññā*, is thoroughly liberated from the *āsavas*, taints, namely, *kāmāsava*, *bhavāsava*, and *avijjāsava*."

Discourse on Four Great Authorities

187. Then, after staying at Bhaṇḍa village as long as he wished, the Bhagavā said to the Venerable Ānanda, "Come, Ānanda, let us go to Hatthi village, and to Amba village, and to Jambu village, and thence to the town of Bhoga."

The Venerable Ānanda respectfully assented, saying "Very well, Venerable Sir." And the Bhagavā, together with a large company of bhikkhus, reached the town of Bhoga.

The Bhagavā stayed at the Ānanda shrine at that Bhoga town. While there, the Bhagavā said to the bhikkhus, "O Bhikkhus, I shall give a discourse on the four Great Authorities.[162] Listen to the discourse and bear it well in mind. I shall speak."

The bhikkhus respectfully assenting, the Bhagavā gave this discourse:

188. O Bhikkhus, in this (matter), if a bhikkhu should say thus:

"Sirs, I have heard and received this (exposition) from the mouth of the Bhagavā: Such and such is the Doctrine; such and such is the *Vinaya*;[163] such and such is the Teacher's (i.e., the Buddha's) Teaching, instructions on methods of removing defilements."

O Bhikkhus, the words of that bhikkhu should not be (immediately) received with approval, nor should they be (immediately) rejected with scorn. Without approval or rejection, those words and phrases (attributed to the Buddha) should be carefully noted and should be

---

(iv) *Dibba-cakkhu*, the Eye of supernormal power, the deva-eye of super-sensuous perception, the "clear" sight of a seer, all pervading and seeing all that proceeds in hidden worlds; and

(v) *Pasāda-cakkhu*, (or *maṃsa-cakkhu*), the physical eye.

162. **Great Authorities**: *Mahāpadesa:* the whole term may be paraphrased as directives for deciding on statements attributed to the Buddha, or to the other three Authorities.

163. **The Vinaya**: this explanation is according to the Commentary, commenting on this para 188.

collated with (lit., put into) the *Sutta*[164] and examined in the light of the *Vinaya.*

If, on thus being collated with the *Sutta* or on being examined in the light of the *Vinaya*, the words and phrases do not fit in with the *Sutta*, or are not in accord with the *Vinaya*, then it must be concluded that 'This assuredly is not an utterance of the Bhagavā; it is only an utterance wrongly learnt by the bhikkhu.' And, thus (coming to this conclusion), bhikkhus, the assertion should be rejected.

If, (however), on being collated with the *Sutta* or on being examined in the light of the *Vinaya*, the (attributed) words and phrases fit in with the *Sutta*, or are in accord with the *Vinaya*, then it must be concluded that 'This assuredly is an utterance of the Bhagavā; it is an utterance learnt aright by the bhikkhu.' Bhikkhus, remember well this first (directive on assertions citing) Great Authority. (1)

Again, O Bhikkhus, in this (matter), if a bhikkhu should say thus:

"There is a community of bhikkhus with elders and a chief bhikkhu at a monastery with such and such a name. I have heard and learnt this (exposition) from that very community of bhikkhus: Such and such is the Doctrine; such and such is the *Vinaya*; such and such is the Teacher's Teaching."

O Bhikkhus, the words of that bhikkhu should not be (immediately) received with approval, nor should they be (immediately) rejected with scorn. Without approval or rejection, the words and phrases (attributed to that community of bhikkhus) should be carefully noted and should be collated with the *Sutta* and examined in the light of the *Vinaya.*

If, on thus being collated with the *Sutta* or on being examined in the light of the *Vinaya*, the words and phrases do not fit in with the *Sutta*, or are not in accord with the *Vinaya*, then it must be concluded that 'This assuredly is not an utterance of the Bhagavā; it is only an utterance wrongly learnt by that community of bhikkhus.' And, thus (coming to this conclusion), bhikkhus, the assertion should be rejected.

If, (however), on being collated with the *Sutta* or on being examined in the light of the *Vinaya*, the (attributed) words and phrases fit in with the *Sutta*, or are in accord with the *Vinaya*, then it must be concluded that 'This assuredly is an utterance of the Bhagavā; it is an utterance learnt aright by that community of bhikkhus.' Bhikkhus, remember well this second (directive on assertions citing) Great Authority. (2)

---

164. **The Sutta**: according to the Commentary, this term in this para 188 means the entire Teaching of the Buddha, encompassing the three Piṭakas.

Again, O Bhikkhus, in this (matter), if a bhikkhu should say thus:

"There are many bhikkhu elders at a monastery with such and such a name, who are of wide learning and knowledge, who can recite by heart (the Pāḷi Texts), having memorized the Doctrine, the *Vinaya*, and the Fundamental Precepts for bhikkhus.[165] I have heard and received this (exposition) from those bhikkhu elders themselves: Such and such is the Doctrine; such and such is the *Vinaya*; such and such is the Teacher's Teaching."

O Bhikkhus, the words of that bhikkhu should not be (immediately) received with approval, nor should they be (immediately) rejected with scorn. Without approval or rejection, the words and phrases (attributed to the bhikkhu elders ... (p) ... then it must be concluded that 'This assuredly is not an utterance of the Bhagavā; it is only an utterance wrongly learnt by those bhikkhu elders.' And, thus (coming to this conclusion), bhikkhus, the assertion should be rejected.

If, (however), on being collated with the *Sutta* ... (p) ... are in accord with the *Vinaya*, then it must be concluded that 'This assuredly is an utterance of the Bhagavā; it is an utterance learnt aright by those bhikkhu elders.' Bhikkhus, remember well this third (directive on assertions citing) Great Authority. (3)

Again, O Bhikkhus, in this (matter), if a bhikkhu should say thus:

"There is a certain bhikkhu elder at a monastery with such and such a name, who is of wide learning and knowledge, who can recite by heart (the Pāḷi Texts), having memorized the Doctrine, the *Vinaya*, and the Fundamental Precepts for bhikkhus. I have heard and received this (exposition) from that very bhikkhu elder: Such and such is the Doctrine; such and such is the *Vinaya*; such and such is the Teacher's Teaching."

O Bhikkhus, the words of that bhikkhu should not be (immediately) received with approval, nor should they be (immediately) rejected with scorn. Without approval or rejection, those words and phrases (attributed to the Buddha) should be carefully noted and should be collated with the *Sutta* and examined in the light of the *Vinaya*.

If, on thus being collated with the Sutta or on being examined in the light of the *Vinaya*, the words and phrases do not fit in with the Sutta, or are not in accord with the *Vinaya* then it must be concluded that 'This assuredly is not an utterance of the Bhagavā; it is only an

165. **Fundamental Precepts**: *Mātikā*, (lit., contents), here means Fundamental Precepts for bhikkhus and bhikkhunīs.

utterance wrongly learnt by the bhikkhu elder.' And, thus (coming to this conclusion), bhikkhus, the assertion should be rejected.

If, (however), on being collated with the *Sutta* or on being examined in the light of the *Vinaya*, the (attributed) words and phrases fit in with the Sutta, or are in accord with the *Vinaya*, then it must be concluded that 'This assuredly is an utterance of the Bhagavā; it is an utterance learnt aright by the bhikkhu elder. Bhikkhus, remember well this fourth (directive on assertions citing) Great Authority. (4)

O bhikkhus, remember these four (citations of) Great Authorities, *Mahāpadesa.*

While the Bhagavā was sojourning at the Ānanda shrine in the town of Bhoga, there, too, he repeatedly expounded to the bhikkhus this very discourse:

"Such is *sīla*, morality; such is *samādhi*, concentration of mind; such is *paññā*, wisdom. *Samādhi*, when based upon *sīla*, is rich in result and of great effect. *Paññā*, when based upon *samādhi*, is rich in result and of great effect. The mind, when developed through *paññā*, is thoroughly liberated from the *āsavas*, taints, namely, *kāmāsava*, the taint of sensuous desire, *bhavāsava*, the taint of hankering after repeated existence, and *avijjāsava*, the taint of ignorance of the true nature of existence as set out in the Four Noble Truths."

Account Concerning Cunda, the Goldsmith's Son

189. Then, after staying at the town of Bhoga as long as he wished, the Bhagavā said to the Venerable Ānanda, "Come Ānanda, let us go to Pāvā."

The Venerable Ānanda respectfully assented, saying, "Very well, Venerable Sir." And the Bhagavā, together with a large company of bhikkhus, went to Pāvā, and stayed at the mango grove of Cunda, the goldsmith's son.

When Cunda, the goldsmith's son heard that the Bhagavā had arrived at Pāvā and was staying at his mango grove, he went to the Bhagavā, and making obeisance, sat at a certain place. To Cunda, thus seated, the Bhagavā gave a discourse, and by his discourse caused him to realize (the benefits of) the Teaching, to become established in (the observance of) the Teaching, and to be filled with gladness and enthusiasm for (the practice of) the Teaching.

After the Bhagavā had caused him to realize (the benefits of) the Teaching, to become established in (the observance of) the Teaching, and to be filled with gladness and enthusiasm for (the practice of) the

Teaching, Cunda, the goldsmith's son said to the Bhagavā, "Venerable Sir, may it please the Bhagavā to accept my offering of food for tomorrow, together with the company of bhikkhus."

The Bhagavā, by silence, signified his acceptance. And Cunda, the goldsmith's son, knowing that the Bhagavā had accepted his request, rose from his seat, made obeisance to the Bhagavā, and left respectfully.

Then Cunda, the goldsmith's son, after that night had passed, caused choice food of both hard and soft kinds, as well as quantities of tender pork,[166] to be prepared at his house, and then informed the Bhagavā that it was time for the meal by the message "Venerable Sir, it is time (to proceed), the food-offering is ready."

Then in the morning the Bhagavā got ready by rearranging his robes and taking alms-bowl and great robe went to the house of Cunda, the goldsmith's son, together with the company of bhikkhus, and (on arriving there) took the seat prepared for him.

Having thus seated himself, the Bhagavā said to Cunda, the goldsmith's son, "Cunda, (you may) serve me the *sūkara-maddava* prepared by you, and (you may) serve the other food prepared by you to the company of bhikkhus."

Cunda, the goldsmith's son assented respectfully, and accordingly served the prepared *sūkara-maddava* to the Bhagavā and the other prepared food to the company of bhikkhus.

Then the Bhagavā said to Cunda, the goldsmith's son, "Cunda, bury the remaining *sūkara-maddava* in a pit. Cunda, apart from the Tathāgata himself, I see no one either in the celestial world of devas, Māra or Brahmās, or in the human world of *samaṇas* (recluses), *brāhmaṇas* (those leading a religious life), rulers and men, who, eating this *sūkara-maddava*, can digest it well."

Cunda the goldsmith's son assented respectfully, saying "Very well, Venerable Sir," and buried the remaining *sūkara-maddava* in a pit. Then he approached the Bhagavā, made obeisance to him, and seated himself

---

166. **Tender pork**: *Sūkara-maddava: sūkara* = pig, *maddava* = *soft*, tender, delicate. The Commentary gives two variant interpretations: (i) soft rice boiled with five differently tasting kinds of cow's milk; or (ii) food prepared with *rasāyana*. (*Rasāyana* may mean an elixir or delicate essence extracted from the roots, leaves, flowers, etc., of a plant.) The Venerable Dhammapāla, in the Udāna Commentary, also has "young bamboo shoots liked by pigs". Other interpretations, based on analogical formations, are "truffles, mushrooms, yams", i.e., the kind of food enjoyed by wild pigs or boars.

at a certain place. And the Bhagavā, by religious discourse to Cunda seated on one side, caused him to realize (the benefits of) the Teaching, to become established in (the observance of) the Teaching, and to be filled with gladness and enthusiasm for (the practice of) the Teaching. Then the Bhagavā rose from his seat and departed.

190. Later, after the Bhagavā had eaten the food offered by Cunda, the goldsmith's son, a severe illness came upon the Bhagavā, a severe attack of dysentery with discharge of blood, and he suffered excessive pain, near unto death. This the Bhagavā endured with mindfulness and deliberation, and without being perturbed.

Then the Bhagavā said to the Venerable Ānanda, "Come Ānanda, let us go to Kusinārā." The Venerable Ānanda assented respectfully, saying "Very well, Venerable Sir."

Separate Verses[167]

I have heard that after partaking of the food offered by Cunda the goldsmith's son, the Enlightened One suffered severe illness and pain, near unto death.

After having eaten the tender pork, there arose in the Teacher excessive pain and illness. Suffering (the attack of) dysentery, the Bhagavā said, 'I shall go to the town of Kusinārā.'

Having Drinking Water Brought

191. Then the Bhagavā left the road and went to the foot of a tree. And he said to the Venerable Ānanda, "Ānanda, fold my double-layered robe fourfold and place it on the ground. I am exhausted; I shall sit down."

The Venerable Ānanda said, "Very well, Venerable Sir," and folding the (Bhagavā's) double-layered robe in four, placed it on the ground. The Bhagavā sat down on the folded robe laid on the ground and said, "Ānanda, go and bring drinking water. I am thirsty. I want to have a drink of water."

On this being said (by the Bhagavā), the Venerable Ānanda said to the Bhagavā, "Venerable Sir, five hundred carts have just now crossed the stream. The shallow water, being stirred up by the cartwheels, flows turbid and muddy. Venerable Sir, the Kakudhā River is not far off.

---

167. **Separate Verses**: i.e., Verses separate from, distinct from the Text. The Commentary says these verses were inserted by the Theras, bhikkhu elders, at the Council.

There, the water is clear, sweet, cool, and free from muddiness. There are good banks (i.e., making the river accessible), and it is a pleasant place. At the Kakudhā River the Bhagavā may drink water, and also may refresh himself."

The Bhagavā said a second time, "Ānanda, go and bring drinking water. I am thirsty. I want to have a drink of water."

For a second time, too, Ānanda said to the Bhagavā, "Venerable Sir, five hundred carts have just now crossed the stream. The shallow water, being stirred up by the cartwheels, flows turbid and muddy. Venerable Sir, the Kakudhā River is not far off. There, the water is clear, sweet, cool, and free from muddiness. There are good banks (i.e., making the river accessible), and it is a pleasant place. At the Kakudhā River the Bhagavā may drink water, and also may refresh himself."

The Bhagavā said a third time, "Ānanda, (I exhort you to) go and bring drinking water. I am thirsty. I want to have a drink of water."

Ānanda, saying "Very well, Venerable Sir, "assented respectfully, and taking the alms-bowl, went to the stream. Then, the shallow water which was flowing turbid and muddy, having been stirred up by the cartwheels, became clear, pure and absolutely free from muddiness.

And this thought occurred to the Venerable Ānanda:

"Wonderful indeed, Sirs, and marvellous indeed, Sirs, is the great power and supernormal (psychic) potency of the Tathāgata! This shallow stream, which was flowing turbid and muddy, having been stirred up by the wheels of the crossing carts, is on my appearance flowing clear, pure and absolutely free from muddiness."

Carrying the drinking water in the alms-bowl, the Venerable Ānanda went back to the Bhagavā, and said:

"Indeed wonderful, Venerable Sir, indeed marvellous. Venerable Sir, is the great power and supernormal (psychic) potency of the Tathāgata! That shallow water of the stream, which was flowing turbid and muddy, having been stirred up just now by the wheels of the crossing carts, became on my approach clear, pure and absolutely free from muddiness. Now let the Bhagavā drink the water. Let the Sugata drink the water."

Then the Bhagavā drank the water.

Account Concerning Pukkusa the Malla Prince

192. At that time, Pukkusa, a Malla prince,[168] who was a disciple of Āḷāra Kālāma (i.e., Āḷāra of the Kālāma clan), was on a long journey from Kusinārā to Pāvā. Seeing the Bhagavā sitting at the foot of a tree, Pukkusa of the Mallas approached the Bhagavā, made obeisance to him, and having sat down on one side, said to the Bhagavā thus:

"Wonderful it is, Venerable Sir, marvellous it is, Venerable Sir, (how) the pabbajitas[169] remain abiding in the attainment of calm.[170]

"Venerable Sir, it happened formerly that Āḷāra Kālāma, while on a long journey, left the road and sat down at the foot of a tree by the roadside, to spend the day. Venerable Sir, at that time, five hundred carts passed by very close to Āḷāra Kālāma.

"Venerable Sir, a certain man who had been following behind those five hundred carts, went up to where Āḷāra Kālāma was and asked him 'Sir, did you see five hundred carts pass by?'

'Friend, I did not see them.'

'Sir, how is it, then? Did you hear the noise (of those carts)?'

'Friend, I did not hear the noise, either.'

'Sir, how is it, then? Were you asleep?'

'Friend, I was not asleep, either.'

'Sir, how is it then? Were you conscious?'

'Yes, friend, (I was conscious).'

'Sir, you say you did not see and did not hear the five hundred carts which passed close by you, even though you were conscious and awake. Yet, isn't your double-layered robe covered all over with dust (from the passing of the carts)?'

'It is so, friend.'

"Venerable Sir, then that man thought thus: 'Wonderful it is, Sirs, marvellous it is, Sirs, the state of calm in which the pabbajitas remain

---

168. **Malla prince**: *Mallaputta*: lit., son of the Mallas. The Mallas were a clan of the ruling Khattiya Class, and thus, princes. It is possible to render *mallaputta* as a Malla youth, or a scion of the Malla princely clan or a young man of Malla lineage.

169. *Pabbajita* means one who has gone out from home, one who has given up worldly life and undertaken the life of a bhikkhu, recluse or ascetic. The term thus can indicate a disciple of the Buddha, but here Āḷāra, a leading ascetic, was not such a disciple. Ascetics also engaged in deep mental cultivation.

170. **Attainment of calm**: *Santa* (instr., *santena*) tranquillity, calmness of mind. *Vihāra* (instr., *vihārena*), in this context, state, condition. It is rendered in the Burmese version as *Samāpatti*, sustained attainment of deep mental absorption.

abiding! This ascetic Āḷāra, although conscious and awake, did not see, did not hear, the five hundred carts which passed close by (him)!' And expressing his feeling of deep reverence for Āḷāra Kālāma, he departed."

193. (The Bhagavā said:) Pukkusa, what do you think of this? Which is the more difficult to achieve (lit., do), the more difficult to happen, (of the case of two persons) (the condition of) one who, though conscious and awake, does not see and does not hear the five hundred carts which pass close by (him), or (the condition of) the the other who, though conscious and awake, does not see and does not hear heavy rain, rumbling thunder, flashing lightning and crashing thunderbolts (close by him)?

"Venerable Sir, it cannot be said that remaining without seeing and hearing the carts passing close by — whether it be five hundred, six hundred, seven hundred, eight hundred, nine hundred, a thousand or even a hundred thousand carts — is more difficult.[171] Indeed, it is much more difficult to remain without seeing and hearing heavy rain, rumbling thunder, flashing lightning and crashing thunderbolts (close by). It is more difficult to do, more difficult to happen."

Pukkusa, at one time I was staying in a straw hut at Ātumā (town). At that time, there was heavy rain, with rumbling thunder and flashes of lightning, and a thunderbolt struck not far from my hut, killing two cultivators, who were brothers, and four oxen. Then, Pukkusa, a multitude of people came out from Ātumā (town) and went up to the place where the two cultivator brothers and four oxen had been killed.

Pukkusa, by that time, I had come out of the straw hut and was walking up and down in the open, near the door of the straw hut. Then, Pukkusa, a man from that crowd of people approached me, and making obeisance to me, stood at a certain place. Pukkusa, I asked that man, 'Friend, why are these many people gathered?'

'Venerable Sir, just now two cultivators, who were brothers, and four oxen have been struck and killed by lightning while it was raining heavily, thunder was rolling and lightning was flashing. That is why this multitude of people has gathered. But, Venerable Sir, where were you?'

'Friend, I have been here all the while.'

'Venerable Sir, how is it, then? Did you see (the happening)?'

'Friend, I did not see it.'

171. This sentence is as paraphrased in the Burmese version. The Pāḷi Text reads: "What can (lit., will) five hundred, six hundred etc., carts do?" That is, the effect of even large numbers of carts will not be comparable to the effect of rain, lightning, thunder, etc.

'Venerable Sir, how is it, then? Did you hear the sound?'

'Friend, I did not hear the sound, either.'

'Venerable Sir, how is it, then? Were you asleep?'

'Friend, I was not asleep, either.'

'Venerable Sir, how is it, then? Were you conscious?'

'Yes, friend, (I was conscious).'

'Venerable Sir, is it that, though conscious and awake, you neither saw nor heard heavy rain, rumbling thunder, flashing lightning and crashing thunderbolts?

That is so, friend.'

Pukkusa, then this thought came to that man: 'Wonderful it is, Sirs, marvellous it is, Sirs, the state of calm in which the pabbajitas remain abiding! This pabbajita (i.e., the Buddha), although conscious and awake, did not see, did not hear heavy rain, rumbling thunder, flashing lightning and crashing thunderbolts'. And expressing his feeling of deep reverence for me, and making obeisance to me, departed respectfully.

When this had been said, Pukkusa the Malla prince said to the Bhagavā:

"Venerable Sir, the deep reverence I felt for Āḷāra Kālāma, I now throw away (as if) scattering it in a great wind, or (as if) letting it be carried away by a strong current.

"Venerable Sir, extremely wonderful (is the Truth)! Surpassingly beautiful (is the Truth)! Venerable Sir, just as if that which has been turned over is turned upright, or that which has been hidden is revealed, or one who has lost his way is informed of the right way, or an oil-lamp is (brought and) held in the darkness so that those with eyes might see objects, even so the Bhagavā has shown me the Truth in many ways.

"Venerable Sir, I take refuge in the Bhagavā, I take refuge in the Dhamma, (the Teaching of the Buddha), I take refuge in the Saṅgha, the community of bhikkhus. May the Bhagavā accept me as a lay-disciple one who has taken refuge, from this day to the end of life."

194. Then, Pukkusa the Malla prince called a man and said to him, "You,[172] do go and bring the pair of fine golden hued pieces of cloth of mine kept for special occasions."

The man replied "Very well, Sir," and went and brought a pair of lengths of fine golden-hued cloth. Then Pukkusa the Malla prince offered the ceremonial pieces of cloth to the Bhagavā, saying "Venerable Sir,

---

172. **You:** *bhaṇe*, a familiar term used in addressing subordinates of inferiors, rendered here by "You," as "Friend," or "My good man" would not be appropriate in tone.

may the Bhagavā accept, out of compassion (for me), this pair of fine ceremonial lengths of cloth."

The Bhagavā said, "In that case, present[173] one to me and one to Ānanda." Pukkusa the Malla prince said, "Very well, Venerable Sir," and presented one to the Bhagavā, and the other (piece of cloth) to the Venerable Ānanda. And then the Bhagavā, by religious discourse, caused Pukkusa the Malla prince to realize (the advantages of) the Teaching, to become established in (the observance of) the Teaching, and to be filled with gladness and enthusiasm for (the practice of) the Teaching.

Thus, by the Bhagavā's discourse, having been caused to realize the advantages of the Teaching, to become established in the observance of the Teaching, and to be filled with gladness and enthusiasm for the practice of the Teaching, Pukkusa the Malla prince arose from his seat, made obeisance to the Bhagavā and departed respectfully.

195. Then, not long after Pukkusa the Malla prince had left, the Venerable Ānanda placed and arranged the pair of fine, golden-hued robes on the body of the Bhagavā. When placed on the (brilliantly shining) body of the Bhagavā, those (golden-hued robes) appeared as though faded.

Then, the Venerable Ānanda said to the Bhagavā, "Most wonderful it is, Venerable Sir, marvellous it is, Venerable Sir, how extremely clear and radiant the Tathāgata's complexion appears! When the pair of golden-hued robes were placed on the Bhagavā's body, they became as though faded."

Ānanda, it is so. Ānanda, it is so. There are two occasions on which the complexion of the Tathāgata appears extremely clear and radiant.

What are these two occasions?

The night, Ānanda, when the Tathāgata attains unsurpassed, supreme Enlightenment, and the night when the Tathāgata passes away, realizing parinibbāna by experiencing the ultimate peace of *anupādisesa nibbāna*, the complete cessation of all the five khandhas.

Ānanda, these are the two occasions on which the complexion of the Tathāgata appears exceedingly clear and radiant.

And now today, Ānanda, in the last watch of this night, in the Sal grove of the Malla princes, at the road-bend leading to Kusinārā town,

173. **Present**: this follows the rendering 'offer or donate' according to the Commentary. The term *acchādehi* literally means "cover, put (something) on (somebody or something)."

the Tathāgata's realization of parinibbāna will take place between two Sal trees. Come, Ānanda, let us go to the Kakudhā river.

The Venerable Ānanda, saying "Very well, Venerable Sir" assented respectfully.

SEPARATE VERSE[174]

Pukkusa brought and offered (to the Buddha) a pair of fine golden-hued robes. Enrobed in them, the Teacher shone in golden radiance.

196. Then the Bhagavā went to the Kakudhā River with a great company of bhikkhus, and went down to the river. He bathed, and drank water. Then he came onto the bank again, and went to the mango grove. He said to the Venerable Cundaka, "Cundaka, fold my double-layered robe in four, and place it on the ground. I am weary, Cundaka. I shall lie down."

The Venerable Cundaka assented respectfully, and placed the folded double-layered robe on the ground. Then the Bhagavā lay down on his right side, nobly (like a lion), placing the left foot over and a little beyond the right foot, with mindfulness and deliberation, and keeping a predetermined time of arising in his mind. The Venerable Cundaka sat there in front of the Bhagavā.

SEPARATE VERSES[175]

Being very weary,[176] the Buddha (the Enlightened), the Incomparable in the world, the Great Teacher, the Tathāgata, went to the Kakudhā river where the water was clear, sweet and clean.

Having come out of the river, after bathing and drinking water, the Bhagavā, the Great Teacher, the Highest, who launched and expounded the Truths (of the Teaching), went to the mango grove, surrounded by and in the midst of the entire group of bhikkhus.

There the Buddha said to the bhikkhu called Cundaka, 'Fold my double-layered robe fourfold and lay it down; I shall lie down.' Thus asked by the Buddha, Cundaka folded the double-layered robe in four

174. **Separate Verse**: inserted by the Elders who collected the Dhamma (texts) at the First Council. (The Commentary)

175. Separate Verses: inserted by the Elders at the First Council.

176. **Being very weary**: The Pāḷi Text here has *akilantarūpo*, which would mean 'as if not weary.' The reading, as in the Udāna Pāḷi Text, *suki-lantarūpo*, 'being very weary' would be more consistent.

and quickly placed it on the ground. The great Teacher, feeling tired, lay down. Cundaka also sat in front of the Buddha.

197. Then the Bhagavā said to the Venerable Ānanda:

Ānanda, someone might cause remorse or regret to Cunda, the goldsmith's son by saying "Friend Cunda, the Tathāgata passed away after eating your food last. Therefore, it is loss and misfortune to you." If that happens, Ānanda, the remorse or regret Cunda might feel should thus be countered: "Friend Cunda, the Tathāgata passed away after eating your food last. Therefore, it is good fortune and good gain to you. Friend Cunda, I heard and received these words from the Bhagavā himself. There are two offerings of food which are of equal fruition and of equal result and which are of much greater fruition and much greater benefit than any other offering of food. What are these two offerings of food?

"The offering of food, after eating which the Tathāgata attains unsurpassed, Perfect Self-Enlightenment. (This is one.)

"The offering of food, after eating which the Tathāgata passes into the ultimate peace of *anupādisesa nibbāna* which is the complete cessation of all the five khandhas. (This is the other.)

"These are the two offerings of food which are of equal fruition and equal result and which are of much greater fruition and much greater benefit than any other offering of food. (Therefore) Respected[177] Cunda, the goldsmith's son has accumulated that *kamma* (force of action) which will bring about long life, which will bring about beautiful appearance, which will bring about well-being and happiness, which will bring about large retinues, which will bring about rebirth in the realms of devas, and which will bring about pre-eminence."

Thus, Ānanda, the remorse or regret of Cunda, the goldsmith's son should be dispelled.

Then the Bhagavā, understanding this matter, at that moment uttered this exultant verse:

To him who gives, merit accumulates.
In him who is self-controlled, hostility cannot grow.
He who is endowed with wisdom, casts off evil.

---

177. **Respected**: this is a paraphrase, to fit in with the context, of *āyasmā* (lit., long-living) in the Pāḷi Text, which is usually translated as Venerable, and which is usually used for and to bhikkhus of standing.

He who thus casts off evil, by the rooting out of passion, anger and mental bewilderment, attains peace (through the extinction of the fires of *kilesā*, moral defilements).

End of the fourth portion for recitation

The Twin Sal Trees

198. Then the Bhagavā said to the Venerable Ānanda, "Come, Ānanda, let us go. We will go to the Sal Grove of the Malla princes at the road-bend leading to Kusinārā town, on the further bank of the Hiraññavatī River." The Venerable Ānanda, saying "Very well, Venerable Sir," assented respectfully.

When the Bhagavā, together with a large company of bhikkhus, got to the Sal Grove of the Malla princes at the road-bend leading to Kusinārā town, on the further bank of the Hiraññavatī River, he said to the Venerable Ānanda, "Ānanda, lay out the couch, with the head to the north, between the pair of Sal trees, I am weary, Ānanda. I shall lie down."

The Venerable Ānanda, saying "Very well, Venerable Sir," assented respectfully, and laid out the couch, with the head to the north, between the pair of Sal trees. Then the Bhagavā lay down on his right side, nobly (like a lion), placing the left foot on and a little beyond the right foot, with mindfulness and deliberation.

At that time, the twin Sal trees blossomed forth all over, though it was out of season. And, in reverence to the Tathāgata, those (trees) rained blossoms, scattering, strewing, and continuously spreading them all over the body of the Tathāgata. Celestial *mandārava* flowers fell from the air above, being scattered, strewn and spread all over the body of the Tathāgata, in reverence to him. And in reverence to the Tathāgata, celestial sandalwood powder fell from the air above, being scattered, strewn and spread all over the body of the Tathāgata.

And in reverence to the Tathāgata, celestial music sounded in the air above.

And in reverence to the Tathāgata, celestial singing in the air above was heard.

199. Then the Bhagavā said to the Venerable Ānanda: Ānanda, the twin Sal trees have blossomed forth all over, though out of season. And, in reverence to the Tathāgata, those (trees) rain blossoms, scattering, strewing and continuously spreading them all over the body of the Tathāgata. And, in reverence to the Tathāgata, celestial *mandārava*

flowers and celestial sandalwood powder fall from the air above, scattering, strewing and spreading all over the body of the Tathāgata.

And in reverence to the Tathāgata, celestial music sounds in the air above.

And in reverence to the Tathāgata, celestial singing in the air above is heard.

Ānanda, mere acts of reverence of this kind cannot be deemed to honour, esteem, venerate, revere, and worship the Tathāgata rightly. (Only) the bhikkhu, or bhikkhunī, or the lay-disciple, or the female lay-disciple, who practices fully according to the Teaching, who is endowed with correctness in the practice of the Teaching, and who lives (lit., walks) in perfect conformity with righteousness and truth,[178] can be deemed to honour, esteem, venerate, revere and worship the Tathāgata in the highest degree.

Therefore, Ānanda, you should thus train and practice, resolving to practice fully according to the Teaching, to be endowed with correctness in the practice of the Teaching, and to live in perfect conformity with righteousness and truth.

Upavāṇa, the Bhikkhu Elder

200. At that time, the Venerable Upavāṇa was standing before the Bhagavā, fanning him. And the Bhagavā caused him to move aside, saying "Move away, bhikkhu, do not stand in front of me."

Then this thought occurred to the Venerable Ānanda:

"This Venerable Upavāṇa had been in attendance on the Bhagavā for a long time, staying near him and always close to him. And yet at this last period of time, the Bhagavā caused him to move aside, saying 'Move away, bhikkhu, do not stand in front of me.' What is the reason for the Bhagavā saying this? What is the cause?"

Then the Venerable Ānanda asked the Bhagavā thus:

"Venerable Sir, this Venerable Upavāṇa had been in attendance on the Bhagavā for a long time, staying near and always close to the Bhagavā. And yet at this last period of time, the Bhagavā caused him to move aside, saying 'Move away, bhikkhu, do not stand in front of me.' What is the reason for the Bhagavā saying this? What is the cause?"

The Bhagavā said:

---

178. **Righteousness and truth**: see footnote to Para 168.

Ānanda, most of the devas in the ten thousand world systems have assembled (here) to see the Tathāgata. Ānanda, for a distance of twelve *yojanās* in and around the Sal Grove of the Malla princes at the road-bend leading to Kusinārā, there is not a spot that could be pierced with the extreme tip of a tail-hair that is not filled by powerful devas.

Ānanda, the devas are grumbling (thus):

"We have come from afar to see the Tathāgata. The Homage-Worthy, Perfectly Self-Enlightened Tathāgatas arise in the world only rarely. And tonight, in the last watch of the night, the parinibbāna of the Tathāgata will take place. This powerful bhikkhu is standing in front of the Bhagavā, obstructing our view. We will not get a view of the Tathāgata at this last period of time."

201. "Venerable Bhagavā, in what condition and in what state of mind are the devas?"

Ānanda, devas who are (standing) in the sky, taking (i.e., transforming) the sky as firm ground, are weeping with dishevelled hair, are weeping with upraised hands, flinging themselves down, rolling forward and backward, rolling hither and thither, (and lamenting) "Too soon is the Bhagavā going to realize parinibbāna! Too soon is the Sugata going to realize parinibbāna! Too soon is the Eye (i e., the Possessor of the Eye of Wisdom) going to disappear from the world!"

Ānanda, devas who are (standing) on the ground, taking (i.e., transforming) the earth as firm ground, are weeping with dishevelled hair, are weeping with upraised hands, flinging themselves down, rolling forward and backward, rolling hither and thither, (and lamenting) "Too soon is the Bhagavā going to realize pari-nibbāna! Too soon is the Sugata going to realize parinibbāna! Too soon is the Eye (i.e., the Possessor of the Eye of Wisdom) going to disappear from the world!"

But those devas who are free from sensual passion can bear it, mindfully and deliberately reflecting: "All conditioned and compounded things have the nature of impermanence. How then can it be possible to get that (permanence) in this (compounded) nature?"

Four Places Arousing Apprehension of the Nature of Impermanence

202. "Venerable Sir, in times past bhikkhus who had ended their residence period of the rains in different places used to come and see (and pay homage to) the Tathāgata. We used to get the privilege of seeing

and honouring[179] these inspiring bhikkhus. But, Venerable Sir, after the Bhagavā has passed away, we shall not get the privilege of seeing and honouring the inspiring bhikkhus."

Ānanda, there are four places which should be (visited and) seen by a person of devotion, and which would cause awareness and apprehension of the nature of impermanence (*saṃvejanīya*). What are these four?

"This (Lumbinī) place is where the Tathāgata was born." Ānanda, this is a place which should be (visited and) seen by a person of devotion, and which would cause awareness and apprehension of the nature of impermanence.

"This (Mahābodhi) place is where the Tathāgata attained unsurpassed Supreme Enlightenment." Ānanda, this also is a place which should be (visited and) seen by a person of devotion, and which would cause awareness and apprehension of the nature of impermanence.

"This (Migadāyavana) place is where the Tathāgata set the unsurpassed Wheel of Truth rolling (i.e., expounded the first sermon, the *Dhammacakka Pavattana Sutta*)." Ānanda, this also is a place which should be (visited and) seen by a person of devotion, and which would cause awareness and apprehension of the nature of impermanence.

"This (Kusinārā) place is where the Tathāgata passed into the ultimate peace of *anupādisesa nibbāna* which is the complete cessation of all the five khandhas." Ānanda, this also is a place which should be (visited and) seen by a person of devotion, and which would cause awareness and apprehension of the nature of impermanence.

Ānanda, these are the four places which should be (visited and) seen by a person of devotion, and which would cause awareness and apprehension of the nature of impermanence.

And, Ānanda, there will come (to these places), bhikkhus, bhikkhunīs, lay-disciples and female lay-disciples, with devotion in their hearts, (reflecting) "Here (in Lumbinī) the Tathāgata was born!" or "Here (at Mahābodhi) the Tathāgata attained unsurpassed, Supreme Enlightenment!" or "Here (at Migadāyavana) the Tathāgata set the unsurpassed Wheel of Truth rolling!" or "Here (at Kusinārā) the Tathāgata passed away, realizing parinibbāna by experiencing the ultimate peace of complete cessation of all the five khandhas!" Ānanda, all those who are on a pilgrimage to (these) shrines, if they should die with devotion in their hearts during the course of the pilgrimage,

---

179. **Honouring:** *payirūpāsanāya* attend on, pay homage to, honour, worship.

will after (their) death and dissolution of the body be reborn in a good destination, a fortunate celestial (deva) realm.

The Venerable Ānanda's Questions

203. "Venerable Sir, how should we conduct ourselves with regard to women?"

Not seeing them, Ānanda.

"If we should (unavoidably) see them, Bhagavā, what should be our conduct?"

Not speaking to them, Ānanda.

"If, Venerable Sir, we should have to speak to them, what should be our conduct?"

You should establish mindfulness, Ānanda.

204. "Venerable Sir, how should we act regarding the body (i.e., the remains) of the Tathāgata?"

Ānanda, do not worry yourselves about doing honour to the body of the Tathāgata. I exhort you, Ānanda: (Only) apply yourselves, exert yourselves in the essential, most excellent practice.[180] Striving ardently, without negligence, in the essential, most excellent practice, resolutely direct your mind (towards the attainment of Nibbāna).[181]

Ānanda, there are wise nobles, wise brahmins, and wise householders, of the utmost devotion to the Tathāgata, who will do honour to the body of the Tathāgata.

205. "But, Venerable Sir, what should be done to the body of the Tathāgata (by the nobles, brahmins and householders)?"

In the same way, Ānanda, as is done to the body of a Universal Monarch.

"But, Venerable Sir, what is done to the body of a Universal Monarch?"

Ānanda, the body of a Universal Monarch is wrapped up in new cloth (made in Kāsi). After being wrapped up in new (Kāsi) cloth, (the body is) wrapped up in carded cotton wool. After being wrapped up in carded cotton wool, (it is) again wrapped up in new (Kāsi) cloth. In this way the body of the Universal Monarch is wrapped up in five hundred successive layers (of cloth and cotton wool).

---

180. **The essential, most excellent practice**: i.e., practice leading to arahatship: *sārattha.* This is rendered in the Burmese Nissaya as "for one's own good, for one's own benefit," from the variant reading *sadattha.*

181. This is as rendered in the Burmese version, following the Commentary, for *pahitatta*, 'sending the mind'.

Then it is enclosed in a golden[182] oil vat covered over by another golden vat. Then a pyre of all kinds of perfumed wood is built, and the body of the Universal Monarch is cremated. A stupa (i.e., a monumental mound with a dome) to (the honour of) the Universal Monarch is built at the junction of four highways.

Ānanda, this is what is done to the body of a Universal Monarch.

Ānanda, in the same way as is done to the body of a Universal Monarch, so should it be done to the body of the Tathāgata. A stupa to (the honour of) the Tathāgata should be built at the junction of four highways.

At that stupa people will make offerings of flowers or incense or scented powder, or will pay homage, or will feel reverence in their minds. To such people, benefit and happiness will accrue for a long time.

Persons Worthy of a Stupa

206. Ānanda, there are four persons who are worthy of a stupa being built to their honour. Who are these four?

A Tathāgata, Homage-Worthy, Perfectly Self-Enlightened, is worthy of a stupa.

A Pacceka Buddha[183] is worthy of a stupa.

An Ariya disciple of a Tathāgata is worthy of a stupa.

A Universal Monarch is worthy of a stupa.

Through what special benefit, Ānanda, is a Tathāgata, Homage-Worthy, Perfectly Self-Enlightened, worthy of a stupa?

Ānanda, many people will feel reverence in their minds, (reflecting) that "This (stupa) is a stupa of that Exalted, Homage-Worthy, Perfectly Self-Enlightened Buddha." After the death and dissolution of these people who feel such reverence and devotion in their minds, they will be reborn in a good destination, a fortunate celestial (deva) realm.

Ānanda, it is through this special benefit that a Tathāgata, Homage-Worthy, Perfectly Self-Enlightened, is worthy of a stupa.

Through what special benefit, Ānanda, is a Pacceka Buddha worthy of a stupa?

---

182. **Golden**: the Burmese version in a footnote says the term *āyasāya* in the Pāḷi text should be translated as "iron"; but as the Commentary has *sovaṇṇāya*, the term "golden" is used here.

183. *Pacceka Buddha*: One who, like the Buddha, is Self-Enlightened in the Four Noble Truths and has uprooted all the *kilesas*. However he cannot teach others. Pacceka Buddhas appear during the absence of the Buddha *sāsanā* or Teaching.

Ānanda, many people will feel reverence in their minds, (reflecting) that "This (stupa) is a stupa of that Exalted, Self-Enlightened Pacceka Buddha." After the death and dissolution of these people who feel such reverence and devotion in their minds, they will be reborn in a good destination, a fortunate celestial (deva) realm.

Ānanda, it is through this special benefit that a Pacceka Buddha is worthly of a stupa.

Through what special benefit, Ānanda, is an Ariya Disciple of the Tathāgata worthy of a stupa?

Ānanda, many people will feel reverence in their minds, (reflecting) that "This (stupa) is a stupa of an Ariya Disciple of that Exalted, Homage-Worthy, Perfectly Self-Enlightened Buddha." After the death and dissolution of these people who feel such reverence and devotion in their minds, they will be reborn in a good destination, a fortunate celestial (deva) realm.

Ānanda, it is through this special benefit that an Ariya Disciple of the Tathāgata is worthy of a stupa.

Through what special benefit, Ānanda, is a Universal Monarch worthy of a stupa?

Ānanda, many people will feel reverence in their minds, (reflecting) that "This (stupa) is a stupa of that righteous monarch who ruled according to the principles of rignteousness." After the death and dissolution of these people who feel such reverence in their minds, they will be reborn in a good destination, a fortunate celestial (deva) realm.

Ānanda, it is through this special benefit that a Universal Monarch is worthy of a stupa.

Ānanda, these are the four persons who are worthy of a stupa.

The Venerable Ānanda

207. Then the Venerable Ānanda went into the pavilion[184] and leaning against the door-post, stood lamenting "I am still a *sekha*,[185] with tasks still to be done (to reach the higher stages of *Magga ñāṇa*). And my Teacher (i.e., the Buddha), who has ever been compassionate towards me, is going to pass away!"

---

184. **Pavilion**: *vihāra*, rendered by the Burmese version as "monastery". The Commentary explains it as *mandala-māla*.

185. *sekha*: one who has still to learn, not yet having attained the final stage of Arahatship. The Venerable Ānanda was only a Sotāpanna, "Stream-Enterer," at that time.

Then the Bhagavā asked the bhikkhus, "O Bhikkhus, where is Ānanda?"

The bhikkhus replied, "Venerable Sir, the Venerable Ānanda has gone into the pavilion, and stands leaning against the door-post, lamenting (thus): I am still a *sekha*, with tasks still to be done. And my Teacher, who has ever been compassionate towards me, is going to pass away."

Then the Bhagavā said to a bhikkhu, "Come bhikkhu, say you to Ānanda in my words: Friend Ānanda, the Teacher calls you." That bhikkhu assented respectfully, saying "Very well, Venerable Sir," and went to the Venerable Ānanda, and said, "Friend Ānanda, the Teacher calls you". The Venerable Ānanda, replying "Very well, friend," to that bhikkhu, went to the Bhagavā, and making obeisance to the Bhagavā, sat at a certain place.

The Bhagavā said to the Venerable Ānanda, seated on one side:

Enough, Ānanda. Do not be grievously anxious, do not lament. Have I not from former times shown that there must be separation (while living), severance (through death) and sundering (through being in different states of existence) from all that are dear and beloved? Ānanda, in this matter, that which has the nature of arising, of appearing, of being compounded, and of decay and dissolution, how can the wish that it, even if it is the body of the Tathāgata, should not disintegrate and disappear be realized? There can be no such possibility.

For a long time now, Ānanda, you have served the Tathāgata faithfully both in his presence and in his absence and with unbounded loving-kindness in deed, to the benefit and welfare (of the Tathāgata); faithfully and with unbounded loving-kindness in words, to the benefit and welfare (of the Tathāgata); faithfully and with unbounded loving-kindness in thought, to the benefit and welfare (of the Tathāgata). You, Ānanda, have gained much merit. Exert yourself in fundamental mental concentration (i.e., *vipassanā* meditation). You will soon become an arahat, free from defilements.

208. Then the Bhagavā said to the bhikkhus:

O Bhikkhus, the attendant bhikkhus of the Exalted, Homage-Worthy, Prefectly Self-Enlightened Buddhas of times past were as (excellent and devoted as) my (attendant) Ānanda.

O Bhikkhus, the attendant bhikkhus of the Exalted, Homage-Worthy, Perfectly Self-Enlightened Buddhas of times to come will be as (excellent and devoted as) my (attendant) Ānanda.

O Bhikkhus, Ānanda is wise and intelligent. He knows: This is the (proper) time for the bhikkhus to approach and see the Tathāgata (or) this is the time for the bhikkhunīs, (or) this is the time for the lay-disciples, (or) this is the time for the female lay-disciples, (or) this is the time for the king, the king's ministers, the teachers of other religions or sects, or their followers (to approach had see the Tathāgata).

Four Marvellous Qualities of Ānanda

203. O Bhikkhus, Ānanda has four marvellous and unprecedentedly wonderful qualities. What are these four?

If, bhikkhus, a company of bhikkhus should come to see Ānanda, they become joyful on seeing him. If Ānanda should discourse to them on the Doctrinc (the Dhamma), they are made joyful by his discourse. When (after the discourse) Ānanda becomes silent, the company of bhikkhus still remains unsatiated.

If, bhikkhus, a company of bhikkhunīs should come to see Ānanda, they become joyful on seeing him. If Ānanda should discourse to them on the Doctrine, they are made joyful by his discourse. When (after the discourse) Ānanda becomes silent, the company of bhikkhunīs still remains unsatiated.

If, bhikkhus, a company of lay-disciples should come to see Ānanda, they become joyful on seeing him. If Ānanda should discourse to them on the Doctrine, they are made joyful by his discourse. When (after the discourse) Ānanda becomes silent, the company of lay-disciples still remains unsatiated.

If, bhikkhus, a company of female lay-disciples should come to see Ānanda, they become joyful on seeing him. If Ānanda should discourse to them on the Doctrine, they are made joyful by his discourse. When (after the discourse) Ānanda becomes silent, the company of female lay-disciples still remains unsatiated.

O Bhikkhus, these are the four marvellous and unprecedentedly wonderful qualities of Ānanda.

O Bhikkhus, a Universal Monarch has four marvellous and unprecedentedly wonderful qualities. What are these four?

If, bhikkhus, a company of nobles should come to see the Universal Monarch, they become joyful on seeing him. If the Universal Monarch should speak to them, they are made joyful by his talk. When (after speaking) the Universal Monarch becomes silent, the company of nobles still remains unsatiated.

If, bhikkhus, a company of brahmins ... (p) ...

If, bhikkhus, a company of (rich) householders ... (p) ...

If, bhikkhus, a company of ascetics should come to see the Universal Monarch, they become joyful on seeing him. If the Universal Monarch should speak to them, they are made joyful by his talk. When (after speaking) the Universal Monarch becomes silent, the company of ascetics still remains unsatiated.

O Bhikkhus, in the same way, Ānanda has four marvellous and unprecedentedly wonderful qualities.

If, bhikkhus, a company of bhikkhus should come to see Ānanda, they become joyful on seeing him. If Ānanda should discourse to them on the Doctrine (the Dhamma), they are made joyful by his discourse. When (after the discourse) Ānanda becomes silent, the company of bhikkhus still remains unsatiated.

If, bhikkhus, a company of bhikkhunīs ... (p) ...

If, bhikkhus, a company of lay-disciples ... (p) ...

If, bhikkhus, a company of female lay-disciples should come to see Ānanda, they become joyful on seeing him. If Ānanda should discourse to them on the Doctrine (the Dhamma,) they are made joyful by his discourse. When (after the discourse) Ānanda becomes silent, the company of female lay-disciples still remains unsatiated.

O Bhikkhus, these are the four marvellous and unprecedentedly wonderful qualities that Ānanda has.

Former Grandeur of Kusinārā

210. When this had been spoken, the Venerable Ānanda said to the Bhagavā:

"Venerable Sir, do not realize parinibbāna in this insignificant, barren, small town. Venerable Sir, elsewhere there are great cities, such as Campā, Rājagaha, Sāvatthi, Sāketa, Kosambī, and Bārāṇasī. Let the Bhagavā realize parinibbāna there (i.e., in one of these great cities). Many rich nobles, many rich brahmins, many rich householders who revere the Tathāgata dwell there. They will render due honour to the remains of the Tathāgata."

Say not so, Ānanda. Do not say 'this insignificant, barren, small town.'

Ānanda, in times long past, there was a king named Mahāsudassana, a Universal Monarch, a Righteous Ruler ruling by the principles of righteousness. Ruler over the four quarters of the earth (lit., the four island-continents bounded by four oceans), Conqueror of all enemies, whose realm was established in security, and who was endowed with the Seven Treasures. And Ānanda, this (Kusinārā) town was then King Mahāsudassana's capital city, called Kusāvatī. From east to west it was twelve yojanas long, and from north to south it was seven yojanas broad.

Ānanda, the capital city Kusāvatī was opulent, prosperous, well-populated, crowded with (all kinds of) people and abundant in provisions. Just as, Ānanda, a capital city of the devas, called Āḷakamandā, is opulent, prosperous, well-populated (with devas), crowded with (all kinds of) yakkha-devas, and abundant in provisions, so the capital city Kusāvatī was opulent, prosperous, well-populated, crowded with (all kinds of) people, and abundant in provisions.

Ānanda, the capital city Kusāvatī was never silent by day and night, (resounding) with ten sounds, namely, the noises of elephants, of horses, of carriages, the sounds of big drums, of tabours, of lutes, of singing, of conches, of small gongs, of cymbals, and tenthly, cries of "Eat, drink, chew."[186]

Go you, Ānanda, enter Kusinārā and say to the Malla princes living in Kusinārā: "Today, Vāseṭṭhas (i.e., Malla princes of the Vāseṭṭha clan), in the last watch of the night (towards dawn), the parinibbāna of the Tathāgata will take place. Come, Vāseṭṭhas, come quickly. Do not feel regret later (with the thought) 'Though the parinibbāna of the Tathāgata took place in our territory, we did not get (the chance) to see him at the very last'."

The Venerable Ānanda assented respectfully, saying "Very well, Venerable Sir," and rearranging his robes, took alms-bowl and great robe, and went into Kusinārā with a companion.

Homage by the Malla Princes

211. At that time the Malla princes of Kusinārā were assembled at the council hall on certain business. Then the Venerable Ānanda approached the council hall of the Malla princes and announced to them: "Today, Vāseṭṭhas, in the last watch of the night, the parinibbāna of the Tathāgata will take place. Come, Vāseṭṭhas, come quickly. Do not feel regret later (with the thought) 'Though the parinibbāna of the Tathāgata took place in our territory, we did not get (the chance) to see him at the very last!"

On hearing these words of the Venerable Ānanda, the Malla princes, their sons (and daughters), daughters-in-law, and their wives felt miserably grief stricken, sad at heart, and oppressively sorrowful in

186. The Pāḷi text lists actually eleven kinds of sounds, the cries of invitation to eat, etc. being the eleventh sound, although mentioned in the text as the last and tenth sound. The sound of small gongs and of cymbals can be combined to count as one sound, according to the Commentary on Buddhavaṃsa.

mind. Some wept with dishevelled hair, with upraised hands, they flung themselves down, and rolled forward and backward, hither and thither; (lamenting) "Too soon is the Bhagavā going to realize parinibbāna! Too soon is the Sugata going to realize parinibbāna! Too soon is the Eye (i.e., the Possessor of the Eye of Wisdom) going to disappear from the world!"

Then the Malla princes, their sons (and daughters), daughters-in-law, and their wives, feeling miserably grief stricken, sad at heart, and oppressively sorrowful in mind, approached the Venerable Ānanda, in the Sal grove of the Mallas at the road-bend (leading) to the town.

Then this thought occurred to the Venerable Ānanda:

"If I should let the Mallas of Kusinārā pay homage to the Bhagavā one by one, the night will have passed into dawn before (all) the Malla princes finish paying reverence to the Bhagavā. it would be well if I should put the Mallas of Kusinārā in (separate) groups according to family, and let them pay homage group by group, (announcing) 'Venerable Sir, the Malla prince of such and such a name, with children, wife, ministers and retinue, pays homage at the feet of the Bhagavā!"

Then the Venerable Ānanda put the Mallas of Kusinārā in groups according to family and let them pay homage to the Bhagavā group by group, (announcing) "Venerable Sir, the Malla prince of such and such a name, with children, wife, ministers and retinue, pays homage at the feet of the Bhagavā."

By this means the Venerable Ānanda enabled (all) the Malla princes to pay homage to the Bhagavā, (finishing) in the very first watch of the night.

Subhadda the Wandering Ascetic

212. At that time Subhadda, a wandering ascetic,[187] was staying at Kusinārā. He heard that "On this day, in the last watch of the night, the parinibbāna of the Samaṇa Gotama[188] will take place." Then Subhadda the wandering ascetic had this thought:

"I have heard it said by old and venerable wandering ascetics, teachers of teachers, that the Homage-worthy. Perfectly Self-Enlightened Tathāgatas arise in the world only sometimes and rarely. Today, in the last watch of the night, the parinibbāna of the Samaṇa Gotama will take place. There is an uncertainty (regarding true doctrine) that has arisen in me. I have this faith in the Samaṇa Gotama that he will be able to expound the Doctrine to me so as to remove this uncertainty."

Then Subhadda the wandering ascetic approached the Venerable Ānanda in the Sal grove of the Malla princes at the road-bend (leading) to Kusinārā, and said to the Venerable Ānanda: "O Ānanda, I have heard it said by old and venerable wandering ascetics, teachers of teachers, that the Homage-Worthy, Perfectly Self-Enlightened Tathāgatas arise in the world only sometimes and rarely. Today, in the last watch of the night, the parinibbāna of the Samaṇa Gotama will take place. There is an uncertainty that has arisen in me. I have this faith in the Samaṇa Gotama that he will be able to expound the Doctrine to me so as to remove this uncertainty. O Ānanda, I request (the chance of getting) to see the Samaṇa Gotama."

On this being said, the Venerable Ānanda replied: "Friend Subhadda, this cannot be allowed. (lit., enough, or, not fitting.) Do not harass the Tathāgata. The Bhagavā is very tired."

For a second time, Subhadda the wandering ascetic said: ... (p) ... (repeated as above).

For a third time, Subhadda the wandering ascetic said: "O Ānanda, I have heard it said by old and venerable wandering ascetics, teachers of teachers, that the Homage-Worthy, Perfectly Self-Enlightened Tathāgatas arise in the world only sometimes and rarely. Today, in the last watch of the night, the parinibbāna of the Samaṇa Gotama will take place. There is an uncertainty that has arisen in me. I have this faith in

---

187. **Wandering ascetic**: *paribbājaka*, a wanderer; wandering religious mendicant; usually not a Buddhist.

188. **Samaṇa Gotama**: a *samaṇa* is a wanderer, a recluse, a person leading a religious life. The Buddha was often mentioned and addressed as a *Samaṇa* by non-Buddhists.

the Samaṇa Gotama that he will be able to expound the Doctrine to me so as to remove this uncertainty. O Ānanda, I request (the chance of getting) to see the Samaṇa Gotama."

For the third time also, the Venerable Ānanda replied: "Friend Subhadda, this cannot be allowed. Do not harass the Tathāgata. The Bhagavā is very tired."

213. The Bhagavā overheard this conversation between the Venerable Ānanda and the wandering ascetic Subhadda, and the Bhagavā said to the Venerable Ānanda:

Ānanda, it is not fitting (to hinder the wandering ascetic). Do not prevent Subhadda (from seeing me). Ānanda, let Subhadda get (the opportunity) to see the Tathāgata. If Subhadda asks me anything, everything he asks will be because he wants to know, and not because he wishes to harass me. When I answer what he asks, he will readily understand that (answer).

Then the Venerable Ānanda said to the wandering ascetic Subhadda, "Go, Friend Subhadda. The Bhagavā has given you permission."

Then Subhadda the wandering ascetic approached where the Bhagavā was, and offered courteous greetings to the Bhagavā. After offering courteous greetings to the Bhagavā, and having said memorable words of felicitation, Subhadda seated himself on one side. When he was seated, Subhadda the wandering ascetic addressed the Bhagavā thus:

"O (Venerable) Gotama, there are samaṇas and brāhmaṇas (i.e., leaders in religious life) who have communities of many disciples, who have large sects of followers, who are leaders of (their) sects, who are renowned, who are famous, who are founders of schools of doctrine, and who are well-esteemed by many people. They are, namely, Pūraṇa Kassapa, Makkhaḷi Gosāla, Ajita Kesakambala, Pakudha Kaccāyana, Sañcaya Belaṭṭhaputta, and Nigaṇṭha Nātaputta. Do all of them have knowledge and understanding, as they themselves have declared? Or do all of them have no knowledge and understanding? Or do some of them have knowledge and understanding, and some have no knowledge and understanding?"

Subhadda, do not ask (this question) (lit., it is not fitting, not proper). Put aside that (question) whether all of them have knowledge and understanding, as they themselves have declared, or whether all of them have no knowledge and understanding, or whether some of them have knowledge and understanding, and some have no knowledge and understanding.

Subhadda, I shall expound the Doctrine to you. Listen and bear it well in mind. I shall speak.

Then to Subhadda, the wandering ascetic, assenting respectfully by saying, "Very well, Venerable Sir," the Bhagavā gave this discourse:

214. Subhadda, in whatsoever Teaching is not found the Noble Path of Eight Constituents, neither in it is there found a Samaṇa of the first stage, (a realizer of the First Magga and Phala, a *sotāpanna*), nor is there found a Samaṇa of the second stage, (a realizer of the Second Magga and Phala, a *sakadāgāmī*), nor is there found a Samaṇa of the third stage, (a realizer of the Third Magga and Phala, an *anāgāmī*), nor is there found a Samaṇa of the fourth stage, (a realizer of the Fourth and Final Magga and Phala, an *arahat*).

And, Subhadda, in whatsoever Teaching is found the Noble Path of Eight Constituents, in it is found a Samaṇa of the first stage (*a sotāpanna*), and in it is found a Samaṇa of the second stage (*a sakadāgāmi*), and in it is found a Samaṇa of the third stage (*an anāgāmī*), and in it is found a Samaṇa of the fourth stage (an *arahat*).

Now, Subhadda, in this Teaching (of mine) there is to be found the Noble Path of Eight Constituents; and in this Teaching alone is found a Samaṇa of the first stage (a *sotāpanna*); in this Teaching alone is found a Samaṇa of the second stage (a *sakadāgāmī*); in this Teaching alone is found a Samaṇa of the third stage (an *anāgāmī*); in this Teaching alone is found a Samaṇa of the fourth stage (an *arahat*). Other systems of Teaching are void of (the twelve)[189] noble samaṇas who have true knowledge. Subhadda, if these (twelve) bhikkhus practice and pass on the Teaching rightly, the world will not be void of arahats.

(VERSE)

Subhadda, at the age of twenty-nine, I renounced the world and became an ascetic to search for Enlightenment (*Sabbaññuta Ñāṇa*). It is over fifty years now, since I became an ascetic. Outside this (Teaching of mine) there is no one who cultivates Insight Practice (*vipassanā*) leading to *Magga Ñāṇa*; (outside of this Teaching) there is no Samaṇa of the first stage (*sotāpanna*); neither is there a Samaṇa of the second stage; nor a Samaṇa of the third stage; nor a Samaṇa of the fourth stage.

---

189. **The twelve**: by this is meant (a) four persons who attain the realization of Magga; (b) four persons who attain the realization of Phala, Fruition; and (c) four persons who are striving through *vipassanā* meditation to attain the four Stages of Realization.

Other systems of teaching are void of (the twelve) noble samaṇas who have true knowledge. Subhadda, if these (twelve) bhikkhus practice and pass on the Teaching, the world will not be void of arahats.

215. When this was said, Subhadda the wandering ascetic addressed the Bhagavā thus: "Venerable Sir, extremely wonderful (is the Doctrine)! Venerable Sir, surpassingly beautiful (is the Doctrine)! Venerable Sir, just as if that which has been turned over is turned upright, or that which has been hidden is revealed, or one who has lost his way is informed of the right way, or an oil-lamp is (brought and) held in the darkness so that those with eyes might see objects, even so the Bhagavā has shown me the Truth in many ways. Venerable Sir, I take refuge in the Bhagavā, I take refuge in the Dhamma (the Teaching of the Buddha), I take refuge in the Saṅgha (the Order of bhikkhus). May I, Venerable Sir, receive from the Bhagavā (lit., in the presence of the Bhagavā) initiation and admission into the Order as a bhikkhu."

Subhadda, if a person who previously has been a believer in other Doctrines wishes to be initiated and to be admitted into this Order as a bhikkhu, he has to live under probation for four months. When the four months have passed, if the bhikkhus are satisfied (with him), that person will be initiated and admitted into the Order, thus becoming a bhikkhu. But in this matter, the individual differences are recognized.

"Venerable Sir, if a person, having been a believer in another Doctrine and wishing to receive initiation and admission into this Order as a bhikkhu, has to live under probation for four months, and if at the end of the four months, the bhikkhus are satisfied and grant him initiation and grant him admission into the Order as a bhikkhu, I am prepared to live under probation even for four years. At the end of four years let the bhikkhus who are satisfied grant me initiation and admission into the Order so as to become a bhikkhu."

Then the Bhagavā said to the Venerable Ānanda, "Since that is so, Ānanda, let Subhadda be initiated into the Order." And the Venerable Ānanda replied, "Very well, Venerable Sir."

After that, Subhadda the wandering ascetic said this to the Venerable Ānanda:

"Fortunate you all are. Friend Ānanda; good gain you all have, Friend Ānanda, in that you all have received in the very presence of the Teacher inauguration as close disciples in this Teaching." (lit., have been sprinkled over with the sprinkling or anointing of close discipleship.)

Subhadda the wandering ascetic then received initiation and admission into the Order as a bhikkhu in the presence of the Bhagavā.

Not long after that, the Venerable Subhadda sought solitary seclusion and remained directing his mind (towards the attainment of Nibbāna) without any remission of awareness and with vigorous resolution.

And soon he attained to and remained abiding in the supreme Arahatta Fruition stage, the goal of the Practice of Purity (*brahmacariya*), having realized this in this very life, by himself and through Magga Insight (*abhiññā*), (a desired goal) for which good people worthily leave the worldly life and become homeless recluses. Thus he knew "Rebirth is no more (for me); I have achieved the goal of the Practice of Purity; what should be done (for the realization of Magga) has been done; and I have nothing more to do (for such realization)." The Venerable Subhadda became one of the arahats, and he was the last one to become a disciple in the presence of the Bhagavā.

End of the fifth portion for recitation

Last Words of the Tathāgata

216. Then the Bhagavā said to the Venerable Ānanda:

It may happen that (some among) you have this thought: 'The Doctrine; (lit. the word) is bereft of the Teacher of the Doctrine; our Teacher is no more." But, Ānanda, it should not be so considered. Ānanda, the Doctrine and Discipline I have taught and laid down to all of you will be your Teacher when I am gone.

Ānanda, when I have passed away, bhikkhus should not address one another as they do at present by the term '*āvuso*' (Friend) (irrespective of seniority). Ānanda, the senior bhikkhus should address the junior bhikkhus by name, or by family name, or by the term '*āvuso*'. And the junior bhikkhus should address the senior bhikkhus by the term '*bhante*' or '*āyasmā*' (Venerable Sir)

Ānanda, after I have passed away, the Saṅgha, the Order of the bhikkhus, may, if it wishes to, abolish lesser and minor Rules of Discipline.

Ānanda, after I have passed away, let the Brahmā penalty be imposed upon Bhikkhu Channa

"But, Venerable Sir, what is the Brahmā penalty?"

Ānanda, let Bhikkhu Channa say whatever he wishes to. The bhikkhus should neither advise him nor admonish him, nor deter him.

217. Then the Bhagavā addressed the bhikkhus thus:

O Bhikkhus, if any bhikkhu should happen to have any uncertainty or perplexity regarding the Buddha, or the Dhamma (the Teaching), or the Saṅgha (the Order of bhikkhus), or Magga, or the Practice, then, bhikkhus, ask (me) questions. Do not let yourselves feel regret later with the thought that 'even though our Teacher was (with us) in our very presence, we were not able to ask him questions personally in return.'

When this was said, the bhikkhus remained silent. For a second time, the Bhagavā said ... (p) ...

For a third time, the Bhagavā said:

O Bhikkhus, if any bhikkhu should happen to have any uncertainty or perplexity regarding the Buddha, or the Dhamma, or the Saṅgha, or Magga, or the Practice, then, bhikkhus, ask (me) questions. Do not let yourselves feel regret later with the thought that 'even though our Teacher was (with us) in our very presence, we were not able to ask him questions personally in return.'

For the third time, too, the bhikkhus remained silent.

Then the Bhagavā said to the bhikkhus:

O Bhikkhus, it may be that you do not ask questions out of respect for the Teacher. Then, bhikkhus, let a bhikkhu tell a companion (his uncertainty or perplexity).

Even when this was said, the bhikkhus continued to remain silent.

Then the Venerable Ānanda said to the Bhagavā: "Wonderful it is. Venerable Sir! Marvellous it is, Venerable Sir! I believe that in this community of bhikkhus not a single bhikkhu has uncertainty or perplexity regarding the Buddha, or the Dhamma, or the Saṅgha, or Magga, or the Practice."

Ānanda, you say this only out of faith. Indeed, Ānanda, the Tathāgata knows for certain that in this community of bhikkhus not a single bhikkhu has uncertainty or perplexity regarding the Buddha, or the Dhamma, or the Saṅgha, or Magga, or the Practice.

Ānanda, amongst these five hundred bhikkhus, even the least (in attainment) is a Sotāpanna, a Stream-enterer, not liable to be reborn in any *apāya* realm of misery, assured (of reaching desirable realms of existence or of reaching the end of *dukkha*), bound for (the three higher levels of Insight, culminating in) Enlightenment.

218. Then the Bhagavā said to the bhikkhus:

O Bhikkhus. I say this now to you: "All conditioned and compounded things (*saṅkhārā*) have the nature of decay and disintegration. With mindfulness endeavour diligently (to complete the task)."[190]

These were the last words of the Tathāgata.

---

190. See footnotes 1 and 2 to para 185.

The Buddha's Parinibbāna

219. Then the Bhagavā entered upon the first *jhāna*. Rising from the first *jhāna*, he entered upon the second *jhāna*. Rising from the second *jhāna*, he entered upon the third *jhāna*. Rising from the third *jhāna*, he entered upon the fourth *jhāna*. Rising from the fourth *jhāna*, he entered upon and became absorbed in the *ākāsānañcāyatana* (Sphere of Infinity of Space). Rising from the *samāpatti*[191] of Infinite Space, he entered upon and became absorbed in the *viññāṇañcāyatana* (Sphere of Infinity of Consciousness). Rising from the *samāpatti* of Infinite Consciousness, he entered upon and became absorbed in the *ākiñcaññāyatana* (Sphere of Nothingness). Rising from the *samāpatti* of Nothingness, he entered upon and became absorbed in the *Nevasaññānāsaññāyatana* (Sphere of Neither *saññā* Nor Non-*saññā*). Rising from the *samāpatti* of Neither *saññā* Nor Non-*saññā*, he entered upon and became absorbed in *Nirodhasamāpatti*, in which *saññā*-and-sensation (i.e., Consciousness) cease.

Then the Venerable Ānanda asked the Venerable Anuruddha, "Bhante Anuruddha, has the Bhagavā passed away?"

(The Venerable Anuruddha replied,) "Āvuso Ānanda the Bhagavā has not passed away. He is absorbed in *Nirodhasamāpatti*."

Then the Bhagavā, rising from the *Nirodhasamāpatti*, entered upon and became absorbed in the Sphere of Neither *saññā* Nor Non-*saññā*. Rising from the *samāpatti* of Neither *saññā* Nor Non-*saññā*, he entered upon and became absorbed in the Sphere of Nothingness. Rising from the *samāpatti* of Nothingness, he entered upon and became absorbed in the Sphere of Infinite Consciousness. Rising from the *samāpatti* of Infinite Consciousness, he entered upon and became absorbed in the Sphere of Infinite Space. Rising from the *samāpatti* of Infinite Space, he entered upon the fourth *jhāna*. Rising from the fourth *jhāna*, he entered upon the third *jhāna*. Rising from the third *jhāna*, he entered upon the

---

191. *Jhāna* is a term used for the state of deep mental absorption in an object of meditation; *samāpatti* is a term used for attainment of sustained deep menial absorption in an object of meditation. When *jhāna* is sustained, it is termed *samāpatti*. The term *jhāna* is usually used for attainment in the first four stages of deep mental absorption, i.e., the four *rūpa jhānas*. The term *samāpatti* is used for attainment in the next stages of deep mental absorption, i.e., the four *arūpa jhānas*, and also for attainment of *phala* and *nirodha*. However, the term *samāpatti* is sometimes used to denote both the *rūpa* and *arūpa jhānas*. In the *nirodha samāpatti* there is no object of meditation, because of the cessation of *saññā*, consciousness.

second *jhāna*. Rising from the second *jhāna*, he entered upon the first *jhāna*. Rising from the first *jhāna*, he entered upon the second *jhāna*. Rising from the second *jhāna*, he entered upon the third *jhāna*. Rising from the third *jhāna*, he entered upon the fourth *jhāna*. Immediately after rising from the fourth *jhāna*, the Bhagavā passed away, realizing parinibbāna.

220. When the Bhagavā passed away, simultaneously with his passing away, a great, terrible, hair-raising and gooseflesh-causing earthquake occurred. Also rolls of thunder burst forth continuously.

When the Bhagavā passed away, at the moment of his passing away, the Sahampati Brahmā recited this verse:

> "Even such an incomparable person as the Self-Enlightened Tathāgata, the Teacher endowed with Ten Strengths (consisting of his perfect comprehension in ten fields of knowledge), has to pass away in this world. All beings in this world must inevitably give up the aggregate of mental and physical phenomena."

221. When the Bhagavā passed away, immediately on his passing away, Sakka, King of the devas, recited this verse:

> "All conditioned and compounded things (*saṅkhārā*) are indeed impermanent. Arising and decay are inherent in them. Having come into existence, they cease. The realization of Nibbāna on their cessation is blissful peace."

222. When the Bhagavā passed away, immediately on his passing away, the Venerable Anuruddha recited these verses:

> "The craving-free Sage has passed away, intent on the peace of Nibbāna. There is no more inhalation or exhalation of breath of the Buddha, he who had a steadfast mind and equanimity.
>
> "The Buddha endured his physical suffering with an unshaken mind. Like a flame extinguished, the mind of that Buddha has found release."

223. When the Bhagavā passed away, immediately on his passing away, the Venerable Ānanda recited this verse:

> "When the Enlightened One, replete with all noble qualities, passed away, then at that moment there occurred the fearsome great earthquake; then at that moment there occurred the hair-raising, gooseflesh-causing great earthquake."

224. When the Bhagavā passed away, some bhikkhus who were at that place and who were not free from the passions wept with upraised hands, flung themselves down, rolled forward and backward, and rolled hither and thither, (lamenting) "Too soon has the Bhagavā realized parinibbāna! Too soon has the Sugata realized parinibbāna! Too soon has the Eye (i.e the Possessor of the Eye of Wisdom) disappeared from the world!"

But those bhikkhus who were free from sensual passion could bear it, mindfully and deliberately reflecting: "All conditioned and compounded things (*saṅkhārā*) are impermanent. How then can it be possible to get that (permanence) in this (compounded nature)?"

225. Then the Venerable Anuruddha said to the bhikkhus: "Enough, friends! Do not grieve, do not lament. Had not the Bhagavā proclaimed from former times that there must be separation (while living), severance (through death) and sundering (through being in different states of existence) from all that are dear and beloved? Friends, in this matter, that which has the nature of arising, of appearing, of being compounded, and of decay and dissolution, how can the wish that it should not disintegrate and disappear be realized? There can be no such possibility. Friends, the devas are reproachful."

"But, Venerable Anuruddha, in what condition and in what state of mind are the devas?"

"Friend Ānanda, devas who are (standing) in the sky, taking (i.e., transforming) the sky as firm ground, weep with dishevelled hair, weep with upraised hands, fling themselves down, roll forward and backward, roll hither and thither, (lamenting) 'Too soon has the Bhagavā realized parinibbāna! Too soon has the Sugata realized parinibbāna! Too soon has the Eye (i.e., the Possessor of the Eye of Wisdom) disappeared from the world!'

"Friend Ānanda, devas who are (standing) on the ground, taking (i.e., transforming) the earth as firm ground, weep with dishevelled hair, weep with upraised hands, fling themselves down, roll forward and backward, roll hither and thither, (lamenting) 'Too soon has the Bhagavā realized parinibbāna! Too soon has the Sugata realized parinibbāna! Too soon has the Eye (i.e., the Possessor of the Eye of Wisdom) disappeared from the world!'

"But those devas who are free from sensual passion can bear it, mindfully and deliberately reflecting: All conditioned and compounded things have the nature of impermanence. How then can it be possible to get that (permanence) in this (compounded nature)?"

Then the Venerable Anuruddha and the Venerable Ānanda spent the rest of the night in religious discourse.

226. Then the Venerable Anuruddha said to the Venerable Ānanda, "Go, Friend Ānanda, enter Kusinārā and tell the Malla princes of Kusinārā 'O Vāseṭṭhas (i.e., Malla Princes), the Bhagavā has passed away. Do now as seems fitting to *you*."

The Venerable Ānanda assented, saying to the Venerable Anuruddha, "Very well, Venerable Sir." He then in the morning rearranged his robes, and taking alms-bowl and great robe entered Kusinārā with a companion.

At that time, the Malla princes were assembled at the council hall on that very business (concerning the Buddha's parinibbāna). Then the Venerable Ānanda went to the council hall of the Kusinārā Malla princes and said to them, "O Vāseṭṭhas, the Bhagavā has passed away. Do now as seems fitting to you."

On hearing those words of the Venerable Ānanda, the Malla princes, their sons, daughters, daughters-in-law, and their wives felt miserably grief stricken, sad at heart and oppressively sorrowful in mind. Some wept with dishevelled hair, with upraised hands; they flung themselves down, and rolled forward and backward, hither and thither, (lamenting) "Too soon has the Bhagavā realized parinibbāna! Too soon has the Sugata realized parinibbāna! Too soon has the Eye (i.e., the Possessor of the Eye of Wisdom) disappeared from the world!"

Last Rites for the Remains of the Buddha

227. Then the Kusinārā Malla princes gave orders to their men, saying "Gather flower-garlands, perfumes and all kinds of musical instruments in Kusinārā."

Then the Kusinārā Malla princes, taking flower-garlands, perfumes and all kinds of musical instruments, as well as five hundred sets of clothing, went to where the body of the Bhagavā was, in the Sal grove of the Mallas at the road-bend. And there they passed the day in paying homage, respect, reverence and honour to the remains of the Bhagavā, with dance, song, music, flowers and perfumes; and they made canopies of cloth and prepared pavilions of cloth.

Then the Kusinārā Malla princes thought: "It is too late today to cremate the remains of the Bhagavā. Tomorrow we shall perform the cremation."

Then the second day also was passed by the Mallas in paying homage, respect, reverence and honour to the remains of the Bhagavā, with dance, song, music, flowers and perfumes, and with the erection of canopies and pavilions of cloth. In the same way the third day also was passed; the fourth day also was passed; the fifth day also was passed; the sixth day also was passed.

Then, on the seventh day, this thought occurred to the Kusinārā Malla princes:

"We shall cremate the body of the Bhagavā south of the town, carrying it to the south side; beyond the town by the Southern road outside the town, paying homage, respect, reverence and honour to the remains of the Bhagavā, with dance, song, music, flowers and perfumes."

228. And thereupon eight foremost elders amongst the Malla princes, after washing their heads and donning new clothes, tried to lift up the body of the Bhagavā, (thinking) "We shall (now) lift up the body of the Bhagavā", but they were not able to do so. Then the Kusinārā Malla princes said to the Venerable Anuruddha, "Venerable Anuruddha, what is the reason, what is the cause that although eight of the foremost elders amongst the Malla princes, after washing their heads and donning new clothes, tried to lift up the body of the Bhagavā, (thinking) 'We shall (now) lift up the body of the Bhagavā', they could not do so?"

"Vāseṭṭhas, (it is because) your intention is different from the intention of the devas."

"What, Venerable Sir, is the intention of the devas?"

"Vāseṭṭhas, your intention is this: 'We shall cremate the body of the Bhagavā south of the town, carrying it to the south side beyond the town by the southern road outside the town, paying homage, respect, reverence and honour to the remains of the Bhagavā, with dance, song, music, flowers and perfumes.' The intention of the devas, however, is this: 'Paying homage, respect, reverence and honour to the remains of the Bhagavā, with celestial dance, song, music, flowers and perfumss, we shall carry the remains of the Bhagavā north of the town by the northern road, then entering the town by the northern gate and proceeding to the centre of the town by the central road, we shall leave by the eastern gate, and shall perform the cremation ceremony at the Makuṭabandhana shrine[192] of the Malla princes on the east side of the town'."

"Venerable Sir, let it be according to the intention of the devas."

229. At that time, all of Kusinārā, including even fence-borders, rubbish heaps and dust bins, became covered knee-deep with celestial

192. **Shrine**: the Commentary says that this was the royal hall where the Malla princes put on the ceremonial dress. It was called a shrine, out of courtesy.

mandārava flowers. Then the devas and the Kusinārā Malla princes, paying homage, respect, reverence and honour to the remains of the Bhagavā, with both celestial and human dance, song, music, flowers and perfumes, carried the remains of the Bhagavā north of the town by the northern road, then entering the town by the northern gate and proceeding to the centre of the town by the central road, they left by the eastern gate, and laid down (the bier with) the body of the Bhagavā at the Makuṭabandhana shrine of the Malla princes on the east side of the town.

230. Then the Kusinārā Malla princes asked the Venerable Ānanda, "Venerable Ānanda, what should be done to the body of the Tathāgata?"

"O Vāseṭṭhas, the body of the Tathāgata should be treated in the same way as is done to the remains of a Universal Monarch."

"Venerable Ānanda, what is done to the remains of a Universal Monarch?"

"O Vāseṭṭhas, the body of a Universal Monarch is wrapped up in new cloth. After being wrapped up in new cloth, (the body is) wrapped up in carded cottonwool. After being wrapped up in carded cotton wool, (it is) again wrapped up in new cloth. In this way the body of the Universal Monarch is wrapped up in five hundred successive layers (of cloth and cotton wool). Then it is enclosed in a golden oil vat and covered over by another golden vat. Then a pyre of all kinds of perfumed wood is built, and the body of the Universal Monarch is cremated. A stupa (i.e., a monumental mound with a dome), to (the honour of) the Universal Monarch is built at the junction of four highways. O Vāseṭṭhas, this is what is done to the body of a Universal Monarch."

"O Vāseṭṭhas, in the same way as is done to the body of a Universal Monarch, so should it be done to the body of the Tathāgata. A stupa to (the honour of) the Tathāgata should be built at the junction of four highways. At that stupa people will make offerings of flowers or incense or scented powder, or will pay homage, or will feel reverence in their minds. To such people, benefit and happiness will accrue for a long time."

Then the Kusinārā Malla princes gave orders to their men, to collect (all) the carded cotton wool of the Malla princes.

Then the Kusinārā Malla princes wrapped up the body of the Bhagavā in new cloth. After being wrapped up in new cloth, (the body was) wrapped up in carded cotton wool. After being wrapped up in carded cotton wool, (it was) wrapped up in new cloth. In this way the body of the Bhagavā was wrapped up in five hundred successive layers (of cloth and cotton wool). Then it was enclosed in a golden oil vat and covered over by another golden vat. Then a pyre of all kinds of perfumed wood was built, and the body of the Bhagavā was placed on the pyre.

THE VENERABLE MAHĀKASSAPA

231. Now at that time the Venerable Mahākassapa was on the way from Pāvā to Kusinārā together with a large company of bhikkhus, numbering five hundred. Then the Venerable Mahākassapa left the road and sat down at the foot of a tree. At that time a certain Ājīvaka, (who was a naked ascetic), was journeying towards Pāvā, taking (with him) a mandārava flower from Kusinārā. Now the Venerable Mahākassapa saw that Ājīvaka coming from a distance and seeing him said to that Ājīvaka, "Friend, do you know our Teacher?"

"Yes, friend, I know of him. It is seven days now since the Samaṇa Gotama passed away. (In fact,) I have brought this celestial mandārava flower from there (i.e., from the place where the Buddha passed away)."

(Thereupon), some of the bhikkhus who were not (yet) free from the passions, from amongst the five hundred bhikkhus with the Venerable Mahākassapa, wept with upraised hands, flung themselves down, rolled forward and backward, and rolled hither and thither, (lamenting) "Too soon has the Bhagavā realized parinibbāna! Too soon has the Sugata realized parinibbāna! Too soon has the Eye (i.e., the Possessor of the Eye of Wisdom) disappeared from the world!"

But those bhikkhus who were free from sensual passion could bear it, mindfully and deliberately reflecting: "All conditioned and compounded things are impermanent. How then can it be possible to get that (permanence) in this (compounded nature)?"

232. Now at that time Subhadda[193] who had become a bhikkhu only in old age was amongst that assembly. And that Subhadda who had become a bhikkhu in his old age said thus to the (other) bhikkhus: "Enough, friends. Do not grieve, do not lament. We are well rid of that great Samaṇa. He had oppressed us by (saying) 'This is proper for you; that is not proper for you'. But now we shall do what we like; we shall not do what we do not like."

Then the Venerable Mahākassapa said to the bhikkhus: "Enough, Āvuso; do not grieve, do not lament. Had not the Bhagavā expounded from long before the (inevitable) facts of separation (while living), severance (through death), and sundering (through being in different

193. This Subhadda is a different person from the wandering ascetic of the same name mentioned in Paras 212–215.

states of existence) from all that are dear and beloved? Āvuso, in this matter, that which has the nature of arising, of appearing, of being compounded, and of decay and dissolution, how can the wish that it, even the body of the Tathāgata, should not disintegrate and disappear be realized? Did not the Bhagavā expound from long before that there can be no such possibility?"

233. Now at that time four foremost Malla princes, after washing their heads and donning new clothes, (thought) "We will set fire to the Bhagavā's funeral Pyre," (and tried to ignite it) but were not able to do so. Then the Kusinārā Malla princes asked the Venerable Anuruddna thus:

"Venerable Anuruddha, what is the reason, what is the cause that although four foremost Malla princes, after washing their heads and donning new clothes, tried to kindle the funeral pyre of the Bhagavā, they were not able to set it on fire?"

"O Vāseṭṭhas, the wish (lit., the intention) of the devas is different."

"Venerable Sir, what is the wish of the devas?"

"O Vāseṭṭhas, the wish of the devas is this: The Venerable Mahākassapa is journeying along the way from Pāvā to Kusinārā, with a great company of bhikkhus, numbering five hundred; let not the Bhagavā's funeral pyre catch fire until the Venerable Mahākassapa has paid homage with his head at the feet of the Bhagavā."

"Venerable Sir, let it be according to the wish of the devas."

234. Then the Venerable Mahākassapa came to the funeral pyre of the Bhagavā at the Makuṭabandhana shrine of the Malla princes in Kusinārā. When he had come up to it, he arranged his robe over one shoulder and under the other, and with the palms of his hands put together and lifted up in reverence he walked three times round the pyre with his right side to it, and paid homage with his head against the feet of the Bhagavā. The five hundred bhikkhus also (who had come with the Venerable Mahākassapa) arranged their robes over one shoulder and under the other, and with their palms put together and lifted up in reverence, they walked three times round the pyre with their right side to it, and paid homage with their heads against the feet of the Bhagavā. When the Venerable Mahākassapa and the five hundred bhikkhus had paid their homage, the funeral pyre of the Bhagavā spontaneously burst into flames.

235. From the outer tegument (thin skin), or the corium (thick under-skin) of the flesh, or the sinews,[194] or the synovic[195] fluid of the body of the Bhagavā which was burnt away, neither ash nor soot[196] was to be seen. Only the bone-relics[197] remained. Just as, for instance, when butter or oil is burnt away, neither ash nor soot is to be seen, so from the outer tegument, or the corium, or the flesh, or the sinews, or the synovic fluid of the body of the Bhagavā which was burnt away, neither ash nor soot was to be seen. Only the bone-relics remained. Of those five hundred sets of cloth wrappings, only two were not consumed by fire, the innermost and the outermost. When the body of the Bhagavā had been burnt up, a stream of water appeared from the sky and extinguished the pyre. A stream of water also spurted out from those Sal trees which had water in them and extinguished the pyre of the Bhagavā. The Kusinārā Malla princes, too, extinguished the pyre with water scented with all kinds of perfumes. Then the Kusinārā Malla princes surrounded the bone-relics of the Bhagavā (placed) in the council hall with a cordon of spearmen and bowmen,[198] and for an entire seven days paid homage, respect, reverence and honour to the relics with dance, song, music and perfumes.

Distribution of the Relics

236. The King of Magadha, Ajātasattu, son of Queen Vedehī, heard that the Bhagavā had passed away at Kusinārā. Then Ajātasattu, son of Queen Vedehī, King of Magadha, sent an envoy to the Kusinārā Malla princes, (saying) "The Bhagavā was of the ruling class. I too am of the ruling class. I too deserve a share of the relics of the Bhagavā. I too shall erect a stupa over the relics of the Bhagavā and shall revere them."

The Licchavī princes of Vesālī heard that the Bhagavā had passed away at Kusinārā. Then the Licchavī princes of Vesālī sent an envoy to the Kusinārā Malla princes, (saying) "The Bhagavā was of the ruling

194. **The sinews**: *nhāru* or *nahāru*: sinew, tendon, muscle.

195. **Synovic or synovial fluid**: *lasikā*: synovia, a greasy albuminous fluid secreted from certain glands in the joints.

196. **Soot**: *masi*: the fine particles of ashes, or soot. The Burmese Nissaya renders it as charred pieces of the Buddha's body.

197. **Bone-relies**: *sarīra*: consisting of small pieces of bones ranging in size from a mustard seed to half a kidney-bean as well as seven larger pieces, namely, the upper fore part of the skull, two collar bones, and four eye-teeth.

198. Lit., with a lattice work of spears and a fence of bows.

class. We too are of the ruling class. We too deserve a share of the relics of the Bhagavā. We too shall erect a stupa over the relics of the Bhagavā and shall revere them."

The Sakya princes living at Kapilavatthu heard that the Bhagavā had passed away at Kusinārā. Then the Sakya princes of Kapilavatthu sent an envoy to the Kusinārā Malla princes, (saying) "The Bhagavā was our highest relative. We too deserve a share of the relics of the Bhagavā. We too shall erect a stupa over the relics of the Bhagavā and shall revere them."

The Buli princes of Allakappa heard that the Bhagavā had passed away at Kusinārā. Then the Buli princes of Allakappa sent an envoy to the Kusinārā Malla princes, (saying) "The Bhagavā was of the ruling class. We too are of the ruling class. We too deserve a share of the relics of the Bhagavā. We too shall erect a stupa over the relics of the Bhagavā and shall revere them."

The Koliya princes of Rāmagāma heard that the Bhagavā had passed away at Kusinārā. Then the Koliya princes of Rāmagāma sent an envoy to the Kusinārā Malla princes, (saying) "The Bhagavā was of the ruling class. We too are of the ruling class. We too deserve a share of the relics of the Bhagavā. We too shall erect a stupa over the relics of the Bhagavā and shall revere them."

The Brahmin of Veṭṭhadīpa heard that the Bhagavā had passed away at Kusinārā. Then the Brahmin of Veṭṭhadīpa sent an envoy to the Kusinārā Malla princes, (saying) "The Bhagavā was of the ruling class. I am of the brahmin class. I too deserve a share of the relics of the Bhagavā. I too shall erect a stupa over the relics of the Bhagavā and shall revere them."

The Malla princes of Pāvā heard that the Bhagavā had passed away at Kusinārā. Then the Pāvā Malla princes sent an envoy to the Malla princes of Kusinārā, (saying) "The Bhagavā was of the ruling class. We too are of the ruling class. We too deserve a share of the relics of the Bhagavā. We too shall erect a stupa over the relics of the Bhagavā and shall revere them."

On these words being said, the Kusinārā Malla princes said thus to that assembly, that group (of envoys), "The Bhagavā passed away in our domain. We will not give you any share of the relics of the Bhagavā."

237. On this being said, the Brahmin Dona addressed that assembly, that group, in verse thus:

"O Sirs, listen to one word of mine. Our Buddha was a believer in forbearance. It would not be at all proper if there should be strife over the sharing of the relics of him who was the noblest of men.

"O Sirs, let us all be united, be harmonious, be in joyful agreement, and divide the relics into eight portions. A great many people have devotion and reverence for the Possessor of the Eye of Wisdom. Let there be stupas (to his honour) widespread in all directions."

238. "Brahmin, in that case, do you yourself divide fairly the relics of the Bhagavā into eight equal portions."

Saying "Very well, Sirs," to that assembly, that group, the Brahmin Dona divided fairly the relics of the Bhagavā into eight equal portions. He then said to that assembly, that group, "Sirs, please give me this vessel (used in measuring out the relics). I too will raise a stupa over it and shall revere it." (Accordingly), the (measuring) vessel was given to the Brahmin Dona by that assembly, that group.

The Moriya princes of Pippalivana heard that the Bhagavā had passed away at Kusinārā. Then the Moriya princes of Pippalivana sent an envoy to the Malla princes of Kusinārā, (saying) "The Bhagavā was of the ruling class. We too are of the ruling class. We too deserve a share of the relics of the Bhagavā. We too shall erect a stupa over the relics of the Bhagavā and shall revere them."

(The Malla princes replied) "No share of the relics of the Bhagavā remains. We have divided (and given) (all) the relics of the Bhagavā. Take the charred pieces of firewood from this place (of cremation)." And they (i.e., the Moriya princes) took away the charred pieces of firewood from that place (of cremation).

Raising the Relic Stupas in Reverence

Then King Ajātasattu of Magadha, son of Queen Vedehī, built at Rājagaha a stupa over the relics of the Bhagavā, in reverence and honour. The Licchavī princes of Vesālī also built at Vesālī a stupa over the relics of the Bhagavā, in reverence and honour. The Sakya princes living at Kapilavatthu also built at Kapilavatthu a stupa over the relics of the Bhagavā, in reverence and honour. The Buli princes of Allakappa also built at Allakappa a stupa over the relics of the Bhagavā, in reverence and honour. The Koḷiya princes of Rāmagāma also built at Rāmagāma a stupa over the relics of the Bhagavā, in reverence and honour. The Brahmin of Veṭṭhadīpa also built at Veṭṭhadīpa a stupa over the relics of the Bhagavā, in reverence and honour. The Malla princes of Pāvā also built at Pāvā a stupa over the relics of the Bhagavā, in reverence and honour. The Malla princes of Kusinārā also built at Kusinārā a stupa over the relics of the Bhagavā, in reverence and honour. The Brahmin Doṇa also built a stupa over the vessel (used in measuring out the relics), in reverence and honour. The Moriya princes of Pippalivana also built at Pippalivana a stupa over the charred pieces of firewood (brought from the place of cremation of the Buddha), in reverence and honour. Thus there came to be in former times ten stupas, eight being stupas of the (Buddha's) relics, the ninth being the vessel-stupa and the tenth being the charcoal-stupa.

VERSES[199]

240. "Of eight measured portions of the relics of the Possessor of the Eye of Wisdom, seven portions (of the relics) of the noblest of men are revered and honoured in the *Jambudīpa* island-continent, and one portion is revered and honoured in Rāmagāma by the King of the Nāgas.[200]

"One eye-tooth[201] is revered and honoured by the Tāvatiṃsa devas. One eye-tooth is revered and honoured in Gandhāra. One eye-tooth is revered and honoured in the realm of the King of Kaliṅga. One eye-tooth is revered and honoured by the king of the Nāgas.

"Through their glorious power, this earth is adorned with (festivals of) reverence and honour to the noble relics. Thus these relics of the Possessor of the Eye of Wisdom are reverentially honoured by the worthiest devas and men.

"Lords of devas, lords of Nāgas and lords of men revere and honour the relics. In the same way the highest monarchs revere and honour the relics. If those (relics) are obtained, pay homage with palms (of hands) put together and lifted up in reverence. Indeed, through hundreds of aeons, it is extremely difficult to meet a Buddha.

"The devas have taken the forty evenly-shaped teeth, all the hair and the hairs of the body, each separately, to all universes in succession."

End of Mahāparinibbāna Sutta, the third sutta from division two (Mahā Vagga)

---

199. The Commentary says that these five verses were added by the *theras*, the bhikkhu elders, in Tambapaṇṇi Island, i.e., Ceylon, present day Sri Lanka.

200. *Nāga*: a serpent-like being gifted with miraculous powers and great strength.

201. **Eye-tooth**: *dāthā:* one of the four sharp-pointed teeth, one on each side of the upper and lower jaws, between the incisors (cutting teeth) and the molars (grinders). The term "eye-teeth" would strictly refer to the two in the upper jaw only, but is used here for all the four teeth, for convenience.

Namo tassa bhagavato arahato sammāsambuddhassa

MAHĀSATIPAṬṬHĀNA SUTTA

IX. MAHĀSATIPAṬṬHĀNA SUTTA

(Great Discourse on Steadfast Mindfulness)

372. Thus have I heard:

The Bhagavā was at one time residing at the market-town called Kammāsadhamma in the Kuru Country. There the Bhagavā addressed the bhikkhus, (saying): "O Bhikkhus," and they replied to him, "Venerable Sir." The Bhagavā said:

SUMMARY

373. Bhikkhus,[202] this is the one and only way for the purification (of the minds) of beings, for overcoming sorrow and lamentation, for the complete destruction of (physical) pain and (mental) distress, for attainment of the noble (*ariya*) Magga, and for the realization of Nibbāna. That (only way) is the practice of the four methods of Steadfast Mindfulness, Satipaṭṭhāna.

What are the four (Satipaṭṭhānas)? Bhikkhus, the bhikkhu (i.e., the disciple) following my Teaching keeps his mind steadfastly on the body (*Kāya*),[203] with diligence, comprehension and mindfulness, (and perceives its impermanent, insecure, soulless, and repulsive nature), thus keeping away covetousness and distress (which will appear if he is not mindful of the five khandhas).

The bhikkhu keeps his mind steadfastly on sensation (*vedanā*), with diligence, comprehension and mindfulness, (and perceives its impermanent, insecure, and soulless nature), thus keeping away covetousness and distress (which will appear if he is not mindful of the five khandhas).

The bhikkhu concentrates steadfastly on the mind (*citta*), with diligence, comprehension and mindfulness, (and perceives its impermanent, insecure, and soulless nature), thus keeping away covetousness and distress (which will appear if he is not mindful of the five khandhas).

---

202. **Bhikkhus**: this term here includes all those dedicated to the practice of the Teaching, (not only those who have been admitted to the Order). (The Commentary)

203. **The body**: strictly speaking, the aggregate of physical phenomena.

The bhikkhu keeps his mind steadfastly on the *dhamma*[204] with diligence, comprehension and mindfulness, (and perceives their impermanent, insecure, and soulless nature), thus keeping away covetousness and distress (which will appear if he is not mindful of the five khandhas).

End of the Summary

Perception of the True Nature of the Body: (i) Section on Breathing

374. Bhikkhus, how does the bhikkhu keep his mind steadfastly on the body?

Bhikkhus, the bhikkhu following the practice of my Teaching, having gone to the forest, or to the foot of a tree, or to an empty, solitary place, sits down cross-legged, keeping his body erect, and sets up mindfulness, orienting it (towards the object of concentration). (Then) with entire mindfulness he breathes in, and with entire mindfulness he breathes out. Breathing in a long inhalation, he is conscious of breathing in a long inhalation, or breathing out a long exhalation, he is conscious of breathing out a long exhalation. Breathing in a short inhalation, he is conscious of breathing in a short inhalation, or breathing out a short exhalation, he is conscious of breathing out a short exhalation. He trains himself to be clearly conscious of the whole stretch of the in-coming breath at its beginning, its middle, and at its end. He trains himself to be clearly conscious of the whole stretch of the out-going breath at its beginning, its middle, and at its end. (By being fully conscious of the inhalation) he trains himself to calm down the strong inhalation as he breathes in. (By being fully conscious of the exhalation) be trains himself to calm down the strong exhalation as he breathes out.[205]

Just as, bhikkhus, a skilful turner or a turner's apprentice knows a long pull (on the string turning the lathe) when a long pull is made, or knows a short pull when a short pull is made, even so, bhikkhus,

---

204. *Dhamma*: the five dhammas consisting of (1) five nīvaraṇas, (2) five khandhas, (3) twelve āyatanas, (4) seven bojjhaṅgas, and (5) four ariya saccas. This will become clear in Paras 382 to 403 of this sutta.

205. No special effect is necessary to calm down the strong inhalation and exhalation. The more one gets mental concentration the more the strong inhalation and exhalation will calm down. When the mental concentration reaches its highest point, inhalation and exhalation will become so delicate that the yogī will feel that his breathing has stopped.

the bhikkhu breathing in a long inhalation is conscious of breathing in a long inhalation, or breathing out a long exhalation is conscious of breathing out a long exhalation, or breathing in a short inhalation is conscious of breathing in a short inhalation, or breathing out a short exhalation is conscious of breathing or a short exhalation. He trains himself to be clearly conscious of the whole stretch of the in-coming breath at its beginning, its middle, and at its end. He trains himself to be clearly conscious of the whole stretch of the out-going breath at its beginning, its middle, and at its end. He trains himself to calm down the strong inhalation as he breathes in. He trains himself to calm down the strong exhalation as he breathes out.

Thus he keeps his mind steadfastly on the aggregate of physical phenomena which is his (own breathing), (and perceives its impermanent, insecure, and soulless nature). (Occasionally) he realizes that the aggregate of physical phenomena (which is the breathing) of others must be of a similar nature. Because of this realization, he can be said to keep his mind steadfastly on the aggregate of physical phenomena (which is the breathing) of others. In this way, he is considered to keep his mind steadfastly on the aggregate of physical phenomena which is his (own breathing) or which is that of others. (When he gains more concentration), he perceives the cause and the actual appearing of the aggregate of physical phenomena (which is the process of breathing). He (also) perceives the cause and the actual dissolution of the aggregate of physical phenomena (which is the process of breathing). He (also) perceives both the actual appearing and the actual dissolution of the aggregate of physical phenomena (which is the process of breathing), with their causes.[206] And further, the bhikkhu is firmly mindful of the fact that there is only the aggregate of physical phenomena (which is inhaling and exhaling). That (mindfulness) is solely for gaining (*vipassanā*) insights progressively, solely for gaining further mindfulness stage by stage. The bhikkhu remains detached from craving and wrong views, without clinging to *any of* the five khandhas (that are continuously deteriorating). Bhikkhus, it is in this way that the bhikkhu keeps his mind steadfastly on the body, (perceiving its true nature).

End of the Section on Breathing

206. The causes of the appearing and dissolution of the aggregate of physical phenomena which is inhalation and exhalation are the existence or the non-existence of the body, the nose and the mind.

Perception of the True Nature of the Body: (ii) Section on Body Movement and Posture

375. And again, bhikkhus, the bhikkhu when walking, is conscious of walking; or when standing, he is conscious of standing; or when sitting, he is conscious of sitting; or when lying down, he is conscious of lying down; or in whatever movement or posture his body is, he is conscious of it.

Thus he keeps his mind steadfastly on the aggregate of physical phenomena which is his body (and perceives its impermanent, insecure, soulless, and repulsive nature). (Occasionally) he realizes that the aggregate of physical phenomena which is the body of others must be of a similar nature. Because of this realization, he can be said to keep his mind steadfastly on the aggregate of physical phenomena which is the body of others. In this way he is considered to keep his mind steadfastly on the aggregate of physical phenomena which is his own body or which is that of others. (When he gains more concentration), he perceives the cause and the actual appearing of the aggregate of physical phenomena which is the body. He (also) perceives the cause and the actual dissolution of the aggregate of physical phenomena which is the body. He (also) perceives both the actual appearing and the actual dissolution of the aggregate of physical phenomena which is the body, with their causes.[207] And further, the bhikkhu is firmly mindful of the fact

---

207. The causes of appearing of physical phenomena are ignorance of the Four Ariya Truths, craving, kamma, and nutriment. They and their effect, i.e., the continuous appearance of physical phenomena, are called five *Samudaya dhammā*. The perception of these five *Samudaya dhammā* is called *Samudaya dhammānupassī*. They are perceived in the following way:

When the bhikkhu can steadfastly keep his mind on the body postures by means of diligence, mindfulness, concentration, comprehension, he perceives the sign or incessant appearance of physical phenomena (*nibbatti lakkhaṇā*): This perception usually begins, when the bhikkhu achieves the second *vipassanā ñāṇa — paccaya pariggaha ñāṇa*. From this perception, the bhikkhu draws the conclusion that rebirths of beings take place in a similar way.

Therefore, while the bhikkhu is perceiving the continuous appearance of physical phenomena he realizes that endless rebirths are due to: (1) ignorance of Four Ariya Truths; (2) craving for pleasure of the senses; (3) *kamma* (deeds, words and thoughts) which has the potency for rebirth as its effect; (4) nutriment which is essential for physical phenomena; (5) mind (*citta*) which is the motivating force; (6) heat and cold. The causes of dissolution of physical phenomena are the absence of the above factors.

that there is only the aggregate of physical phenomena (without soul or *atta* directing it).[208] That (mindfulness) is solely for gaining (*vipassanā*) insights, progressively, solely for gaining further mindfulness stage by stage. The bhikkhu remains detached from craving and wrong views, without clinging to any of the five khandhas (that are continuously deteriorating). Bhikkhus, it is also in this way that the bhikkhu keeps his mind steadfastly on the body, (perceiving its true nature).

End of the Section on Body Movement and Posture

Perception of the True Nature of the Body: (III) Section on Clear Comprehension

376. And again, bhikkhus, the bhikkhu, in moving forward and in moving backward does so with clear comprehension; in looking straight ahead and sideways, he does so with clear comprehension; in bending and in stretching his limbs, he does so with clear comprehension; in carrying or wearing the great robe, alms-bowl and the other two robes, he does so with clear comprehension; in eating, drinking, chewing and savouring, he does so with clear comprehension; in defecating and

---

The bhikkhu then realizes that extinction of ignorance of Four Ariya Truths will cause the extinction of the endless appearance of physical phenomena. The actual perception of the sign of *change* or *disappearance* or *deterioration* of physical phenomena will begin when the bhikkhu achieves the third *vipassanā ñāṇa — Sammasana ñāṇa*. The sign of change is called *viparināma lakkhaṇā*. In fact, the perception of the appearance and disappearance of physical phenomena, by means of *nibbatti* and *viparināma lakkhaṇā*, becomes clearer when the bhikkhu achieves the fourth *vipassanā ñāṇa — Udayabbaya ñāṇa*. However, the perception of only the disappearance of physical phenomena becomes stronger, when he achieves the fifth *vipassanā ñāṇa — bhaṅga ñāṇa*.

208. This shows the mental state of the bhikkhu when his mindfulness is at its height. Before he reaches this mental state, he occasionally imagines, in spite of his efforts to be mindful, a) that body and limbs are his; b) that his *jīva* (soul or *atta*) is directing them to make postures. Occasionally, he even feels proud of and pleased with "his" body and limbs.

These false views of the body and limbs begin to disappear when he achieves the fifth *vipassanā ñāṇa — bhaṅga ñāṇa*. From that stage the bhikkhu perceives only the deterioration of the body. And he is no longer conscious of the body and the limbs as such. And therefore he does not take pride and pleasure in them.

With this perception of the non-existence of the body and limbs, he fully (and finally) achieves the eleventh *vipassanā ñāṇa — saṅkhār'upekkhā ñāṇa*.

urinating, he does so with clear comprehension; in walking, standing, sitting, falling asleep, waking, speaking or in keeping silent, he does so with clear comprehension.

Thus he keeps his mind steadfastly on the aggregate of physical phenomena which is his body ... (p) ... (that are continuously deteriorating). Bhikkhus, it is also in this way that the bhikkhu keeps his mind steadfastly on the body, (perceiving its true nature).

End of the Section on Clear Comprehension

Perception of the True Nature of the Body: (iv) Section on Consideration of Repulsiveness

377. And again, bhikkhus, the bhikkhu examines and reflects closely upon this very body, from the soles of the feet up and from the tips of the hair down, enclosed by the skin and full of manifold impurities, (thinking thus:) "There are in this body: hair of the head, hair of the body, nails, teeth, skin, flesh, sinews, bones, marrow, kidneys, heart, liver, membranes (including the pleura, the diaphragm and other forms of membrane in the body), spleen, lungs, large intestine, small intestine, contents of the stomach, faeces, (brain),[209] bile, phlegm, pus, blood, sweat, solid fat, tears, liquid fat, saliva, nasal mucus, synovial fluid (i.e., lubricating oil of the joints) and urine."

Just as if, bhikkhus, there were a bag with an opening at each end, and full of various kinds of grain such as hill-paddy, paddy, green gram, cow-pea, sesame and husked rice; and a man with sound eyes, having opened it, should examine and reflect (on the contents) thus: "This is hill-paddy, this is paddy, this is green gram, this is cow-pea, this is sesame, this is husked rice," even so, bhikkhus, the bhikkhu examines and reflects on this very body, from the soles of the feet up and from the tips of the hair down, enclosed by the skin and full of manifold impurities, (thinking thus:) "There are in this body: hair of the head, ... (p) ... urine."

Thus he keeps his mind steadfastly on the aggregate of physical phenomena which is his body ... (p) ... (that are continuously deteriorating).

Bhikkhus, it is also in this way that the bhikkhu keeps his mind steadfastly on the body, (perceiving its true nature).

End of the Section on Consideration of Repulsiveness

---

209. 'the brain' is not included in the Pāḷi Text of this Sutta; but is included in the Paṭisaṃbhidā Magga.

Perception of the True Nature of the Body: (v) Section on Consideration of the Primary Elements

378. And again, bhikkhus, the bhikkhu examines and reflects on this body, in whatever position it remains or is placed, as composed of the primary elements:[210] "There are in this body (only) the earth element, the water element, the fire element, and the air element."

Just as if, bhikkhus, a skilful butcher or a butcher's apprentice, having slaughtered a cow and cut it up into portions should be sitting at the junction of four main roads, (so that only pieces of meat are seen and not the cow as such), even so the bhikkhu examines and reflects on this very body in whatever position it remains or is placed, as composed of the primary elements: "There are in this body (only) the earth element, the water element, the fire element, and the air element."

Thus he keeps his mind steadfastly on the aggregate of physical phenomena which is his body ... (p) ... (that are continuously deteriorating). Bhikkhus, it is also in this way that the bhikkhu keeps his mind steadfastly on the body, (perceiving its true nature).

End of the Section on Consideration of the Primary Elements

Perception of the True Nature of the Body: (vi) Section on Nine Kinds of Corpses

379. And again, bhikkhus, as if the bhikkhu is seeing a body, one day dead, or two days dead, or three days dead, swollen, turning black and

---

210. **The primary elements**: *dhātu*, 'element', is a force of Nature which behaves in accordance with the Laws of Nature. The four primary elements literally translated above for the sake of brevity as 'earth, water, fire, and air elements' are:

(1) *Pathavi-dhātu*: a force of Nature that has the attribute of causing hardness. (It is sometimes translated as the element of solidity or of extension);

(2) *Āpo-dhātu*: a force of Nature that has the attributes of causing cohesion and of causing fluidity. (It is sometimes translated as the element of cohesion);

(3) *Tejo-dhātu*: a force of Nature that has the attribute of causing heat or cold, i.e., thermal energy. (It is sometimes translated as the element of heat);

(4) *Vāyo-dhātu*: a force of Nature that has the attribute of causing motion or impetus. (It is sometimes translated as the element of motion).

The *pathavi-dhātu* is predominant in the first twenty items of the list given in Section (iv). The *apo-dhātu* is predominant in the last twelve items. The *tejo-dhātu* consists of four kinds of heat in the body and *vāyo-dhātu* consists of six kinds of *vāyo* in the body.

blue, and festering, abandoned in the charnel-ground, he applies (this perception) to his own body thus: "Indeed, this body of mine, too, is of the same nature; it will become like that; it cannot escape such (a fate)."

Thus he keeps his mind steadfastly on the aggregate of physical phenomena which is his body ... (p) ... (that are continuously deteriorating). Bhikkhus, it is also in this way that the bhikkhu keeps his mind steadfastly on the body, (perceiving its true nature).

And again, bhikkhus, as if the bhikkhu is seeing a body abandoned in the charnel-ground, being devoured by crows, being devoured by hawks, being devoured by vultures, being devoured by herons, being devoured by dogs, being devoured by tigers; being devoured by leopards, being devoured by jackals, or being devoured by various kinds of worms, he applies (this perception) to his own body thus: "Indeed, this body of mine, too, is of the same nature; it will become like that: it cannot escape such (a fate)."

Thus he keeps his mind steadfastly on the aggregate of physical phenomena which is his body ... (p) ... (that are continuously deteriorating). Bhikkhus, it is also in this way that the bhikkhu keeps his mind steadfastly on the body, (perceiving its true nature).

And again, bhikkhus, as if the bhikkhu is seeing a body abandoned in the charnel-ground —

(reduced to) a skeleton held together by the tendons, with some flesh and blood still adhering to it, ... (p) ...

(reduced to) a skeleton held together by the tendons, blood-besmeared, fleshless, ... (p) ...

(reduced to) a skeleton still held together by the tendons, without flesh and blood, ... (p) ...

(reduced to) loose bones scattered in all directions, — at one place bones of a hand, at another place bones of a foot, at another place ankle-bones, at another place shin-bones, at another place thigh-bones, at another place hip-bones, at another place rib-bones, at another place spinal-bones, at another place shoulder-bones, at another place neck-bones, at another place the jawbone, at another place the teeth, at another place the skull, he applies (this perception) to his own body thus: "Indeed, this body of nine, too, is of the same nature; it will become like that; it cannot escape such (a fate)."

Thus he keeps his mind steadfastly on the aggregate of physical phenomena which is his body ... (p) ... (that are continuously deteriorating). Bhikkhus, it is also in this way that the bhikkhu keeps his mind steadfastly on the body, (perceiving its true nature).

And again, bhikkhus, as if the bhikkhu is seeing a body abandoned in the charnel-ground –

(reduced to) bleached bones of conch-like colour, ... (p) ...

(reduced to) bones more than a year old, lying in a heap, ... (p) ...

(reduced to) rotted bones, crumbling to dust, he then applies (this perception) to his own body thus: "Indeed, this body of mine, too, is of the same nature; it will become like that; it cannot escape such (a fate)."

Thus he keeps his mind steadfastly on the aggregate of physical phenomena which is his body (and perceives its impermanent, insecure, soulless, and repulsive nature). (Occasionally) he realizes that the aggregate of physical phenomena which is the body of others must be of a similar nature. Because of this realization, he can be said to keep his mind steadfastly on the aggregate of physical phenomena which is the body of others. In this way, he is considered to keep his mind steadfastly on the aggregate of physical phenomena which is his own body or which is that of others. (When he gains more concentration), he perceives the cause and the actual appearing of the aggregate of physical phenomena which is the body. He (also) perceives the cause and the actual dissolution of the aggregate of physical phenomena which is the body. He (also) perceives both the actual appearing and the actual dissolution of the aggregate of physical phenomena which is the body, with their causes. And further, the bhikkhu is firmly mindful of the fact that there is only the aggregate of physical phenomena (without soul or *atta* directing it). That (mindfulness) is solely for gaining (*vipassanā*) insights progressively, solely for gaining further mindfulness stage by stage. The bhikkhu remains detached from craving and wrong views without clinging to any of the five khandhas (that are continuously deteriorating). Bhikkhus, it is also in this way that the bhikkhu keeps his mind steadfastly on the body, (perceiving its true nature).

End of the Section on Nine Kinds of Corpses

End of the fourteen ways[211] *of perception of the true nature of the body*

---

211. **Fourteen Ways**: consisting of one way of perception in each of the first five sections and nine ways of perception in the sixth and last section.

Perception of the True Nature of Sensation

380. Bhikkhus, how does the bhikkhu keep his mind steadfastly on sensation, *vedanā*, (and perceive its impermanent, insecure, and soulless nature)?

Bhikkhus, the bhikkhu who follows my Teaching, when experiencing a pleasant sensation, knows that a pleasant sensation is experienced; or when experiencing an unpleasant sensation, knows that an unpleasant sensation is experienced; or when experiencing a sensation neither pleasant nor unpleasant, knows that a sensation neither pleasant nor unpleasant is experienced.

When experiencing a pleasant sensation associated with sensual desires, he knows that a pleasant sensation associated with sensual desires is experienced; or when experiencing a pleasant sensation not associated with sensual desires, he knows that a pleasant sensation not associated with sensual desires is experienced; when experiencing an unpleasant sensation associated with sensual desires, he knows that an unpleasant sensation associated with sensual desires is experienced; or when experiencing an unpleasant sensation not associated with sensual desires, he knows that an unpleasant sensation not associated with sensual desires is experienced; when experiencing a sensation neither pleasant nor unpleasant associated with sensual desires, he knows that a sensation neither pleasant nor unpleasant associated with sensual desires is experienced; or when experiencing a sensation neither pleasant nor unpleasant not associated with sensual desires, he knows that a sensation neither pleasant nor unpleasant not associated with sensual desires is experienced.

Thus he keeps his mind steadfastly on sensation, *vedanā*, experienced by himself (and perceives its impermanent, insecure, and soulless nature). (Occasionally) he realizes that sensation experienced by others must be of a similar nature. Because of this realization, he can be said to keep his mind steadfastly on sensation experienced by others. In this way, he is considered to keep his mind steadfastly on sensation experienced by himself or by others. (When he gains more concentration), he perceives the cause and the actual appearing of sensation. He (also) perceives the cause and the actual dissolution of sensation. He (also) perceives both the actual appearing and the actual dissolution of sensations, with their causes.[212] And further, the bhikkhu

212. The causes of the appearing of sensation are: ignorance of the Four Ariya

is firmly mindful of the fact that there is only sensation (without soul or *atta*). That (mindfulness) is solely for gaining (*vipassanā*) insights progressively, solely for gaining further mindfulness stage by stage. The bhikkhu remains detached from craving and wrong views, without clinging to any of the five khandhas (that are continuously deteriorating). Bhikkhus, it is also in this way that the bhikkhu keeps his mind steadfastly on sensation, (perceiving its true nature).

End of Perception of the True Nature of Sensation

PERCEPTION OF THE TRUE NATURE OF MIND

381. Bhikkhus, how does the bhikkhu concentrate steadfastly on the mind, *citta*, (and perceive its impermanent, insecure, and soulless nature)?

Bhikkhus, the bhikkhu following my Teaching knows (i.e., is aware of) the mind accompanied by passion, *rāga*[213] as 'Mind with passion'; he knows the mind unaccompanied by passion, as 'Mind without passion'; he also knows the mind accompanied by anger, *dosa*,[214] as 'Mind with anger'; he also knows the mind unaccompanied by anger, as 'Mind without anger'; he also knows the mind accompanied by bewilderment, *moha*,[215] as 'Mind with bewilderment'; he also knows the mind unaccompanied by bewilderment, as 'Mind without bewilderment'; he also knows the

---

Truths, craving, *kamma* and contact (*phassa*). These result in the appearing of sensation. The disappearance of these causes results in the dissolution or absence of sensation.

213. *Raga*: passion, pleasure in or craving for something. In *vipassanā bhāvanā*, the bhikkhu is liable to misunderstand passion. He may think that he is required to be mindful of strong forms of passion only. He is, in fact, required to be mindful of all forms of passion — weak, medium, strong. In *vipassanā*, it is a very important point. Whatever takes place in the six senses, however insignificant, however wholesome or unwholesome it is, he is required to be mindful of it.

214. *Dosa*: mental violence, hatred, frustration, desire to ill-treat, desire to destroy, desire to kill, are all covered by this term, *dosa*.

215. *Moha*: usually defined as stupidity, dullness of mind, bewilderment, infatuation, delusion. *Moha* is a *cetasika* that makes *citta* (mind) incapable of choosing between right and wrong, incapable of perceiving the four Noble Truths, incapable of practicing correctly for the preception of the four Noble Truths, incapable of adopting a proper mental attitude. It is called *micchā-ñāṇa*, the intellect that is capable of giving only evil counsel in all matters. *Moha* makes a person blind to the nature and consequences of a demeritorious deed.

indolent state of mind, *saṃkhitta citta,*[216] as 'Indolent state of mind'; he also knows the distracted state of mind, *vikkhitta citta,*[217] as 'Distracted state of mind'; he also knows the developed state of mind, *mahaggata citta,*[218] as 'Developed state of mind'; he also knows the undeveloped state of mind, *amahaggata citta,*[219] as 'Undeveloped state of mind' ; he also knows the inferior state of mind, *sa-uttara citta*, as 'Inferior state of mind'; he also knows the superior state of mind, *anuttara citta,*[220] as 'Superior state of mind'; he also knows the mind in a state of concentration, *samāhita citta,*[221] as 'Mind in a state of concentration'; he also knows the mind not

---

216. *Saṃkhitta citta*: (lit., shrunken mind); this means indolence, lethargy, slothfulness, lack of interest in anything. (The Commentary)

217. *Vikkhitta citta*: A diffused or restless state of mind resulting in lack of concentration. (The Commentary)

218. *Mahaggata citta*: The loftiness of mind experienced in *rūpa jhāna* and *arūpa jhāna*. (The Commentary)

219. *Amahaggata citta*: (*Kāmāvacara citta*): The mind as generally found in the sensuous realms. (The Commentary)

220. '*sa-uttara*', and '*anuttara*' are relative terms, indicating inferior and superior states of mind. A state of mind that has some other state of mind superior to it, and is therefore inferior, is *sa-uttara citta*; a state of mind that is superior to some other state of mind is *anuttara citta*. *Kāmāvacara citta*, the state of mind of the sensuous realms, is inferior to the *rūpa* and *arūpa jhāna* states of mind. The *rūpa jhāna* state of mind is inferior to the *arūpa jhāna* state of mind, but is superior to the *kāmāvacara* state of mind. In *vipassanā* practice, the *arūpa jhāna* state of mind is superior to both the *rūpa jhāna* and the *kāmāvacara* states of mind. Within the stages of the *jhānas* themselves, each *jhāna* is relatively inferior or superior, progressing to the *nevasaññānāsaññāyatana jhāna* which is the highest state of mind.

An ordinary yogi who has no experience of *jhāna* cannot concentrate on the *mahaggata* or *anuttara* states of mind.

As a matter of fact, *anuttara* is normally an epithet for *lokuttara citta* or *magga-phala citta*. However, in *vipassanā* practice, the yogi can concentrate only on the five *upādānakkhandhas*, the five aggregates which form the objects of clinging. He cannot concentrate on *magga-phala citta*. Therefore, *jhānas* are given the epithet *anuttara*. (The Commentary)

221. *samāhita citta*: is the mind that has *samādhi*, which is mental concentration on an object. According to the Commentary, *samāhita citta* has (1) *upacāra samādhi*, and (2) *appanā samādhi*, (i.e., *jhāna*). *Upacāra samādhi* is *samādhi* that precedes, and is close to *appanā samādhi*, helping the latter to take place. *Appanā samādhi* fixes the mind on the mental object. The mind with *upacāra samādhi* generally belongs to the sensuous state of existence. The mind with *appanā samādhi* belongs to the *rūpa* (fine material) and *arūpa* (non-material) *jhānas*.

in a state of concentration, *asamāhita citta*,[222] as 'Mind not in a state of concentration'; he also knows the liberated state of mind, *vimuttacitta*,[223] as 'Liberated state of mind; he also knows the unliberated state of mind, *avimutta citta*,[224] as 'Unliberated state of mind'.

Thus the bhikkhu concentrates steadfastly on his own mind, *citta*, (and perceives its impermanent, insecure, and soulless nature). (Occasionally) he realizes that the mind of others must be of a similar nature. Because of this realization, he can be said to concentrate steadfastly on the mind of others. In this way, he is considered to concentrate steadfastly on his own mind or on the mind of others. (When he gains more concentration), he perceives the cause and the actual appearing of the mind. He (also) perceives the cause and the actual dissolution of the mind. He (also) perceives both the actual appearing and the actual dissolution of the mind, with their causes.[225] And further, the bhikkhu is firmly mindful of the fact that there is only Mind (without soul or *atta*). That (mindfulness) is solely for gaining (*vipassanā*) insights progressively, solely for gaining further mindfulness stage by stage. The bhikkhu remains detached from craving and wrong views, without clinging to any of the five *khandhas* (that are continuously deteriorating). Bhikkhus, it is also in this way that the bhikkhu concentrates steadfastly on the mind, (perceiving its true nature).

End of Perception of the True Nature of Mind

Perception of the True Nature of Dhammā: (i) Section on the Hindrances

382. Bhikkhus, how does the bhikkhu keep his mind steadfastly on dhamma, mental and physical phenomena, (and perceive that they are just phenomena without any entity or soul)? Bhikkhus, the bhikkhu following my Teaching keeps his mind steadfastly on the mental

---

222. *Asamāhita citta*: The mind without the two kinds of *samādhi*. (The Commentary)

223. *Vimutta citta*: Here it means the mind temporarily liberated from moral defilements (*kilesas*). (The Commentary)

224. *Avimutta citta*: The mind not liberated from moral defilements. (The Commentary)

225. The causes of the appearing of the mind are: ignorance of the four Ariya Truths, craving, kamma, the complex of mental and physical aggregates (*nāma-rūpa*). The disappearance of these causes result in the dissolution of the mind.

phenomena of the five *nīvaraṇas*,[226] Hindrances. And how does the bhikkhu keep his mind steadfastly on the five *nīvaraṇas*, Hindrances, (and perceive their soulless nature)?

Bhikkhus, when sense-desire *kāmacchaṇda*, is present in him, the bhikkhu following my Teaching knows 'There is sense-desire in me'; or when sense-desire is not present in him, he knows 'There is no sense-desire in me'. Besides, he knows how the sense-desire which has not yet arisen comes to arise; and he knows how the sense-desire that has arisen comes to be discarded; and he knows how the discarded sense-desire will not arise in the future.

"When ill will, *byāpāda*, is present in him, he knows 'There is ill will in me'; or when ill will is not present in him, he knows 'There is no ill will in me'. Besides, he knows how the ill will which has not yet arisen comes to arise; and he knows how the ill will that has arisen comes to be discarded; and he knows how the discarded ill will will not arise in the future.

When sloth and torpor, *thīna-middha*, are present in him, he knows 'There are sloth and torpor in me'; or when sloth and torpor are not present in him, he knows. There are no sloth and torpor in me'. Besides, he knows how the sloth and torpor which have not yet arisen come to arise; and he knows how the sloth and torpor that have arisen come to be discarded; and he knows how the discarded sloth and torpor will not arise in the future.

When distraction and worry, *uddacca-kukkucca*, are present in him, he knows 'There are distraction and worry in me'; or when distraction and worry are not present in him, he knows 'There are no distraction and worry in me'. Besides, he knows how the distraction and worry which have not yet arisen come to arise; and he knows how the distraction and

---

226. *Nīvaraṇa*: obstacles in the path of one's spiritual progress. They are hindrances to doing good deeds and to the achievement of *jhānas* and of the four *magga* Insights. There are five hindrances:

(a) *Kāmacchanda*: all forms of *taṇhā* and *lobha*, craving and desire.

(b) *Byāpāda*: ill will; harbouring evil desires to ill-treat or destroy others, or to bring others into trouble.

(c) *Thīna-middha*: sloth and torpor; feeling of indolence, particularly for doing good and meritorious deeds.

(d) *Uddacca-kukkucca*: distraction (or agitation) and worry. This has two aspects: flitting about of the mind (series of thought moments) in all directions, and worrying over past commissions and omissions.

(e) *Vicikicchā*: doubt or wavering of mind.

worry that have arisen come to be discarded; and he knows how the discarded distraction and worry will not arise in the future.

When doubt or wavering or the mind, *vicikicchā*, is present in him, he knows 'There is doubt in me'; or when doubt is not present in him, he knows 'There is no doubt in me'. Besides, he knows how the doubt which has not yet arisen comes to arise; and he knows how the doubt that has arisen comes to be discarded; and he knows how the discarded doubt will not arise in the future.

Thus he keeps his mind steadfastly on the *dhammā*, mental and physical phenomena, in himself (and perceives that they are just phenomena without any entity or soul). (Occasionally) he realizes that the *dhammā* in others must be of a similar nature. Because of this realization, he can be said to keep his mind steadfastly on the *dhammā* in others. In this way, he is considered to keep his mind steadfastly on the *dhammā* in himself or in others. (When he gains more concentration), he perceives the cause and the actual appearing of the *dhammā*. He (also) perceives the cause and the actual dissolution of the *dhammā*. He (also) perceives both the actual appearing and the actual dissolution of the *dhammā*, with their causes.[227] And further, the bhikkhu is firmly mindful of the fact that there are only *dhammā* (without soul or *atta*). That (mindfulness) is solely for gaining (*vipassanā*) insights progressively, solely for gaining further mindfulness stage by stage. The bhikkhu remains detached from craving and wrong views, without clinging to any of the five *khandhas* (that are continuously deteriorating). Bhikkhus, it is also in this way that the bhikkhu keeps his mind steadfastly on the five *nīvaraṇa dhammā* (perceiving their true nature).

End of the Section on the Hindrances

---

227. The arising of the Hindrances is due to *ayoniso manasikāra*, wrong perception of phenomena, resulting from taking any phenomenon as permanent, pleasurable, endowed with soul, and non-repulsive. In the case of craving and desire, the *nīvaraṇa* is due to taking what is actually repulsive as non-repulsive; in the case of ill will, the *nīvaraṇa* is due to taking something as being offensive. The non-appearance or disappearance of the Hindrances is brought about by *yoniso manasikāra*, right perception of phenomena, viewing all phenomena as impermanent, unpleasurable, soulless, and repulsive.

The discarded *kāmacchanda* will not arise again due to Arahatta Magga. The discarded *byāpāda* will not arise again due to Anāgāmi Magga. The discarded *thīna-middha* will not arise again due to Arahatta Magga. The discarded *uddhacca kukkucca* will not arise again due to Arahatta Magga and Anāgāmi Magga respectively. The discarded *vicikiccā* will not arise again due to Sotāpatti Magga.

Perception of the True Nature of Dhammā: (ii) Section on the Five Khandhas

383. And again, bhikkhus, the bhikkhu keeps his mind steadfastly on the mental and physical phenomena of the five *upādānakkhandhas*,[228] aggregates which are the objects of clinging, (and perceives that they are just phenomena without any entity or soul). Bhikkhus, how does the bhikkhu keep his mind steadfastly on the five *upādānakkhandhas*, aggregates, which are the objects of clinging?

Bhikkhus, the bhikkhu following my Teaching perceives thus: 'Such is *rūpa*, physical phenomenon; such is the origination of physical phenomenon; such is the disappearance of physical phenomenon. Such is *vedanā*, sensation; such is the origination of sensation; such is the disappearance of sensation. Such is *saññā*, perception (i.e., assimilation of sensation); such is the origination of perception; such is the disappearance of perception. Such is *saṅkhāra*, mental formations; such is the origination of mental formations; such is the disappearance of mental formations. Such is *viññāna*, consciousness; such is the origination of consciousness; such is the disappearance of consciousness.'

Thus he keeps his mind steadfastly on the *dhammā*, mental and physical phenomena, in himself (and perceives that they are just phenomena without any entity or soul). (Occasionally) he realizes that the *dhammā* in others must be of a similar nature. Because of this realization, he can be said to keep his mind steadfastly on the *dhammā* in others. In this way, he is considered to keep his mind steadfastly on the *dhammā* in himself or in others. (When he gains more concentration), he perceives the cause and the actual appearing of the *dhammā*. He (also) perceives the cause and the actual dissolution of the *dhammā*. He (also) perceives both the actual appearing and the actual dissolution

---

228. *Upādānakkhandhas* are the five *khandha*, aggregates, which are the objects of grasping or clinging. The five *khandhas* are:

(1) *rūpakkhandha*, the aggregate of physical phenomena, or the body;

(2) *vedanākkhandha*, the aggregate of sensation or feeling;

(3) *saññākkhandha*, the aggregate of perception;

(4) *saṅkhārakkhandha*, the aggregate of volitional thought and action or mental formations, (with the exception of *vedanā* and *saññā*); and

(5) *viññāṇakkhandha*, the aggregate of consciousness.

But the *magga-phala citta* (*lokuttara citta*) is not an object of Clinging. Therefore, only the *viññāṇakkhandha* which does not include *magga-phala citta* can be the object of clinging (*upādāna*).

of the *dhammā*, with their causes.[229] And further, the bhikkhu is firmly mindful of the fact that there are only *dhammā*. That (mindfulness) is solely for gaining (*vipassanā*) insights progressively, solely for gaining further mindfulness stage by stage. The bhikkhu remains detached from craving and wrong views, without clinging to any of the five *khandhas* (that are continuously deteriorating). Bhikkhus, it is also in this way that the bhikkhu keeps his mind steadfastly on these five *upādānakkhandha dhammā*, (perceiving their true nature).

End of the Section on the Five Khandhas

PERCEPTION OF THE TRUE NATURE OF DHAMMĀ: (III) SECTION ON THE TWELVE SENSE-BASES

384. And again, bhikkhus, the bhikkhu keeps his mind steadfastly on the mental and physical phenomena of the six internal and the six external *āyatanas*, sense-bases, (and perceives that they are just phenomena without any entity or soul). Bhikkhus, how does the bhikkhu keep his mind steadfastly on the six internal and the six external *āyatana dhammā*?

Bhikkhus, the bhikkhu following my Teaching is conscious of the eye, is also conscious of visible objects, and knows any fetter[230] that arises

229. The causes for the appearing and dissolution of the aggregate of physical phenomena are the same as those for body movement and posture, (see footnote to paragraph 375); for sensation, perception, and mental formations, the same as for sensation (see footnote to paragraph 380); or consciousness the same as for the mind (see footnote to paragraph 381).

230. **Fetter**: *saṃyojana*: a fetter that binds one to endless *dukkha*. There are ten *saṃyojanās*:

(1) *kāmarāga*, craving for sensual pleasure;

(2) *paṭigha*, anger, disappointment, fear, grief, ill will;

(3) *māna*, pride, conceit;

(4) *sakkāya-diṭṭhi*, belief in the illusion, that there is Self, Soul;

(5) *vicikicchā*, doubt, wavering, scepticism, (see footnote on the hindrances in paragraph 382);

(6) *sīlabbataparāmāsa*, the misleading belief that there are paths, other than the Ariya Path of Eight Constituents, that can liberate one from *dukkha*;

(7) *bhavarāga*, craving to become a Brahmā with mind and body (*rūparaga*) or craving to become a Brahmā with only mind and no body (*arūparāga*);

(8) *issā*, jealousy, envy;

(9) *macchariya*, meanness and stinginess;

(10) *avijjā*, ignorance of the Four Noble Truths.

This list is according to the Adhidhamma classification.

dependent on both (the eye and the visible object). Besides, he knows how a fetter which has not yet arisen comes to arise; and he knows how the fetter that has arisen comes to be discarded; and he knows how the discarded fetter will not arise in the future.

He is conscious of the ear, is also conscious of sounds, and knows any fetter that arises dependent on both (the ear and the sound). Besides, he knows how a fetter which has not yet arisen comes to arise; and he knows how the fetter that has arisen comes to be discarded; and he knows how the discarded fetter will not arise in the future.

He is conscious of the nose, is also conscious of odours, and knows any fetter that arises dependent on both (the nose and the odour). Besides, he knows how a fetter which has not yet arisen comes to arise; and he knows how the fetter that has arisen comes to be discarded; and he knows how the discarded fetter will not arise in the future.

He is conscious of the tongue, is also conscious of tastes, and knows any fetter that arises dependent on both (the tongue and the taste). Besides, he knows how a fetter which has not yet arisen comes to arise; and he knows how the fetter that has arisen comes to be discarded; and he knows how the discarded fetter will not arise in the future.

He is conscious of the body, is also conscious of tactile objects, and knows any fetter that arises dependent on both (the body and the tactile object). Besides, he knows how a fetter which has not yet arisen comes to arise; and he knows how the fetter that has arisen comes to be discarded; and he knows how the discarded fetter will not arise in the future.

He is conscious of the mind, is also conscious of mind-objects, and knows any fetter that arises dependent on both (the mind and the mind-objects). Besides, he knows how a fetter which has not yet arisen comes to arise; and he knows how the fetter that has arisen comes to be discarded: and he knows how the discarded fetter will not arise in the future.[231]

Thus he keeps his mind steadfastly on the *dhammā* in himself (and perceives that they are just phenomena without any entity or soul). (Occasionally) he realizes that the *dhammā* in others must be of a similar nature. Because of this realization, he can be said to keep his mind steadfastly on the *dhammā* in others. In this way, he is considered to keep his mind steadfastly on the *dhammā* in himself or in others. (When he gains

---

231. A fetter which has not yet arisen comes to arise due to *ayoniso-manasikāra*; the fetter that has arisen comes to be discarded through *yoniso-manasikāra*; due to one of the four Ariya Maggas the discarded fetter will not arise in the future.

more concentration), he perceives the cause and the actual appearing of the *dhammā*. He (also) perceives the cause and the actual dissolution of the *dhammā*. He (also) perceives both the actual appearing and the actual dissolution of the *dhammā*, with their causes.[232] And further, the bhikkhu is firmly mindful of the fact that there are only *dhammā*. That (mindfulness) is solely for gaining (*vipassanā*) insights progressively, solely for gaining further mindfulness stage by stage. The bhikkhu remains detached from craving and wrong views, without clinging to any of the five *khandhas* (that are continuously deteriorating). Bhikkhus, it is also in this way that the bhikkhu keeps his mind steadfastly on the six internal and the six external *āyatana dhammā*, (perceiving their true nature).

End of the Section on the Twelve Sense-Bases

Perception of the True Nature of Dhammā: (iv) Section on Bojjhaṅgā

385. And again, bhikkhus, the bhikkhu keeps his mind steadfastly on the mental phenomena of the seven *bojjhaṅgā*[233] (factors which enable one to comprehend the four Ariya Truths), and perceives that they are just phenomena without any entity or soul. And, bhikkhus, how does the bhikkhu keep his mind steadfastly on the seven *bojjhaṅgā*, and perceive their soulless nature?

Bhikkhus, when *sati-saṃbojjhaṅga*[234] the enlightenment-factor of mindfulness, is present in him, the bhikkhu following my Teaching knows

---

232. The causes for the appearing of the physical sense-bases are ignorance of the four Noble Truths, craving, kamma, and nutriment; and the dissolution of those physical sense-bases is due to the disappearance of these causes. The causes for the appearing and the dissolution of the mind base are the same as those for the Mind; (see footnote to Para 381). The causes for the appearing and the dissolution of the mind-object base, which are not already included in the physical sense-bases, are the same as those for Sensation; (see footnote to Para 380).

233. *Bojjhaṅgā*, pl. of *bojjhaṅga*: from *Bodhi* + *aṅga*. *Bodhi* = knowledge of the four Ariya Truths, Enlightenment, through *vipassanā insight*, and *magga-phala* insight. *Aṅga* = factor leading to such knowledge. *Bojjhaṅga* is generally translated as factor of enlightenment or enlightenment-factor.

234. *Sati-saṃbojjhaṅga*: This is a combination of three words, namely, *sati* = steadfast mindfulness + *saṃ* = well, positively, clearly + *bojjhaṅga* = one of the seven *bojjhaṅgā*. *Sati-saṃbojjhaṅga* is the *bojjhaṅga* of steadfast mindfulness that enables one to comprehend clearly the four Ariya Truths.

"*sati-saṃbojjhaṅga* is present in me"; or when *sati-saṃbojjhaṅga* is not present in him, he knows '*sati-saṃbojjhaṅga* is not present in me'. Besides, he knows how the *sati-saṃbojjhaṅga* which has not arisen before comes to arise;[235] and he knows how the complete fulfilment in developing[236] the arisen sati-saṃbojjhaṅga comes about.

When *dhammavicaya-saṃbojjhaṅga,*[237] enlightenment-factor of investigative knowledge of phenomena, is present in him, he knows "*dhammavicaya-saṃbojjhaṅga* is present in me"; or when *dhammavicaya-saṃbojjhaṅga* is not present in him, he knows '*dhammavicaya-saṃbojjhaṅga* is not present in me'. Besides, he knows how the *dhammavicaya-saṃbojjhaṅga* which has not arisen before comes to arise; and he knows how the complete fulfilment in developing the arisen *dhammavicaya-saṃbojjhaṅga* comes about.

When *viriya-saṃbojjhaṅga,*[238] the enlightenment-factor of effort, is present in him, he knows '*viriya-saṃbojjhaṅga* is present in me; or when *viriya-saṃbojjhaṅga* is not present in him, he knows '*viriya-saṃbojjhaṅga* is not present in me'. Besides, he knows how the *viriya-saṃbojjhaṅga* which has not yet arisen before comes to arise; and he knows how the complete fulfilment in development the arisen *viriya-saṃbojjhaṅga* comes about.

When *pīti-saṃbojjhaṅga,*[239] the enlightenment-factor of delightful satisfaction, is present in him, he knows '*pīti-saṃbojjhaṅga* is present

---

235. This is due to *yoniso manasikāra*: *yoniso = proper + manasikāra =* attention to the object. (See footnote to paragraph 382). This also applies to the other factors of enlightenment.

236. This is due to *arahatta-magga*: the fourth and final stage of *magga* insight, *magga ñāṇa*, in which all the *kilesas*, moral defilements, are eradicated. This also applies to the other factors of enlightenment.

237. *Dhammavicaya* is a combination of two words, namely, *dhamma + vicaya. Dhamma* means the five *khandhas*, or *nāmarūpa*, mental and physical phenomena. *Vicaya* means knowledge through proper investigation. Here, investigation means *vipassanā bhāvanā*. So *dhammavicaya* means knowledge of the true nature of the five *khandhas* by means of *vipassanā bhāvanā*.

238. *Viriya-saṃbojjhaṅga*: *Viriya* means the right effort to be mindful. It is a well-balanced effort which is neither unduly strong nor unduly weak. If the effort is unduly weak, the bhikkhu cannot achieve mental concentration (*samādhi*). If it is unduly strong, he will become so exhausted that *samādhi*, which he has already achieved, can be impaired.

239. *Pīti*: when one's *viriya*, effort, becomes well-balanced, after attaining *sati*, steadfast mindfulness, and *dhamma-vicaya*, knowledge of the true nature of

in me'; or when *pīti-saṃbojjhaṅga* is not present in him, he knows '*pīti-saṃbojjhaṅga* is not present in me'. Besides, he knows how the *pīti-saṃbojjhaṅga* which has not arisen before comes to arise; and he knows how the complete fulfilment in developing the arisen *pīti-saṃbojjhaṅga* come about.

When *passaddhi-saṃbojjkaṅga,*[240] the enlightenment-factor of serenity, is present in him, he knows '*passaddhi-saṃbojjhaṅga* is present in me'; or when *passaddhi-saṃbojjhaṅga* is not present in him, he knows '*passaddhi-saṃbojjhaṅga* is not present in me'. Besides, he knows how the *passaddhi-saṃbojjhaṅga* which has not arisen before comes to arise; and he knows how the complete fulfilment in developing the arisen *passaddhi-saṃbojjhaṅga* comes about.

When *samādhi-saṃbojjhaṅga,*[241] the enlightenment-factor of concentration, is present in him, he knows '*samādhi-saṃbojjhaṅga* is present in me'; or when *samādhi-saṃbojjhaṅga* is not present in him, he knows '*samādhi-saṃbojjhaṅga* is not present in me'. Besides, he knows how the *samādhi-saṃbojjhaṅga* which has not arisen before comes to arise; and he knows how the complete fulfilment in developing the arisen *samādhi-saṃbojjhaṅga* comes about.

When *upekkhā-saṃbojjhaṅga,*[242] the enlightenment factor of equanimity, is present in him he knows '*upekkhā-saṃbojjhaṅga* is present in me'; or when *upekkhā-saṃbojjhaṅga* is not present in him, he knows '*upekkhā-saṃbojjhaṅga* is not present in me'. Besides, he knows how the *upekkhā-saṃbojjhaṅga* which has not arisen before comes to arise; and he knows how the complete fulfilment in developing the arisen *upekkhā-saṃbojjhaṅga* comes about.

---

nāmarūpa, one gets *pīti*, joy and satisfaction which may thrill one through and through.

240. *Passaddhi-saṃbojjhaṅga*: after one has got *pīti-saṃbojjhaṅga*, one naturally gets *passaddhi-saṃbojjhaṅga*. Before this stage, one has to start the meditation process by making a definite effort to be steadfastly mindful. However, when this *passaddhi* stage has been once reached, mindfulness takes place without much effort.

241. *Samādhi-saṃbojjhaṅga*: *Samādhi-saṃbojjhaṅga* is a logical consequence of *pīti-saṃbojjhaṅga* and *passaddhi-saṃbojjhaṅga*. When the bhikkhu achieves it, he is instantly and closely aware of every object as it appears in his mind.

242. *Upekkhā-saṃbojjhaṅga*: *Upekkhā-saṃbojjhaṅga* is a *bojjhaṅga* that keeps a balance between *saddhā* (faith) and *paññā* (knowledge of the true nature of the five *khandhas* by means of *vipassanā bhāvanā*). It also keeps a balance between *vīriya* and *samādhi*.

Thus he keeps his mind steadfastly on the *dhammā* in himself (and perceives that they are just phenomena without any entity or soul). (Occasionally) he realizes that the *dhammā* in others must be of a similar nature. Because of this realization, he can be said to keep his mind steadfastly on the *dhammā* in others. In this way, he is considered to keep his mind steadfastly on the *dhammā* in himself or in others. (When he gains more concentration), he perceives the cause and the actual appearing of the *dhammā*. He (also) perceives the cause and the actual dissolution of the *dhammā*. He (also) perceives both the actual appearing and the actual dissolution of the *dhammā*, with their causes.[243] And further the bhikkhu is firmly mindful of the fact that there are only *dhammā*. That (mindfulness) is solely for gaining (*vipassanā*) insights progressively, solely for gaining further mindfulness stage by stage. The bhikkhu remains detached from craving and wrong views, without clinging to any of the five *khandhas* (that are continuously deteriorating). Bhikkhus, it is also in this way that the bhikkhu keeps his mind steadfastly on the seven *bojjhaṅgā*, perceiving their true nature.

End of the Section on the Seven Bojjhaṅgā

PERCEPTION OF THE TRUE NATURE OF DHAMMĀ: (V) SECTION ON THE FOUR NOBLE TRUTHS

386. And again, bhikkhus, the bhikkhu keeps his mind steadfastly on the mental and physical phenomena of the four Noble Truths (and perceives that they are just phenomena without any entity or soul). And, bhikkhus, how does the bhikkhu keep his mind steadfastly on the four Noble Truths?

Bhikkhus, the bhikkhu following my Teaching knows 'This is *dukkha*' as it really is; he knows 'This is the origin of *dukkha*' as it really is; he knows 'This is the cessation of *dukkha*' as it really is; he knows 'This is the practice of the Path leading to the cessation of *dukkha*' as it really is.

End of the First Portion for Recitation

243. The arising of the *bojjhaṅgā*, factors of enlightenment, is due to *yoniso-manasikāra*, right perception of phenomena, viewing all phenomena as impermanent, unpleasurable, soulless and repulsive. The non-appearance or disappearance of a *bojjhaṅga* is due to *ayoniso-manasikāra*, wrong perception of phenomena, viewing all phenomena as permanent, pleasurable, endowed with soul, and non-repulsive.

Exposition of the Noble Truth of Dukkha

387. Bhikkhus, what is the Noble Truth of Dukkha?[244] Birth (i.e., repeated rebirth) is *dukkha*. Ageing also is *dukkha*. Death also is *dukkha*. Grief, lamentation, pain, distress, and despair are also *dukkha*. To have to associate with those (persons or things) one dislikes is also *dukkha*; to be separated from those one loves or likes is also *dukkha*; the craving for what one cannot get[245] is also *dukkha*; in short, the five Aggregates which are the objects of Clinging are *dukkha*.

3S8. And, bhikkhus, what is birth (*jāti*)? The coming into existence (of *nāmarūpa*), the complete origination, the conception, the arising up in new form, the appearance of the Aggregates (*khandhas*), the acquisition of the sense-bases of various beings in various categories, — this, bhikkhus, is called birth.

389. And, bhikkhus, what is ageing (*jarā*)? The process of ageing, the decrepitude, the decay and loss of teeth, the greying of hair, the wrinkling of skin, the failing of the life-force, the wearing out of the sense-faculties (such as sight) of various beings in various categories, — this, bhikkhus, is called ageing.

390. And, bhikkhus, what is death (*maraṇa*)? The falling away from existence, the passing away from existence, the dissolution, the disappearance, the end of life, the passing away due to completion of the life-span, the breaking up of the aggregates (*khandhas*), the discarding of the body, the destruction of the life-faculty of various beings in various categories, — this, bhikkhus, is called death.

391. And, bhikkhus, what is grief (*soka*)? The grievous anxiety, the sorrowful and anxious state of mind, the sorrowfulness and anxiety, the inward grief, the inward wretchedness of one who is beset by some ruinous loss or other, who encounters some painful misfortune or other, — this, bhikkhus, is called grief.

392. And, bhikkhus, what is lamentation (*parideva*)? The weeping and lamenting, the act of weeping and lamenting, the condition of weeping and

244. Dukkha as a Noble Truth is left untranslated. "Suffering" and "ill" are inadequate renderings. Dukkha is inherent in existence. The five aggregates which are the objects of clinging therefore embody *dukkha*. Dukkha has connotations of impermanence, insubstantiality, unsatisfactoriness, emptiness, imperfection, insecurity, besides the obvious ones of suffering, physical pain (as in paragraph 393) and mental affliction.

245. According to the Commentary.

lamenting by one who is beset by some ruinous loss or other, who encounters some painful misfortune or other, — this, bhikkhus, is called lamentation.

393. And, bhikkhus, what is pain (*dukkha*)? The bodily pain and bodily unpleasantness, the painful and unpleasant feeling produced by contact of the body, — this, bhikkhus, is called pain.

394. And, bhikkhus, what is distress (*domanassa*)? The mental pain and mental unpleasantness, the painful and unpleasant feeling produced by contact of the mind, — this, bhikkhus, is called distress.

395. And, bhikkhus, what is despair (*upāyāsa*)? The sorrowful trouble and tribulation, the troubled state, the state of tribulation of one who is beset by some ruinous loss or other, who encounters some painful misfortune or other, — this, bhikkhus, is called despair.

396. And, bhikkhus, what is the *dukkha* of having to associate with those (persons or things) one dislikes (*appiyehi sampayogo dukkho*)? Having to meet, remain together, be in close contact, or intermingle, with sights, sounds, odours, tastes, tactile objects and mind-objects in this world which are undesirable, unpleasant or unenjoyable, or with those who desire one's disadvantage, loss, discomfort, or state of harmful bondage (to *kilesas*, moral defilements), — this, bhikkhus, is called the *dukkha* of having to associate with those (persons or things) one dislikes.

397. And, bhikkhus, what is the *dukkha* of being separated from those one loves or likes (*piyehi vippayogo dukkho*)? Not being able to meet, remain together, be in close contact, or intermingle, with sights, sounds, odours, tastes, tactile objects and mind-objects in this world which are desirable, pleasant or enjoyable, or with mother or father or brothers or sisters or friends or companions or maternal and paternal relatives who desire one's advantage, benefit, comfort or freedom from harmful bondage (to *kilesas*, moral defilements), — this, bhikkhus, is called the *dukkha* of being separated from those one loves or likes.

398. And bhikkhus, what is the *dukkha* of the craving for what one cannot get? In beings subject to birth the wish arises: 'Oh that we were not subject to birth! Oh that (new) birth would not happen to us!' But it is not possible to get such a wish. This is the *dukkha* of the craving for what one cannot get. Bhikkhus, in beings subject to ageing the wish arises: 'Oh that we were not subject to ageing! Oh that ageing would not happen to us!' But it is not possible to get such a wish. This also is the *dukkha* of the craving for what one cannot get. Bhikkhus, in beings subject to illness, the wish arises: 'Oh that we were not subject to illness! Oh that illness would not happen to us!' But it is not possible to get such a wish. This

also is the *dukkha* of the craving for what one cannot get. Bhikkhus, in beings subject to death the wish arises: 'Oh that we were not subject to death! Oh that death would not happen to us!' But it is not possible to get such a wish. This also is the *dukkha* of the craving for what one cannot get. Bhikkhus, in beings subject to grief, lamentation, pain, distress and despair, the wish arises: 'Oh that we were not subject to grief, lamentation, pain, distress and despair! Oh that grief, lamentation, pain, distress and despair would not happen to us!' But it is not possible to get such a wish. This also is the *dukkha* of the craving for what one cannot get.

399. And, bhikkhus, what is (meant by) 'In short, the five aggregates which are the objects of clinging are *dukkha*'? They are the aggregate of corporeality, the aggregate of sensation, the aggregate of perception, the aggregate of mental formations, and the aggregate of consciousness, as objects of clinging. These, bhikkhus, are what is meant by 'In short, the five aggregates which are the objects of clinging are *dukkha*'.

Bhikkhus, this is called the Noble Truth of Dukkha.

Exposition of the Noble Truth of the Origin of Dukkha

400. And, bhikkhus, what is the Noble Truth of the origin of *dukkha*? The origin of *dukkha* is the craving (*taṇhā*)[246] which gives rise to fresh rebirth, and, accompanied by pleasure and passion, finds great delight in this or that existence, namely, craving for pleasures of the senses (*kāma-taṇhā*), craving for (better) existence (*bhava-taṇhā*), and craving for non-existence (*vibhava-taṇhā*).

But, bhikkhus, when this craving arises, where does it arise? When it establishes itself, where does it establish itself? When this craving arises and establishes[247] itself, it does so in the delightful and pleasurable characteristics of the *upādānakkhandhas.*[248]

---

246. *Kāma-taṇhā* is hankering after and becoming attached to pleasures of the senses. *Bhava-taṇhā* is hankering after and becoming attached to continued existence, either the current sensual existence or a better and higher existence in the *rūpa* (fine material) or *arūpa* (non-material) Brahmā realms, or becoming attached to the *rūpa* and *arūpa jhānas*. *Vibhava-taṇhā* is hankering after and becoming attached to the idea that there is no *kamma* for rebirth, and hence no future existence.

247. **Establishes**: *nivisati* = recurs again and again. (The Commentary)

248. *Upādānakkhandhas*: In the Pāḷi text *loka*, which the Commentary explains as the aggregates which are the object of clinging.

What are the delightful and pleasurable characteristics of the *upādānakkhandhas*?

In the *upādānakkhandhas*, the eye has the characteristic of being delightful and pleasurable. When this Craving arises, it arises there (i.e., in the eye); when it establishes itself, it establishes itself there. In the *upādānakkhandhas*, the ear ... (p) ... In the *upādānakkhandhas*, the nose ... (p) ... In the *upādānakkhandhas*, the tongue ... (p) ... In the *upādānakkhandhas*, the body ... (p) ... In the *upādānakkhandhas*, the mind has the characteristic of being delightful and pleasurable. When this Craving arises, it arises there; when it establishes itself, it establishes itself there.

In the *upādānakkhandhas*, visible objects ... (p) ... In the *upādānakkhandhas*, sounds... In the *upādānakkhandhas*, odours ... (p) ... In the *upādānakkhandhas*, tastes ... (p) ... In the *upādānakkhandhas*, tactual objects ... (p) ... In the *upādānakkhandhas*, mind-objects have the characteristic of being delightful and pleasurable. When this craving arises, it arises there; when it establishes itself, it establishes itself there.

In the *upādānakkhandhas*, eye-consciousness (i.e., consciousness arising in the eye) ... (p) ... In the *upādānakkhandhas*, ear-consciousness ... (p) ... In the *upādāna-kkhandhas*, nose-consciousness ... (p) ... In the *upādānak-khandhas*, tongue-consciousness... In the *upādānak-khandhas*, body-consciousness ... (p) ... In the *upādānak-khandhas*, mind-consciousness has the characteristic of being delightful and pleasurable. When this craving arises, it arises there; when it establishes itself, it establishes itself there.

In the *upādānakkhandhas*, eye-contact (i.e., contact with the sense of sight) ... (p) ... In the *upādānakkhandhas*, ear-contact (i.e., contact with the sense of hearing) ... (p) ... In the *upādānakkhandhas*, nose-contact (i.e., contact with the sense of smell) ... (p) ... In the *upādānakkhandhas*, tongue-contact ... (p) ... In the *upādānakkhandhas*, body-contact ... (p) ... In the *upādānakkhandhas*, mind-contact has the characteristic of being delightful and pleasurable. When this craving arises, it arises there; when it establishes itself, it establishes itself there.

In the *upādānakkhandhas*, the sensation born of eye-contact ... (p) ... In the *upādānakkhandhas*, the sensation born of ear-contact ... (p) ... In the *upādānakkhandhas*, the sensation born of nose-contact ... (p) ... In the *upādānakkhandhas*, the sensation born of tongue-contact ... (p) ... In the *upādānakkhandhas*, the sensation born of body-contact ... (p) ... In the *upādānakkhandhas*, the sensation born of mind-contact has the characteristic of being delightful and pleasurable. When this craving arises, it arises there; when it establishes itself, it establishes itself there.

In the *upādānakkhandhas*, perception of visible objects ... (p) ... In the *upādānakkhandhas*, perception of sounds ... (p) ... In the *upādānakkhandhas*, perception of odours ... (p) ... In the *upādānakkhandhas*, perception of tastes ... (p) ... In the *upādānakkhandhas*, perception of tactile objects ... (p) ... In the *upādānakkhandhas*, perception of mind-objects has the characteristic of being delightful and pleasurable. When this craving arises, it arises there; when it establishes itself, it establishes itself there.

In the *upādānakkhandhas*, volition (*sañcetanā*) focussed on visible objects ... (p) ... In the *upādānakkhandhas*, volition focussed on sounds ... (p) ... In the *upādānakkhandhas*, volition focussed on odours ... (p) ... In the *upādānakkhandhas*, volition focussed on tastes ... (p) ... In the *upādānakkhandhas*, volition focussed on tactile objects ... (p) ... In the *upādānakkhandhas*, volition focussed on mind-objects has the characteristic of being delightful and pleasurable. When this craving arises, it arises there; when it establishes itself, it establishes itself there.

In the *upādānakkhandhas*, craving for visible objects ... (p) ... In the *upādānakkhandhas*, craving for sounds ... (p) ... In the *upādānakkhandhas*, craving for odours ... (p) ... In the *upādānakkhandhas*, craving for tastes ... (p) ... In the *upādānakkhandhas*, craving for tactile objects ... (p) ... In the *upādānakkhandhas.*, craving for mind-objects has the characteristic of being delightful and pleasurable. When this craving arises, it arises there; when it establishes itself, it establishes itself there.

In the *upādānakkhandhas*, *vitakka*,[249] initial application of the mind to visible objects ... (p) ... In the *upādānakkhandhas*, initial application of the mind to sounds ... (p) ... In the *upādānakkhandhas*, initial application of the mind to odours ... (p) ... In the *upādānakkhandhas*, initial application of the mind to tastes ... (p) ... In the *upādānakkhandhas*, initial application of the mind to tactile objects ... (p) ... In the *upādānakkhandhas*, initial application of the mind to mind-objects has the characteristic of being delightful and pleasurable. When this craving arises, it arises there; when it establishes itself, it establishes itself there.

In the *upādānakkhandhas*, *vicāra*, sustained application of the mind to visible objects ... (p) ... In the *upādānakkhandhas*, sustained application of the mind to sounds ... (p) ... In the *upādānakkhandhas*, sustained application of the mind to odours ... (p) ... In the *upādānakkhandhas*, sustained application of the mind to tastes ... (p) ... In the *upādānakkhandhas*,

---

249. *Vitakka* is the initial turning of the mind towards the object of attention. It is also rendered as 'reflection', 'thinking' or 'thought-conception'. *Vicāra* is the deliberate investigation or examination by the mind of the object of attention.

sustained application of the mind to tactile objects ... (p) ... In the *upādānakkhandhas*, sustained application of the mind to mind-objects has the characteristic of being delightful and pleasurable. When this craving arises, it arises there; when it establishes itself, it establishes itself there.

Bhikkhus, this is called the Noble Truth of the Origin of Dukkha.

Exposition of the Noble Truth of the Cessation of Dukkha

401. And, bhikkhus, what is the Noble Truth of the Cessation of Dukkha?

It is the complete extinction and cessation of this very craving, its abandoning and discarding, the liberation and detachment from it. (This, in fact, is realization of *nibbāna.*)

But, bhikkhus, when this craving is abandoned, where is it abandoned? When it ceases, where does it cease? When this craving is abandoned or ceases, it is abandoned, or it ceases in the delightful and pleasurable characteristics of the *upādānakkhandhas.*

What are the delightful and pleasurable characteristics of the *upādānakkhandhas*?

In the *upādānakkhandhas*, the eye has the characteristic of being delightful and pleasurable. When this Craving is abandoned, it is abandoned there (i.e., in the eye); when it ceases, it ceases there. In the *upādānakkhandhas*, the ear ... (p) ... In the *upādānakkhandhas*, the nose ... (p) ... In the *upādānakkhandhas*, the tongue ... (p) ... In the *upādānakkhandhas*, the body ... (p) ... In the *upādānakkhandhas*, the mind has the characteristic of being delightful and pleasurable. When this craving is abandoned, it is abandoned there; when it ceases, it ceases there.

In the *upādānakkhandhas*, visible objects ... (p) ... In the *upādānakkhandhas*, sounds ... (p) ... In the *upādānakkhandhas*, odours ... (p) ... In the *upādānakkhandhas*, tastes ... (p) ... In the *upādānakkhandhas*, tactile objects ... (p) ... In the *upādānakkhandhas*, mind-objects have the characteristic of being delightful and pleasurable. When this craving is abandoned, it is abandoned there; when it ceases, it ceases there.

In the *upādānakkhandhas*, eye-consciousness, ear-consciousness, nose-consciousness, tongue-consciousness, body-consciousness, mind-consciousness, (each) has the characteristic of being delightful and pleasurable. When this craving is abandoned, it is abandoned there; when it ceases, it ceases there.

In the *upādānakkhandhas*, eye-contact, ear-contact, nose-contact, tongue-contact, body-contact, mind-contact, (each) has the characteristic of being delightful and pleasurable. When this craving is abandoned, it is abandoned there; when it ceases, it ceases there.

In the *upādānakkhandhas*, the sensation born of eye-contact, the sensation born of ear-contact, the sensation born of nose-contact, the sensation born of tongue-contact, the sensation born of body-contact, the sensation born of mind-contact, (each) has the characteristic of being delightful and pleasurable. When this craving is abandoned, it is abandoned there; when it ceases, it ceases there.

In the *upādānakkhandhas*, perception of visible objects, perception of sounds, perception of odours, perception of tastes, perception of tactile objects, perception of mind-objects, (each) has the characteristic of being delightful and pleasurable. When this craving is abandoned, it is abandoned there; when it ceases, it ceases there.

In the *upādānakkhandhas*, volition focussed on visible objects, volition focussed on sounds, volition focussed on odours, volition focussed on tastes, volition focussed on tactile objects, volition focussed on mind-objects, (each) has the characteristic of being delightful and pleasurable. When this craving is abandoned, it is abandoned there; when it ceases, it ceases there.

In the *upādānakkhandhas*, craving for visible objects, craving for sounds, craving for odours, craving for tastes. craving for tactile objects, craving for mind-objects, (each) has the characteristic of being delightful and pleasurable. When this craving is abandoned, it is abandoned there; when it ceases, it ceases there.

In the *upādānakkhandhas*, *vitakka*, initial application of the mind to visible objects, to sounds, to odours, to tastes, to tactile objects, to mind-objects, (each) has the characteristic of being delightful and pleasurable. When this craving is abandoned, it it abandoned there; when it ceases, it ceases there.

In the *upādānakkhandhas*, *vicāra*, sustained application of the mind to visible objects, to sounds, to odours, to tastes, to tactile objects, to mind-objects, (each) has the characteristic of being delightful and pleasurable. When this craving is abandoned, it is abandoned there; when it ceases, it ceases there.

Bhikkhus, this is called the Noble Truth of the Cessation of Dukkha.

Exposition of the Noble Truth of the Path Leading to the Cessation of Dukkha

402. And, bhikkhus, what is the Noble Truth of the Path leading to the Cessation of Dukkha?

It is the Noble Path of Eight Constituents, namely, *sammādiṭṭhi*, Right View, *sammāsaṅkappa*, Right Thinking, *sammāvācā*, Right Speech, *sammākammanta*, Right Action, *sammā-ājiva*, Right Livelihood, *sammāvāyāma*, Right Effort, *sammāsati*, Right Mindfulness, *sammāsamādhi*, Right Concentration.

And, bhikkhus, what is Right View?

Insight-knowledge of *dukkha*, insight-knowledge of the origin of *dukkha*, insight-knowledge of the cessation of *dukkha* (i.e., *nibbāna*), insight-knowledge of the path leading to the cessation of *dukkha* (i.e., the Path leading to *nibbāna*). This, bhikkhus, is called Right View.

And, bhikkhus, what is Right Thinking?

Thoughts directed to liberation from sensuality, thoughts free from ill will (i.e., thoughts of loving-kindness), and thoughts free from cruelty (i.e., thoughts of compassion). This, bhikkhus, is called Right Thinking.

And, bhikkhus, what is Right Speech?

Abstaining from falsehood, from back-biting, from coarse speech, from vain and unbeneficial talk. This, bhikkhus, is called Right Speech.

And, bhikkhus, what is Right Action?

Abstaining from killing, from taking what is not given, from wrongful indulgence in sexual pleasures. This, bhikkhus, is called Right Action.

And, bhikkhus, what is Right Livelihood?

Bhikkhus, the *ariya* disciple following my Teaching completely abstains from a wrong way of livelihood, and makes his living by a right means of livelihood. This, bhikkhus, is called Right Livelihood.

And, bhikkhus, what is Right Effort?

Bhikkhus, the bhikkhu following my Teaching generates will, makes effort, rouses energy, applies his mind, and strives most ardently to prevent the arising of evil demeritorious states of mind that have not yet arisen. He generates will, makes effort, rouses energy, applies his mind, and strives most ardently to abandon evil demeritorious states of mind that have arisen. He generates will, makes effort, rouses energy, applies his mind, and strives most ardently to attain meritorious states of mind that have not yet arisen. He generates will, makes effort, rouses energy, applies his mind, and strives most ardently to maintain the meritorious states of mind that have arisen, to prevent their lapsing, to increase them, to cause them to grow, to make them develop in full (in *samatha* & *vipassanā* meditation). This, bhikkhus, is called Right Effort.

And, bhikkhus, what is Right Mindfulness?

Bhikkhus, the bhikkhu (i.e., the disciple) following my Teaching keeps his mind steadfastly on the body (*kāya*), with diligence, comprehension and mindfulness, (and perceives its impermanent, insecure, soulless and repulsive nature), thus keeping away covetousness and distress (which will appear if he is not mindful of the five *khandhas*).

The bhikkhu keeps his mind steadfastly on sensation (*vedanā*), with diligence, comprehension and mindfulness, (and perceives its impermanent, insecure, and soulless nature), thus keeping away covetousness and distress (which will appear if he is not mindful of the five *khandhas*).

The bhikkhu concentrates steadfastly on the mind (*citta*), with diligence, comprehension and mindfulness, (and perceives its impermanent, insecure, and soulless nature), thus keeping away covetousness and distress (which will appear if he is not mindful of the five *khandhas*).

The bhikkhu keeps his mind steadfastly on the *dhammā*, with diligence, comprehension and mindfulness, (and perceives their impermanent, insecure, and soulless nature), thus keeping away covetousness and distress (which will appear if he is not mindful of the five *khandhas*). This, bhikkhus, is called Right Mindfulness.

And, bhikkhus, what is Right Concentration?

Bhikkhus, the bhikkhu who follows my Teaching, being detached from sensual pleasures and demeritorious factors, achieves and remains in the first *jhāna*, which has *vitakka* (initial application of the *mind*), *vicāra* (sustained application of the mind), *pīti* (delightful satisfaction) and *sukha* (bliss), born of detachment from the hindrances (*nīvaraṇas*).

Having got rid of *vitakka* and *vicāra*, the bhikkhu achieves and remains in the second *jhāna*, with internal tranquillity, with enhancement of one-pointedness of concentration, devoid of *vitakka* and *vicāra*, but with *pīti* and *sukha* born of concentration.

Having been detached from *pīti*, that bhikkhu dwells in equanimity with mindfulness and clear comprehension, and experiences *sukha* in mind and body. He achieves and remains in the third *jhāna*, that which causes a person who attains it to be praised by the Noble Ones as one who has equanimity and mindfulness, one who abides in *sukha*.

By dispelling both pain and pleasure, and by the previous disappearance of sadness and gladness, that bhikkhu achieves and remains in the fourth *jhāna*, a state of equanimity and absolute purity of mindfulness, without pain or pleasure. This, bhikkhus, is called Right Concentration.

Bhikkhus, this is called the Noble Truth of the Path leading to the Cessation of Dukkha.

403. Thus he keeps his mind steadfastly on the *dhammā* in himself (and perceives that they are just phenomena without any entity or soul). (Occasionally) he realizes that the *dhammā* in others must be of a similar nature. Because of this realization, he can be said to keep his mind steadfastly on the *dhammā* in others. In this way, he is considered to keep his mind steadfastly on the *dhammā* in himself or in others. (When he gains more concentration), he perceives the cause and the actual appearing of the *dhammā*. He (also) perceives the cause and the actual dissolution of the *dhammā*. He (also) perceives both the actual appearing and the actual dissolution of the *dhammā*, with their causes. And further the bhikkhu is firmly mindful of the fact that there are only *dhammā*. That (mindfulness) is solely for gaining (*vipassanā*) insights progressively, solely for gaining further mindfulness stage by stage. The bhikkhu remains detached from craving and wrong views, without clinging to any of the five *khandhas* (that are continuously deteriorating). Bhikkhus, it is also in this way that the bhikkhu keeps his mind steadfastly on the Four Noble Truths, (perceiving their true nature).

End of the Section on the Noble Truths

End of "Perception of the True Nature of Dhammā"

The Benefits of Practicing the Four Methods of Mindfulness

404. Indeed, bhikkhus, whosoever practices these four methods of Steadfast Mindfulness in this manner for seven years, one of two results is to be certainly expected in him: arahatship (*aññā*, the knowledge of final emancipation, *arahatta phala*) in this very existence, or if there yet be any trace of clinging left, the state of an *anāgāmī* (the state of non-return to the world of sense-existence, *anāgāmī phala*).

Let alone seven years, bhikkhus, whosoever practices these four methods of Steadfast Mindfulness in this manner for six years ... (p) ... for five years ... (p) ... for four years ... (p) ... for three years ... (p) ... for two years ... (p) ... for one year.

Let alone one year, bhikkhus, whosoever practices these four methods of Steadfast Mindfulness in this manner for seven months, one of two results is to be certainly expected in him: arahatship in this very existence, or if there yet be any trace of clinging left, the state of an *anāgāmī.*

Let alone seven months, bhikkhus, whosoever practices these four methods of Steadfast Mindfulness in this manner for six months ... (p) ... for five months ... (p) ... for four months ... (p) ... for three months ... (p) ... for two months ... (p) ... for one month ... (p) ... for a half month.

Let alone a half month, bhikkhus, whosoever practices these four methods of Steadfast Mindfulness in this manner for seven days, one of two results is to he certainly expected in him: arahatship in this very existence, or if there yet be any trace of Clinging left, the state of an *anāgāmī.*

405. Because of these beneficial results. I have declared (at the beginning) thus: "Bhikkhus, this is the one and only way for the purification (of the minds) of beings, for overcoming sorrow and lamentation, for the complete destruction of (physical) pain and (mental) distress, for attainment of the noble (Ariya) Magga, and for the realization of Nibbāna. That (only way) is the practice of the four methods of Steadfast Mindfulness, Satipaṭṭhāna."

Thus spoke the Bhagavā. Delighted, the bhikkhus received the words of the Buddha with respectful appreciation.

End of the Mahāsatipaṭṭhāna Sutta, the ninth sutta from division two (Mahā Vagga)

Ten Suttas from

Dīgha Nikāya

Collection of Long Discourses of the Buddha

FOUR SUTTAS

FROM

PĀTHIKA VAGGA

Pāthika Division

Cakkavatti Sutta
Saṃpasādanīya Sutta
Pāsādika Sutta
Siṅgāla Sutta

Namo tassa bhagavato arahato sammāsambuddhassa

CAKKAVATTI SUTTA

III. CAKKAVATTI SUTTA

BEING ONE'S OWN FIRM SUPPORT, BEING ONE'S OWN REFUGE

80. Thus have I heard:

At one time the Bhagavā was staying at the town of Mātulā in the country of Magadha. Then the Bhagavā addressed the bhikkhus as 'Bhikkhus', and they replied respectfully 'Venerable Sir'. And the Bhagavā spoke as follows:

Be your own firm support (lit., island), bhikkhus, be your own refuge; do not take any other refuge. Let the Dhamma be your firm support, let the Dhamma be your refuge; do not take any other refuge.

And how, bhikkhus, does a bhikkhu take himself as his own firm support, as his own refuge, and not any other refuge? How does he take the Dhamma as his firm support and his refuge, and not any other refuge?

Bhikkhus, the bhikkhu (i.e., the disciple) following the practice of my Teaching keeps his mind steadfastly on the body (*kāya*) with diligence, comprehension and mindfulness (and perceives its impermanent, insecure, soulless and unpleasant nature), thus keeping away covetousness and distress (which will appear if he is not mindful of the five *khandhas*).

The bhikkhu keeps his mind steadfastly on sensation (*vedanā*) ... (p) ... (and perceives its impermanent, insecure, and soulless nature)

The bhikkhu concentrates steadfastly on the mind (*citta*) ... (p) ... (and perceives its impermanent, insecure, and soulless nature)

The bhikkhu keeps his mind steadfastly on the Dhamma with diligence, comprehension and mindfulness (and perceives its impermanent, insecure, and soulless nature), thus keeping away covetousness and distress (which will appear if he is not mindful of the five *khandhas*).

In this way, bhikkhus, a bhikkhu takes himself as his own firm support, himself as a refuge, and not any other refuge; and he takes the Dhamma as his firm support and his refuge, not any other refuge.

Keep yourselves, bhikkhus, within your own range[1] of contemplation as has been taught and instructed by the Buddha (lit., the father).

1. Range: *gocara*, lit., pasture, resort, range. Here, range of contemplation

Bhikkhus, if you keep yourselves within the range of contemplation as has been taught and instructed by the Buddha, evil (such as moral defilements) will have no opportunity, no ground to arise in you.

Bhikkhus, it is by cultivation of wholesome Dhammas that meritorious results accrue and develop.

Daḷhanemi, the Universal Monarch

81. Bhikkhus, this happened a long time ago. At that time, there was a Universal Monarch named Daḷhanemi, a king by right, who ruled in a righteous manner over the four continents bounded by the four oceans, the conqueror of all foes, the promoter of peace and stability in his territories, the possessor of seven precious treasures. He possessed these seven precious treasures, namely, the Wheel Treasure, the Elephant Treasure, the Horse Treasure, the Gem Treasure, the Queen Treasure, the Rich Man Treasure, and seventhly, the Eldest Son Treasure. The king had more than a thousand sons, all brave men of heroic features, able to conquer hosts of enemies. He ruled over the Earth to the extent of its ocean boundaries, having conquered territories not by force or by arms but by righteousness.

82. Bhikkhus, after a lapse of many years, many hundreds of years, many thousands of years, King Daḷhanemi instructed a certain man, saying, 'O Man, if you should see this mighty Wheel Treasure make the slightest shift from its resting place, slipping down a little, bring me word.'

'Very well, Your Majesty,' replied the man.

Bhikkhus, after a lapse of many years, many hundreds of years, many thousands of years, the man saw the mighty Wheel Treasure make a slight shift from its resting place, slipping down a little.

On seeing that, the man went to King Daḷhanemi and said, 'May it please Your Majesty to know for a truth that the mighty Wheel Treasure had made a slight shift from its resting place, slipping down a little.'

Upon this, bhikkhus, King Daḷhanemi sent for his eldest son and said to him, 'Dear son, my mighty Wheel Treasure has made a slight shift from its resting place, slipping down a little. I have heard it said thus: "Should the mighty Wheel Treasure of a Universal Monarch make a slight shift from its resting place, slipping down a little, the king has not much longer to live."

---

means objects of steadfast mindfulness. The bhikkhus, are exhorted to keep their minds occupied with these four objects of steadfast mindfulness.

'I have had my full share of human pleasures; it is time now for me to seek celestial bliss. Come, my dear son, take over charge of ruling the Earth bounded by the ocean. As for me, shaving off my hair and beard and putting on the bark-dyed robes, I shall go forth from the household life into the homeless life of an ascetic.'

83. Then, bhikkhus, King Daḷhanemi, after giving his son full instructions on kingship, shaved off his hair and beard, put on the bark-dyed robes and went forth from the household life into the homeless life of an ascetic. On the seventh day after the royal ascetic had gone forth, the mighty Wheel Treasure disappeared.

Then a certain man went to the anointed king of the Khattiya caste, and said to him, 'May it please Your Majesty to know for a truth that the mighty Wheel Treasure has disappeared.'

Thereupon, the anointed king of the Khattiya caste was stricken with grief over the disappearance of the mighty Wheel Treasure, and showed great distress. And he went to the royal ascetic and reported to him, 'Know for a truth, Your Majesty that the mighty Wheel Treasure has disappeared.'

Then, bhikkhus, the royal ascetic said to the anointed king of the Khattiya caste, 'Grieve not, my dear son, show no distress over the disappearance of the mighty Wheel Treasure. The mighty Wheel Treasure is not a paternal heritage of yours. Come, now, dear son, fulfil the noble duties required of a Universal Monarch. On Sabbath day, the fifteenth day of the month, perform the ceremonial ablution of your head, then ascend to the uppermost terrace of your palace and observe the moral precepts, in fulfilment of the noble duties required of a Universal Monarch. There is reason to believe that the mighty Wheel Treasure will then appear to you with its thousand spokes, rim and hub and with all parts complete.

The Noble Duties of a Universal Monarch

84. 'Your Majesty, what may be the noble duties of a Universal Monarch?'

'Dear son, making the Dhamma your only support, honouring the Dhamma, esteeming it, adoring it, paying homage to it, revering it, holding aloft the banner of the Dhamma, making it the pinnacle, taking it as your guide and master, you should in a righteous manner arrange to provide protection, shelter and security for your own folk and family, for the fighting forces, for kings and vassals dependent on you, for brahmins and householders, for dwellers of towns and villages, for samaṇas and brāhmaṇas and for birds and beasts.

'Dear son, let there not be any lawlessness in your kingdom. Make offerings of gifts to the needy in your kingdom. There are, in your kingdom, religious teachers who are not over-bearing, not remiss and heedless in their actions; they remain devoted to the practice of forbearance, leading a life of moral restraint and gentleness; they discipline their own mind, making it tranquil, trying to bring it to perfect peace. Approach them at an appropriate time and ask of them, enquire from them:

"Venerable Sirs, what constitutes a meritorious act, what constitutes a demeritorious act? What is a blameworthy act? What is a faultless act? What should be resorted to and embraced? What should not be resorted to and embraced? What line of action adopted by me would prove to be unbeneficial and distressful for a long time? What line of action adopted by me would prove to be beneficial and conducive to happiness for a long time?" Having heard their advice, keep away from that which is demeritorious; take up that which is meritorious and practice it. These, then, dear son, are the noble duties of a Universal Monarch.'

The Wheel Treasure Appears

85. Bhikkhus, the anointed king of the Khattiya caste, saying 'Very well, Your Majesty!' in assent, fulfilled the noble duties required of a Universal Monarch. On Sabbath day, the fifteenth day of the month, he performed the ceremonial ablution of his head, then ascended to the uppermost terrace of his palace and observed the moral precepts in fulfilment of the noble duties required of a Universal Monarch. To him thus engaged there appeared the mighty Wheel Treasure, with its thousand spokes, rim and hub and with all parts complete.

On seeing the mighty Wheel Treasure, the anointed king of the Khattiya caste thought thus: "I have heard it said, 'If the anointed king of the Khattiya caste, who, on Sabbath day, the fifteenth day of the month, performs, the ceremonial ablution of the head, then ascends to the uppermost terrace of his palace and observes the moral precepts in fulfilment of the noble duties required of a Universal Monarch, if to him there appears the mighty Wheel Treasure with its thousand spokes, rim and hub and with all parts complete, then that king is indeed a Universal Monarch.' Could it be that I am a Cakkavatti, a Universal Monarch?"

Then the anointed king of the Khattiya caste rose from his seat, arranged his upper robe over one shoulder, and holding a gold pitcher (of water) in his left hand, sprinkled water with his right hand on the Wheel Treasure, saying. 'May the august Wheel Treasure turn and roll on! May the august Wheel Treasure be triumphant!'

Then, bhikkhus, the Wheel Treasure rolled on towards the Eastern region. The Universal Monarch followed it with his army of four components (i.e., an army consisting of elephants, chariots, cavalry and infantry). Bhikkhus, where the Wheel Treasure came to rest, there the Universal Monarch encamped with his army of four components. Then, bhikkhus, the rival kings of the Eastern region came to the Universal Monarch and said, 'Welcome, O Great King! O Great King, your coming is auspicious! O Great King, please consider this country as your own. Great King, may it please Your Majesty to instruct and advise us.'

Upon this, the Universal Monarch said thus: 'Refrain from taking life; take not what is not given; indulge not in sexual misconduct; speak not what is not true; and avoid taking intoxicating drinks. Continue to enjoy your revenues as you have been wont to.'

Thereby, bhikkhus, all the rival kings of the Eastern region became vassals to the Universal Monarch.

86. Bhikkhus, the Wheel Treasure then descended on the Eastern Ocean, rose up again and rolled on towards the Southern region ... (p) ... the Wheel Treasure then descended on the Southern Ocean, rose up again and rolled on towards the Western region. The Universal Monarch followed it with his army of four components. Bhikkhus, where the Wheel Treasure came to rest, there the Universal Monarch encamped with his army of four components. Then, bhikkhus, the rival kings of the Western region came to the Universal Monarch and said, 'Welcome, O Great King! O Great King, your coming is auspicious! Great King, please consider this country as your own. Great King, may it please Your Majesty to instruct and advise us.'

Upon this, the Universal Monarch said thus: 'Refrain from taking life; take not what is not given; indulge not in sexual misconduct; speak not what is not true; and avoid taking intoxicating drinks. Continue to enjoy your revenues as you have been wont to.'

Thereby, bhikkhus, all the rival kings of the Western region became vassals to the Universal Monarch.

87. Bhikkhus, the Wheel Treasure then descended on the Western Ocean, rose up again and rolled on towards the Northern region. The

Universal Monarch followed it with his army of four components. Bhikkhus, where the Wheel Treasure came to rest, there the Universal Monarch encamped with his army of four components. Then, bhikkhus, the rival kings of the Northern region came to the Universal Monarch and said, 'Welcome, O Great King! O Great King, your coming is auspicious! Great King, please consider this country as your own. Great King, may it please Your Majesty to instruct and advise us.'

Upon this, the Universal Monarch said thus: 'Refrain from taking life; take not what is not given; indulge not in sexual misconduct; speak not what is not true; and avoid taking intoxicating drinks. Continue to enjoy your revenues as you have been wont to.'

Thereby, bhikkhus, all the rival kings of the Northern region became vassals to the Universal Monarch.

Then, bhikkhus, the Wheel Treasure, having been triumphant over all the Earth bounded by the ocean, returned to the royal city of the Universal Monarch and it stood, as if it were a wheel fixed on an axle, at the entrance to the Front Hall of the palace, adorning with its glory the royal palace of the Universal Monarch.

The Second and Subsequent Universal Monarchs

88. Bhikkhus, after a lapse of many years, many hundreds of years, many thousands of years, the second Universal Monarch ... (p) ... the third Universal Monarch ... (p) ... the fourth Universal Monarch ... (p) ... the fifth Universal Monarch ... (p) ... the sixth Universal Monarch ... (p) ... the seventh Universal Monarch instructed a certain man, saying, 'O man, if you should see this mighty Wheel Treasure make the slightest shift from its resting place, slipping down a little, bring me word.'

'Very well, Your Majesty,' replied the man.

Bhikkhus, after a lapse of many years, many hundreds of years, many thousands of years, the man saw the mighty Wheel Treasure make a slight shift from its resting place, slipping down a little.

On seeing that, the man went to the Universal Monarch and reported, 'May it please Your Majesty to know for a truth that the mighty Wheel Treasure has made a slight shift from its resting place, slipping down a little.'

89. Upon this, bhikkhus, the Universal Monarch sent for his eldest son and said to him 'Dear son, my mighty Wheel Treasure has made a slight shift from its resting place, slipping down a little. I have heard it said thus: Should the mighty Wheel Treasure of a Universal Monarch

make a slight shift from its resting place, slipping down a little, the king has not much longer to live.

'I have had my full share of human pleasures; it is time now for me to seek celestial bliss. Come, dear son, take over charge of ruling the Earth bounded by the ocean. As for me, shaving off my hair and beard and putting on the bark-dyed robes, I shall go forth from household life into the homeless life of an ascetic.'

Then, bhikkhus, the Universal Monarch, after giving his son full instructions on kingship, shaved off his hair and beard, put on the bark-dyed robes, and went forth from household life into the homeless life of an ascetic. On the seventh day after the royal ascetic had gone forth, the mighty Wheel Treasure disappeared.

90. Then a certain man went to the anointed king of the Khattiya caste, and said to him, 'May it please Your Majesty to know for a truth that the mighty Wheel Treasure has disappeared.'

Thereupon, the anointed king of the Khattiya caste was stricken with grief over the disappearance of the mighty Wheel Treasure, and showed great distress. But that king did not go and enquire of the royal ascetic the noble duties required of a Universal Monarch. He ruled over his country in accordance with his own ideas. Being ruled thus according to his own ideas, the different parts of his country did not make uniform progress as they used to when they were governed by the former kings who had carried out the noble duties required of a Universal Monarch.

Then, bhikkhus, the executive ministers, counsellors, finance ministers, elder statesmen, army officers, officers of palace guards and legal advisors assembled and came to the anointed king of the Khattiya caste. They said to him, 'Your Majesty, the different parts of Your Majesty's country being governed in accordance with your own ideas are not uniformly progressing as they used to when they were governed by the former kings who had carried out the noble duties required of a Universal Monarch. There are in your kingdom the executive ministers, counsellors, finance ministers, elder statesmen, army officers, officers of the palace guards and legal advisors, as well as others, who have preserved the knowledge of the noble duties required of a Universal Monarch. May it please Your Majesty to enquire of us concerning the noble duties required of a Universal Monarch. If we are asked, we are prepared to inform you of the noble duties required of a Universal Monarch.'

Decline in Life Expectation and Deterioration in Physical Appearance

91. Then the anointed king of the Khattiya caste caused the executive ministers, counsellors, finance ministers, elder statesmen, army officers, officers of the palace guards and legal advisors to be assembled and enquired of them the noble duties required of a Universal Monarch. When thus asked by the king, the ministers explained to him the noble duties required of a Universal Monarch.

Having heard them, the king took measures to provide, in a righteous manner, protection, shelter and security to (the people of) his kingdom. He failed, however, to provide for the needs of the poor. When the needy and the destitute were thus neglected and not cared for, poverty became widespread in the land. When poverty became widespread, a certain man took, with intention to steal, what was not given him. The king's men caught him and brought him to the presence of the anointed king, saying, 'Your Majesty, this man took, with intention to steal, what was not given him.'

Thereupon, bhikkhus, the anointed king asked the man, 'Is it true that you took, with intention to steal, what was not given you?'

'It is true, Your Majesty', answered the man.

'And why did you do so?' asked the king.

The man replied, 'Because, Your Majesty, I do not have sufficient means of livelihood.'

Then, bhikkhus, the anointed king of the Khattiya caste provided the man with money, saying, 'O man, with this money, maintain yourself, look after your parents and support your family, too. Engage in trading and business and give the samaṇas and brāhmaṇas such donations as will promote spiritual welfare leading to higher realms of existence and such alms as will produce beneficial results, namely, happiness and rebirth in deva realms.'

Bhikkhus, that man said, 'Very well, Your Majesty,' to the anointed king of the Khattiya caste.

Now, bhikkhus, another man took, with intention to steal, what was not given him. The king's men caught him and brought him to the presence of the anointed king of the Khattiya caste, saying, 'Your Majesty, this man took, with intention to steal, what was not given him.'

Thereupon, bhikkhus, the anointed king of the Khattiya caste asked the man, 'Is it true that you took, with intention to steal, what was not given you?'

'It is true, Your Majesty,' answered the man.

'And why did you do so?' asked the king.

The man replied, 'Because, Your Majesty, I do not have sufficient means of livelihood.'

Then, bhikkhus, the anointed king of the Khattiya caste provided the man with money, saying, 'O man, with this money, maintain yourself, look after your parents and support your family, too. Engage in trading and business and give the samaṇas and brāhmaṇas such donations as will promote spiritual welfare leading to higher realms of existence and such alms as will produce beneficial results, namely, happiness and rebirth in deva realms.'

Bhikkhus, that man replied, 'Very well, Your Majesty', to the anointed king of the Khattiya caste.

92. Bhikkhus, men heard: 'Friends, to them who have taken, with intention to steal, what was not given, the king is giving away money'. Then, this thought occurred to them: 'Well, what if we also take, with intention to steal, what is not given?'

At that time, a certain man took, with intention to steal, what was not given him. The king's men caught him and brought him to the presence of the anointed king of the Khattiya caste, saying, 'Your Majesty, this man took, with intention to steal, what was not given him.'

Thereupon, bhikkhus, the anointed king of the Khattiya caste asked the man, 'Is it true that you took, with intention to steal, what was not given you?'

'It is true, Your Majesty,' answered the man.

'And why did you do so?' asked the king.

The man replied, 'Because, Your Majesty, I do not have sufficient means of livelihood.'

Then this thought occurred to the anointed king of the Khattiya caste: 'If I keep on giving money to anyone who took, with intention to steal, what was not given, then acts of thievery will go on increasing. It would be well if I were to inflict the utmost punishment on this thief, and eliminate him once and for all by cutting off his head.'

Then, bhikkhus, the anointed king of the Khattiya caste ordered his men: 'Men, in that case, tie up this man's hands firmly behind his back with stout ropes, shave off his head and beating loud drums lead him around from street to street, from crossroads to crossroads. Then, take him out of the town by the Southern gate and on the South side of the town, give him the utmost punishment; eliminate him once and for all; cut off his head.'

Bhikkhus, the men said, 'Very well, Your Majesty,' to the anointed king of the Khattiya caste. They tied up the man's hands firmly behind his back with stout ropes, shaved off his head and beating loud drums, led him around from street to street, from crossroads to crossroads. Then, they took him out of the town by the Southern gate, and on the Southern side of the town, gave him the utmost punishment to eliminate him once and for all. They cut off his head,

93. Now, bhikkhus, men heard: 'On them that took, with intention to steal, what was not given, the king has inflicted severest punishment, to eliminate them once and for all. Their heads were cut off.' On hearing this, the thought occurred to them: 'Let us have sharp swords made; having made the sharp swords we will take, with the intention to steal, what is not given us. We will inflict the severest injury on those who do not give us their property; we will eliminate them completely; we will cut off their heads.'

Then they had sharp swords made. Having made the sharp swords, they took to marauding villages; they took to marauding towns also; they took to marauding cities also; they took to committing highway robberies, too.

They took, with intention to steal, what was not given. They inflicted the severest injury on those who did not give them their property; they eliminated them completely; they cut off their heads.

94. In this manner, bhikkhus, when money was not bestowed on the destitute, poverty increased; with increase in poverty, there was a rise in thefts. With the rise in thefts, lethal weapons grew in number. As lethal weapons multiplied, killings and murders became widespread. When killings and murders became widespread, the life span of those people declined. Their physical appearance deteriorated. When their life span declined and their physical appearance deteriorated, the children of those people whose life span was eighty thousand years lived only for forty thousand years.

Bhikkhus, among those who lived for forty thousand years, a certain man took, with intention to steal, what was not given him. The king's men caught him and brought him to the presence of the anointed king of the Khattiya caste, saying, 'Your Majesty, this man took, with intention to steal, what was not given him.'

Thereupon, bhikkhus, the anointed king of the Khattiya caste asked the man, 'Is it true that you took, with intention to steal, what was not given you?'

'No, Your Majesty, it is not true,' he lied intentionally.

95. In this manner, bhikkhus, when money was not bestowed on the destitute, poverty increased; with increase in poverty, there was a rise in thefts. With the rise in thefts, lethal weapons grew in number. As lethal weapons multiplied, killings and murders became widespread. When killings and murders became widespread, lying became common. As lying became common, the life span of those people declined and their physical appearance deteriorated. When their life span declined and their physical appearance deteriorated, the children of those people whose life span was forty thousand years lived only for twenty thousand years.

Bhikkhus, among those who lived for twenty thousand years, a certain man took, with intention to steal, what was not given him. Then another man reported, with malicious intent, to the anointed king of the Khattiya caste, 'Your Majesty, 'such and such a man has taken, with intention to steal, what was not given him.'

96. In this manner, bhikkhus, when money was not bestowed on the destitute, poverty increased; with increase in poverty, there was a rise in thefts. With the rise in thefts, lethal weapons grew in number. As lethal weapons multiplied, killings and murders became widespread. When killings and murders became widespread, lying became common. When lying became common, speaking maliciously of others became common, too. As malicious speech grew rife, the life span of those people declined and their physical appearance deteriorated. When their life span declined and their physical appearance deteriorated, the children of those people whose life span was twenty thousand years lived only for ten thousand years.

Bhikkhus, of those people whose life span was ten thousand years, some were comely in appearance; some were ugly in appearance. The ugly ones, coveting the comely ones, committed misconduct with the wives of others.

97. In this manner, bhikkhus, when money was not bestowed on the destitute, poverty increased; with increase in poverty, ... (p) ... sexual misconduct became widely prevalent.

With widely prevalent sexual misconduct, the life span of those people declined and their physical appearance deteriorated. When their life span declined and their physical appearance deteriorated, the children of those people whose life span was ten thousand years lived only for five thousand years.

98. Bhikkhus, among those people whose life span was five thousand years, two things developed, namely, harsh speech and frivolous talk. With the increase in the practice of harsh speech and frivolous talk, the life span of those people declined and their physical appearance deteriorated, and some of the children of those people whose life span was five thousand years lived only for two thousand five hundred years and some only for two thousand years.

99. Bhikkhus, among those people, whose life span was two thousand five hundred years, covetousness and ill will began to develop. When covetousness and ill will increased, the life span of those people declined and their physical appearance deteriorated. As their life span declined and their physical appearance deteriorated, the children of those people whose life span was two thousand five hundred years lived only for one thousand years.

100. Bhikkhus, those people whose life span was one thousand years began to entertain wrong beliefs.[2] When wrong beliefs grew, the life span of those people declined and their physical appearance deteriorated. As their life span declined and their physical appearance deteriorated, the children of those people whose life span was one thousand years lived only for five hundred years.

101. Bhikkhus, among those people whose life span was five hundred years, three things became rampant, namely, abominable lust, incest and inordinate passion When these things became rife, the life span of those people declined and their physical appearance deteriorated. As their life span declined and their physical appearance deteriorated, some of the children of those people whose life span was five hundred years lived only for two hundred and fifty years, and some only for two hundred years. Among the people whose life span was two hundred and fifty years, these things developed: failure to do filial duties towards mother and father; failure to do religious duties towards samaṇas and brāhmaṇas; and failure to show reverential regard for the elders in the family and clan.

102. In this manner, bhikkhus, when money was not bestowed on the destitute, poverty increased; with increase in poverty, there was a rise in thefts. With the rise in thefts, lethal weapons grew in number.

---

2. Wrong beliefs, consisting of *natthika diṭṭhi*, the belief that no action, good or bad, produces any results either here or hereafter; *ahetuka diṭṭhi*, the belief that there is no past cause, that the present is not the result of the past; *akiriya diṭṭhi*, the belief that there is no good or bad action as such.

As lethal weapons multiplied, killings and murders became widespread. When killings and murders became widespread, lying became common. As lying became common, speaking maliciously of others became common, too. As malicious speech grew rife, sexual misconduct became widely prevalent. When sexual misconduct became widely prevalent, two things developed, namely, harsh speech and frivolous talk. When these two things developed, covetousness and ill will began to develop. With the development of covetousness and ill will, there arose wrong beliefs. When wrong beliefs grew, these three things became rampant: abominable lust, incest and inordinate passion. When these three things became rife, people failed to do filial duties towards mother and father, failed to do religious duties towards samaras and brāhmaṇas and failed to show reverential regard for the elders in the family and clan.

When these things developed, the life span of those people declined and their physical appearance deteriorated. As their life span declined and their physical appearance deteriorated, the children of those people whose life span was two hundred and fifty years lived only for one hundred years.

Life Span of Ten Years

103. Bhikkhus, the time will come when the children of these people will have a life span of only ten years. When the life span has come down to ten years, young maids of five years will be of marriageable age. Bhikkhus, to them whose life span is only ten years, these savoury tastes, namely, clarified butter, fresh butter, sesamum oil, honey, molasses and salt will have disappeared.

Bhikkhus, the best food available to the people with a life span of ten years will be the meal prepared from millet (*kudrūsa*). Just as today, *sāli* rice cooked with meat is the best food, so will the meal made from millet be for those people with the life span of ten years.

Bhikkhus, for the people with a life span of ten years only, the ten meritorious deeds productive of wholesome effect will have completely disappeared; ten evil deeds productive of unwholesome results will flourish exceedingly. Even the word 'merit' will disappear from the vocabulary of the people with a ten-year span of life; how then could there be anyone performing meritorious deeds! Among such people with a life span of ten years, they who fail to do their filial duties towards mother and father, religious duties towards samaṇas and brāhmaṇas and who fail to show reverential regard for the elders in the family and clan, will be the recipients of honour and praise. Bhikkhus, just as in the present day, those who fulfil their filial duties towards mother and father, religious duties towards samaṇas and brāhmaṇas and who show reverential regard for the elders in the family and clan, are the recipients of honour and praise; in those days when the life span will be only ten years, those who fail to do their filial duties towards mother and father, religious duties towards samaṇas and brāhmaṇas, and who fail to show reverential regard for the elders in the family and clan, will be the recipients of honour and praise.

Bhikkhus, among such people with only a ten-year span of life, there will be no thoughts of reverence for one's mother, mother's sisters, wives of uncles, wives of teachers, or wives of elders who deserve to be respected.

Promiscuous relationship will be the rule in the world then, just as amongst goats, sheep, fowl, swine, dogs and jackals.

Bhikkhus, among such people with only a ten-year span of life, there will develop intense animosity, intense ill will, intense hatred with violent thoughts of killing one another, in a mother towards a son, in a son towards a mother, in a father towards a son, in a son towards a father, in a brother towards a sister, in a sister towards a brother, there will develop intense animosity, intense ill will, intense hatred with violent thoughts of killing one another. Bhikkhus, just as intense animosity, intense ill will, intense hatred with violent thoughts of killing develop in the hunter on seeing game, so will intense animosity, intense ill will, intense hatred with violent thoughts of killing one another develop among the people with only a ten-year span of life. In a mother towards a son, in a son towards a mother, in a father towards a son, in a son towards a father, in a brother towards a sister, in a sister towards a brother, there will develop intense animosity, intense ill will intense hatred with violent thoughts of killing one another.

104. Bhikkhus, among such people with only a ten-year span of life, world-wide armed conflicts will rage on for seven days, during which they will look upon one another as prey. Powerful weapons will appear in their hands. With these powerful weapons, thinking 'This is prey; this is prey,' they will set about killing one another.

Bhikkhus, then, this thought will occur to some of them: 'Let us not kill anyone; let not anyone kill us, either. It would be well if we were to repair to thickets of tall grass, dense jungle of creepers, forested woodland, inaccessible mid-river islands and mountain valleys and sustain ourselves on wild roots and fruits.' And they will repair to thickets of tall grass, dense jungle of creepers, forested woodland, inaccessible mid-river islands and mountain valleys and sustain themselves on wild roots and fruits for seven days. At the end of seven days, coming out of thickets of tall grass, dense jungle of creepers, forested woodland, inaccessible mid-river islands and mountain valleys, they will embrace one another and in a spirit of harmony and concord give solace to one another saying, 'O friends, we still see living beings; you are still alive like us! O friends, we still see living beings; you are still alive like us!'

Increase in Life Span and Improvement in Physical Appearance

105. Then this thought will occur to these beings: 'As a consequence of our evil deeds, we have suffered this heavy loss of our kith and kin. It would be well if we were to do good deeds. And now, what good deeds should we do? Let us refrain from taking life. It would be well to perform that good deed!' So thinking, they will abstain from killing; they will perform that good deed. In consequence of performing such good deeds, their life span will expand; their physical appearance will improve. When their life span thus expands and their physical appearance improves, the children of those people whose life span is ten years will live for twenty years.

Bhikkhus, to them this thought will occur: 'By virtue of good deeds, our life span has expanded; we have improved in physical appearance. It would be well if we were to perform more and more of good deeds; and what good deeds should we do? Let us abstain from taking what is not given, abstain from sexual misconduct, from telling lies, from speaking maliciously, from using harsh language, and from engaging in frivolous talk; let us give up covetousness, ill will, wrong views; let us give up three things, namely, abominable lust, incest and inordinate passion. And let us fulfil our filial duties towards mother and father, religious duties towards samaṇas and brāhmaṇas and show reverential regard for the elders of the family and clan. It would be well for us to perform such good deeds.' And they will become dutiful towards mother and father, towards samaṇas and brāhmaṇas; and they will show reverential regard for the elders of the family and clan. They will perform such good deeds.

By virtue of performing such good deeds, their life span will expand; their physical appearance will improve. When their life span thus expands and their physical appearance improves, the children of those people whose life span is twenty years will live for forty years. And the children of those people whose life span is forty years will live for eighty years; the children of those people whose life span is eighty years will live for one hundred and sixty years; the children of those people whose life span is one hundred and sixty years will live for three hundred and twenty years; the children of those people whose life span is three hundred and twenty years will live for six hundred and forty years; the children of those people whose life span is six hundred and forty years will live for two thousand years; the children of those people whose life span is two thousand years will live for four thousand years; the children of those people whose life span is four thousand years will live for eight thousand years; the children of those people whose life span is eight thousand years will live for twenty thousand years; the children of those people whose life span is twenty thousand years will live for forty thousand years; the children of those people whose life span is forty thousand years will live for eighty thousand years. Bhikkhus, the maiden daughters of those who live for eighty thousand years will be of marriageable age when they are five hundred years old.

[The Pāḷi Text ends the description of the progressive increase of the life span of people at this point, namely, the life span of eighty thousand years. According to the Commentary, this process of life span expansion goes on and on till it reaches a life span of an incalculable number of years, *asaṅkhyeyya āyu*. Then the process of recession of the life span begins again until it reaches a life span of ten years. It is at the point when the life span is eighty thousand years during the process of recession that the events mentioned in the next and subsequent paragraphs (106 to 108) will occur. Buddhas appear only in a period of recession of the life span, and never in a period of expansion of the life span.]

The Universal Monarch Saṅkha

106. Bhikkhus, those people whose life span is eighty thousand years will have only three kinds of affliction, namely, hunger, sluggishness after meals[3] and ageing. Bhikkhus, for those people with a life span of eighty thousand years, this continent of Jambudīpa will become rich and prosperous; the villages, towns and royal cities will be so close as to be within the flying distance of a cockerel. Bhikkhus, at that time when men will live for eighty thousand years, the whole continent of Jambudīpa will be so teaming with people as to have no empty space, like a jungle thickly overgrown with reeds and grass.

Bhikkhus, at that time when people will live for eighty thousand years this city of Bārāṇasī will become the royal city of Ketumatī, very rich and prosperous, thickly populated with people of all races, a city of bounteous food supplies and provisions. Bhikkhus, at that time when people will live for eighty thousand years, there will be eighty-four thousand towns in this Jambudīpa with the royal city of Ketumatī at their head. Bhikkhus, at that time when people will live for eighty thousand years, there will arise at the royal city of Ketumatī, a Universal Monarch, named Saṅkha, a king by right, who will rule in a righteous manner over the four continents bounded by the four oceans, the conqueror of all foes, the promoter of peace and stability in his territories, the possessor of seven precious treasures. He will possess these seven precious treasures, namely, the Wheel Treasure, the Elephant Treasure, the Horse Treasure, the Gem Treasure, the Queen Treasure, the Rich Man Treasure and seventhly the Eldest Son Treasure. The king will have more than a thousand sons, all brave men of heroic features, able to conquer hosts of enemies. He will justly rule over the Earth to the extent of its ocean boundaries, having conquered territories not by force or by arms but by righteousness.

Appearance of Metteyya Buddha

107. Bhikkhus, just as I, who am *Arahaṃ*, being worthy of special veneration; *Sammāsambuddha*, having truly comprehended all Dhammas by my own intellect and insight; *Vijjācaraṇa Saṃpanna*, being endowed with supreme knowledge and perfect practice of morality; *Sugata*, speaking only words that are true and beneficial; *Lokavidū*, knowing all the three lokas; *Anuttaropurisa-dammasārathi*, being incomparable in

---

3. This is the Commentary interpretation of *icchā* and *anasana*.

taming those who deserve to be tamed; *Satthādevamanussānaṃ*, being the Teacher of devas and men; *Buddha*, being the Enlightened One, knowing and teaching the Four Noble Truths; and *Bhagavā*, being the Most Exalted One, have at the present period appeared in this world, so also, bhikkhus, when the life span of people becomes eighty thousand years, there will appear in the world a *Bhagavā* called Metteyya who is *Arahaṃ*, being worthy of special veneration; *Sammā-sambuddha*, having truly comprehended Dhammas by his own intellect and insight; *Vijjācaraṇa Sampanna*, being endowed with supreme knowledge and perfect practice of morality; *Sugata*, speaking only words that are true and beneficial; *Lokavidū*, knowing all the three lokas; *Anuttaro-purisadammasārathi*, being incomparable in taming those who deserve to be tamed; *Satthādevamanussānaṃ*, being the Teacher of devas and men; *Buddha*, being the Enlightened One, knowing and teaching the Four Noble Truths; and *Bhagavā*, being the Most Exalted One.

Just as I, having by myself realized, through Perfect Wisdom, the nature of the universe with its devas, māras and brahmās, and also the world of human beings with its samaṇas, brāhmaṇas and kings and men, expound on it, so also that Metteyya Buddha, having by himself realized, through Perfect Wisdom, the nature of the universe with its devas, māras and brahmās, and also the world of human beings with its samaṇas, brāhmaṇas and kings and men, will expound on it.

Just as I now teach the Dhamma, which is good in the beginning, good in the middle, and good in the end, rich in meaning and words, and just as I make clear the completeness and purity of the Noble Practice, so also that Metteyya Buddha will teach the Dhamma, which is good in the beginning, good in the middle, and good in the end, rich in meaning and words, and make clear the completeness and purity of the Noble Practice. Just as I am accompanied by hundreds of bhikkhus (when travelling), so will that Metteyya Buddha be accompanied by thousands of bhikkhus (when travelling).

108. At that time, King Saṅkha will cause the palatial building formerly built for King Mahāpanāda to rise again and will dwell in that palace. But afterwards he will give it away as alms to samaṇas, brāhmaṇas, helpless ones, wayfarers, destitutes and beggars. Then in the presence of the Exalted, the Homage-Worthy, the Perfectly Self-Enlightened Metteyya Buddha, he will shave off his hair and beard, and putting on bark-dyed robes, he will go forth from the household life into the homeless life of an ascetic. After thus renouncing the world, he will dwell alone and in seclusion, vigilant and zealous, will incline his mind

(to *nibbāna*), and will soon attain, by himself, in this very life, by virtue of Magga-Knowledge, the fruits of the noblest and the most supreme Arahatship, the ultimate goal for which men of good family forsake hearth and home to lead the homeless life.

109. Be your own firm support (lit., island), bhikkhus, be your own refuge; do not take any other refuge. Let the Dhamma be your firm support, let the Dhamma be your refuge; do not take any other refuge.

And how, bhikkhus, does a bhikkhu take himself as his own firm support, as his own refuge, and not any other refuge? How does he take the Dhamma as his firm support and his refuge, and not any other refuge?

Bhikkhus, the bhikkhu (i.e., the disciple) following the practice of my Teaching keeps his mind steadfastly on the body (*kāya*) with diligence, comprehension and mindfulness (and perceives its impermanent, insecure, soulless and unpleasant nature), thus keeping away covetousness and distress (which will appear if he is not mindful of the five *khandhas*).

The bhikkhu keeps his mind steadfastly on Sensation (*vedanā*) ... (p) ... (and perceives its impermanent, insecure, and soulless nature) ... (p) ...

The bhikkhu concentrates steadfastly on the mind (*citta*) ... (p) ... (and perceives its impermanent, insecure, and soulless nature) ....

The bhikkhu keeps his mind steadfastly on the Dhammas[4] with diligence, comprehension and mindfulness (and perceives their impermanent, insecure, and soulless nature), thus keeping away covetousness and distress (which will appear if he is not mindful of the five *khandhas*).

In this way, bhikkhus, a bhikkhu takes himself as his own firm support, as his own refuge, and not any other refuge; and he takes the Dhamma as his firm support and his refuge, not any other refuge.

Increases in Length of Life and Improvement in Physical Appearance of Bhikkhus

110. Keep yourselves, bhikkhus, within your own range of contemplation as has been taught and instructed by the Buddha (lit., the father). Bhikkhus, if you keep yourselves within your own range of contemplation as has been taught and instructed by the Buddha, you

4. **The Five Dhammas** consisting of: (i) nīvaraṇas, (ii) five khandhas, (iii) twelve āyatanas, (iv) seven bojjhaṅgas, (v) the Four Ariya Truths.

will increase in length of life, improve in your physical appearance, increase in happiness, grow in wealth and gain in strength and power.

Bhikkhus, what is meant by the length of 'life' of a bhikkhu? Herein, bhikkhus, a bhikkhu develops the basis of psychic power by means of concentration of will (*chanda*) combined with right exertion; he develops the basis of psychic power by means of concentration of energy (*vīriya*) combined with right exertion; he develops the basis of psychic power by means of concentration of thought (*citta*) combined with right exertion; he develops the basis of psychic power by means of concentration of investigative knowledge (*vimaṃsā*) combined with right exertion. Bhikkhus, by developing these four bases of psychic power and practicing them over and over again, he could, if he so wishes, live on for the whole of the life span or even beyond the life span. This, bhikkhus, is what is meant by the length of 'life' of a bhikkhu.

What, bhikkhus, is meant by the 'physical appearance' of a bhikkhu? Herein, bhikkhus, a bhikkhu is well established in morality (*sīla*). He practices self-restraint in accordance with the fundamental precepts of the Order (*Pāṭimokkhasaṃvara sīla*)', he is endowed with good practice and resorts only to a suitable subject for constant meditation; he senses danger in the slightest transgression or lapse of conduct; he takes particular care not to make any breach of the rules of training. This, bhikkhus, is what is meant by the 'physical appearance' of a bhikkhu.

What, bhikkhus, is meant by the 'happiness' of a bhikkhu? Herein, bhikkhus, keeping himself detached from pleasures of five senses, and from evil, he achieves and remains in the first *jhāna*, which is accompanied by *vitakka* (initial application of the mind), *vicāra* (sustained application of the mind), and which has *pīti* (delightful satisfaction) and *sukha* (bliss), born of detachment from hindrances (*nīvaraṇa*). Then having got rid of *vitakka* and *vicāra*, he achieves and remains in the second *jhāna* ... (p) ... in the third *jhāna* ... (p) ... in the fourth *jhāna*. This, bhikkhus, is what is meant by the 'happiness' of a bhikkhu.

What, bhikkhus, is meant by the 'wealth' of a bhikkhu? Herein, bhikkhus, a bhikkhu abides suffusing one direction with loving-kindness. Likewise, the second, the third, and the fourth direction; thus above, below, around, everywhere, treating all sentient beings of the whole world as himself, he abides suffusing them with loving-kindness which is abounding, lofty, infinite, free from anger and free from ill will.

A bhikkhu abides suffusing one direction with compassion ... (p) ... with sympathetic joy ... (p) ... with equanimity.

Likewise, the second, the third, and the fourth direction; thus above, below, around, everywhere, treating all sentient beings of the world as himself, he abides suffusing them with equanimity which is abounding, lofty, infinite, free from anger and free from ill will. This, bhikkhus, is what is meant by the 'wealth' of a bhikkhu.

Bhikkhus, what is meant by the 'strength' of a bhikkhu? Herein, bhikkhus, a bhikkhu, consequent on complete destruction of *āsavas*, moral intoxicants or taints, becomes an Arahat, who realizes and attains by himself in the present life the taint-free emancipation of the mind (*Arahattaphala Samādhi*) as well as the Insight emancipation (*Arahattaphala Paññā*) through *Magga*-Knowledge. This, bhikkhus, is what is meant by the 'strength' of a bhikkhu.

Bhikkhus, I do not see any power as hard to conquer as that of Māra. (The only power that can subdue this force of Māra is the power of the *Arahattaphala*.) Bhikkhus, it is by cultivation of wholesome Dhammas that meritorious results thus accrue and develop.

Thus spoke the Bhagavā. And the bhikkhus, glad at heart, rejoiced at the words of the Bhagavā.

End of Cakkavatti Sutta, the third sutta from division three (*Pāthika Vagga*)

Namo tassa bhagavato arahato sammāsambuddhassa

SAṂPASĀDANĪYA SUTTA

V. SAṂPASĀDANĪYA SUTTA

(Faith Inspiring Discourse)

BRAVE UTTERANCE OF THE VENERABLE SĀRIPUTTA

141. Thus have I heard:

Once the Bhagavā was dwelling in the mango grove of (the rich man) Pāvārika at Nāḷandā. At that time the Venerable Sāriputta went to the Bhagavā and after paying obeisance to him, sat down at a suitable place and spoke to him thus:

"Venerable Sir, this faith I have in the Bhagavā: that there never has been, there will not be, nor is there now, any samaṇa or brāhmaṇa who can excel the Bhagavā in Enlightenment".

142. Indeed, Sāriputta, you make a noble, fearless speech, a definite statement (as if with personal knowledge), and a bold utterance (like a lion's roar) thus: 'Venerable Sir, this faith I have in the Bhagavā: that there never has been, there will not be, nor is there now, any samaṇa or brāhmaṇa who can excel the Bhagavā in Enlightenment.'

Sāriputta, how is this? Are all those Homage-Worthy, Perfectly Self-Enlightened Bhagavās of bygone times rightly and fully known to you through knowing their minds with your mind thus: 'Such was their *sīla*, practice of morality; such was their concentration (*samādhi pakkhiya dhamma*); such was their *paññā*, wisdom; such was how they abided in the attainment of cessation of consciousness (*nirodhasamāpatti*); such was their emancipation'?

"Not so, Venerable Sir."

And how is this, Sāriputta? Are all those Homage-Worthy, Perfectly Self-Enlightened Bhagavās of times to come rightly and fully known to you through knowing their minds with your mind thus: 'Such will be their *sīla*, practice of morality; such will be their concentration (*samādhi pakkhiya* dhamma); such will be their *paññā*, wisdom; such is how they will abide in the attainment of cessation of consciousness (*nirodha samāpatti*); such will be their emancipation'?

"Not so. Venerable Sir."

And how is this, Sāriputta? Am I, the present Homage-Worthy, Perfectly Self-Enlightened Bhagavā, rightly and fully known to you through knowing my mind with your mind thus: 'Such is the *sīla*, the practice of morality of the Bhagavā; such is his concentration (*samādhi pakkhiya dhamma*); such is his *paññā* wisdom; such is how he abides in the attainment of cessation of consciousness (*nirodha samāpatti*); such is his emancipation'?

"Not so, Venerable Sir."

Sāriputta, you do not have *cetopariya ñāṇa*, personal knowledge of the minds of the Homage-Worthy, Perfectly Self-Enlightened Bhagavās of the past, the future and the present time. Then Sāriputta, without such knowledge how can you make a noble, fearless speech, a definite statement (as if with personal knowledge), and a bold utterance (like a lion's roar) thus: 'Venerable Sir, this faith I have in the Bhagavā: that there never has been, there will not be, nor is there now, any samaṇa of brāhmaṇa who can excel the Bhagavā in Enlightenment'?

143. "Venerable Sir, I do not have *cetopariya ñāṇa*, personal knowledge of the minds of the past, the future and the present Homage-Worthy, Perfectly Self-Enlightened Bhagavās. Nevertheless, I do have the *dhammanvaya ñāṇa*, knowledge by inference from personal experience.

"Suppose, Venerable Sir, there is a frontier fortress town of the king, with firm foundations, strongly fortified with ramparts and a single arched gateway. And there is a gate keeper, wise, intelligent, prudent, who would keep out the strangers he does not know and admit only those he knows. And as he patrols the path that encircles the fortress, he does not perceive a hole or a gap in the rampart wide enough to allow even a cat to pass through. Then this thought might occur to the gate keeper: Whatever big living things enter or leave the city they do so by this gate only. In the same way, Venerable Sir, I have come to possess the *dhammanvaya ñāṇa*, knowledge by inference from personal experience.

"Venerable Sir, all the Homage-Worthy, the Perfectly Self-Enlightened Bhagavās of the past had abandoned the Hindrances that defile the mind and weaken the intellect, had well established their minds in the practice of the Four Methods of Steadfast Mindfulness, had truly cultivated the Seven Factors of Enlightenment and had fully attained the unsurpassed knowledge of the highest Path, and the supreme Enlightenment.

"And Venerable Sir, all the Homage-Worthy, the Perfectly Self-Enlightened Bhagavās of the future will abandon the Hindrances that defile the mind and weaken the intellect, will have their minds well established in the practice of the Four Methods of Steadfast Mindfulness, will truly cultivate the Seven Factors of Enlightenment and will fully attain the unsurpassed knowledge of the highest Path, and the supreme Enlightenment.

"And Venerable Sir, the present Homage-Worthy and Perfectly Self-Enlightened Bhagavā also has abandoned the Hindrances that defile the mind and weaken the intellect, has well established his mind in the practice of the Four Methods of Steadfast Mindfulness, has truly cultivated the Seven Factors of Enlightenment and has fully attained the unsurpassed knowledge of the highest Path, and the supreme Enlightenment."

144. "Venerable Sir, (at one time) I approached the Bhagavā to listen to the exposition on the Dhamma. The Bhagavā then taught me the Dhammas, each one of which gets higher and higher and nobler and nobler, comparing and contrasting that which is pure and white (meritorious *dhammā*) with that which is impure and dark (demeritorious *dhammā*).

"Venerable Sir, the Bhagavā having taught me in diverse ways the Dhammas, each one of which gets higher and higher and nobler and nobler, comparing and contrasting that which is pure and white with that which is impure and dark, I have achieved Magga Knowledge in some of the Dhammas (*i.e.*, those pertaining to *ariya* disciples) and perfection the understanding of the Four Noble Truths; thus I came to be convinced that the Bhagavā knows truly and well all the Dhammas, that the Dhamma has been taught well by the Bhagavā and that the disciples of the Bhagavā practice well what is taught them. And with this conviction comes my faith and devoted confidence in the Teacher."

Exposition on the Faultless Dhammas

145. "Furthermore, Venerable Sir, the Bhagavā teaches the faultless Dhammas[5] by an exposition which is of the highest excellence. And what are the faultless Dhammas? They are the Four Methods of Steadfast Mindfulness, the Four Supreme Efforts, the Four Bases of Psychic Potency, the Five Controlling Faculties, the Five Powers, the Seven Factors of Enlightenment and the Noble Path of Eight Constituents.

"In this Teaching, Venerable Sir, because of the destruction of the *āsavas*, moral intoxicants or taints, the bhikkhu realizes and attains by himself in the present life, the taint-free emancipation of the mind (*arahattaphala samādhi*) as well as the insight emancipation (*arahattaphala paññā*), through Magga Knowledge.

5. **Faultless Dhammas**: *kusalā dhammā*: The Commentary explains *kusala* here as *anavajja*, free from 'fault'. The Aṭṭhasālinī defines 'fault' as *kilesa*, moral defilements.

"Venerable Sir, most excellent is this exposition on the faultless Dhammas. And the Bhagavā knows all these Dhammas in their entirety; there is nothing more to know beyond what the Bhagavā knows. And there is no one, whether samaṇa or brāhmaṇa, who can surpass the Bhagavā in the knowledge of these faultless Dhammas."

Exposition on Classification of the Āyatanas, the Sense Bases

146. "Furthermore, Venerable Sir, the Bhagavā teaches the Dhamma on the Classification of the Āyatanas, the sense bases, by an exposition which is of the highest excellence. Venerable Sir, these internal sense bases and external sense bases are each of six kinds, namely,

1. Sensing part of the eye; visible object.
2. Sensing part of the ear; sound.
3. Sensing part of the nose; odour.
4. Sensing part of the tongue; taste.
5. Sensing part of the body; tangible object
6. Mind; cognizable object.

"Venerable Sir, most excellent is this exposition on Classification of the Āyatanas. And the Bhagavā knows all these Dhammas in their entirety; there is nothing more to know beyond what the Bhagavā knows. And there is no one, whether samaṇa or brāhmaṇa, who can surpass the Bhagavā in the knowledge of the Classification of the Āyatanas."

Exposition on Modes of Taking Conception in a Mother's Womb

147. "Furthermore, Venerable Sir, the Bhagavā teaches the Dhamma on the modes of taking conception in a mother's womb, by an exposition which is of the highest excellence. Venerable Sir, there are four modes of taking conception in a mother's womb.

"Venerable Sir, in this world, a certain individual takes conception in a mother's womb unknowingly, remains in it unknowingly, and leaves it unknowingly. This is the first mode of taking conception in a mother's womb. (This refers to the conception of an ordinary person.)

"Again, Venerable Sir, in this world, a certain individual takes conception in a mother's womb knowingly, remains in it unknowingly, and leaves it unknowingly. This is the second mode of taking conception in a mother's womb. (This refers to the conception of the eighty Great Disciples.)

"Again, Venerable Sir, in this world, a certain individual takes conception in a mother's womb knowingly, remains in it knowingly, and leaves it unknowingly. This is the third mode of taking conception in a mother's womb. (This refers to the conception of the two Chief Disciples and of a Pacceka Buddha.)

"Again. Venerable Sir, in this world, a certain individual takes conception in a mother's womb knowingly, remains in it knowingly and leaves it knowingly. This is the fourth mode of taking conception in a mother's womb. (This refers to the conception of a Supremely Enlightened Buddha.) Venerable Sir, most excellent is this exposition on the modes of taking conception in a mother's womb."

Exposition on Modes of Reading Another Person's Mind

148. "Furthermore, Venerable Sir, the Bhagavā teaches the Dhamma on the modes of reading another person's mind, by an exposition which is of the highest excellence. Venerable Sir, there are four modes of reading another person's mind.

"Venerable Sir, in this world, a certain individual reads another person's mind by means of visible signs and omens and says, 'You are thinking in this way; you have this thought in your mind. Your mind is thus.' In this way, he makes numerous readings of other people's minds and his readings turn out to be correct, not otherwise. This is the first mode of reading another person's mind.

"Venerable Sir, then again in this world, a certain individual reads another person's mind not by visible signs and omens, but by hearing sounds uttered by humans, non-humans or devas and says, 'You are thinking in this way; you have this thought in your mind. Your mind is thus.' In this way, he makes numerous readings of other people's minds and his readings turn out to be correct, not otherwise. This is the second mode of reading another person's mind.

"Venerable Sir, then again in this world, a certain individual reads another person's mind not by visible signs and omens nor by hearing sounds uttered by humans, non-humans or devas but by hearing the mental vibrations produced by processes of initial thinking about an object (*vitakka*) and continued fixation of attention on it (*vicāra*) of the person concerned. Reading thus, he says, 'You are thinking in this way; you have this thought in your mind. Your mind is thus.' In this way, he makes numerous readings of other people's minds and his readings turn out to be correct, not otherwise. This is the third mode of reading another person's mind.

"Venerable Sir, then again in this world, a certain individual reads another person's mind not by means of visible signs and omens, nor by hearing sounds uttered by humans, non-humans or devas, nor by hearing the mental vibrations produced by processes of initial thinking about an object (*vitakka*) and continued fixation of attention on it (*vicāra*) of the person concerned. With his mind free from *vitakka* and *vicara*, and fully concentrated, he discriminatively knows with his mind the mind of another person, thus: This good person, having well established himself in volitional activities (such as sensation and perception), will be immediately directing his mind to (further) stages (such as *jhānas* and *maggas*).' In this way he makes numerous readings of other people's minds and his readings turn out to be correct, not otherwise. This is the fourth mode of reading another person's mind. Venerable Sir, this exposition on the mode of reading another person's mind is of the highest excellence."

Exposition on Attainment of Insight

149. "Venerable Sir, the Bhagavā then teaches the Dhamma on the attainment of different stages of Insight, by an exposition which is of the highest excellence. Venerable Sir, these are the four such stages of Insight.

"Venerable Sir, in this world, a certain samaṇa or brāhmaṇa, in consequence of striving strenuously, steadfastly and perseveringly with mindfulness and right attentiveness, attains to the first *jhāna* concentration. When the mind has become concentrated in this way, the recluse contemplates on this body, from the soles of the feet up and from the crown of the head down, enclosed by the skin and full of multifarious impurities. 'There are in this body, hair of the head, hairs of the body, nails, teeth, skin, flesh, sinews, bones, marrow, kidneys, heart, liver, pleura, spleen, lungs, large intestine, small intestines, contents of the stomach, faeces, bile, phlegm, pus, blood, sweat, fat, tears, grease, saliva, nasal mucus, oil of the joints, urine. This is the attainment of the first stage of Insight.

"Then again, Venerable Sir, in this world, a certain samaṇa or brāhmaṇa, in consequence of striving strenuously, steadfastly and perseveringly, with mindfulness and right attentiveness, attains to the first *jhāna* concentration. When the mind has become concentrated in

this way, ... (p) ... oil of the joints, urine.' Then without contemplating on the skin, flesh and blood of the person, he contemplates on the skeleton. This is the attainment of the second stage of Insight.

"Then again, Venerable Sir, in this world, a certain samaṇa or brāhmaṇa, in consequence of striving strenuously, steadfastly and perseveringly, with mindfulness and right attentiveness, attains to the first *jhāna* concentration. When the mind has become concentrated in this way, ... (p) ... oil of the joints, urine.' Then without contemplating on the skin, flesh and blood of the person, he contemplates on the skeleton. He knows the continuous flow of the stream of consciousness of a person from moment to moment. He also knows that the consciousness of a person not yet free from *taṇhā* is present both in this existence and the next. This is the attainment of the third stage of Insight.

"Then again, Venerable Sir, in this world, a certain samaṇa, or brāhmaṇa, after striving strenuously, steadfastly and perseveringly, with mindfulness and right attentiveness, attains to the first *jhāna* concentration. When the mind has been concentrated in this way, ... (p) ... oil of the joints, urine.' Then without contemplating on the skin, flesh and blood of the person, he contemplates on the skeleton. He knows the continuous flow of the stream of consciousness of a person from moment to moment. He also knows that the consciousness which is unaccompanied by *kamma* of a person free from *taṇhā* is not present in this existence or the next. This is the attainment of the fourth stage of Insight. Venerable Sir, this exposition on attainment of Insight is of the highest excellence."

EXPOSITION ON CLASSIFICATION OF INDIVIDUALS

150. "Venerable Sir, furthermore, the Bhagavā teaches the Dhamma on the classification of individuals, by an exposition which is of the highest excellence. Venerable Sir, there are these seven classes of individuals, namely, *Ubhatobhāga Vimutta*, one who becomes free from defilements both by the attainment of *Arūpa Samāpatti* and by the attainment of fruition knowledge (*Arahatta-phala*); *Paññā Vimutta*, one who is liberated by fruition knowledge (*Arahatta-phala*) through *Vipassanā* Insight only; *Kāya Sakkhi*, one who progresses in attainment from *Sotāpatti-phala* to *Arahatta-magga* through *Vipassanā* meditation after achieving all eight *jhāna* attainments; *diṭṭhippatta*, one who progresses in attainment from *Sotapatti-phala* to *Arahatta-magga* with Insight Knowledge predominant in his striving but without *jhāna* attainments; *Saddha Vimutta*, one

who progresses in attainment from *Sotāpatti-phala* to *Arahatta-magga* with faith predominant in his striving but without *jhāna* attainments; *Dhammānusārī*, one who attains *Sotāpatti-magga* with Insight Knowledge predominant in his striving; *Saddhānusārī*, one who attains *Sotāpatti-magga* with faith in the Four Noble Truths predominant in his striving.

"Venerable Sir, this exposition on the classification of individuals is of the highest excellence."

Exposition on Striving for Development of Factors of Enlightenment

151. "Furthermore, Venerable Sir, the Bhagavā teaches the Dhamma on striving for development of the Factors of Enlightenment, by an exposition which is of the highest excellence. Venerable Sir, these are the Seven Factors of Enlightenment: *sati-saṃbojjhaṅga*, the enlightenment-factor of Mindfulness; *dhammavicaya-saṃbojjhaṅga*, the enlightenment-factor of Investigative Knowledge of phenomena; *viriya-saṃbojjhaṅga*, the enlightenment-factor of Effort; *pīti-saṃbojjhaṅga*, the enlightenment-factor of Delightful Satisfaction; *passaddhi-saṃbojjhaṅga*, the enlightenment-factor of Serenity; *samādhi-saṃbojjhaṅga*, the enlightenment-factor of Concentration; *upekkhā-saṃbojjhaṅga*, the enlightenment-factor of Equanimity.

"Venerable Sir, this exposition on striving for development of Factors of Enlightenment is of the highest excellence."

Exposition on Practice of the Path

152. "Furthermore, Venerable Sir, the Bhagavā teaches the Dhamma on the modes of practice of the Path, by an exposition which is of the highest excellence. Venerable Sir, these are the four modes of practice of the Path, namely, difficult practice ending in slow acquisition of Insight Knowledge; difficult practice ending in swift acquisition of Insight Knowledge; facile practice ending in slow acquisition of Insight Knowledge; facile practice ending in swift acquisition of Insight Knowledge.

"Venerable Sir, of those four modes of practice of the Path, when the practice is difficult and Insight Knowledge is acquired slowly, the mode of practice is regarded as poor for two reasons: difficulty in practice and slowness in acquisition of Insight Knowledge. When the practice is difficult and Insight Knowledge is acquired swiftly, the mode of practice is regarded as poor because of difficulty in practice.

When the practice is facile and Insight Knowledge is acquired slowly, the mode of practice is regarded as poor because of slowness in acquisition of Insight Knowledge. When the practice is facile and the acquisition of Insight Knowledge is swift, the mode of practice is regarded as good for two reasons: facility in practice and swiftness in acquisition of Insight Knowledge.

"Venerable Sir, this exposition on the modes of practice of the Path is of the highest excellence."

Exposition on Right Conduct in Speech

153. "Furthermore, Venerable Sir, the Bhagavā teaches the Dhamma on right conduct in speech, by an exposition which is of the highest excellence. Venerable Sir, in this world, a certain individual (with right conduct in speech) does not utter falsehood, does not indulge in calumny, avoids slander, does not speak disdainfully, nor merely to win an argument. He speaks only words of wisdom worthy to be treasured in the mind, and only at an appropriate time.

"Venerable Sir, this exposition on right conduct in speech is of the highest excellence."

Exposition on Right Moral Conduct

"Furthermore, Venerable Sir, the Bhagavā teaches the Dhamma on right moral conduct, by an exposition which is of the highest excellence. Venerable Sir, in this world, a certain individual (with right moral conduct) speaks only the truth; is endowed with faith; refrains from deceitful pretensions (of attainments he does not possess), from flattery; does not practice subtle insinuation by signs and indications (for gain); does not use pressure (to get offerings); does not seek for more gain by cunning offer of gifts. He is well guarded as to the sense faculties; moderate in eating; upright in deeds, words and thoughts. He applies himself to the practice and development of vigilance and is free of indolence or sloth. Strenuous and resolute, he abides in *jhāna* state and he is endowed with retentive memory. He is pleasant of speech and is intellectually equipped to attain to higher knowledge (not reached before), to carry and retain the Dhamma that has been learnt or heard, to draw inferences with mature wisdom. He remains free from sensual desire, is endowed with mindfulness and Insight knowledge.

"Venerable Sir, this exposition on right conduct is of the highest excellence."

Exposition on Modes of Instruction

154. "Furthermore, Venerable Sir, the Bhagavā teaches the Dhamma on modes of instruction, by an exposition which is of the highest excellence. Venerable Sir, these are the four modes of Instruction.

"Venerable Sir, the Bhagavā by the proper exercise of his own intuition knows in respect of another person: 'If this individual practices the Dhamma as taught by me, he will, consequent on complete destruction of the three fetters, become a *Sotāpanna*, a Stream-enterer, who is not liable to fall into miserable existences and states of woe and is assured of attaining the three higher levels of the Path.'

"Venerable Sir, the Bhagavā by the proper exercise of his own intuition knows in respect of another person: 'If this individual practices the Dhamma as taught by me, he will, consequent on complete destruction of the three fetters and attenuation of the grosser forms of passion, hatred and delusion, become a *Sakadāgāmī*, a Once-returner, who will in time achieve the complete ending of *dukkha*, after returning to this realm of human beings only once.'

"Venerable Sir, the Bhagavā by the proper exercise of his own intuition knows in respect of another person: 'If this individual practices the Dhamma as taught by me, he will, consequent on complete destruction of all the five fetters which lead to rebirth in the lower sensuous planes, become an *Anāgāmi*, a Non-returner, who will reappear as a spontaneously manifesting being in the Brahmā realm, whence he will not return but pass away into *nibbāna*'.

"Venerable Sir, the Bhagavā by the proper exercise of his own intuition knows in respect of another person: 'If this individual practices the Dhamma as taught by me, he will, consequent on complete destruction of the *āsavas*, moral intoxicants or taints, become an *Arahat* who realizes and attains by himself in the present life the taint-free emancipation of the mind (*Arahattaphala Samādhi*) as well as the Insight emancipation (*Arahattaphala Paññā*), through *Magga* Knowledge.'

"Venerable Sir, this exposition on modes of Instruction is of the highest excellence."

Exposition on Emancipation-Knowledge Attainable by Other Individuals

155. "Furthermore, Venerable Sir, the Bhagavā teaches the Dhamma on emancipation-knowledge attainable by other individuals, by an exposition which is of the highest excellence.

"The Bhagavā by the proper exercise of his own intuition knows in respect of another person: 'This individual, consequent on complete destruction of the three fetters, will become a *Sotāpanna*, a Stream-enterer, who is not liable to fall into miserable existences and states of woe and is assured of attaining the three higher levels of the Path.'

"Venerable Sir, the Bhagavā by the proper exercise of his own intuition knows in respect of another person: 'This individual, consequent on complete destruction of the three fetters and attenuation of the grosser forms of passion, hatred and delusion, will become a *Sakadāgāmī*, a Once-returner, who will in time achieve the complete ending of *dukkha*, after returning to this realm of human beings only once.'

"Venerable Sir, the Bhagavā by the proper exercise of his own intuition knows in respect of another person: 'This individual, consequent on complete destruction of all the five fetters which lead to rebirth, in the lower sensuous planes, will become an *Anāgāmī*, a Non-returner, who will reappear as a spontaneously manifesting being in the Brahmā realm, whence he will not return but pass away into *nibbāna*.'

"Venerable Sir, the Bhagavā by the proper exercise of his own intuition knows in respect of another person: 'This individual will, consequent on the complete destruction of the *āsavas*, moral intoxicants, become an *Arahat*, who realizes and attains by himself in the present life the taint-free emancipation of the mind (*Arahattaphala Samādhi*) as well as the Insight emancipation (*Arahattaphala paññā*), through *Magga* Knowledge.'

"Venerable Sir, this exposition on emancipation-knowledge attainable by other individuals is of the highest excellence."

Exposition on Eternity View

156. "Furthermore, Venerable Sir, the Bhagavā teaches the Dhamma on Eternity View, by an exposition which is of the highest excellence. Venerable Sir, there are these three types of Eternity View.

"Venerable Sir, in this world, a certain samaṇa or brāhmaṇa, after striving strenuously, steadfastly and perseveringly, with mindfulness and right attentiveness, attains to the fourth *jhāna* concentration. When the mind has become concentrated in this way, he can recall many past existences. And what can he recollect?

"He remembers one past existence, or two, or three, or four, or five, or ten, or twenty, or thirty, or forty, or fifty, or a hundred, a thousand, a hundred thousand existences, or many hundred, many thousand, many hundred thousand existences in this way: 'There I was, such a name I had, such a clan I belonged to, such appearance I had, such food I ate, such pleasures I enjoyed and such pains I suffered, and such a life span I had. Passing away from that existence, I was born in another existence. In that (new) existence, too, such a name I had, such a clan I belonged to, such appearance I had, such food I ate, such pleasures I enjoyed and such pains I suffered, and such a life span I had. Passing away from that existence, I was born in this existence.' in this manner, he remembers many a former existence with full characteristic details and related facts (such as names and clans).

"And he says (to himself) 'The world had undergone dissolution; it had undergone formation. I know thus the time that had passed. The world will undergo dissolution; it will undergo formation. I know thus the time to come, too. *Atta* as well as *loka* is eternal, barren, as steadfast as a mountain peak, firmly fixed as a gate post. Though these sentient beings pass on from one existence to another, faring on, vanishing (from this existence) and reappearing (in that existence), *atta* as well as *loka* remains permanent like things of an unchanging and enduring nature.' This is the first type of Eternity View.

"Furthermore, Venerable Sir, in this world, a certain samaṇa or brāhmaṇa, after striving strenuously, steadfastly and perseveringly, with mindfulness and right attentiveness, attains to the fourth *jhāna* concentration. When the mind has become concentrated in this way, he can recall many past existences. And what can he recollect?

"He remembers one cycle of world dissolution and formation, two cycles of world dissolution and formation, three cycles of world dissolution and formation, four cycles of world dissolution and formation, five cycles of world dissolution and formation, ten cycles of world dissolution and formation; he remembers thus: 'There I was, such a name I had, such a clan 1 belonged to, such appearance I had, such food I ate, such pleasures I enjoyed and such pains I suffered, and such a life span I had. Passing away from that existence, I was born in another existence. In that (new) existence, too, such a name I had, such a clan I belonged to, such appearance I had, such food I ate, such pleasures I enjoyed and such pains I suffered, and such a life span I had. Passing away from that existence, I was born in this existence.' In this manner, he remembers many a former existence with full characteristic details and related facts (such as names and clans).

"And he says (to himself) 'The world had undergone dissolution; it had undergone formation. I know thus the time that had passed. The world will undergo dissolution; it will undergo formation. I know thus the time to come, too. *Atta* as well as *loka* is eternal, barren, as steadfast as a mountain peak, firmly fixed "as a gate post. Though these sentient beings pass on from one existence to another, faring on, vanishing (from this existence) and reappearing (in that existence), *atta* as well as *loka* remains permanent like things of an unchanging and enduring nature.' This is the second type of Eternity View.

"Furthermore, Venerable Sir, in this world, a certain samaṇa or brāhmaṇa, after striving strenuously, steadfastly and perseveringly, with mindfulness and right attentiveness, attains to the fourth *jhāna* concentration. When the mind has become concentrated in this way, he can recall many past existences. And what can he recollect?

"He remembers ten cycles of world dissolution and formation, twenty cycles of world dissolution and formation, thirty cycles of world dissolution and formation, forty cycles of world dissolution and formation; he remembers thus: 'There I was, such a name I had, such a clan I belonged to, such appearance I had, such food I ate, such pleasure I enjoyed and such pains I suffered, and such a life span I had. Passing away from that existence, I was born in another existence. In that (new) existence, too, such a name I had, such a clan I belonged to, such appearance I had, such food I ate, such pleasures I enjoyed and such pains I suffered, and such a life span I had. Passing away from that existence, I was born in this existence.' In this manner, he remembers many a former existence with full characteristic details and related facts (such as names and clans).

"And he says (to himself) 'The world had undergone dissolution: it had undergone formation. I know thus the time that had passed. The world will undergo dissolution; it will undergo formation. I know thus the time to come, too. *Atta* as well as *loka* is eternal, barren, as steadfast as a mountain peak, firmly fixed as a gate post. Though these sentient beings pass on from one existence to another, faring on, vanishing (from this existence) and reappearing (in that existence), *atta* as well as *loka* remains permanent like things of an unchanging and enduring nature.' This is the third type of Eternity View. Venerable Sir, this exposition on the Eternity View is of the highest excellence."

Exposition on Knowledge of Past Existences

157. "Furthermore, Venerable Sir, the Bhagavā teaches the Dhamma on knowledge of past existences, by an exposition which is of the highest excellence.

"Venerable Sir, in this world, a certain samaṇa or brāhmaṇa, after striving strenuously, steadfastly and perseveringly, with mindfulness and right attentiveness, attains to the fourth *jhāna* concentration. When the mind has become concentrated in this way, he can recall many past existences. And what can he recollect?

"He remembers one existence, or two, or three, or four, or five, or ten, or twenty, or thirty, or forty, or fifty, or a hundred, or a thousand, or a hundred thousand existences, or many cycles of world dissolution many cycles of world formation, many cycles of world dissolution and formation thus: 'There I was, such a name I had, such a clan I belonged to, such appearance I had, such food I ate, such pleasures I enjoyed and such pains I suffered, and such a life span I had. Passing away from that existence, I was born in another existence. In that (new) existence, too, such a name I had, such a clan I belonged to, such appearance I had, such food I ate, such pleasures I enjoyed and such pains I suffered, and such a life span I had. Passing away from that existence, I was born in this existence.' In this manner, he remembers many a former existence with full characteristic details and related facts (such as names and clans).

"Venerable Sir, there are Brahmās whose life span cannot be measured in simple numerical figures or mathematically reckoned in tens or hundreds. As a matter of fact, whether the being has passed through existences where there is corporeality or no corporeality, where there is *saññā* or no *saññā*, where there is neither *saññā* nor non-*saññā* he can recollect all these existences: 'There I was, such a name I had, such a clan I belonged to, such appearance I had, such food I ate, such pleasures I enjoyed and such pains I suffered, and such a life span I had. Passing away from that existence, I was born in another existence. In that (new) existence, too, such a name I had, such a clan I belonged to, such appearance I had, such food I ate, such pleasures I enjoyed and such pains I suffered, and such a life span I had. Passing away from that existence, I was born in this existence.' In this manner he remembers many a former existence with full characteristic details and related facts (such as names and clans).

"Venerable Sir, this exposition of the Bhagavā on Knowledge of Past Existences is of the highest excellence."

Exposition on Knowledge of the Passing Away and Arising of Beings

158. "Furthermore, Venerable Sir, the Bhagavā teaches the Dhamma on the knowledge of the passing away and arising of beings, by an exposition which is of the highest excellence.

"Venerable Sir, in this world, a certain samaṇa or brāhmaṇa, after striving strenuously, steadfastly and perseveringly, with mindfulness and right attentiveness, attains to the fourth *jhāna* concentration. When the mind has become concentrated in this way, he sees with divine power of sight, which is extremely clear and surpassing the sight of man, beings in the process of passing away and also of arising, inferior or superior beings, beautiful or ugly beings, beings with good or bad destinations. He knows beings arising according to their own kamma action thus:

> 'Friends, these beings were full of evil conduct in deed, word and thought. They maligned the Ariyas, held wrong views, and performed actions according to wrong views. After death and dissolution of the body, they re-appeared in wretched destinations (*duggatiṃ*), miserable existences (*apāya*), states of ruin (*vinipāta*), realms of continuous suffering (*niraya*). But friends, there were also those who were endowed with good conduct in deed, word and thought. They did not malign the Ariyas: they held right views and performed actions according to right views. After death and dissolution of the body, they re-appeared in good destinations, the happy world of the devas.'

"In this way, with the divine power of sight which is extremely clear, surpassing the sight of man, he sees beings in the process of passing away and also of arising, inferior or superior beings, beautiful or ugly beings, beings with good or bad destinations, and beings arising according to their own kamma action.

"Venerable Sir, this exposition on the knowledge of the passing away and arising of beings is of the highest excellence."

Exposition on Supernormal Psychic Powers

159. "Furthermore, Venerable Sir, the Bhagavā teaches the Dhamma on supernormal psychic powers, by an exposition which is of the highest excellence. Venerable Sir, there are two kinds of supernormal psychic powers. Venerable Sir, there is the supernormal psychic power which

is blameworthy, harmful and not noble; and there is the supernormal psychic power which is blameless, harmless and noble.

"What, Venerable Sir, is the supernormal psychic power which is blameworthy, harmful and not noble?

"Venerable Sir, a certain samaṇa or brāhmaṇa, after striving strenuously ... (p) ... attains to the fourth *jhāna* concentration. When the mind has become concentrated in this way, he wields a variety of supernormal psychic powers."

"Being one, he becomes many, and from being many, he becomes one. He becomes visible or invisible at will. He goes through a wall, a rampart or a mountain, unhindered as though going through space. He plunges into or out of the earth as though plunging into or out of water. He walks on water, without sinking, as though on earth. He travels in space, seated cross-legged, like a winged bird. He touches and strokes with his hand the moon and the sun which are so mighty and powerful. He has mastery over his body at will (to reach) even as far as the Brahmā world.

"This, Venerable Sir, is the supernormal psychic power which is blameworthy, harmful and not noble.

"And what, Venerable Sir, is the supernormal psychic power which is blameless, harmless and noble?

"Venerable Sir, in this world, if the bhikkhu desires to perceive pleasantness in things that are unpleasant, he dwells perceiving pleasantness even in things that are unpleasant.[6]

"If the bhikkhu desires to perceive unpleasantness in things that are pleasant, he dwells perceiving unpleasantness even in things that are pleasant.[7]

"If the recluse desires to perceive pleasantness in things that are unpleasant as well as in things that are pleasant, he dwells perceiving only pleasantness in things that are unpleasant as well as in things that are pleasant.

"If the bhikkhu desires to perceive unpleasantness in things that are pleasant as well as in things that are unpleasant, he dwells perceiving only unpleasantness both in things that are pleasant as well as in things that are unpleasant.

---

6. The Commentary explains that he dwells suffusing loving-kindness on unpleasant beings and regarding unpleasant objects as mere elements.

7. The Commentary explains that on pleasant beings and objects, he dwells practising *asubha bhāvanā*, contemplation on the 'foulness' of the body and meditating on their impermanent nature.

"If the bhikkhu desires to remain in equanimity[8] with mindfulness and clear comprehension, towards both unpleasant and pleasant objects, he dwells contemplating on both these objects with equanimity and mindfulness.

"Venerable Sir, this is the supernormal psychic power which is blameless, harmless and noble.

"Venerable Sir, this exposition on the supernormal psychic powers is of the highest excellence. The Bhagavā knows this Dhamma truly and completely in its entirety. There is nothing more to know beyond what the Bhagavā knows.

"There is no one whether samaṇa or brāhmaṇa, who surpasses the Bhagavā in the knowledge of the supernormal psychic powers."

Other Virtues of the Teacher

160. "Venerable Sir, whatever (Lokuttara Dhamma) should be attained by an aspirant (for Buddhahood) who has faith and energetic resolution and who is endowed with vigour, manly exertion, manly endeavour, manly strength, and manly endurance to accomplish onerous tasks, the Bhagavā has achieved that (Lokuttara Dhamma).

"The Bhagavā does not indulge in, nor is attached to sensuous pleasures, which are low, vulgar, common, ignoble, and unbeneficial. The Bhagavā does not practice self-mortification which is painful, ignoble and unbeneficial.

"The Bhagavā acquires at will without difficulty and with ease, the four Rūpāvacara Jhānas which are conducive to well-being and happiness in this very life and which transcend the state of Kāmāvacara Consciousness."[9]

Answers to Different Questions

161. "Venerable Sir, should anyone ask me 'Friend Sāriputta, was there any samaṇa or brāhmaṇa, in times past, who excelled the Bhagavā in Enlightenment?' I would say 'No, there was not'.

---

8. The Commentary explains that he remains mindful, contemplative and equanimous, not developing hatred (dislike) on unpleasant objects nor craving (liking) for pleasant objects.

9. *Kāmāvacara* Consciousness: consciousness that belongs mostly to the Sensuous Plane.

"Venerable Sir, should anyone ask me 'Friend Sāriputta, will there be any samaṇa or brāhmaṇa, in times to come, who will excel the Bhagavā in Enlightenment?' I would say 'No, there never will be.'

"Venerable Sir, should anyone ask me 'Friend Sāriputta, is there at the present time any samaṇa or brāhmaṇa, who excels the Bhagavā in Enlightenment?' I would say 'No, there is not.'

"Venerable Sir, should anyone ask me 'Friend Sāriputta, was there any samaṇa or brāhmaṇa, in times past, who was equal to the Bhagavā in Enlightenment? I would say 'Yes, there was.'

"Venerable Sir, should anyone ask me 'Friend Sāriputta, will there be any samaṇa or brāhmaṇa, in times to come, who will be the equal of the Bhagavā in Enlightenment?' I would say 'Yes, there will be.'

"Venerable Sir, should anyone ask me 'Friend Sāriputta, is there at the present time, any samaṇa or brāhmaṇa, who is the equal of the Bhagavā in Enlightenment?' I would say, 'No, there is not.'

"Venerable Sir, should anyone ask me 'Friend Sāriputta, how is that you answer in the affirmative to some questions and in the negative to others?' I would reply 'Friend, I have heard it said by the Bhagavā himself, I have received it from the Bhagavā himself, that there were Homage-Worthy, Perfectly Self-Enlightened Bhagavās in the past who were the equal of the present Bhagavā in Enlightenment.'

"Friend, I have heard it said by the Bhagavā himself, I have received it from the Bhagavā himself, that there will be Homage-Worthy, Perfectly Self-Enlightened Bhagavās in times to come who will be the equal of the present Bhagavā in Enlightenment.'

"Friend, I have heard it said by the Bhagavā himself, I have received it from the Bhagavā himself, that it is not possible for two Homage-Worthy, Perfectly Self-Enlightened Bhagavās to arise simultaneously in the same group of world systems.'

"How is that, Venerable Sir? Should I be questioned in such a manner and should I reply in the manner described, would I be repeating the teaching as taught by the Bhagavā; or would it amount to misrepresenting the Bhagavā with what is not true? Would I be stating the practice in accordance with the Lokuttara Dhamma, or would any doctrine of the Bhagavā be open to censure or criticism because of my explanation?"

In fact, Sāriputta, should you be questioned in such a manner and should you give the reply in the manner described, you would be repeating the Teaching as taught by the Bhagavā; it would not amount to misrepresenting the Bhagavā with what is not true. You would be stating the practice in accordance with the Lokuttara Dhamma and none of the doctrine will be open to censure or criticism because of your explanation.

Marvellous and Unprecedented Event

162. When the Bhagavā had spoken thus, the Venerable Udāyī said these words to the Bhagavā:

"Venerable Sir, marvellous it is, wonderful it is that the Tathāgata is without any craving, is well contented and is free from moral defilements. Mighty as he is, powerful as he is, the Tathāgata is unassuming and un-ostentatious. Venerable Sir, if wandering ascetics of other faiths could find in themselves even just one of these virtues, they would loudly proclaim it round the town with a flourish of banners. Marvellous it is, wonderful it is that the Tathāgata is without any craving, is well contented and is free from moral defilements. Mighty as he is, powerful as he is, the Tathāgata is unassuming and ostentatious."

(The Buddha said:) See, Udāyī, how a Tathāgata is without craving, is well contented and is free from moral defilements. Mighty as he is, powerful as he is, a Tathāgata is unassuming and un-ostentatious. If wandering ascetics of other faiths could find in themselves even just one of these virtues, they would loudly proclaim it round the town with a flourish of banners. See, Udāyī, how a Tathāgata is without any craving, is well contented and is free from moral defilements.

163. Then, the Bhagavā advised the Venerable Sāriputta: Therefore, Sāriputta, you should repeatedly keep on giving this discourse to the bhikkhus and the bhikkhunīs, to the laymen and laywomen. Wherever there may be foolish ones (without Magga Knowledge) who entertain doubt and scepticism about the Tathāgata, they will have their doubt and scepticism banished by hearing this discourse.

In this manner, the Venerable Sāriputta declared in the presence of the Bhagavā his faith and confidence in the Bhagavā, Therefore, this discourse in the form of questions and answers is designated as Saṃpasādanīya Sutta, the discourse which inspires faith.

End of Saṃpasadanīya Sutta, the fifth sutta from division three (*Pāthika Vagga*)

Namo tassa bhagavato arahato sammāsambuddhassa

PĀSĀDIKA SUTTA

VI. PĀSĀDIKA SUTTA

(Delectable Discourse)

164. Thus have I heard:

At one time the Bhagavā was staying at the mansion in the mango grove of Vedhaññā, the Sakyan, in the country of Sakka.

AFTER NIGAṆṬHA NĀTAPUTTA'S DEATH

Nigaṇṭha Nātaputta had just passed away at Pāvā. His death had caused a schism among his disciples who, split into two parties, were engaged in strife and disagreements, quarrelling and arguing over doctrines:

"You do not know this Doctrine and Discipline. I know this Doctrine and Discipline. How can you ever know this Doctrine and Discipline? Your practice is wrong. My practice is right. My speech is coherent and sensible. Your speech is not coherent and sensible. What you should say first, you say last; and what you should say last, you say first. What you have long practiced to say has been upset now. I have exposed the fault in your doctrine. You stand rebuked. Try to escape from this censure or explain it if you can."

It seemed that these disciples of Nigaṇṭha Nātaputta had only one thought, that of destroying one another.

Just as one gets wearied of, is displeased with and has no more high regard for a teaching which is not well taught, not well imparted, not conducive to attainment of the Path and Fruition, nor to eradication of defilements, which is taught by one who is not perfectly enlightened, and which has lost its mainstay and is devoid of any refuge, even so Nigaṇṭha Nātaputta's white-robed lay followers became disgusted with and displeased with the disciples of Nigaṇṭha Nātaputta; they lost respect for them.

165. Then Cunda Samaṇuddesa[10] having passed the rains retreat at Pāvā, cane to see the Venerable Ānanda in the village of Sāma. After paying respectful homage to the Venerable Ānanda, he sat down at a certain place. So seated, he addressed the Venerable Ānanda in these words:

---

10. Cunda Samaṇuddesa: Cunda Samaṇera, meaning, Cunda, the novice. A younger brother of the Venerable Sāriputta who was still called by this name although by that time he had become a bhikkhu.

"Venerable Sir, Nigaṇṭha Nātaputta has just passed away at Pāvā. His death has caused a schism ... (p) ... Nigaṇṭha Nātaputta's white-robed lay followers became disgusted with and displeased with the disciples of Nigaṇṭha Nātaputta; they lost respect for them."

Thus informed, the Venerable Ānanda said to Cunda Samaṇuddesa, "Friend Cunda, this is a matter about which we should see the Bhagavā. Come Cunda, let us go to the Bhagavā and report to him about this."

"Very well, Venerable Sir", said Cunda Samaṇuddesa.

Then the Venerable Ānanda and Cunda went to the Bhagavā. After paying respectful homage to the Bhagavā, they sat down at a certain place; and having sat down, the Venerable Ānanda addressed the Bhagavā thus:

"Venerable Sir, Cunda Samaṇuddesa told me 'Venerable Sir, Nigaṇṭha Nātaputta has just passed away at Pāvā. His death has caused a schism ... (p) ... the Nātaputta's white-robed lay followers became disgusted with and displeased with the disciples of Nigaṇṭha Nātaputta; they lost respect for them."

The Teaching of One Who Is Not Perfectly Enlightened

166. Cunda, it is natural and to be expected that this should happen so with a teaching which is not well taught, not well imparted, not conducive to attainment of the Path and Fruition, nor to eradication of defilements, and which is taught by one who is not perfectly enlightened.

Cunda, in this matter, there is the teacher who is not perfectly enlightened; there is the doctrine which is not well taught, not well imparted, not conducive to attainment of the Path and Fruition, nor to eradication of defilements, and which is taught by one who is not perfectly enlightened.

And there is a disciple who does not practice in conformity with that doctrine of that teacher, does not sincerely and devotedly practice the doctrine, does not practice in accordance with the doctrine of the teacher, and keeps deviating from the doctrine.

To such a disciple, one should say, 'Friend, you have been fortunate; you have had good luck. Your teacher is one who is not perfectly enlightened; the doctrine is one which is not well taught, not well imparted, not conducive to attainment of the Path and Fruition, nor to eradication of defilements, and which is taught by one who is not perfectly enlightened. But you do not practice in conformity with that doctrine, you do not sincerely and devotedly practice the doctrine, you do not practice in accordance with the doctrine of the teacher, and you keep deviating from the doctrine.'

Indeed, Cunda, as said before, in that case, the teacher is to be censured; his doctrine is to be censured; but the disciple is to be praised.

Suppose, Cunda, the teacher says to such a disciple, 'Come, friend, practice according to the doctrine taught and prescribed by your teacher.' In this way the teacher exhorts the disciple, the disciple is exhorted by the teacher; and the disciple, exhorted by the teacher, practices as instructed. All such teachers and disciples accumulate much demerit.

And why so? It is because, Cunda, the teaching is not well taught, not well imparted, not conducive to attainment of the Path and Fruition, nor to eradication of defilements, and is taught by one who is not perfectly enlightened.

167. Cunda, in this matter, there is the teacher who is not perfectly enlightened; there is the doctrine which is not well taught, not well imparted, not conducive to attainment of the Path and Fruition, nor to eradication of defilements, and which is taught by one who is not perfectly enlightened.

And there is a disciple who practices in conformity with that doctrine of the teacher, sincerely and devotedly practices the doctrine, practices in accordance with the doctrine of the teacher.

To such a disciple, one should say, 'Friend, you have been unfortunate, you have had poor luck. Your teacher is one who is not perfectly enlightened; the doctrine is one which is not well taught, not well imparted, not conducive to attainment of the Path and Fruition, nor to eradication of defilements, and which is taught by one who is not perfectly enlightened. But you practice in conformity with the doctrine, you sincerely and devotedly practice the doctrine, you practice in accordance with the doctrine of the teacher.'

Indeed, Cunda, as said before, in that case, the teacher is to be censured; his doctrine is to be censured; and the disciple also is to be censured.

Suppose, Cunda, the teacher says to such a disciple, 'Friend, you are engaged in the practice of attaining liberation, indeed you will succeed in fully attaining liberation. 'In this way the teacher encourages and praises his disciple; the disciple is encouraged and praised by the teacher; and the disciple, encouraged and praised in this manner by the teacher, puts forth strenuous energy in his endeavour. All such teachers and disciples accumulate much demerit.

And why so? It is because, Cunda, the teaching is not well taught, not well imparted, not conducive to attainment of the Path and Fruition, nor to eradication of defilements, and is taught by one who is not perfectly enlightened.

The Teaching of One Who Is Perfectly Enlightened

168. Cunda, in this matter, there is the Teacher who is perfectly self-enlightened; there is the Doctrine which is well taught, well imparted, conducive to attainment of the Path and Fruition and to eradication of defilements, and which is taught by one who is perfectly self-enlightened.

But there is a disciple who does not practice in conformity with that Doctrine of the Teacher, does not sincerely and devotedly practice the Doctrine, does not practice in accordance with the Doctrine of the Teacher, and keeps deviating from the Doctrine.

To such a disciple, one should say, 'Friend, you have been unfortunate, you have had poor luck. Your Teacher is one who is perfectly self-enlightened; the Doctrine is one which is well taught, well imparted, conducive to attainment of the Path and Fruition and to eradication of defilements, and which is taught by one who is perfectly self-enlightened, But you do not practice in conformity with that Doctrine, you do not sincerely and devotedly practice the Doctrine, you do not practice in accordance with the Doctrine of the Teacher, and you keep deviating from the Doctrine.'

Indeed, Cunda, as said before, in that case, the Teacher is praiseworthy, the Doctrine is praiseworthy, but the disciple is to be censured.

Suppose, Cunda, the teacher says to such a disciple, 'Come, friend, practice according to the doctrine taught and prescribed by your teacher.' In this way, the teacher exhorts the disciple, the disciple is exhorted by the teacher; and the disciple, exhorted by the teacher, practices as instructed. All such teachers and disciples accumulate much merit.

And why so? It is because, Cunda, the Teaching is well taught, well imparted, conducive to attainment of the Path and Fruition, and to eradication of defilements, being taught by one who is perfectly self-enlightened.

169. Cunda, in this matter, there is the Teacher who is perfectly self-enlightened; there is the Teaching which is well taught, well imparted, conducive to attainment of the Path and Fruition, and to eradication of defilements, and which is taught by one who is perfectly self-enlightened.

And there is a disciple who practices in conformity with the Doctrine of that Teacher, sincerely and devotedly practices the Doctrine, practices in accordance with the Doctrine of the Teaching.

To such a disciple, one should say, 'Friend, you have been fortunate, you have had good luck. Your Teacher is one who is perfectly self-enlightened; the Doctrine is one which is well taught, well imparted, conducive to attainment of the Path and Fruition, and to eradication of defilements, and which is taught by one who is perfectly self-enlightened. And you practice in conformity with the Doctrine and you sincerely and devotedly practice the Doctrine, you practice in accordance with the Doctrine of the Teacher.'

Indeed, Cunda, as said before, in that case, the Teacher is praiseworthy, the Doctrine is praiseworthy and the disciple is to be praised, too.

Suppose, Cunda, the teacher says to such a disciple, 'Friend, you are engaged in the practice of attaining the Path and Fruition; indeed you will succeed in fully attaining liberation.' In this way, Cunda, the Teacher encourages and praises his disciple; the disciple is encouraged and praised by the Teacher; the disciple, encouraged and praised in this manner by his Teacher, puts forth strenuous energy in his endeavour. All such teachers and disciples accumulate much merit.

And why so? It is because, Cunda, the Teaching is well taught, well imparted, conducive to attainment of the Path and Fruition, and to eradication of defilements, and is taught by one who is perfectly self-enlightened.

The Teacher over Whose Death the Disciples Become Anguished

170. Cunda, in this world, there arises a Teacher who is Homage-Worthy and Perfectly Self-Enlightened. And his Doctrine is well taught, well imparted, conducive to attainment of the Path and Fruition, and to eradication of defilements, and is taught by one who is perfectly self-enlightened.

But his disciples in that Teaching have not yet attained the knowledge of the Four Truths; the Life of Purity in its entirety has not yet been fully explained and made clear to these disciples; the various sections of doctrine and practice in the Teaching have not yet been brought together and incorporated into one complete whole, have not yet been formulated as the Dhamma on liberation from the round of existences, have not yet been well proclaimed in the realms of devas and men, when that Teacher of these disciples passes away. Cunda, when such a Teacher passes away, his disciples become anguished over his death.

And why so? (The disciples might say:) It is because in this world there arises to us a Teacher who is Homage-Worthy and Perfectly Self-Enlightened. And his Doctrine is well taught, well imparted, conducive to attainment of the Path and Fruition, and to eradication of defilements, taught by one who is perfectly self-enlightened. But in that system of Teaching of ours, we have not yet attained the knowledge of the Four Truths; the Life of Purity in its entirety has not yet been fully explained and made clear to us; the various sections of doctrine and practice in the Teaching have not yet been brought together and incorporated into one complete whole, have not yet been formulated as the Dhamma on liberation from the round of existences, have not yet been well proclaimed in the realms of devas and men. Now our Teacher has passed away.

Cunda, when such a Teacher passes away, his disciples become anguished over his death, having failed to achieve the attainment for which they need his guidance and assistance.

The Teacher over Whose Death the Disciples Do Not Get Anguished

171. Cunda, in this world, there arises a Teacher who is Homage-Worthy and Perfectly Self-Enlightened. And his Doctrine is well taught, well imparted, conducive to attainment of the Path and Fruition, and to eradication of defilements, and is taught by one who is perfectly self-enlightened.

And his disciples in that Teaching have attained the knowledge of the Four Truths; the Life of Purity in its entirety has been fully explained and made clear to these disciples; the various sections of doctrine and practice in the Teaching have been brought together and incorporated into one complete whole, have been formulated as the Dhamma on liberation from the round of existences, have been well proclaimed in the realms of devas and men, when the Teacher of these disciples passes away. Cunda, when such a Teacher passes away, his disciples do not become anglished over his death.

And why so? (The disciples might say:) It is because in this world there arises to us a Teacher who is Homage-Worthy and Perfectly Self-Enlightened. And his Doctrine is well taught, well imparted, conducive to attainment of the Path and Fruition, and to eradication of defilements, taught by one who is perfectly self-enlightened. And in that system of Teaching of ours, we have attained the knowledge of the Four Truths; the Life of Purity in its entirety has been fully explained and made clear to us; the various sections of doctrine and practice in the Teaching have been brought together and incorporated into one complete whole, have been formulated as the Dhamma on liberation from the round of existences, have been well proclaimed in the realms of devas and men. Now our Teacher has passed away.

Cunda, when such a Teacher passes away, his disciples do not become anguished over his death, having achieved the desired attainments with his guidance and assistance.

Imperfections of a System of Teaching

172. Cunda, in a system of Teaching, even though the Doctrine is fully endowed with those characteristics mentioned before, (such as being well taught) if the Teacher is one who is not well established in the virtues of an Elder Bhikkhu, nor of ripe experience and long standing in the Order, without mature knowledge of old times and not far advanced in age, then that system of Teaching is by this circumstance imperfect.

But, Cunda, in a system of Teaching, when the Doctrine is fully endowed with those characteristics mentioned before, and the Teacher is one who is well established in the virtues of an Elder Bhikkhu and is of ripe experience and seniority in the Order, with mature knowledge of old times and far advanced in age, then that system of Teaching is by this circumstance perfect.

173. Cunda, in a system of Teaching, even though the Doctrine is fully endowed with those characteristics mentioned before, and the Teacher is one who is well established in the virtues of an Elder Bhikkhu and is of ripe experience and seniority in the Order, with mature knowledge of old times, and far advanced in age, if the senior bhikkhu disciples of the Teacher are not yet accomplished in the knowledge of the Path, not yet fully trained (in the discipline and practice), nor fully confident (in the interpretation of the Dhamma), have not yet attained the Fruition (*Arahattaphala*) through the cessation of all moral intoxicants, are not competent yet to propagate the Teaching, are not capable of refuting any opposing doctrine that may arise and crushing it with the authority of the Doctrine, and are not able to teach the Dhamma which promotes liberation from the round of existences, then that system of teaching is by this circumstance imperfect.

But Cunda, in a system of Teaching, when the Doctrine is fully endowed with those characteristics mentioned before, and the Teacher is one who is well established in the virtues of an Elder Bhikkhu and is of ripe experience and seniority in the Order, with mature knowledge of old times, and far advanced in age, and the senior bhikkhu disciples of the Teacher are accomplished in the knowledge of the Path, fully trained (in the discipline and practice), fully confident (in the interpretation of the Dhamma), have attained the Fruition (*Arahattaphala*) through the cessation of all moral intoxicants, are competent to propagate the Teaching, are capable of refuting any opposing doctrine that may arise and crushing it with the authority of the Doctrine, and are able to teach the Dhamma which promotes liberation from the round of existences, then that system of Teaching is by this circumstance perfect.

174. Cunda, in a system of Teaching, even though the Doctrine is endowed with those characteristics mentioned before, and the Teacher is one who is well established in the virtues of an Elder Bhikkhu and is of ripe experience and seniority in the Order, with mature knowledge of old times, and far advanced in age, and the senior bhikkhu disciples of the Teacher are accomplished in the knowledge of the Path, fully trained (in the discipline and practice), fully confident (in the interpretation of the Dhamma), have attained the Fruition, (*Arahattaphala*) through the cessation of all moral intoxicants, are competent to propagate the Teaching, are capable of refuting any opposing doctrine that may arise and crushing it with the authority of the Doctrine, and are able to teach the Dhamma which promotes liberation from the round of existences, if the bhikkhu disciples of middle standing are not yet accomplished in the knowledge of the Path, then that system of Teaching is by that circumstance imperfect. Though the bhikkhu disciples of middle standing are accomplished in the knowledge of the Path, if the bhikkhu disciples of junior standing are not yet accomplished in the knowledge of the Path ... (p) ... Though the bhikkhu disciples of junior standing are accomplished in the knowledge of the Path, if the bhikkhunī[11] disciples of senior sending are not yet accomplished in the knowledge of the Path ... (p) ... Though the bhikkhunī disciples of senior standing are accomplished in the knowledge of the Path, if the bhikkhunī disciples of middle standing are not yet accomplished in the knowledge of the Path ... (p) ... Though the bhikkhunī disciples of middle standing are accomplished in the knowledge of the Path, if the bhikkhunī disciples of

11. *Bhikkhunī*: a female member of the Buddhist Order.

junior standing are not yet accomplished in the knowledge of the Path ... (p) ...

Though the bhikkhunī disciples of junior standing have become accomplished in the knowledge of the Path, if the lay disciples of that Teacher, who are white-robed laymen who practice the Life of Purity, are not yet accomplished in the knowledge of the Path ... (p) ... Though the lay disciples of the Teacher, who are white-robed laymen who practice the Life of Purity, have become accomplished in the knowledge of the Path, if the lay disciples of that Teacher, who are white-robed laymen who still indulge in sensual pleasures, are not yet accomplished in the knowledge of the Path ... (p) ... Though the lay disciples of the Teacher, who are white-robed laymen who still indulge in sensual pleasures, have become accomplished in the knowledge of the Path, if the lay disciples of that Teacher, who are white-robed laywomen who practice the Life of Purity, are not yet accomplished in the knowledge of the Path ... (p) ... Though the lay disciples of the Teacher, who are white-robed laywomen who practice the Life of Purity, have become accomplished in the knowledge, of the Path, if the lay disciples of that Teacher, who are white-robed laywomen who still indulge in sensual pleasures, are not yet accomplished in the knowledge of the Path ... (p) ...

Though the lay disciples of the Teacher, who are white-robed laywomen who still indulge in sensual pleasures, have become accomplished in the knowledge of the Path, if the system of Teaching of that Teacher has not yet fully developed, not yet become prosperous, nor widespread and well-known, not yet well proclaimed in the realms of devas and men ... (p) ... Though the system of Teaching of that Teacher has fully developed, become prosperous, widespread and well-known and well proclaimed in the realms of devas and men, if it has not attained the foremost place with regard to gain, fame and followers, then that system of Teaching is by that circumstance imperfect.

But, Cunda, in a system of Teaching, when the Doctrine is fully endowed with those characteristics mentioned before, and the Teacher is one who is well established in the virtues of an Elder Bhikkhu, and is of ripe experience and seniority in the Order, with mature knowledge of old times, and far advanced in age, and the senior bhikkhu disciples of the Teacher are accomplished in the knowledge of the Path, fully trained (in the discipline and practice), fully confident (in the interpretation of the Dhamma), have attained the Fruition (*Arahattaphala*) through the cessation of all moral intoxicants, and are competent to propagate the Teaching, are capable of refuting any opposing doctrine that may arise and crushing it with the authority of the Teaching, and are able to teach the Dhamma which promotes liberation from the round of existences, and the disciples of that Teacher who are bhikkhus of middle standing are accomplished in the knowledge of the Path, and the disciples of that Teacher who are bhikkhus of junior standing are accomplished in the knowledge of the Path, and the disciples of that Teacher who are bhikkhunīs of senior standing are accomplished in the knowledge of the Path, and the disciples of that Teacher who are bhikkhunīs of middle standing are accomplished in the knowledge of the Path, and the disciples of that Teacher who are bhikkhunīs of junior standing are accomplished in the knowledge of the Path, and the lay disciples of that Teacher, who are white-robed laymen who practice the Life of Purity, are accomplished in the knowledge of the Path, and the lay disciples of that Teacher who are white-robed laymen who still indulge in sensual pleasures are accomplished in the knowledge of the Path, and the lay disciples of that Teacher who are white-robed laywomen who practice the Life of Purity are accomplished in the knowledge of the Path, and the lay disciples of that Teacher who are white-robed lay-women who still indulge in sensual pleasures are accomplished in the knowledge of the Path, and the system of Teaching of that Teacher has fully developed, become prosperous, widespread and well-known and has been well proclaimed in the realms of devas and men; and it has reached the foremost place with regard to gain, fame, and following, then that system of Teaching is, by this circumstance, perfect.

175. Cunda, now I have appeared in the world as a Teacher who is Homage-Worthy and Perfectly Self-Enlightened; the Teaching is one which is well taught, well imparted, conducive to attainment of the Path and Fruition, and to eradication of defilements, taught by one who is perfectly self-enlightened.

And the disciples in my system of Teaching have attained the knowledge of the Four Truths; the Life of Purity in its entirety has been explained fully and made clear to the disciples; the various sections of doctrine and discipline in the Teaching have been brought together and incorporated into one complete whole, have been formulated as the Dhamma on liberation from the round of existences, and have been well proclaimed in the realms of devas and men.

Cunda, I, the Teacher, am well established in the virtues of an Elder Bhikkhu, and I am of ripe experience and seniority in the Order, with mature knowledge of old times, and far advanced in age now.

Cunda, there are now senior bhikkhu disciples of mine who are accomplished in the knowledge of the Path, fully trained in the discipline and practice, fully confident, having attained the Fruition (the *Arahattaphala*), competent to propagate the Teaching, capable of refuting any opposing doctrine that may arise and crushing it with the authority of the Teaching, able to teach the Dhamma which promotes liberation from the round of existences. Cunda there are now bhikkhu disciples of mine who are or middle standing (who are accomplished in the knowledge of the Path); Cunda, there are now bhikkhu disciples of mine who are of junior standing ... (p) ... Cunda, there are now bhikkhunī disciples of mine who are of senior standing ... (p) ... Cunda, there are now bhikkhunī disciples of mine who are of middle standing ... (p) ... Cunda, there are now bhikkhunī disciples of mine who are of junior standing ... (p) ... Cunda, there are now my laymen disciples who are white-robed and who practice the Life of Purity ... (p) ... Cunda, there are now my laymen disciples who still indulge in sensual pleasures ... (p) ... Cunda, there are now my laywomen disciples who are white-robed and who practice the Life of Purity ... (p) ... Cunda, there are now my laywomen disciples who still indulge in sensual pleasures (who are accomplished in the knowledge of the Path); Cunda, my system of Teaching has now fully developed, become prosperous, widespread and well-known and has been well proclaimed in the realms of devas and men.

176. Cunda, various Teachers have also appeared in this world now. But, Cunda, I do not see anyone amongst them who has reached the topmost place like me with regard to gain, fame, and followers.

Cunda, various orders and sects have appeared in this world now. But, Cunda, I do not see any other order which has reached the topmost place like my Order of Bhikkhus with regard to gain, fame, and followers.

Cunda, if someone wishes to describe a Teaching as perfect in every sense, complete in every detail, requiring nothing to add to or substract from, well taught and well imparted, then he can describe only this Teaching of mine as perfect in every sense ... (p) ... well imparted.

Cunda, Udaka Rāmaputta had said, "Seeing, one does not see. On seeing what, does one not see?[12] Of a well sharpened razor, one sees the blade but not the edge." Cunda, it is of such a well sharpened razor that it is said, (by Udaka, son of Rama) "Seeing, one does not see." But, Cunda,

12. Udaka posed this riddle to his disciples who could not solve it; he therefore answered it himself after some time.

these words of Udaka son of Rāma, are low, vulgar, common, not uttered by *ariyas*, unbeneficial.

Cunda, whoever wants rightly to say 'Seeing, one does not see' he should say it only of this Teaching of mine.

Here, on seeing what, does one not see? As explained above, there is the Teaching which is perfect in every sense, complete in every detail, which requires nothing to add to or substract from, well taught and well imparted, it is this Teaching which one sees.

And there is no feature in the Teaching which, when taken out, will make it purer; thus one does not see any feature which needs taking out. And there is no feature which, when added to the Teaching, will make it more complete; thus one does not see any feature which needs to be added to the Teaching.

Thus, here, 'seeing' means seeing the Teaching, and 'not seeing' is not seeing what needs to be taken out from or added to the Teaching.

Cunda, if someone wishes to describe any Teaching as perfect ... (p) ... well imparted, then he can describe only this Teaching of mine as perfect in every sense, complete in every detail, requiring nothing to add to or substract from, well taught and well imparted.

The Dhammas Which Should Be Recited and Imparted Uniformly

177. Therefore, Cunda, there are these Dhammas which I have taught after realizing them through Magga-Knowledge and Enlightenment. All of you, my disciples, should come together, assemble in a congregation and recite and impart these Dhammas in a uniform version, collating meaning with meaning, wording with wording, without dissension. In this way, this Teaching will endure and last long for the welfare and happiness of many, for the good of the world, for the benefit, welfare, and happiness of devas and men.

Cunda, what are these Dhammas?

"I have taught these Dhammas after realizing them through Magga-Knowledge and Enlightenment. All of you, my disciples, should come together, assemble in a congregation, and recite and impart these Dhammas in a uniform version, collating meaning with meaning, wording with wording, without dissension. In this way, this Teaching will endure and last long for the welfare and happiness of many, for the good of the world, for the benefit, welfare, and happiness of devas and men."

(And what are these Dhammas?) They are:
The Four Methods of Steadfast Mindfulness
The Four Great Efforts
The Four Bases of Psychic Potency
The Five Faculties
The Five Powers
The Seven Factors of Enlightenment
The Noble Path of Eight Constituents

Cunda, these are the Dhammas I have taught after realizing them with Magga-Knowledge and Enlightenment. All of you, my disciples, should come together, assemble in a congregation, and recite and impart these Dhammas in a uniform version, collating meaning with meaning, wording with wording, without dissension. In this way, this Teaching will endure and last long for the welfare and happiness of many, for the good of the world, for the benefit, welfare, and happiness of devas and men.

On Handling Differences of Opinion

178. Cunda, from amongst you who are living in concord, harmony, non-dissension, and Practice of Purity, if a fellow-bhikkhu happens to speak on the Dhamma amidst the company of bhikkhus, it may occur to you that the said respected bhikkhu has taken hold of a wrong meaning, and has presented a wrong wording, then you should neither approve nor reject what he says. Without approving or rejecting, you should only say, 'Friend, as to the wording to convey this meaning, should it be these or those words? Which would better fit in with the meaning? Or, friend, as to the meaning of this expression, should it be taken this way or that way? Which would fit in with the expression best?'

Whereupon the said respected bhikkhu might say, 'Friends, of the various expressions to convey this meaning, only this wording will suit the meaning best. I, therefore, choose this wording. And amongst the various meanings of this expression, only this meaning seems to fit in best with the wording. I, therefore, choose this meaning.'

In that case, you should neither praise nor censure him. Without praising or censuring him, you should properly let that bhikkhu know and bear in mind the (correct) meaning and wording.

179. Cunda, if another fellow-bhikkhu happens to speak on the Dhamma amidst the company of bhikkhus, it may occur to you that the said respected bhikkhu has taken hold of a wrong meaning and

has presented a correct wording; then you should neither approve nor reject what he says. Without approving or rejecting, you should only say, 'Friend, as to the meaning of this expression, should it be taken in this way or that way? Which would fit in with the expression best?'

Whereupon the said bhikkhu might say, 'Friends, of the various meanings for this expression, only this meaning will suit the expression best.'

In that case, you should neither praise nor censure him. Without praising or censuring him, you should properly let that bhikkhu know and bear in mind the (correct) meaning.

180. And again, Cunda, if another fellow-bhikkhu happens to speak on the Dhamma amidst the company of bhikkhus, it may occur to you that the said respected bhikkhu has taken hold of a correct meaning but has presented a wrong wording; then you should neither approve nor reject what he says. Without approving or rejecting, you should only say, 'Friend, as to the wording to convey this meaning, should it be these or those words? Which would fit in with the meaning best?'

Whereupon the said bhikkhu might say, 'Friends, of the various expressions for this meaning, only this wording will suit the meaning best.'

In that case, you should neither praise nor censure him. Without praising or censuring him, you should properly let that bhikkhu know and bear in mind the (correct) wording.

181. Cunda, if another fellow-bhikkhu happens to speak on the Dhamma amidst the company of bhikkhus, it may occur to you that the said respected bhikkhu has taken hold of a correct meaning and has also presented a correct wording.

In that case, you should gladly approve of his words, saying 'Well said (Sādhu)!' After gladly approving of his words, saying 'Well said (Sādhu)!', you should tell him, 'Oh, friend, we have been fortunate. It is fortunate for the community that we see such a venerable fellow-bhikkhu who is so highly proficient in both the meaning and the wording (of the Dhamma).'

Sanctioning of (Four) Requisites

182. Cunda, I teach the Dhamma not just to guard against moral intoxicants arising in the present world.

Cunda, I teach the Dhamma not just to prevent moral intoxicants from arising in the next world.

Cunda, I teach the Dhamma to guard against moral intoxicants arising in the present world as well as to prevent moral intoxicants from arising in the next world.

Therefore, Cunda, in this Teaching, I have sanctioned the robe for you. It can protect you from cold; it can protect you from heat; it can protect you from gadflies, mosquitoes, wind, the sun's heat and reptiles; it can conceal and cover up the private parts of the body for the sake of decency. (I have permitted it so that you may practice the Life of Purity after warding off such discomforts as cold and heat.)[13]

I have sanctioned the alms-food for you. It can sustain the body and keep it going; it can remove the discomforts of hunger; and it can help in the practice of the Life of Purity. (I have permitted the alms-food so that you may practice the Life of Purity after reflecting thus:)[13] 'By this alms-food I shall get rid of the discomfort of hunger; I shall prevent the arising of the discomfort due to immoderate eating; I shall be living a blameless life with good health.'

I have sanctioned the dwelling place (monestary) for you. It can protect you from cold; it can protect you from heat; it can protect you from gadflies, mosquitoes, wind, the sun's heat and reptiles; it can ward off the rigours of weather and will enable you to enjoy meditating in solitary retreat. (I have permitted the use of a dwelling place, so that you may practice the Life of Purity after warding off such discomforts as cold and heat.)[13]

I have sanctioned for you the medicine which cures illness and serves as a protector of life. It can remove affliction produced by disturbances of body constituents and provide freedom from pains of illnesses and disease. (I have permitted the use of medicine so that you may practice the Life of Purity after warding off pains and afflictions.)[13] (last note)

Enjoyment of Pleasure

183. Cunda, there is this possibility that the wandering ascetics of other faiths might say, 'The samaṇas of the Sakyan clan (i.e., the bhikkhu disciples of the Buddha) are engaged in enjoyment of pleasure.'

Cunda, to these wandering ascetics of other faiths who would make such remarks, you should reply, 'Friends, what is the enjoyment of pleasure? There are many forms and varieties of enjoyment of pleasure.'

13. The Commentary.

Cunda, there are these four forms, of enjoyment of pleasure which are low, vulgar, common, ignoble, unbeneficial; not conducive to disillusionment with the five *khandhas,* nor to abandonment of attachment, nor to cessation of *dukkha*, nor to extinction of defilements, nor to attainment of *Magga*-Knowledge, nor to realization of the Four Noble Truths, nor to realization of *Nibbāna.*

And what are these four forms? In this world, a certain foolish person finds pleasure and gratification in killing, in taking the life of other beings. This is the first form of enjoyment of pleasure.

Again, in this world, a certain foolish person finds pleasure and gratification in stealing, in taking what is not given. This is the second form of enjoyment of pleasure.

And then in this world, a certain foolish person finds pleasure and gratification in telling lies, in saying what is not true. This is the third form of enjoyment of pleasure.

Then, in this world, a certain foolish person enjoys full gratification in the pleasures of the five senses. This is the fourth form of enjoyment of pleasure.

Cunda, these four forms of enjoyment of pleasure are low, vulgar, common, ignoble, unbeneficial; not conducive to disillusionment with the five *khandhas,* nor to abandonment of attachment, nor to cessation of *dukkha,* nor to extinction of defilements, nor to attainment of *Magga*-Knowledge, nor to realization of the Four Noble Truths, nor to realization of *Nibbāna.*

Cunda, there is this possibility that the wandering ascetics of other faiths might say, 'The samaṇas of the Sakyan clan (i.e., the bhikkhu disciples of the Buddha) are engaged in these four forms of enjoyment of pleasure.'

You should tell these wandering ascetics, 'Say not so!' These wandering ascetics would not be telling the truth about you; they would be alleging what is not true, what has no foundation.

184. Cunda, there are these four forms of enjoyment of pleasure which are conducive to disillusionment with the five *khandhas,* to abandonment of attachment, to cessation of *dukkha,* to extinction of defilements, to attainment of *Magga*-Knowledge, to realization of the Four Noble Truths, and to realization of *Nibbāna.*

And what are these four forms?

Cunda, the bhikkhu in this Teaching, being detached from the sensual pleasures and demeritorious factors, achieves and remains in the first *jhāna* which is accompanied by *vitakka* (initial application of the mind), *vicāra* (sustained application of the mind), and which has *pīti* (delightful satisfaction) and *sukha* (bliss) born of detachment from hindrances (*nīvaraṇas*). This is the first form of enjoyment of pleasure.

Then, Cunda, the bhikkhu, having got rid of *vitakka* and *vicāra*, achieves and remains in the second *jhāna*, with internal tranquillity, with enhancement of one-pointedness of concentration, devoid of *vitakka* and *vicāra*, but with *pīti* and *sukha* born of concentration. This is the second form of enjoyment of pleasure.

Then again, Cunda, because *pīti* (delightful satisfaction) fades away, the bhikkhu achieves and remains in the third *jhāna*, that which causes a person who attains it to be praised by the Noble Ones as one who has equanimity and one who abides in *sukha*. This is the third form of enjoyment of pleasure.

Then, Cunda, the bhikkhu, having given up both pain and pleasure, and by the previous disappearance of sadness and gladness, achieves and remains in the fourth *jhāna*, without pain and pleasure, a state of equanimity and absolute purity of mindfulness. This is the fourth form of enjoyment of pleasure.

Cunda, these four forms of enjoyment of pleasure are conducive to disillusionment with the five *khandhas*, to abandonment of attachment, to cessation of *dukkha*, to extinction of defilements, to attainment of *Magga*-Knowledge, to realization of the Four Noble Truths, and to realization of *Nibbāna*.

Cunda, there is the possibility that the wandering ascetics of other faiths might say, 'The samaṇas of the Sakyan clan are engaged in these four forms of enjoyment of pleasure.' You should say to these wandering ascetics, 'It is true.' These wandering ascetics would be telling the truth about you; they would not be alleging what is not true, what has no foundation.

Benefits of Enjoyment of Pleasure

185. Cunda, there is the possibility that the wandering ascetics of other faiths might ask what benefits and what advantages are to be expected by those who are engaged in these four forms of enjoyment of pleasure.

Then, Cunda, you should reply to these wandering ascetics of other faiths thus: "Friends, four benefits and advantages are to be expected by those who are engaged in these four forms of enjoyment of pleasure.

"And what are these four benefits?

"Friends, in this Teaching, the bhikkhu, having completely eradicated the three fetters, becomes a *Sotāpanna*, a Stream-enterer, not liable to fall into miserable existences and states of woe, and is assured of attaining the three higher levels of Insight. This is the first benefit, the first advantage.

"And the bhikkhu, consequent on complete eradication of the three fetters and attenuation of the grosser forms of passion, hatred and delusion, becomes a *Sakadāgāmī*, a Once-returner, who will achieve the complete ending of *dukkha* after returning only once to this human world. This is the second benefit, the second advantage.

"And then, the bhikkhu, consequent on complete destruction of all the five fetters which lead to rebirth in the lower sensuous planes, becomes an *Anāgāmī*, a Non-returner, who will reappear as a spontaneously manifesting being in the Brahmā realm, whence he will not return but pass away into *Nibbāna*. This is the third benefit, the third advantage.

"And then, the bhikkhu, consequent on complete destruction of *āsavas*, moral intoxicants or taints, becomes an *Arahat* who realizes and attains by himself in the present life the taint-free emancipation of the mind (*Arahattaphala Samādhi*) as well as the Insight emancipation (*Arahattaphala Paññā*) through *Magga* Insight. This is the fourth benefit, the fourth advantage. Friends, these are the four benefits and advantages to be expected by those who are engaged in these four forms of enjoyment of pleasure."

Evil Deeds Not Committed by One Free of Moral Intoxicants

186. Cunda, there is this possibility that the wandering ascetics of other faiths might say that the samaṇas of the Sakyan clan (i.e., the disciples of the Buddha) are not firmly fixed in their doctrines.

Cunda, you should reply to these wandering ascetics of other faiths thus: "Friends, the Bhagavā, the One who knows, the One who perceives, the Homage-Worthy, the Perfectly Self-Enlightened, has taught and prescribed fundamental precepts which the disciples should not transgress throughout their life. Just as a stone pillar or an iron pillar, fixed deeply and firmly in the ground, is immovable, unshakable, so also fundamental precepts taught and prescribed by the Bhagavā, the One who knows, the One who perceives, the Homage-Worthy, the Perfectly Self-Enlightened, remain immovable, unshakable.

"Friends, the bhikkhu who has become worthy of special veneration, liberated from moral intoxicants, having carried out the noble practice of the Path, having already done what should be done, having laid down the burden (of the *kilesas*, moral defilements), having attained his own goal, *Arahattaphala*, having cut off the fetter of craving for rebirth, and being fully liberated because of perfect knowledge, will not commit these nine evil deeds:

"Friends, the bhikkhu who has been liberated from moral intoxicants will not intentionally take the life of a being;

"The bhikkhu who has been liberated from moral intoxicants will not take, with the intention of stealing, what is not given;

"The bhikkhu who has been liberated from moral intoxicants will not indulge in sexual intercourse;

"The bhikkhu who has been liberated from moral intoxicants will not deliberately tell lies;

"The bhikkhu who has been liberated from moral intoxicants will not collect and store material things for later use and enjoyment, as was his wont in lay life;

"The bhikkhu who has been liberated from moral intoxicants will not take a wrong course of action through partiality;

"The bhikkhu who has been liberated from moral intoxicants will not take a wrong course of action through ill will;

"The bhikkhu who has been liberated from moral intoxicants will not take a wrong course of action through ignorance of what is right or wrong;

"The bhikkhu who has been liberated from moral intoxicants will not take a wrong course of action through fear.

"Friends, the bhikkhu who has become worthy of special veneration, liberated from moral intoxicants, having carried out the noble practice of the Path, having already done what should be done, having laid down the burden (of the *kilesas*, moral defilements), having attained his own goal, *Arahattaphala*, having cut off the fetter of craving for rebirth and being fully liberated because of perfect knowledge, will not commit these nine evil deeds."

Dealing with Problems

187. Cunda, there is this possibility that the wandering ascetics of other faiths might say thus: 'Samaṇa Gotama manifests an infinite knowledge and insight concerning the past; but concerning the future,

he does not manifest such knowledge and insight. Why is it so? What is the reason for this?'

The wandering ascetics of other faiths, just like stupid and foolish persons, are under the impression that knowledge and insight of a certain set of things should be similarly manifested in knowledge and insight of another set of things.

Cunda, concerning the past, the Tathāgata has the knowledge and mindfulness by which he recollects previous existences. He can recall existences as far back as he wishes.

Cunda, concerning the future, reflective Insight arises, by virtue of the knowledge of the Path, to the Tathāgata at the foot of the Bodhi tree, that 'This is the last existence. There is no more rebirth.'

Cunda, concerning the past, should it be false, untrue and unbeneficial, the Tathāgata would not deal with it.

Cunda, concerning the past, should it be right and true, but unbeneficial, the Tathāgata would not deal with it, either.

Cunda, concerning the past, should it be right and true and also beneficial, the Tathāgata knows the proper time to deal with the problem.

Cunda, concerning the future, should it be false, untrue and unbeneficial, the Tathāgata would not deal with it ... (p) ...

Cunda, concerning the future, should it be right and true and also beneficial, the Tathāgata knows the proper time to deal with the problem.

Cunda, concerning the present, should it be false, untrue and unbeneficial, the Tathāgata would not deal with it.

Cunda, concerning the present, should it be right and true, but unbeneficial, the Tathāgata would not deal with it, either.

Cunda, concerning the present, should it be right and true and also beneficial, the Tathāgata knows the proper time to deal with the problem.

188. Cunda, in this manner, the Tathāgata is One who talks about the past, the future and the present only at the appropriate time, on what is true, what is beneficial and only on matters concerning the Doctrine and the Discipline. Hence, the appellation 'Tathāgata.'

Cunda, in the deva world with its devas, māras and Brahmās and in the human world with its samaṇas, brāhmaṇas, kings and men, there are objects which are seen, heard, felt, known, achieved, sought after and repeatedly thought over, the Tathāgata has the penetrative Insight into all these objects. Hence the appellation 'Tathāgata.'

Cunda, from that night when the Tathāgata attains the Supreme Enlightenment to that night when the Tathāgata realizes the *Nibbāna Dhātu* with complete extinction of the *khandha* aggregates (i.e., with no more rebirth), during the whole of that intervening period, the Tathāgata teaches, expounds and instructs all that is true and not otherwise. Hence, the appellation 'Tathāgata.'

Cunda, the Tathāgata practices what he preaches, and preaches only what he himself practices. Hence, for practicing what is preached and preaching what is practiced, the appellation 'Tathāgata.'

Cunda, in the deva world with its devas, māras and Brahmās and in the human world with its samaṇas, brāhmaṇas, kings and men, the Bhagavā conquers all, is invincible and is one who indeed sees and who can exercise authority over others. Hence, the appellation 'Tathāgata'.

What Is Not Explained

189. Cunda, there is this possibility that the wandering ascetics of other faiths might say thus: 'A being exists after death. This alone is the truth; any other view is false. Friends, what do you think of this?'

Cunda, to these wandering ascetics of other faiths who say thus, you should reply: Friends, the Bhagavā does not say 'A being exists after death. This alone is the truth; any other view is false.'

Cunda, there is this possibility that the wandering ascetics of other faiths might say thus: 'A being does not exist after death. This alone is the truth; any other view is false. Friends, what do you think of this?'

Cunda, to these wandering ascetics of other faiths who say thus, you should reply: Friends, the Bhagavā does not say 'A being does not exist after death. This alone is the truth; any other view is false.'

Cunda, there is this possibility that the wandering ascetics of other faiths might say thus: 'A being both exists and does not exist after death. This alone is the truth; any other view is false. Friends, what do you think of this?'

Cunda, to these Wandering ascetics of other faiths who say thus, you should reply: Friends, the Bhagavā does not say 'A being both exists and does not exist after death. This alone is the truth; any other view is false.

Cunda, there is this possibility that the wandering ascetics of other faiths might say thus: 'A being both does not exist and does not not-exist after death. This alone is the truth; any other view is false. Friends, what do you think of this?'

Cunda, to these wandering ascetics of other faiths who say thus, you should reply: Friends, the Bhagavā does not say 'A being both does not exist and does not not-exist after death. This alone is the truth; any other view is false.'

Cunda, there is this possibility that the wandering ascetics of other faiths might say thus: 'Friends, why is it that the Samaṇa Gotama does not deal with these?'

Then Cunda, you should reply to these wandering ascetics of other faiths thus: 'Friends, the Bhagavā does not deal with them because they are not in consonance with one's benefit; they are not in consonance with the *dhamma* (i.e., *Lokuttara dhamma*); they are not even the beginning of the Noble Practice; they are not conducive to disillusionment with the five *khandhas*, nor to abandonment of attachment, nor to cessation of *dukkha*, nor to extinction of defilements, nor to attainment of *Magga*-Knowledge, nor to realization of the Four Noble Truths, nor to realization of *Nibbāna*. That is why the Bhagavā does not deal with them.

What Is Explained

190. Cunda, there is this possibility that wandering ascetics of other faiths might say thus: 'Friends, what has the Samaṇa Gotama declared?'

Cunda, you should tell these wandering ascetics of other faiths: Friends, the Bhagavā has declared, 'This is Dukkha.'

Friends, the Bhagavā has declared, 'This is the cause of Dukkha.'

Friends the Bhagavā has declared, 'This is the cessation of Dukkha.'

Friends, the Bhagavā has declared, 'This is the Path leading to the cessation of Dukkha.'

Cunda, there is this possibility that the wandering ascetics of other faiths might say thus: 'Friends, why has the Samaṇa Gotama declared them?'

Cunda, to these wandering ascetics of other faiths who say thus, you should reply: 'Friends, the Bhagavā has declared them because they are in consonance with one's benefit; they are in consonance with the *dhamma* (*i.e.*, *Lokuttara dhamma*); they are the beginning of the Noble Practice; they are conducive to disillusionment with the five *khandhas*, to abandonment of attachment, to cessation of *dukkha*, to extinction of defilements, to attainment of *Magga*-Knowledge, to realization of the Four Noble Truths, and to realization of *Nibbāna*. That is why the Bhagavā deals with them.'

Wrong Views Based on Speculations About the Past

191. Cunda, there are certain wrong views based on speculations about the Past. Concerning these wrong views, I have declared to you that which should indeed be declared to you. And that which should not declared, why should I declare them to you?

And what are these wrong views based on speculations about the Past?

Cunda, there are certain samaṇas and brāhmaṇas who hold and declare the view, '*Atta* as well as *loka* is eternal. This alone is the truth; any other view is false.'

But Cunda, there are certain samaṇas and brāhmaṇas who hold and profess the view, '*Atta* as well as *loka* is not eternal ... (p) ... *Atta* as well as *loka* is both eternal and not eternal ... (p) ... *Atta* as well as *loka* is neither eternal nor not-eternal ... (p) ... *Atta* as well as *loka* is made by oneself ... (p) ... *Atta* as well as *loka* is made by others ... (p) ... *Atta* as well as *loka* is made by oneself as well as by others ... (p) ... *Atta* as well *loka* is made neither by oneself nor by others and arises without a cause. This alone is the truth; any other view is false.'

Cunda, there are also samaṇas and brāhmaṇas who hold and profess the view, 'Pleasure and pain are eternal ... (p) ... Pleasure and pain are not eternal ... (p) ... Pleasure and pain are both eternal and not eternal ... (p) ... Pleasure and pain are neither eternal nor not-eternal ... (p) ... Pleasure and pain are made by oneself ... (p) ... Pleasure and pain are made by others ... (p) ... Pleasure and pain are made by oneself as well as by others ... (p) ... Pleasure and pain are made neither by oneself nor by others and arise without a cause. This alone is the truth; any other view is false.'

192. Cunda, there are those samaras and brāhmaṇas who hold and profess the view, '*Atta* as well as *loka* is eternal. This alone is the truth; any other view is false.' I approached and said to them, 'Friends, you maintain that *atta* as well as *loka* is eternal. Is this so, friends?' And they replied, 'This alone is the truth; any other view is false.' I do not admit this claim of theirs. And why so? It is because, Cunda, in this matter there are also certain beings with other kinds of birth-linking consciousness.

Cunda, in the matter of expounding these various views (which are mere relative terms), I see no one who is my equal, not to say of one who can surpass me. Indeed with regard to exposition of ultimate truths also, I remain supreme.

193. Cunda, there are those samaṇas and brāhmaṇas who hold and profess the view, '*Atta* as well as *loka* is not eternal ... (p) ... *Atta* as well as *loka* is both eternal and not eternal ... (p) ... *Atta* as well as *loka* is neither eternal nor not eternal ... (p) ... *Atta* as well as *loka* is made by oneself ... (p) ... *Atta* as well as *loka* is made by others ... (p) ... *Atta* as well as *loka* is made by oneself as well as by others ... (p) ... *Atta* as well as *loka* is made neither by oneself nor by others and arises without a cause ... (p) ...

'Pleasure and pain are eternal ... (p) ... Pleasure and pain are not eternal ... (p) ... Pleasure and pain are both eternal and not eternal ... (p) ... Pleasure and pain are neither eternal nor not eternal ... (p) ... Pleasure and pain are made by oneself ... (p) ... Pleasure and pain are made by others ... (p) ... Pleasure and pain are made by oneself as well as by others ... (p) ... Pleasure and pain are made neither by oneself nor by others and arise without a cause. This alone is the truth; any other view is false.' I approached and said to them "Friends, you say 'Pleasure and pain are not made by oneself nor by others and arise without a cause.' Is this so, friends?" Those samaṇas and brāhmaṇas replied, 'This alone is the truth; any other view is false.' I do not admit this claim of theirs. And why so? It is because, Cunda, in this matter there are also certain beings with other kinds of birth-linking consciousness.

Cunda, in the matter of expounding these various views (which are mere relative terms), I see no one who is my equal, not to say of one who can surpass me. Indeed with regard to exposition of ultimate truths, I remain supreme.

Cunda, these are wrong views based on speculations about the Past. Concerning these wrong views, I have declared to you that which should indeed be declared to you. And that which should not be declared to you, why should I declare them to you?

Wrong Views Based on Speculations About the Future

194. Cunda, there are certain wrong views based on speculations about the Future. Concerning these wrong views, I have declared to you that which should indeed be declared to you. And that which should not declared, why should I declare them to you?

And what are the wrong views based on speculations about the Future? Cunda, there are certain samaṇas and brāhmaṇas who hold and profess the view, '*Atta* is corporeal; it remains eternal after death. This alone is the truth; any other view is false.'

Then again, Cunda, there are other samaṇas and brāhmaṇas who hold and profess the view, '*Atta* is incorporeal ... (p) ... *Atta* is both corporeal and incorporeal ... (p) ... *Atta* is neither corporeal nor incorporeal ... (p) ... *Atta* is saññā ... (p) ... *Atta* is not saññā ... (p) ... *Atta* neither is nor is not saññā ... (p) ... *Atta* ceases, is destroyed on death; it does not exist after death. This alone is the truth; any other view is false.'

Cunda, there are those samaṇas and brāhmaṇas who hold and profess the view, '*Atta* is corporeal; it remains eternal after death. This alone is the truth; any other view is false.' I approached and said to them, 'Friends, you say that *atta* is corporeal; it remains eternal after death. Is this so, friends?' Those samaṇas and brāhmaṇas replied, 'This alone is the truth; any other view is false.' I do not admit this claim of theirs. And why so? It is because, Cunda, in this matter, there are also certain beings with other kinds of birth-linking consciousness.

Cunda, in the matter of expounding these various views (which are mere relative terms), I see no one who is my equal, not to say of one who can surpass me. Indeed with regard to exposition of ultimate truths also, I remain supreme.

195. Cunda, there are those samaṇas and brāhmaṇas who hold and profess these views, '*Atta* is not corporeal ... (p) ... *Atta* is both corporeal and incorporeal ... (p) ... *Atta* is neither corporeal nor incorporeal ... (p) ... *Atta* is saññā ... (p) ... *Atta* is not saññā ... (p) ... *Atta* neither is nor is not saññā. *Atta* ceases, is destroyed on death; it does not exist after death. This alone is the truth; any other view is false.' I approached and said to them, 'Friends, you say that *atta* ceases, is destroyed on death; it does not exist after death. Is this so, friends?' Those samaṇas and brāhmaṇas replied, 'This alone is the truth; any other view is false.' I do not admit this claim of theirs. And why so? It is because, Cunda, in this matter, there are also certain beings with other kinds of birth-linking consciousness.

Cunda, in the matter of expounding these various views (which are mere relative terms), I see no one who is my equal, not to say of one who can surpass me. Indeed with regard to exposition of ultimate truths also, I remain supreme.

Cunda, these wrong views are based on speculations about the Future. Concerning these wrong views, I have declared to you that which should be declared to you. And that which should not be declared to you, why should I declare them to you?

196. Cunda, in order to reject and overcome these wrong views based on speculations about the Past and speculations about the Future, I have taught and laid down these Four Methods of Steadfast Mindfulness.[14] And what are these Four?

Cunda, the bhikkhu (i.e., the disciple) following the practice of my Teaching keeps his mind steadfastly on the body (*kāya*) with diligence, comprehension and mindfulness, (and perceives its impermanent, insecure, soulless, and unpleasant nature), thus keeping away covetousness and distress (which will appear if he is not mindful of the five *khandhas*).

The bhikkhu keeps his mind steadfastly on sensation (*vedanā*) (and perceives its impermanent, insecure, and soulless nature) ... (p) ...

The bhikkhu concentrates steadfastly on the mind (*citta*) (and perceives its impermanent, insecure, and soulless nature) ... (p) ...

The bhikkhu keeps his mind steadfastly on the *dhamma* (and perceives its impermanent, insecure, and soulless nature) thus keeping away covetousness and distress (which will appear if he is not mindful of the five *khandhas*).

Cunda, in this manner I have taught and laid down these Four Methods of Steadfast Mindfulness in order to reject and overcome the wrong views based on speculations about the Past and speculations about the Future.

197. At that time, the Venerable Upavāṇa was standing behind the Bhagavā, fanning him. And he addressed the Bhagavā in these words: 'Marvellous it is, Venerable Sir! Wonderful it is, Venerable Sir! This discourse is indeed delectable; this discourse is indeed most delightful. By what name, Venerable Sir, should this discourse be known?'

Upavāṇa, since this discourse arouses such pious devotion and delight, let it be known as the 'Delectable Discourse'. So said the Bhagavā and the Venerable Upavāṇa, glad at heart, rejoiced at the words of the Bhagavā.

End of Pāsādika Sutta, the sixth sutta from division three (*Pāthika Vagga*)

14. See the translation of the Mahāsatipaṭṭhāna Sutta in this collection.

Namo tassa bhagavato arahato sammāsambuddhassa

SIṄGĀLA SUTTA

VIII. SIṄGĀLA SUTTA

(Discourse to Siṅgāla)

242. Thus have I heard:

At one time the Bhagavā was staying near Rājagaha in (the monastery of) the Bamboo Grove, the sanctuary where black squirrels were fed. Now at that time, Siṅgālaka (*i.e.*, the young Siṅgāla), the son of a householder, rising early in the morning, and having gone out from Rājagaha, in wet clothes and with wet hair, worshipped with palms together the various directions such, as the East, the South, the West, the North, the Nadir and the Zenith.

243. Then the Bhagavā, having rearranged his robes in the morning, took his alms-bowl and great robe and entered Rājagaha on his alms round. On seeing Siṅgālaka, the son of a householder, who had risen early in the morning and had come out from Rājagaha in wet clothes and with wet hair, worshipping with palms together the various directions such as the East, the South, the West, the North, the Nadir and the Zenith, the Bhagavā spoke to him thus:

> Young householder, rising early in the morning having come out from Rājagaha, in wet clothes and with wet hair, wherefore do you worship with palms together the various directions such as the East the South, the West, the North, the Nadir and the Zenith?

"Venerable Sir, my father said to me on his death-bed, 'My dear son, worship the directions! Venerable Sir, respecting, revering, reverencing and honouring my father's words, I rise early in the morning, go out from Rājagaha in wet clothes and with wet hair, worship with palms together the various directions such as the East, the South, the West, the North, the Nadir and the Zenith."

THE SIX DIRECTIONS

244. Young householder, in the Ariyan Teaching the six directions are not to be worshipped in this manner.

"How then Venerable Sir, are the six directions to be worshipped in the Ariyan Teaching? May it please the Bhagavā to teach me the six directions which are to be worshipped in the Ariyan Teaching."

In that case, young householder, listen and bear it well in mind. I shall teach you.

"Very well, Venerable Sir, "replied Siṅgālaka, the householder's son. And the Bhagavā spoke as follows:

> Young householder, the noble disciple refrains from four acts of defilement; he does no evil which is instigated by four factors; and he does not indulge in six practices causing dissipation of wealth. Thus avoiding these fourteen evil things, he covers the six directions and follows the path for success in both the worlds. He has accomplished his tasks for this world as well as for the next. After death and dissolution of the body, he is reborn in a happy deva world.

The Four Acts of Defilement

245. And what are the four acts of defilement that the noble disciple abstains from?

The destruction of life, young householder is an act of defilement; stealing is an act of defilement; sexual misconduct is an act of defilement; telling lies is an act of defilement. These are the four evil acts of defilement which the noble disciple abstains from.

After the Bhagavā had spoken these words, he uttered these verses:

> Young householder, killing, stealing, telling lies and committing adultery are called the four evil acts of defilement. The wise never praise them.

Four Factors Instigating Evil Acts

246. What are the four factors by which the noble disciple is not led astray to commit evil acts? Instigated by partiality, evil is committed; instigated by anger, evil is committed; instigated by ignorance (of what is right or wrong), evil is committed; and instigated by fear, evil is committed. But, young householder, as the noble disciple is not led astray by these four factors, namely, partiality, anger, ignorance and fear, he does not commit evil.

After the Bhagavā had spoken these words, he uttered these verses:

> Young householder, whosoever commits an evil act out of partiality, anger, fear or ignorance, his fame and following will fade away just like the moon in the waning half of the month; whosoever does not commit evil out of partiality, anger, fear or ignorance, his fame and following will grow day by day even as the moon in the waxing half of the month.

Six Practices Causing Dissipation of Wealth

247. And what are the six practices causing dissipation of wealth which the noble disciple does not indulge in?

Young householder, indulgence in intoxicants which cause inebriety and negligence leads to dissipation of wealth; sauntering in streets at unseemly hours leads to dissipation of wealth; frequenting shows and entertainments leads to dissipation of wealth; addiction to gambling which causes negligence leads to dissipation of wealth; associating with bad companions leads to dissipation of wealth; habitual idleness leads to dissipation of wealth.

Six Evil Consequences of Indulgence in Intoxicants

248. Young householder, there are these six evil consequences of indulgence in intoxicants which cause inebriety and negligence: actual loss of wealth in this very life; liability to be involved in quarrels; susceptibility to illness and disease; loss of good name and reputation; indecent exposure of body; impairment of intelligence. Young householder, these are the six evil consequences of indulgence in intoxicants which cause inebriety and negligence.

Six Evil Consequences of Sauntering in Streets at Unseemly Hours

249. Young householder, there are these six evil consequences of a person sauntering in streets at unseemly hours: he himself becomes unprotected and unguarded; his wife and children become unprotected and unguarded; his property becomes unprotected and unguarded; he becomes suspected of committing crimes and evil deeds; he becomes subjected to false accusations; he will have to face many troubles. Young householder, these are the six evil consequences of sauntering in streets at unseemly hours.

Six Evil Consequences of Frequenting Shows and Entertainments

250. Young householder, there are these six evil consequences of a person frequenting shows and entertainments: "Where is the dancing? Where is the singing? Where is the music? Where is the recitation? Where is the playing of cymbals? Where is the beating of drums?" He makes

these enquiries and goes there (thereby neglecting his responsibilities). Young householder, these are the six evil consequences of frequenting shows and entertainments.

Six Evil Consequences of Gambling

251. Young householder, there are these six evil consequences of a person being addicted to gambling which causes negligence: as a winner he begets enmity; as a loser he grieves over his loss; there is actual loss of wealth in this very life; his word is not relied upon in a court of law; he is despised by his friends and companions; he is not sought after as a partner in marriage because people say, 'He is a gambler, he cannot support a wife'. Young householder, these are the six evil consequences of gambling which causes negligence.

Six Evil Consequences of Associating with Bad Companions

252. Young householder, there are these six evil consequences of a person associating with bad companions; there are those who gamble, those who are libertines, those who are drunkards, those who are swindlers, those who are cheats, and those who are aggressive and violent. Only these people form his circle of friends and companions. (He therefore suffers, in this life and in the next, the evil consequences of associating with them.) Young householder, these are the six evil consequences of associating with bad companions.

Six Evil Consequences of Habitual Idleness

253. Young householder, there are these six evil consequences of a person indulging in habitual idleness: he does no work, saying it is too cold; he does no work, saying it is too hot; he does no work, saying it is too late in the evening; he does no work, saying it is too early in the morning; he does no work, saying he is too hungry; he does no work, saying he is too full. Thus making such lame excuses, he leaves many duties undone, not acquiring new wealth, but wasting away such wealth as he has already accumulated. Young householder, these are the six evil consequences of habitual idleness.

After the Bhagavā had spoken these words, he uttered these verses:

There are drinking companions; there are those who are friends only in one's presence. (These are not true friends.) There is one who proves to be a comrade in times of crisis. This is indeed a true friend.

Sleeping till the sun is high; committing adultery; begetting enmity; engaging in unbeneficial activities; keeping evil companions and being extremely stingy. These are the six causes bringing ruin to a man.

He who has bad friends and evil companions who is given to bad ways and is moving in bad circles is heading for ruin both in this world and the next.

Playing dice, womanizing, drinking, dancing and singing; sleeping during daytime; sauntering at unseemly hours: (evil companions and stinginess); these six causes bring ruin to a man.

Playing dice: indulging in drinking; misbehaving with women who are dear as life to other men, with women who are sought after by the base and are shunned by the wise; the fame and following of such people fade away just like the moon in the waning half of the month.

The destitute drunkard, feeling thirsty, frequents liquor shops. As a stone sinks in water, he becomes immersed in debt to be soon disowned and rejected by his relatives.

He who habitually sleeps in the day, is not wakeful at night,[15] is always drunk, and is debauched cannot manage a household.

Chances and opportunities pass by the young man who says it is too hot, too cold, too late and leaves things undone.

But for him who does not consider cold or heat any more than a blade of grass and who dutifully attends to the affairs of men, happiness and prosperity do not decline.

False Friend

254. Young householder, these four should be regarded as false friends pretending to be true friends: a person who only takes from one (and does not give in return); a person who only renders lip-service by making empty promises; a person who flatters; and a person who is an associate in activities that lead to loss of wealth.

255. Young householder, a person who only takes from one should be known as a false friend pretending to be a true friend, by four characteristics: he only takes from one (and does not give in return); he wants much in return for giving only a little; he renders service only when he gets into trouble; he attends on one only for his own advantage.

---

15. **Is not wakeful** at night: this follows the Commentary which has '*rattinuṭṭhāna dessinā*', lit., 'is not in the habit of rising at night.' The Pāḷi Text has '*rattimuṭṭhāna dessinā*' which would mean 'dislikes rising at night.'

Young householder, a person who only takes from one (and does not give in return) should be known as a false friend pretending to be a true friend, by these four characteristics.

256. Young householder, a person who only renders lip-service by making empty promises should be known as a false friend pretending to be a true friend, by four characteristics: he speaks about what he could have done for one; he speaks about what he would do in the future for one; he tries to please one with empty promises; and when occasion actually arises to render his assistance, be expresses his inability to do so.

Young householder, a person who only renders lip-service by making empty promises should be known as a false friend pretending to be a true friend, by these four characteristics.

257. Young householder, a person who flatters should be known as a false friend pretending to be a true friend, by four characteristics: he approves of the evil actions of his friend; he approves also of the good actions of his friend; he praises him in his presence; and he speaks ill of him in his absence.

Young householder, a person who flatters should be known as a false friend pretending to be a true friend, by these four characteristics.

258. Young householder, a person who is an associate in activities that lead to loss of wealth should be known as a false friend pretending to be a true friend, by four characteristics: he is a companion when indulging in intoxicants that cause inebriety and negligence; he is a companion when sauntering in streets at unseemly hours; he is a companion when frequenting shows and entertainments; and he is a companion when indulging in gambling which causes negligence.

Young householder, a person who is an associate in activities that lead to loss of wealth should be known as a false friend pretending to be a true friend, by these four characteristics.

259. Thus spoke the Bhagavā. And having spoken these words, he uttered these verses:

The friend who only takes, the friend who only renders lip service, the friend who flatters, and the friend who brings about loss of wealth, — the wise should know these four as false friends and avoid them from a distance as from a path of danger.

TRUE FRIEND

260. Young householder, these four should be regarded as true-hearted friends: he who is helpful; he who is the same in prosperity

and adversity; he who gives good counsel; and he who understands and sympathizes.

261. Young householder, he who is helpful should be known as a true-hearted friend, by four characteristics: he protects the inebriated friend; he protects the property of the inebriated friend; he is a refuge for the friend who is in trouble; and when unforeseen needs arise, he comes to the aid of the friend with twice the required assistance.

Young householder, he who is helpful should be known as a true-hearted friend, by these four characteristics.

262. Young householder, he who is the same in prosperity and adversity should be known as a true-hearted friend, by four characteristics: he confides his secrets in his friend; he keeps the secrets of his friend; he does not forsake his friend when in trouble; he sacrifices even his life for the sake of his friend.

Young householder, he who is the same in prosperity and adversity should be known as a true-hearted friend, by these four characteristics.

263. Young householder, he who gives good counsel should be known as a true-hearted friend, by four characteristics: he restrains his friend from doing evil; he encourages his friend to do good; he tells him about profound matters which his friend has not heard before; and he shows his friend the way to the realm of the devas.

Young householder, he who gives good counsel should be known as a true-hearted friend, by these four characteristics.

264. Young householder, he who understands and sympathizes should be known as a true-hearted friend, by four characteristics: he does not rejoice in the misfortunes of his friend; he rejoices over his friend's prosperity; he restrains others from speaking ill of his friend; and he commends those who speak well of his friend.

Young householder, he who understands and sympathizes should be known as a true-hearted friend, by these four characteristics.

265. Thus spoke the Bhagavā. And having spoken these words, he uttered these verses:

The friend who is helpful, the friend who is the same in prosperity and adversity, the friend who gives good counsel, and the friend who understands and sympathizes, — the wise should know these four as true-hearted friends and cherish them with devotion as a mother cherishes the child of her own bosom.

The wise man of virtue shines bright like a blazing fire. The riches of a person who acquires his wealth in harmless ways like a bee which gathers honey without damaging the flowers grow as an ant hill grows.

Having acquired wealth in this manner, the young man able to set up a household should divide his wealth into four portions; in this manner he can make friends:

He should spend and enjoy one portion; he should use two portions to run his business; and the fourth should be reserved for use in emergencies.

Covering the Six Directions

266. Young householder, how does the noble disciple cover the six directions? Young householder, these six directions should be known thus: the parents should be looked upon as the East, the teachers as the South, wife (and children) as the West, friends and associates as the North, servants and employees as the Nadir and samaṇas and brāhmaṇas as the Zenith.

267. Young householder, in five ways should a son minister to the parents as the Eastern quarter thus: My parents have supported me I shall support them in turn; I shall manage affairs on their behalf; I shall maintain the honour and tradition of the family; I shall make myself worthy of the inheritance; and furthermore, I shall offer alms on behalf of the departed parents.

Young householder, the parents, attended upon in these five ways as the Eastern quarter by their children, look after the children in five ways: they restrain them from evil, they encourage them to do good, they give them education and professional training, they arrange suitable marriages for the children, and hand over property as inheritance to them at the proper time.

Young householder, in these five ways the children attend upon their parents and the parents look after their children in these five ways. It is thus that the Eastern quarter is covered and made safe and secure.

268. Young householder, in five ways should a pupil minister to a teacher as the Southern quarter: by rising from the seat to greet and salute the teacher; by attending and waiting upon the teacher; by obeying the words of the teacher; by offering personal service to the teacher and by learning and receiving the teacher's instructions with respectful attention.

Young householder, the teacher, attended upon in these five ways as the Southern quarter by the pupil, looks after the pupil in five ways: he instructs the pupil well in what should be instructed; he teaches well what should be taught; he trains the pupil in all the arts and sciences; he entrusts the pupil to his friends and associates, and provides for protection in every quarter.

Young householder, in these five ways the pupil attends upon his teacher as the Southern quarter and the teacher looks after the pupil in these five ways. It is thus that the Southern quarter is covered and made safe and secure.

269. Young householder, in five ways should a husband minister to a wife as the Western quarter: by being courteous to her and addressing her in endearing terms; by showing respect to her and not disparaging her; by being faithful to her; by giving her control and authority over domestic matters; by providing her with clothing and ornaments.

Young householder, the wife, looked after in these five ways as the Western quarter by the husband, attends upon the husband in five ways: she discharges well her various duties; she is hospitable and generous to kith and kin from both sides of the family; she is faithful to her husband; she manages well what he earns and brings to her; she is skilled and industrious in performing all her tasks.

Young householder, in these five ways the husband looks after his wife as the Western quarter and the wife also attends upon her husband in these five ways. It is thus that the Western quarter is covered and made safe and secure.

270. Young householder, in five ways should a man of good family minister to his friends and associates as the Northern quarter: by giving generously; by being pleasant and courteous in speech; by being helpful; by treating them as he treats himself; by being true to his words and promises.

Young householder, the friends and associates, looked after in these five ways as the Northern quarter by a man of good family, look after him (in return) in five ways: they protect the inebriated friend; they guard over his property when he is inebriated; they become a refuge when he is in trouble; they do not forsake him in his troubles; they even help his descendants.

Young householder, in these five ways a man of good family looks after his friends and associates as the Northern quarter, and the friends and associates also look after him in these five ways. It is thus that the Northern quarter is covered and made safe and secure.

271. Young householder, in five ways should a master minister to his servants and employees as the Nadir: by assigning the work in accordance with their ability and physical strength; by giving them food and remuneration; by looking after them in sickness; by sharing with them choice food; by granting them leave at times.

Young householder, the servants and employees, ministered to as the Nadir by their master in these five ways, attend upon him in five ways: they rise before him; they go to sleep after him; they take only what is given; they perform their duties well; they uphold his good name and fame.

Young householder, in these five ways the master looks after his servants and employees as the Nadir, and the servants and employees in return also attend upon their master in these five ways. It is thus that the Nadir is covered and made safe and secure.

272. Young householder, in five ways should a man of good family minister to the samaṇas and brāhmaṇas as the Zenith: by deeds of loving kindness; by words of loving kindness; by thoughts of loving kindness; by keeping the house open to them; by supplying them with material needs (such as alms-food).

Young householder, the samaṇas and brāhmaṇas, ministered to in these five ways as the Zenith by a man of good family, bring benefit to him in six ways: they restrain him from evil; they exhort him to do good; they protect him with loving kindness; they teach him (the profound matters) that he has not heard before; they explain and make clear to him (the profound matters) which he has heard before; they show him the path to the realm of the devas.

Young householder, in these five ways a man of good family ministers to the samaṇas and the brāhmaṇas as the Zenith and the samaṇas and the brāhmaṇas also bring benefit to him in these six ways. It is thus that the Zenith is covered and made safe and secure.

273. Thus spoke the Bhagavā. And having spoken these words, he uttered these verses:

The mother and the father are the East; the teachers are the South; wife and children are the West; friends and associates are the North.

Servants and employees are the Nadir; samaṇas and brāhmaṇas are the Zenith; the man of good family who is the head of a household should worship these six directions.

Whoever is skilled and wise (in worshipping these six directions), and is full of moral virtues, gentle and keen-witted, meek and humble, gains fame and followers.

Whoever is energetic and not indolent, unshaken in adversity, constantly employed in making a livelihood, endowed with, resourceful intelligence gains fame and followers.

Whoever is benevolent, seeks and makes good friends, understands what is spoken (by a benefactor), is not stingy or jealous, leads and guides by giving helpful counsel and reasoned advice, gains fame and followers.

There are these benevolent practices, namely: generosity and charitableness, pleasant speech, helpfulness to others, impartial treatment to all as to oneself as the case demands; in this world, these four benevolent practices are like the lynchpin of a moving carriage.

Were these benevolent practices non-existent (in the world), the mother would not receive honour and respect from her children; the father would not receive honour and respect from his children.

Because the wise observe these four benevolent practices in every way, they reach eminence, and gain praise and admiration.

274. When the Bhagavā had spoken thus, Siṅgāla, the young householder, said as follows:

"Venerable Sir, excellent (is the dhamma)! Excellent (is the dhamma)! Venerable Sir, it is as if that which is overturned is set right, or that which has been hidden is revealed, as if someone were pointing out the road to one who has gone astray, or holding a lamp amidst the darkness so that 'those who have eyes may see', even so has the Bhagavā shown the Dhamma in various ways.

"Venerable Sir, I take refuge in the Buddha, I take refuge in the Dhamma, I take refuge in the Saṅgha. May it please the Bhagavā to receive me as a lay disciple from this very day to the end of life."

End of Siṅgāla Sutta, the eighth sutta from division three (*Pāthika Vagga*)

Appendices

APPENDIX A 1

On Four Grounds[1]

There are four different groups of samaṇas and brāhmaṇas. Each group formulates its own view of the eternalism of *atta* as well as *loka.*

In the first group, there are samaṇas and brāhmaṇas whose range of recollection, by means of *pubbenivāsānussati ñāṇa*, does not go beyond several hundred thousand existences, in a cycle of dissolution.

In the second group, there are samaras and brāhmaṇas whose range of recollection, by means of *pubbenivāsānussati ñāṇa*, does not go beyond several million existences, in ten cycles of dissolution.

In the third group, there are samaṇas and brāhmaṇas whose range of recollection, by means of *pubbenivāsānussati ñāṇa*, does not go beyond several million existences, in forty cycles of dissolution.

In the fourth group, there are samaṇas and brāhmaṇas who rely on observation and speculation, since they do not have *pubbenivāsānussati ñāṇa.*

The views of the above four groups are taken as the four grounds.

The duration of a cycle of dissolution should also be explained. Once a bhikkhu requested the Buddha to explain to him how long was the duration of a world. The Buddha replied that it would not be possible to explain the duration of a world in terms of years. Again the bhikkhu asked if it would not be possible to explain it by means of an example.

Then the Buddha explained how long the duration of a world was by means of an example. Suppose, there was, for example, a huge stone, which was a yojana long, a yojana wide and a yojana high (a yojana-about seven miles). If a person rubbed it gently with a piece of delicate velvet, once in a hundred years, the huge stone would, at long last, diminish and disappear as a result of rubbing. However, the world would not yet have come to an end by that time.

The first kind of dissolution takes place as the result of the appearance of seven suns in the sky. Then huge fires take place in fourteen out of thirty-one *bhūmis* in a *cakkavāḷa* (a world system). The fourteen bhūmis are is follows: (1) Three first *jhāna Brahmā bhūmis*; (2) Six *deva bhūmis*, one *manussa bhūmi*, four *apāya bhūmis*. The fire rages so long as there is even a tiny scrap to burn.

---

1. Paragraph 30, Brāhmajāla Sutta.

The second kind of dissolution takes place as the result of heavy downpour of rain. The rain water dissolves everything it touches. The downpour takes place in the three second *jhāna Brahmā bhūmis* in addition to the fourteen *bhūmis* mentioned in the first kind of dissolution. It will continue so long as there is even a tiny scrap to dissolve.

The third kind of dissolution takes place as the Result of a violent storm which can blow anything out of existence. The storm takes place in the three third *jhāna Brahmā bhūmis*, in addition to the seventeen *bhūmis* mentioned in the second kind of dissolution. The storm rages so long as there is even a tiny scrap to be blown out of existence.

The beings of the *bhūmis* that are destroyed are reborn in the *bhūmis* which are not destroyed, respectively in accordance with their *jhāna* at the time of death.

APPENDIX A 2

Power of Recollection[2]

(Pubbenivāsānussati ñāṇa)

1. Power of recollection: Ability to recollect many past existences through utmost mental concentration.

Ability to recollect many past existences is of two kinds: (i) by tracing the details of successive past lives, going back from the immediate past life to innumerable existences beyond it; (ii) by recollecting only the moments of death and the preceding moments of birth of successive existences without going through the details of the intervening period (until the particular existence which needs to be recollected is reached). This power is achieved through utmost mental concentration (*ceto samādhi*) by dint of ardent, steadfast, persevering exertion, mindfulness and right attentiveness.

Ardent exertion means strenuous effort to rid oneself of mental defilements; *steadfast exertion* means continuing on with strenuous effort; *persevering exertion* means persevering with strenuous effort.

While striving thus, one has to maintain constant mindfulness so as not to lose sight of the original object of meditation. At the same time, through right attentiveness (*Sammā manasikāra*), one keeps to the correct method of meditation.

These three kinds of exertion, together with constant mindfulness and right attentiveness, will result first in access-concentration of the

2. Paragraph 31, Brāhmajāia Sutta.

first *jhāna*; and then in advancement from the first *jhāna* to the fourth *jhāna*; and then, after repeated practice of entering into and arising from each *jhāna*, in achievement of utmost mental concentration which will lead to the power of recollecting many past existences.

Utmost mental concentration means the concentrated mind has become purified, pellucid, unblemished, undefiled, malleable, pliable, firm and imperturbable to the extent that the yogi can gain the power of recollecting past existences.

2. Who gains the power of recollection?

By going through the above process resulting in utmost mental concentration, the following persons acquire the power of recollection:

(1) Recluses and ascetics outside a Buddha's Teaching
(2) Ordinary disciples of a Buddha
(3) The Great Disciples
(4) The Chief Disciples
(5) Paccekabuddhas and
(6) The Supremely Enlightened Buddhas

The recluses and ascetics (such as samaras and brāhmaṇas mentioned in this Sutta) can recollect up to only forty kappas, and not any further, because their power of Insight is weak; they have no discriminative knowledge of *nāma* and *rūpa*. The ordinary disciples can recollect up to one hundred or one thousand kappas; the eighty great disciples up to one hundred thousand kappas; the chief disciples up to one *asaṅkhyeyya* and one hundred thousand kappas; the Paccekabuddhas up to two *asaṅkhyeyya* and one hundred thousand kappas; the Supremely Enlightened Buddhas have no limits to their power of recollection. The disciples, great disciples, chief disciples and Paccekabuddhas differ in their power of recollection because of the differences in the *pāramīs* they have fulfilled.

3. Differences in power and method of recollection.

The recluses and ascetics of other beliefs recollect past existences by tracing each successive past existence one after another. They have no power to recollect by the method of recalling the moment of death in a particular existence and jumping back to the birth moment of that particular existence without going through the details between these two moments. Just like a blind man who has to depend on a walking stick, they cannot leave out tracing past existences in succession. They cannot jump over the intervening period between the death moment and the birth moment of an existence.

The ordinary disciples and the great disciples recollect by means of both these methods of recollecting. The two chief disciples and Paccekabuddhas have no need to rely upon recollecting successive existences. They recollect by recalling only the death moments and the birth moments of successive existences.

The Supremely Enlightened Buddhas have no limits at all on their power of recollection, both with regard to the length of time or method of recollecting. They can focus exactly on any moment of any existence and see what happened then and there.

The power of recollection of an ascetic may be likened to the light produced by a fire-fly; that of the disciples to the light produced by an oil lamp; that of the great disciples to a beacon light; that of the chief disciples to the morning star; that of Paccekabuddhas to moonlight and the power of recollection of a Buddha to sunlight.

APPENDIX A 3

Note on "In the Wrong Way"[3]

He does not view the eightfold Ariya Path with *taṇhā, māna, diṭṭhi*. If he finds pleasure in the discovery of the path and is, therefore, attached to it, it is called viewing the path with *taṇhā*. *Taṇhā* means hunger for six objects, namely, *rūpa* (form), *sadda* (sound), *gandha* (odour), *rasa* (taste), *phoṭṭhabba* (tangible thing), *dhamma* (idea), that will give one *vedayita sukha* (pleasurable feelings).

Taṇhā, in the present context, is *dhamma taṇhā*, because it is the hunger for ideas that gives samaṇas and brāhmaṇas pleasurable feelings.

Taṇhā causes *upādāna*, which means strong steadfast attachment to objects that give one pleasurable feelings.

If he thinks that only he can discover the path and is, therefore, proud of it, it is called viewing the path with *māna*. If he believes that it is "I", who discover the path, it is called viewing the path with *diṭṭhi*.

APPENDIX A 4

Note on "Feeling (Vedanā)"[4]

The samaṇas and brāhmaṇas view their theories of eternalism with *taṇhā, māna, diṭṭhi*. Therefore, they find pleasure in their theories and as a result, are deeply attached to them. This attachment to pleasurable

3. Paragraph 36, Brāhmajāla Sutta.
4. Paragraph 36, Brāhmajāla Sutta.

feeling is dangerous. It will lead one to endless rebirths, involving rebirths in nether regions, where mental and bodily suffering is intense. Even when one does not have rebirths in these nether regions, he will have old age, disease, death, separation, etc., whenever he has rebirths.

Cause of Feeling

Ignorance of the Four Ariya Truths is the cause of rebirth. Rebirth is the cause of contact between sense organ, object and mind. Contact is the cause of feeling.

Cause of Extinction

When contact becomes extinct, feeling becomes extinct. When rebirth becomes extinct, contact becomes extinct. When ignorance becomes extinct, rebirth becomes extinct.

Fault of Vedanā

Vedanā causes *taṇhā*. *Taṇhā* causes *upādāna*. *Upādāna* causes *bhavo*. The real meaning of *bhava* is rebirth. However, in the theory of cause and effect, *bhava* is used figuratively and is defined as *kamma* that cause rebirth. When there are rebirths, there will naturally be old age, disease, death, separation, mental as well as bodily pain, etc. (Deeds which one does, words which one speaks, thoughts which one conceives, are called *kammas*.)

A Very Important Paragraph

This, the third sub-paragraph of paragraph 36, is a very important paragraph. The readers should have a very clear understanding of the idea that underlies this paragraph. Otherwise, they will definitely miss the importance of this paragraph.

The Underlying Idea

According to Buddhism, the eyes, the form and the mind that sees the form are *dukkha*. Similarly, the ears, the sound and the mind that hears the sound; the nose, the odour and the mind that smells the odour; the tongue, the taste and the mind that tastes the taste; the body, the tangible object and mind that feels the touch; the *mano-dvāra* that receives the idea, the idea and the *manodvārāvajjana* that is mindful of the idea – all of them are *dukkha* (mental and bodily suffering), because all of them are in a flux, impermanent, continuously deteriorating.

Many *puthujjana* Buddhists (those who have not yet achieved any of the *maggas*), accept the above conception, only because it is the teaching of the Buddha. They cannot be said to believe the above teaching genuinely. From the time they get up from bed in the morning, till the time they go to bed at night, they are striving bodily, verbally, mentally, to get all or some of the following *sukha-vedanās* (feelings that give pleasures).

1. To see forms that will give them pleasures of the eyes,
2. To hear sounds that will give them pleasures of the ears,
3. To smell odours that will give them pleasures of the nose,
4. To taste tastes that will give them pleasures of the tongue,
5. To feel the touches that will give them pleasures of the body,
6. To receive the ideas that will give them pleasures of the mind.

Some Ariyas are also Struggling

Even some Ariyas, (those who have achieved *Maggas*) such as *Sotāpannas* and *Sakadāgāmis*, who have uprooted two out of seven seeds of major defilements, namely, false views of mind and body, and doubts, will still be striving to achieve these pleasurable feelings, though their efforts will be in a lesser degree.

Anāgāmīs are the *Ariyas* who are next to the *Arahats*. They have uprooted four out of seven seeds of major defilements, namely, false views, doubts, attachment to sensual pleasures, anger. Since attachment to sensual pleasures has been uprooted, they have absolutely no attachment to the pleasures of the eyes, ears, nose, tongue, body. But these *anāgāmīs* are very much attached to the sixth *sukha-vedanā*, (feelings of pleasure), namely, *mano-samphassajā sukha-vedanā*, (the pleasures of the mind) which can be achieved by means of *jhānas*.

One becomes free from attachments to these *sukha-vedanās*, only when one becomes an *Arahat*, who has uprooted all of the seven anusayas (seeds of strong defilements).

Significance of Vedanā

If one studies Abhidhamma, one will come across such words as *citta*, *cetasika*, *rūpa* and *Nibbāna*. *Cetasika* means a concomitant of mind. There are altogether fifty-two *cetasikas*. *Vedanā* (feeling) and *saññā* (perception) are two of these fifty-two mental concomitants. The Buddha singled out only these two *cetasikas* and mentioned them as two of the five *Khandhas*. They are given such significance because the first gives rise to *taṇhā* (hunger for pleasures) and the other gives rise to *diṭṭhi* (belief in soul), which are the causes of endless rebirths.

Liberation from Vedanā

The Ariya Path to liberation from attachment to *vedanā* has three major constituents.

The first constituent of the Ariya Path is *Sīla*. There are two kinds of *Sīla*, namely, *Sīla* for the laymen and *Sīla* for bhikkhus. *Sīla* requires one to refrain from doing and saying what is not right.

The second constituent is *Samādhi* (mental concentration). The Buddha laid down forty methods for acquiring mental concentration. These are called forty *bhāvanās*.

The third constituent is *Paññā*. It means the four *Maggas*. They will give one liberation from attachment to *vedanā*. One can achieve these four *Maggas* by means of a method which requires him to maintain steadfast mindfulness on his body as well as bodily movement, on feelings arising from mental as well as bodily contacts, on mind as well as any mental states which arise in the mind, and on all ideas. This method is called Satipaṭṭhāna method.

The Discoverer of the Ariya Path

The Buddha had, by himself, discovered the Ariya Path and liberated himself from attachment to *vedanā*. The Paccekabuddha was also a Buddha, because he also had, by himself, discovered the Ariya Path and liberated himself from attachment to *vedanā*. However, he did not achieve *sabbaññuta ñāṇa*. This deficiency made him unable to proclaim the truth. Therefore he was known as Paccekabuddha.

Sabbaññuta ñāṇa enabled the Buddha to know all there was to know about the four realities in the ultimate sense, namely, *citta* (mind), *cetasikas* (mental concomitants), *rūpa* (matter), *Nibbāna* (the perfect peace of extinction of *taṇhā*, craving). *Sabbaññuta ñāṇa* also gave the Buddha an extraordinary mastery over language. The combination of the supreme knowledge of *citta*, *cetasikas*, *rūpa*, *Nibbāna*, with the extraordinary mastery over language, enabled the Buddha to use various methods in his discourses for the liberation of human beings, devas and brahmās from attachment to *vedanā*.

APPENDIX A 5

The Thirty-One Planes of Existence (Bhūmi)[5]

'*Bhūmi*' in Paḷi means 'Plane of Existence'. In the Buddhist concept of 'existence' (*bhava*) there are thirty-one planes (*bhūmis*) of existence.

5. Paragraph 39, Brāhmajāla Sutta.

These thirty-one planes of existence are divided into three categories, viz, (1) (*kāma bhūmi*), sensual plane of existence dominated by pleasures of the senses (this comprises also corporeal existence); (2) (*rūpa bhūmi*), corporeal plane of existence with fine materially; and (3) (*arūpa bhūmi*), non-corporeal plane of existence i.e., formless, non-material existence.

(1) *Kāma bhūmi* comprises the four *apāya bhūmis*, the one *manussa bhūmi*, and the six *deva bhūmis*. The four *apāya bhūmis* are (i) *niraya* (the realm of continuous intense suffering), (ii) *tiracchāna* (the realm of animals), (iii) *peta* (the realm of miserable and ever hungry beings), and (iv) *asura* (the realm of miserable and frightened beings). The *manussa bhūmi* is the plane of human beings. The six *deva bhūmis are* (i) *Cātumahārājika* (the abode of the Four Guardian Devas), (ii) *Tāvatiṃsa* (the abode of the Thirty-three Devas), (iii) *Yāmā* (the abode of misery-freed beings), (iv) *Tusita* (the abode of happy dwellers), (v) *Nimmanarati* (the abode of those who rejoice in their own creations), and (vi) *Paranimmitavasavatti* (the abode of those who indulge in pleasures created to their liking by others). Of these eleven *kāma bhūmis*, the four *apāya bhūmis* are known as unfortunate destinations (*duggati*), and the remaining seven (i.e., *manussa bhūmi* and the six *deva bhūmis*) are known as fortunate destinations (*sugati*).

Above the eleven *kāma bhūmis* are the twenty *Brahmā bhūmis*. Of these, sixteen are corporeal *Brahmā bhūmis* of fine materiality, of which fifteen are the realms of Brahmās with both mind and body, and one is the realm of Brahmās with only body and no Consciousness. The other four are non-corporeal *Brahmā bhūmis*. The sixteen Corporeal *Brahmā bhūmis* are: three first-*jhāna bhūmis*, namely, bhūmis of *Brahmāpārisajjā*, (Attendents of the Great Brahmās), *Brahmapurohitā*, (Counsellors of the Great Brahmās), and *Mahābrahmā*, (Great Brahmās); three second-*jhāna bhūmis*, namely, *bhūmis* of *Parittābhā* (Brahmās of lesser radiance), *Appamāṇabhā* (Brahmās of limitless radiance), *Abhassara* (Brahmās of flashing radiance): three third-*jhāna bhūmis*, namely, *bhūmis* of *Parittasubhā* (Brahmās of lesser massive radiance), *Appamāṇasubhā* (Brahmās of limitless massive radiance), *Subhakiṇhā* (Brahmās of multi-hued glittering radiance); seven fourth-*jhāna bhūmis*, namely, *bhūmis* of *Vehapphalā* (Brahmās enjoying great reward of *jhāna* practice), *Asaññasattā* (Brahmās devoid of Consciousness) and five *Suddhāvāsa Brahmā bhūmis*, namely, *bhūmis* of *Avihā* (Brahmās whose position is durable), *Atappā* (Serene Brahmās), *Sudassā* (Brahmās of inspiring appearance), *Sudassī* (Brahmās of extremely pure appearance), and *Akaniṭṭhā* (Incomparable Brahmās).

Those who retain the first-*jhāna* concentration at death are reborn in the first-*jhāna Brahmā bhūmis*; those who retain the second-*jhāna* concentration at death are reborn in the second-*jhāna Brahmā bhūmis*; those who retain the third-*Jhāna* concentration at death are reborn in the third-*jhāna Brahmā bhūmis*; and those who retain the fourth-*Jhāna* concentration at death are reborn in the *fourth-Jhāna Brahmā bhūmis.* Only those who have attained the *Anāgāmi Magga* are reborn in one of the five *Suddhāvāsa Brahmā bhūmis*, the planes of the pure, clean and undefiled. Later, they attain Arahatship and live in those planes till their *parinibbāna.*

All *Rūpa Brahmās* look like male human beings. They are resplendent with the light from their own bodies. Their bodies are extremely delicate, and they do not have the need to take any nutriment. These Brahmās, with the exception of *Asaññasatta* Brahmās, subsist on *pīti* born of their *jhāna* mind.

The four non-corporeal Brahmā *bhūmis* are: (i) *Ākāsānañcāya tana Brahmā bhūmi*, (ii) *Viññāṇañcāyatana Brahmā bhūmi*, (iii) *Ākiñcaññāyatana Brahmā bhūmi*, and (iv) *Nevasaññānāsaññāyatana Brahmā bhūmi.* Those who have achieved and retained the *Ākāsānañcāyatana jhāna* at death are reborn in the *Ākāsañañcāyatana Brahmā bhūmi;* those who have achieved and retained *Viññāṇañcāyatana jhāna* at death are reborn in the *Viññāṇañcāyatana Brahmā bhumi*; those who have achieved and retained *Ākiñcaññāyatana jhāna* at death are reborn in the *Ākiñcaññāyatana Brahmā bhūmi*; and those who have achieved and retained the *Nevasaññānāsaññāyatana jhāna* at death are reborn in the *Nevasaññānāsaññāyatana Brahmā bhūmi.*

Non-corporeal Brahmās are so-called because they have no body. They have only mind. *Arūpa Brahmās*, in their previous existences, firmly believed that the body (*i.e.*, corporeality) was the root cause of all *dukkha*, and they had a deep and abiding abhorrence of the body. Therefore they practiced meditation for the attainment of *Arūpa jhāna*, and eventually are reborn in these non-corporeal *Brahmā bhūmis.*

APPENDIX A 6

Paṭibhāga Nimitta[6]

In meditation practice, out of forty kinds of meditation, there are ten kinds of *kasiṇa* meditation using earth, water, fire, air, dark-blue colour, yellow colour, red colour, white colour, light and space as *kasiṇa* objects.

---

6. Paragraph 54, Brāhmajāla Sutta.

In the earth *kasiṇa* (*pathavī kasiṇa*) meditation, the yogi makes a disc of reddish yellow earth, uses it as an object of his *kasiṇa* meditation and builds up his concentration by gazing hard at it. As his concentration becomes steadfast, he sees the earth disc with his eyes shut or open: with his eyes open, he sees the actual *kasiṇa* object of the earth disc which is termed the '*parikamma nimitta*', and with his eyes shut, he sees with his mind's eye the identical image of the earth disc, with all its faults and impurities, and that image is termed the '*uggaha nimitta*'. When the concentration is so developed as to see the '*uggaha nimitta*', with his eyes shut (or even open in a darkroom), the yogi puts away his earth disc, and meditates only on the '*uggaha nimitta*' which again develops into a very clear and well defined image, without the original faults of the '*uggaha nimitta*' and this new purified mental image is termed the '*paṭibhāga nimitta*' The yogi meditates on this '*paṭibhāga nimitta*' and keeps away such hindrances as sensual desire (*kāmacchanda*), desire to harm others (*byāpāda*), sloth and torpor (*thīna middha*), distraction and worry (*uddhacca-kukkucca*), and doubt (*vicikicchā*). In this way the yogi attains *jhāna*.

If the original *kasiṇa* object (*parikamma nimitta*) is small, the purified mental image (*paṭibhāga nimitta*) also is small. If the original *kasiṇa* object is large, the purified mental image also is large. If the yogi continues to strive, he may attain *jhāna* concentration. Before or after the attainment of *jhāna*, he may extend this purified mental image in three ways: (i) seeing its limits; (ii) not seeing its limits; and (iii) seeing its limits vertically but not seeing its limits horizontally.

The yogi who attains this *jhāna* state takes this image for *loka* or the world. Therefore, (i) for one whose extended mental image is limited, the world is finite; (ii) for one whose extended mental image is limitless, the world is infinite, and (iii) for one whose extended mental image is limited vertically but limitless horizontally, the world is finite as well as infinite.

The yogi adopts this process for mediation on each of the remaining nine *kasiṇa* objects.

APPENDIX A 7

Dukkha[7]

As expounded in paragraph 387 of *Mahāsatipaṭṭhāna Sutta*, the Noble Truth of Dukkha is explained as: Birth (*i.e.*, repeated birth) is *dukkha*. Ageing also is *dukkha*. Death also is *dukkha*. Grief, lamentation, pain, distress, and despair are also *dukkha*. To have to associate with those

7. Paragraph 248, Sāmaññaphala Sutta.

(persons or things) one dislikes is also *dukkha*; to be separated from those one loves or likes is also *dukkha*; the craving for what one cannot get is also *dukkha*; in short, the five Aggregates of Clinging are *dukkha*.

Dukkha as a Noble Truth is left untranslated. "Suffering" and "ill" are inadequate renderings. Dukkha is inherent in existence. The five Aggregates of Clinging therefore embody *dukkha*. Dukkha has connotations of impermanence, insubstantiality, unsatisfactoriness, emptiness, imperfection, insecurity, besides the obvious ones of 'suffering', physical pain and mental affliction.

APPENDIX B 1

Saṃyojana or Fetters[8]

Saṃyojanas are bonds or fetters binding all beings to the wheel of existence. They are broken or eliminated in stages which mark the progress of a person towards emancipation. When they are completely eliminated, emancipation results.

The ten fetters are:

(1) *sakkāya diṭṭhi:* belief in *atta* or soul; illusion of self-hood; self-belief; ego illusion; the view that the body and mind is "myself".

(2) *vicikicchā*: doubt or wavering concerning the Buddha's Enlightenment, his Teaching, and his Order.

(3) *Sīlabbataparāmāsa:* the belief that there are practices and paths other than the Ariya Path of Eight Constituents, that can liberate one from *dukkha.*

(4) *kāmarāga*: sensual desire; sensuous passion; attachment to and satisfaction in sensual objects such as colours, shapes, sounds, odours, tastes, tactile objects.

(5) *paṭigha*: ill will, including feelings of hatred, anger, resentment, revulsion, dissatisfaction, aversion, annoyance, disappointment.

(6) *rūparāga*: (a) craving for existence in the Fine-Material (Brahmā) realms; (b) desire for the bliss, the tranquillity, the attractive flavor or the various stages of concentration on forms, or colours, or materiality.

(7) *arūparāga*: (a) craving for existence in the Formless (i.e., with only mind and no body) (Brahmā) realms; (b) desire for the bliss, the tranquillity, the attractive flavor of full concentration on objects other than forms, such as space or Consciousness or emptiness.

8. Paragraph 157, Mahāparinibbāna Sutta.

(8) *māna*: pride; awareness of superiority or inferiority; the illusion of having this or that status relative to one another.
(9) *uddhacca*: restlessness; agitation; mental unrest, distraction, lack of peace and quiet (arising from curiosity, inquisitiveness).
(10) *avijjā:* ignorance, lack of real, correct knowledge as to the nature of existence, as to the Four Noble Truths. It is the main root of *dukkha* and of rebirth.

Of these ten, the first five are called lower or grosser fetters, because they bind beings to the realms of sense-gratification (*kāma loka*).

One who has destroyed the first three fetters, namely, (i) illusion of self-hood, ego-illusion, (belief that there is Self), (ii) doubt and uncertainty, (iii) belief in practices and paths other than the Ariya Path of Eight Constituents — as in the case of the woman devotee Sujātā of Nātika village — becomes a *Sotāpanna*, Stream-enterer, or Stream-winner. Such a person, being confirmed in the knowledge of the truth, based on *sīla*, *samādhi* and *paññā*, has entered the stream that leads surely to *Nibbāna*; he or she has attained *sotāpatti magga*, 'the path' of one who has entered the current of emancipation. This is followed immediately by *sotāpatti phala*, 'the fruit' or 'fruition' or stream-entering. Such a person, being incapable of committing demeritorious deeds which lead to rebirth in sub-human realms of existence, cannot be reborn in any realm lower than the human, and if he does not attain full emancipation earlier, he is bound to do so within the course of seven lives at the most.

When, in addition to the destruction of the first three fetters as above, the next two fetters, namely, sensual desire, (sensuous passion), and ill will, as well as *moha*, (i.e., having no proper attitude to right or wrong and to the Noble Truths), are lessened or very much weakened, one becomes a *Sakadāgāmī*, or Once-Returner — as in the case of the devotee Sudatta of Nātika village. A Once-Returner is so called because even if he fails to realize *Nibbāna* in the current life, he is bound to do so in the next birth (the next life). He will not have to endure more than one rebirth in the sensuous realms.

The third stage is that of the *Anāgāmī*, the Non-Returner — such as the bhikkhunī Nandā of Nātika village — who has completely destroyed the first five fetters, the lower or grosser fetters, including even the subtle remnants of sensual desire and ill will. He or she will not be born again in the sensuous realms (*kāma loka*). If he does not gain *Nibbāna* before he dies, he will realize it in his next birth, which takes place in *Suddhāvāsa*, the Pure Abodes of the Brahmās. There he attains *Arahatship*, complete emancipation, and realizes *Nibbāna* without returning to the sensuous realms.

The fourth and last stage is that of the *Arahat* – such as the bhikkhu Sālha of Nātika village – who has broken all the fetters, including the subtle fetters (vi) to (x) in the above list, who has burned out all the moral defilements and impurities or taints. For him there is no rebirth. While the mental and bodily formations (the five *khandhas*) continue to function, he experiences *sa-upādisesa nibbāna*, or *nibbāna* with the elements of existence still present. At death, this becomes *anupādisesa nibbāna*, or *parinibbāna*, the complete extinction of the life-asserting, life-sustaining factors.

These four stages of the Noble Individual (*ariya puggala*) are sometimes separated by intervals, sometimes they follow immediately after one another, but at each stage 'the fruit' or 'fruition', *phala* or attainment, follows instantly upon the realization of *Magga* in the series of thought moments. The flash of Insight into *Nibbāna* is *magga ñāṇa*, and the repeated experience of Insight into *Nibbāna*, Fruition is *phala ñāṇa.* Starting with the *Sotāpanna*, those who have reached any or all of these four stages are called *Ariyas* or Noble Individuals.

APPENDIX B 2

General Comments on Eight Abhibhāyatana Jhānas[9]

A *bhāvanā* (meditation) has three stages. They are:

(1) *parikamma.* It is the stage when the yogi begins to concentrate on an object, in order to get mental concentration. *Parikamma* means preparation for meditation. The first sign of mental concentration is the appearance of a mental picture of the object in the eyes of the yogi, when he closes them. This mental picture is called *uggaha nimitta.*

(2) *upacāra.* It is the stage when the yogi's mind reaches the immediate vicinity of *appanā samādhi* (*jhāna*). In that stage, the yogi's mind becomes devoid of five *nīvaraṇas*, namely, sensuality, ill will, torpor of mind or body, worry, wavering. The mental picture that appears at this stage is called *paṭibhāga nimitta.* While *uggaha nimitta* is identical with the original *kasiṇa* object, *paṭibhāga* nimitta is clear and bright.

(3) *appanā.* It is the stage when the mind achieves *jhāna*. Then the mind becomes fixed on the object.

Let us now see what yogis in each of the eight jhānas do.

9. Paragraph 173, Mahāparinibbāna Sutta.

First abhibhāyatana jhāna

Yogis, in this category, concentrate, as *parikamma bhāvanā*, on the colour of some parts of their body. If they choose dark colour, they concentrate, for instance, on hair, which has dark colour and mentally repeat "*nīlaṃ, nīlaṃ*". If they choose golden colour, they concentrate, for instance, on skin, which has golden colour and mentally repeat "*pītaṃ, pītaṃ*". If they choose red colour, they concentrate, for instance, on blood, which has red colour and mentally repeat "*lohitaṃ, lohitaṃ*". If they choose white colour, they concentrate, for instance, on bone, which has white colour and mentally repeat "*odataṃ, odataṃ.*"

Since objects of *parikamma bhāvanā* are parts of the body of yogis, they are called *ajjhatta* (personal) objects. *Uggaha nimitta* (mental picture) which yogis get concentrating on *ajjhatta* objects, is not very clear. It can by no means help yogis to achieve *upacāra samādhi*. Therefore, yogis give up *uggaha nimitta* as soon as *parikamma samādhi* becomes sufficiently strong. Then they choose a small *bahiddha* (external) object, the colour of which is either good or bad, and concentrate on it.

Being highly gifted persons, they quickly overcome obstacles and achieve *upacāra* and *appanā samādhi*, one after another, in quick succession.

Second abhibhāyatana jhāna

Yogis, in this category, also concentrate, as *parikamma bhāvanā*, on *ajjhatta* objects. They also give up *ajjhatta* objects when *parikamma samādhi* becomes sufficiently strong, and concentrate on large *bahiddha* objects, the colour of which is either good or bad.

Being highly gifted persons, they quickly overcome obstacles and achieve *upacāra* and *appanā samādhi*, one after another, in quick succession.

Third abhibhāyatana jhāna

Yogis, in this category, concentrate, as *parikamma bhāvanā*, on small *bahiddha* objects, the colour of which is either good or bad.

Being highly gifted parsons, they quickly overcome obstacles and achieve *parikamma, upacāra, appanā samādhi* in quick succession.

Fourth abhibhāyatana jhāna

Yogis, in this category, concentrate, as *parikamma bhāvanā*, on large *bahiddha* objects, the colour of which is either good or bad.

Being highly gifted persons, they quickly overcome obstacles and achieve *parikamma, upacāra, appanā samādhi*, one after another, in quick succession.

Fifth abhibhāyatana jhāna

Yogis, in this category, concentrate, as *parikamma bhāvanā*, on *bahiddha* objects, the colour of which is as dark blue as the flower of the butterfly pea or dark blue fine cloth made in Bārāṇasī.

Being highly gifted persons, they quickly overcome obstacles and achieve *parikamma, upacāra, appanā samādhi*, one after another, in quick succession.

Sixth abhibhāyatana jhāna

Yogis, in this category, concentrate, as *parikamma bhāvanā*, on *bahiddha* objects, the colour of which is as golden-yellow as the wild champac flower or golden-yellow fine cloth made in Bārānāsī.

Being highly gifted persons, they overcome obstacles and achieve *parikamma, upacāra, appanā samādhi*, one after another, in quick succession.

Seventh abhibhāyatana jhāna

Yogis, in this category, concentrate, as *parikamma bhāvanā*, *bahiddha* objects, the colour of which is as red as *bandhujīvaka* flower or red fine cloth made in Bārāṇasī.

Being highly gifted persons, they overcome obstacles and achieve *parikamma, upacāra, appanā samādhi*, one after another, in quick succession.

Eighth abhibhāyatana jhāna

Yogis, in this category, concentrate, as *parikamma bhāvanā*, on *bahiddha* objects, the colour of which is as white as the morning star or white fine cloth made in Bārāṇasī.

Being highly gifted persons, they overcome obstacles and achieve *parikamma, upacāra, appanā samādhi*, one after another, in quick succession.

Abhibhāyatana jhānas and dispositions

The first *abhibhāyatana jhāna* is suitable for yogis who are strongly inclined towards reflection (*vitakka*).

The second *abhibhāyatana jhāna* is suitable for yogis who "are strongly inclined towards stubborness (*moha*).

The colour of the third *jhāna* is either good or bad. The good colour is suitable for yogis who are strongly inclined towards irritability (*dosa*).

The colour of the object of the fourth *jhāna* is also either good or bad. The bad colour is suitable for yogis who are strongly inclined towards passion (*rāga*).

APPENDIX B 3
General Comments on Eight Vimokkhas[10]
(Eight kinds of release)

The first three vimokkhas

Vimokkha means complete freedom from *nīvaraṇas* (as long as yogis have *jhānas*).

It also means complete fixation of mind on the object of meditation, without any interference (as long as yogis have *jhānas*).

Out of eight *vimokkhas*, the first three refer to *rūpa jhānas*. (They are so called because these *jhānas* are achieved by concentrating on corporeal objects.)

Out of these three categories of *rūpa jhānas*, the first is achieved by concentrating on *ajjhatta* (internal) as well as *bahiddha* (external) objects.

The second is achieved by concentrating on *bahiddha* objects.

The third is achieved by concentrating on kasiṇas (objects of meditation) of very good and clean colour, namely, *nīla*, *pīta*, *lohita*, *odāta* (dark blue, golden, red, white). While yogis in this category are having *jhānas*, they do not have such a thought as "It is exquisite." Since, however, they are concentrating on "exquisite" objects, it appears as if they have such a thought.

The next four vimokkhas

The next four *vimokkhas*, namely, the fourth, the fifth, the sixth, the seventh refer to four *arūpa jhānas*. (They are so called because there four *jhānas* are achieved by concentrating on incorporeal objects.) These four *arūpa jhānas* are also named *vimokkha*, firstly because yogis, who have them, are completely free from any thoughts that pertain to corporeal objects, and secondly because their minds are completely fixed on incorporeal objects without any interference.

---

10. Paragraph 174, Mahāparinibbāna Sutta.

The last vimokkha

The last *vimokkha*, namely, the eighth, refers to *nirodha samāpatti*.

Nirodha means cessation. It is cessation of the *nāmarūpa* process, with the exception of three kinds of *rūpas*. While one is in *nirodha samāpatti*, his mind and its concomitants (*citta* and *cetasikas*) completely cease.

However, out of the four kinds of rūpas, namely: 1. *kammaja rūpa*, 2. *cittaja rūpa*, 3. *utuja rūpa*, 4. *āhāraja rūpa*, which the body is composed of, *cittaja rūpa* ceases. The other three carry on as usual.

Samāpatti means attainment.

Qualifications

1. One who wishes to have *nirodha samāpatti* must be, at least, an *anāgāmī* (one who has got *anāgāmī magga*).
2. He must have dexterity to achieve any of the four *rūpa jhānas* and the four *arūpa jhānas*, as he pleases.

Step by Step

One who has the above mentioned two qualifications take the following steps, one by one.

1. The maximum duration of *nirodha samāpatti* is seven days. Before one goes into *nirodha samāpatti* he must determine the duration of *nirodha samāpatti*. For instance, he wishes to remain in it throughout the maximum duration. He must declare this wish as the first step. However, in order to ensure that he does not expire while he is in *nirodha samāpatti*, he is required to ascertain the span of his life before he makes the wish. Only when he sees that he will live more than seven days, he declares the wish that he wants to remain in *nirodha samāpatti* during its entire length. If, for instance, he sees that he has only five days to live, he may declare the wish that he wants to remain in it for four days.
2. He takes up the appropriate *kasiṇa bhāvanā* for the achievement of the four *rūpa* and the four *arūpa jhānas*. He may remain in the four *rūpa jhānas* and the first, the second, the third *arūpa jhānas*, as long as he wishes. When, however, he goes into the fourth and the final *arūpa jhāna*, namely, *nevasaññānāsaññāyatana jhāna*, he cannot remain in it for more than one or two thought-moments. His strong wish to be in *nirodha samāpatti* impels him into it. (See Paragraph 414 of *Poṭṭhapāda Sutta* of *Sīlakkhandha Vagga*.)

SIMILARITIES AND DIFFERENCES BETWEEN *NIRODHA SAMĀPATTI* AND DEATH

Similarities

(a) A dead person is motionless.
A person in *nirodha samāpatti* is also motionless.

(b) A dead person does not breathe.
A person in *nirodha samāpatti* also does not breathe These two points are similarities between a dead person and a person in *nirodha samāpatti.*

Differences

(a) A dead person becomes cold some time after death. A person in *nirodha samapātti* is warm throughout the full duration of the *samāpatti.*

(b) *Pasādas*, sensitive layers that enable eyes to see, ears to hear, nose to smell, tongue to taste, body to feel are destroyed, some time after the death of a person.

Pasādas of a person in *nirodha samāpatti* remain intact throughout the full duration of the *nirodha samāpatti.*

ABOUT PARIYATTI

Pariyatti is dedicated to providing affordable access to authentic teachings of the Buddha about the Dhamma theory (*pariyatti*) and practice (*paṭipatti*) of Vipassana meditation. A 501(c)(3) nonprofit charitable organization since 2002, Pariyatti is sustained by contributions from individuals who appreciate and want to share the incalculable value of the Dhamma teachings. We invite you to visit www.pariyatti.org to learn about our programs, services, and ways to support publishing and other undertakings.

PARIYATTI PUBLISHING IMPRINTS

Vipassana Research Publications (focus on Vipassana as taught by S.N. Goenka in the tradition of Sayagyi U Ba Khin)
BPS Pariyatti Editions (selected titles from the Buddhist Publication Society, copublished by Pariyatti)
MPA Pariyatti Editions (selected titles from the Myanmar Pitaka Association, copublished by Pariyatti)
Pariyatti Digital Editions (audio and video titles, including discourses)
Pariyatti Press (classic titles returned to print and inspirational writing by contemporary authors)

PARIYATTI ENRICHES THE WORLD BY

- disseminating the words of the Buddha,
- providing sustenance for the seeker's journey,
- illuminating the meditator's path.

Printed in Great Britain
by Amazon

61429443R00248